Fundamentals of Computer Networking

Principles, Protocols and Practice

Fundamentals of Computer Networking

Principles, Protocols and Practice

Halima Yusuf
Dawit Alemu

Kruger Brentt
Publishers
2026

Kruger Brentt Publishers UK. LTD.

Company Number 9728962

Regd. Office: 68 St Margarets Road, Edgware, Middlesex HA8 9UU

ISBN: 978-1-78715-651-7

For information on all our publications visit our website at http://krugerbrentt.com/

Preface

Fundamentals of Computer Networking: Principles, Protocols, and Practice offers a structured and comprehensive introduction to the essential concepts that govern modern communication networks. As digital connectivity becomes indispensable across industries, understanding how networks operate—how data moves, how devices communicate, and how security is maintained—has become a fundamental requirement for students, IT professionals, and practitioners.

This book begins with the foundational principles of networking, explaining how networks are structured, how communication occurs at various layers, and how the Internet functions as a large interconnected system. Through clear explanations and intuitive diagrams, readers are guided from the basics of signals, switching, and transmission media to the architectural design and layered structure of the TCP/IP and OSI models.

Subsequent chapters delve into core protocols and mechanisms, including IP addressing, routing algorithms, congestion control, error detection, flow control, LAN technologies, wireless networks, and transport-layer services. The book also emphasizes hands-on understanding of modern tools and technologies such as routers, switches, DHCP, DNS, Wi-Fi protocols, firewalls, VPNs, and cloud networking.

With the rapid evolution of networked systems, the book covers contemporary developments such as software-defined networking (SDN), network virtualization, 5G networks, IoT communication architectures, and cybersecurity essentials. Examples, case studies, and practical scenarios reinforce learning and enable readers to understand how theory translates into operational networks.

Written to provide clarity, depth, and practical relevance, this book serves as a reliable text for computer science and engineering students, competitive exam aspirants, and IT professionals seeking a strong grounding in networking principles and practices.

Halima Yusuf

Dawit Alemu

Contents

CHAPTER

Introduction

1

When the first computers were built during the second world war, they were expensive and isolated. However, after about twenty years, as their prices gradually decreased, the first experiments began to connect computers together. In the early 1960s, researchers including Paul Baran, Donald Davies or Joseph Licklider independently published the first papers describing the idea of building computer networks [Baran] [Licklider1963]. Given the cost of computers, sharing them over a long distance was an interesting idea. In the US, the *ARPANET* started in 1969 and continued until the mid 1980s [LCCD09]. In France, Louis Pouzin developed the Cyclades network [Pouzin1975]. Many other research networks were built during the 1970s [Moore]. At the same time, the telecommunication and computer industries became interested in computer networks. The telecommunication industry bet on the X25. The computer industry took a completely different approach by designing Local Area Networks (LAN). Many LAN technologies such as Ethernet or Token Ring were designed at that time. During the 1980s, the need to interconnect more and more computers led most computer vendors to develop their own suite of networking protocols. Xerox developed [XNS] , DEC chose DECNet [Malamud1991] , IBM developed SNA [McFadyen1976], Microsoft introduced NetBIOS [Winston2003], Apple bet on Appletalk [SAO1990]. In the research community, ARPANET was decommissioned and replaced by TCP/IP [LCCD09] and the reference implementation was developed inside BSD Unix [McKusick1999]. Universities who were already running Unix could thus adopt TCP/IP easily and vendors of Unix workstations such as Sun or Silicon Graphics included TCP/IP in their variant of Unix. In parallel, the *ISO,* with support from the governments, worked on developing an open [1] Suite of networking protocols. In the end, TCP/IP became the de facto standard that is not only used within the research community. During the 1990s and the early 2000s, the growth of the usage of TCP/IP continued, and today proprietary protocols are seldom used. As shown by the figure below, that provides the estimation of the number of hosts attached to the Internet, the Internet has sustained large growth throughout the last 20+ years.

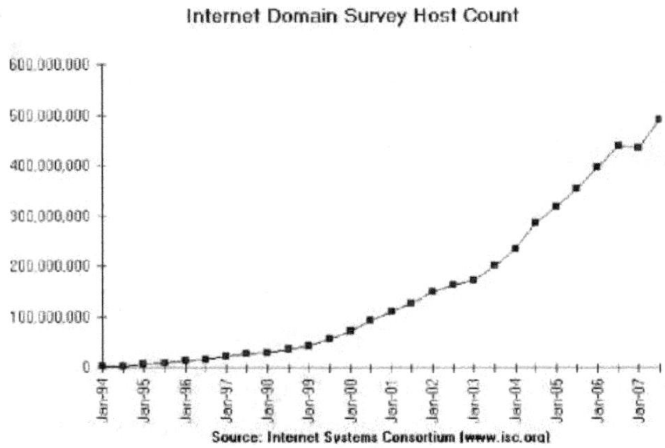

Figure 1.1: Estimation of the number of hosts on the Internet

Recent estimations of the number of hosts attached to the Internet show a continuing growth since 20+ years. However, although the number of hosts attached to the Internet is high, it should be compared to the number of mobile phones that are in use today. More and more of these mobile phones will be connected to the Internet. Furthermore, thanks to the availability of TCP/IP implementations requiring limited resources such as uIP [Dunkels2003], we can expect to see a growth of TCP/IP enabled embedded devices.

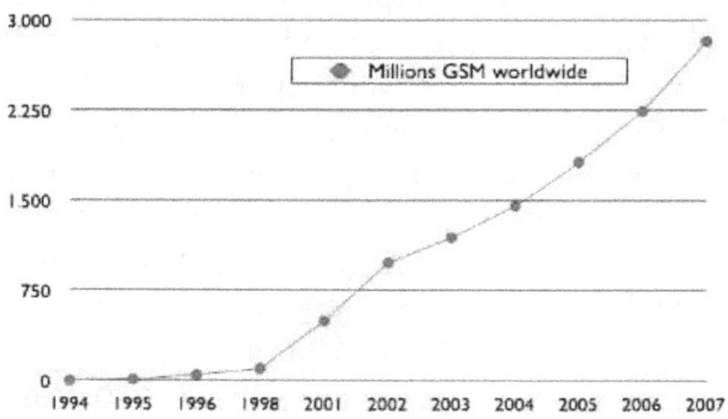

Figure 1.2: Estimation of the number of mobile phones

Before looking at the services provided by computer networks, it is useful to agree on some terminology that is widely used in networking literature. First of all, computer networks are often classified in function of the geographical area that they cover

- *LAN* : a local area network typically interconnects hosts that are up to a few or maybe a few tens of kilometers apart.
- *MAN* : a metropolitan area network typically interconnects devices that are up to a few hundred kilometers apart
- *WAN* : a wide area network interconnect hosts that can be located anywhere on Earth

Another classification of computer networks is based on their physical topology. In the following figures, physical links are represented as lines while boxes show computers or other types of networking equipment.

Computer networks are used to allow several hosts to exchange information between themselves. To allow any host to send messages to any other host in the network, the easiest solution is to organise them as a full-mesh, with a direct and dedicated link between each pair of hosts. Such a physical topology is sometimes used, especially when high performance and high redundancy is required for a small number of hosts. However, it has two major drawbacks :

- for a network containing *n* hosts, each host must have *n-1* physical interfaces. In practice, the number of physical interfaces on a node will limit the size of a full-mesh network that can be built
- for a network containing n hosts, $\frac{n \times (n-1)}{2}$ links are required. This is possible when there are a few nodes in the same room, but rarely when they are located several kilometers apart

The second possible physical organisation, which is also used inside computers to connect different extension cards, is the bus. In a bus network, all hosts are attached to a shared medium, usually a cable through a single interface. When one host sends an electrical signal on the bus, the signal is received by all hosts attached to the bus. A drawback of bus-based networks is that if the bus is physically cut, then the network is split into two isolated networks. For this reason, bus-based networks are sometimes considered to be difficult to operate and maintain, especially when the cable is long and there are many places where it can break. Such a bus-based topology was used in early Ethernet networks.

A third organisation of a computer network is a star topology. In such topologies, hosts have a single physical interface and there is one physical link between each host and the center of the star. The node at the center of the star can be either a piece of equipment that amplifies an electrical signal, or an active device, such as a piece of equipment that understands the format of the messages exchanged through the network. Of course, the failure of the central node implies the failure of the network. However, if one physical link fails (e.g. because the cable has been cut), then only one node is disconnected from the network. In practice, star-shaped networks are easier to operate and maintain than bus-shaped networks. Many network administrators also appreciate the fact that they can control the network from a central point. Administered from a Web interface, or through a console-like connection, the center of the star is a useful point of control (enabling or disabling devices) and an excellent observation point (usage statistics).

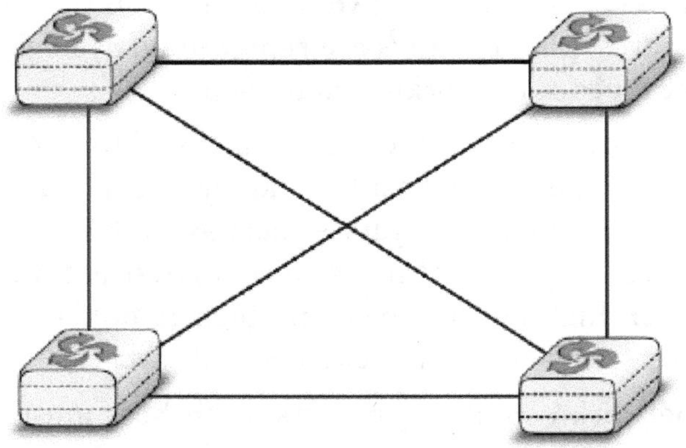

Figure 1.3: A Full mesh network

Figure 1.4: A network organised as a Bus

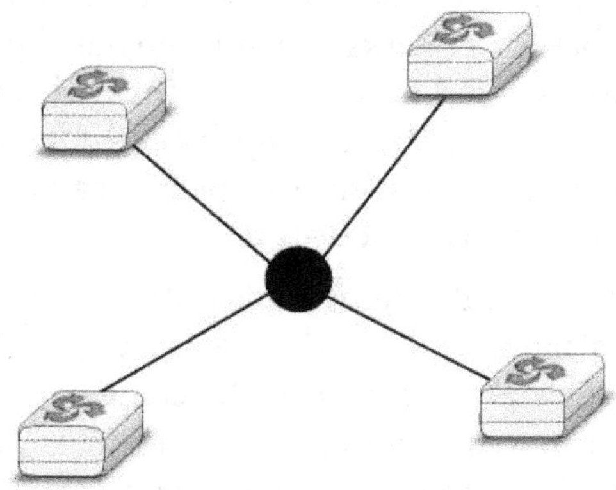

Figure 1.5: A network organised as a Star

A fourth physical organisation of a network is the Ring topology. Like the bus organisation, each host has a single physical interface connecting it to the ring. Any signal sent by a host on the ring will be received by all hosts attached to the ring. From a redundancy point of view, a single ring is not the best solution, as the signal only travels in one direction on the ring; thus if one of the links composing the ring is cut, the entire network fails. In practice, such rings have been used in local area networks, but are now often replaced by star-shaped networks. In metropolitan networks, rings are often used to interconnect multiple locations. In this case, two parallel links, composed of different cables, are often used for redundancy. With such a dual ring, when one ring fails all the traffic can be quickly switched to the other ring.

A fifth physical organisation of a network is the tree. Such networks are typically used when a large number of customers must be connected in a very cost-effective manner. Cable TV networks are often organised as trees.

In practice, most real networks combine part of these topologies. For example, a campus network can be organised as a ring between the key buildings, while smaller buildings are attached as a tree or a star to important buildings.

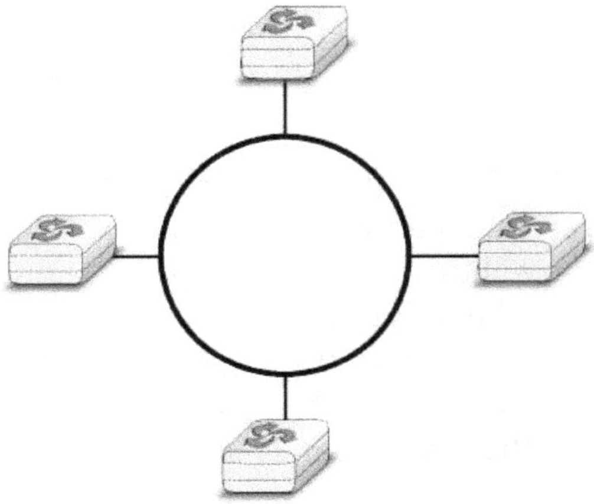

Figure 1.6: A network organised as a Ring

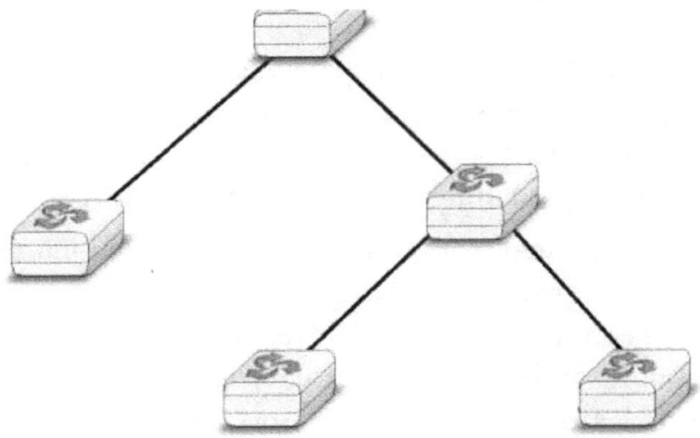

Figure 1.7: A network organised as a Tree

Or an ISP network may have a full mesh of devices in the core of its network, and trees to connect remote users.

Throughout this book, our objective will be to understand the protocols and mechanisms that are necessary for a network such as the one shown below.

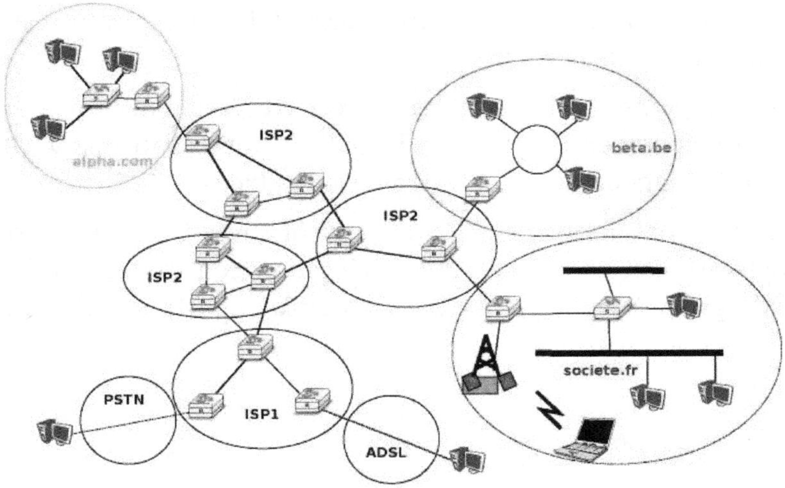

Figure 1.8: A simple internetwork

The figure above illustrates an internetwork, i.e. a network that interconnects other networks. Each network is illustrated as an ellipse containing a few devices. We will explain throughout the book the different types of devices and their respective roles enabling all hosts to exchange information. As well as this, we will discuss how networks are interconnected, and the rules that guide these interconnections. We will also analyse how the bus, ring and mesh topologies are used to build real networks.

The last point of terminology we need to discuss is the transmission modes. When exchanging information through a network, we often distinguish between three transmission modes. In TV and radio transmission, *broadcast* is often used to indicate a technology that sends a video or radio signal to all receivers in a given geographical area. Broadcast is sometimes used in computer networks, but only in local area networks where the number of recipients is limited.

The first and most widespread transmission mode is called *unicast*. In the unicast transmission mode, information is sent by one sender to one receiver. Most of today's Internet applications rely on the unicast transmission mode. The example below shows a network with two types of devices : hosts (drawn as computers) and intermediate nodes (drawn as cubes). Hosts exchange information via the intermediate nodes. In the example below, when host *S* uses unicast to send information, it sends it via three intermediate nodes. Each of these nodes receives the information from its upstream node or host, then processes and forwards it to its downstream node or host. This is called *store and forward* and we will see later that this concept is key in computer networks.

A second transmission mode is *multicast* transmission mode. This mode is used when the same information must be sent to a set of recipients. It was first used in LANs but later became supported in wide area networks. When a sender uses multicast to send information to *N* receivers, the sender sends a single copy of the information and the network nodes duplicate this information whenever necessary, so that it can reach all recipients belonging to the destination group.

To understand the importance of multicast transmission, consider source *S* that sends the same information to destinations *A*, *C* and *E*. With unicast, the same information passes three times on intermediate nodes *1* and *2* and twice on node 4. This is a waste of resources on the intermediate nodes and on the links between them. With multicast transmission, host *S* sends the information to node *1* that forwards it downstream to node *2*. This node creates a copy of the received information and sends one copy directly to host *E* and the other downstream to node *4*. Upon reception of the information, node *4* produces a copy and forwards one to node *A* and another to node *C*. Thanks to multicast, the same information can reach a large number of receivers while being sent only once on each link.

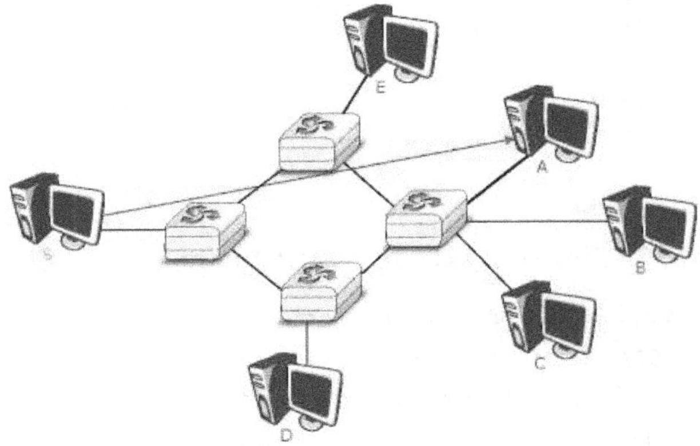

Figure 1.9: Unicast transmission

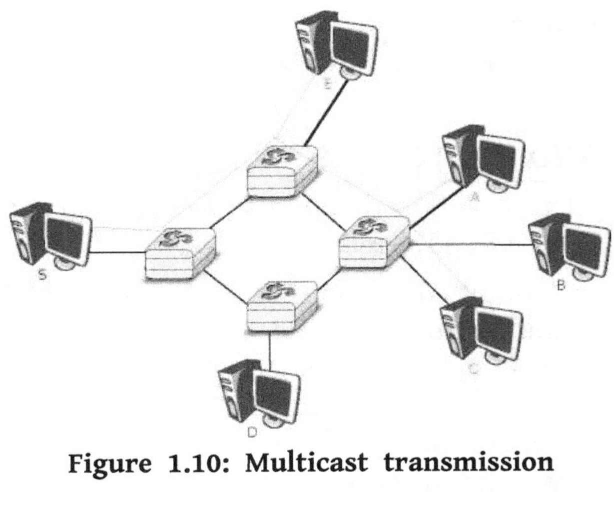

Figure 1.10: Multicast transmission

The last transmission mode is the *anycast* transmission mode. It was initially defined in **RFC 1542.** In this transmission mode, a set of receivers is identified. When a source sends information towards this set of receivers, the network ensures that the information is delivered to *one* receiver that belongs to this set. Usually, the receiver closest to the source is the one that receives the information sent by this particular source. The anycast transmission mode is useful to ensure redundancy, as when one of the receivers fails, the network will ensure that information will be delivered to another receiver belonging to the same group. However, in practice supporting the anycast transmission mode can be difficult.

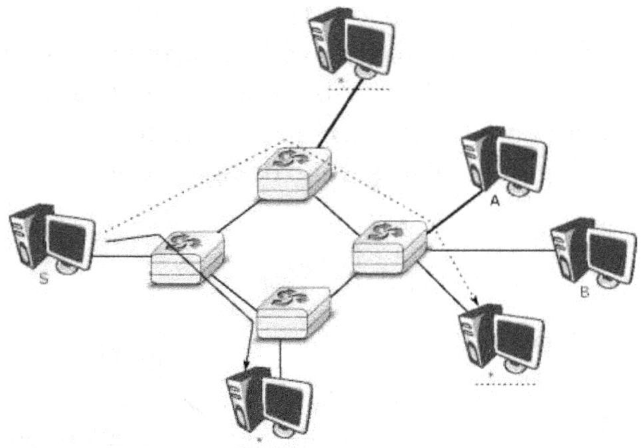

Figure 1.11: Anycast transmission

In the example above, the three hosts marked with * are part of the same anycast group. When host *S* sends information to this anycast group, the network ensures that it will reach one of the members of the anycast group. The dashed lines show a possible delivery via nodes *1, 2* and *4*. A subsequent anycast transmission from host S to the same anycast group could reach the host attached to intermediate node *3* as shown by the plain line. An anycast transmission reaches a member of the anycast group that is chosen by the network in function of the current network conditions.

1.1 SERVICES AND PROTOCOLS

An important aspect to understand before studying computer networks is the difference between a *service* and a *protocol.*

In order to understand the difference between the two, it is useful to start with real world examples. The traditional Post provides a service where a postman delivers letters to recipients. The Post defines precisely which types of letters (size, weight, etc) can be delivered by using the Standard Mail service. Furthermore, the format of the envelope is specified (position of the sender and recipient addresses, position of the stamp). Someone who wants to send a letter must either place the letter at a Post Office or inside one of the dedicated mailboxes. The letter will then be collected and delivered to its final recipient. Note that for the regular service the Post usually does not guarantee the delivery of each particular letter, some letters may be lost, and some letters are delivered to the wrong mailbox. If a letter is important, then the sender can use the registered service to ensure that the letter will be delivered to its recipient. Some Post services also provide an acknowledged service or an express mail service that is faster than the regular service.

In computer networks, the notion of service is more formally defined in [X200]. It can be better understood by considering a computer network, whatever its size or complexity, as a black box that provides a service to *users* , as shown in the figure below. These users could be human users or processes running on a computer system.

Many users can be attached to the same service provider. Through this provider, each user must be able to exchange messages with any other user. To be able to deliver these messages, the service provider must be able to unambiguously identify each user. In computer networks, each user is identified by a unique *address,* we will discuss later how these addresses are built and used. At this point, and when considering unicast transmission, the main characteristic of these *addresses* is that they are unique. Two different users attached to the network cannot use the same address.

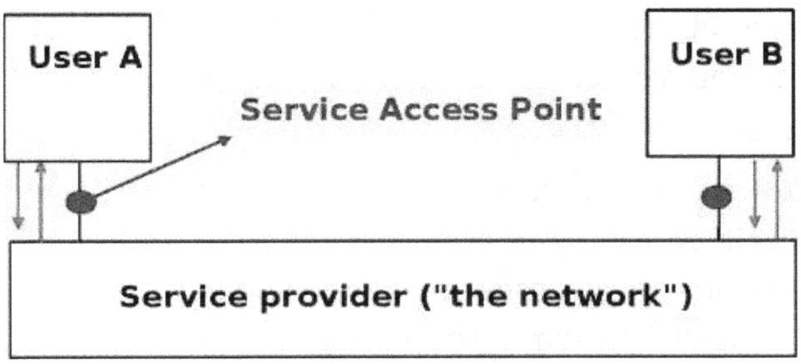

Figure 1.12: Users and service provider

Throughout this book, we will define a service as a set of capabilities provided by a system (and its underlying elements) to its user. A user interacts with a service through a *service access point.* Note that as shown in the figure above, users interact with one service provider. In practice, the service provider is distributed over several hosts, but these are implementation details that are not important at this stage. These interactions between a user and a service provider are expressed in [X200] by using primitives, as show in the figure below. These primitives are an abstract representation of the interactions between a user and a service provider. In practice, these interactions could be implemented as system calls for example.

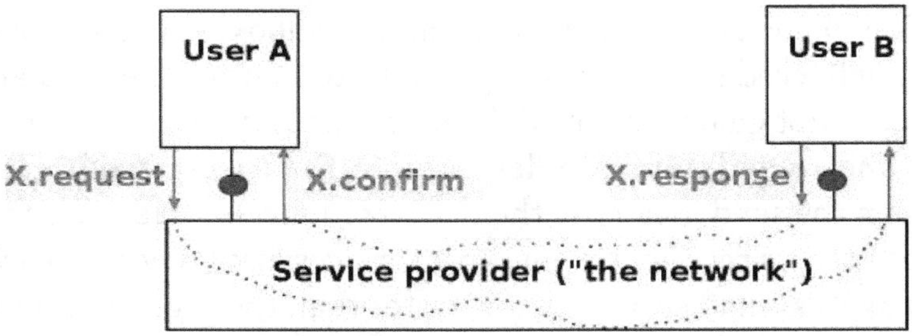

Figure 1.13: The four types of primitives

Four types of primitives are defined :

- *X.request.* This type of primitive corresponds to a request issued by a user to a service provider
- *Vindication.* This type of primitive is generated by the network provider and delivered to a user (often related to an earlier and remote *X.request* primitive)
- *X.response.* This type of primitive is generated by a user to answer to an earlier *Vindication* primitive
- *X.confirm.* This type of primitive is delivered by the service provide to confirm to a user that a previous *X.request* primitive has been successfully processed.

Primitives can be combined to model different types of services. The simplest service in computer networks is called the *connectionless service.* This service can be modelled by using two primitives:

- *Data.request(source,destination,SDU).* This primitive is issued by a user that specifies, as parameters, its (source) address, the address of the recipient of the message and the message itself. We will use *Service Data Unit* (SDU) to name the message that is exchanged transparently between two users of a service.
- *Data.indication(source,destination,SDU).* This primitive is delivered by a service provider to a user. It contains as parameters a *Service Data Unit* as well as the addresses of the sender and the destination users.

When discussing the service provided in a computer network, it is often useful to be able to describe the interactions between the users and the provider graphically. A frequently used representation is the *time-sequence diagram.* In this chapter and later throughout the book, we will often use diagrams such as the figure below. A time-sequence diagram describes the interactions between two users and a service provider. By convention, the users are represented in the left and right parts of the diagram while the service provider occupies the middle of the diagram. In such a time-sequence diagram, time flows from the top, to the bottom of the diagram. Each primitive is represented by a plain horizontal arrow, to which the name of the primitive is attached. The dashed lines are used to represent the possible relationship between two (or more) primitives. Such a diagram provides information about the ordering of the different primitives, but the distance between two primitives does not represent a precise amount of time.

The figure below provides a representation of the connectionless service as a *time-sequence diagram.* The user on the left, having address *S,* issues a *Data.request* primitive containing SDU *M* that must be delivered by the service provider to destination D. The dashed line between the two primitives indicates that the *Data. indication* primitive that is delivered to the user on the right corresponds to the *Data.request* primitive sent by the user on the left.

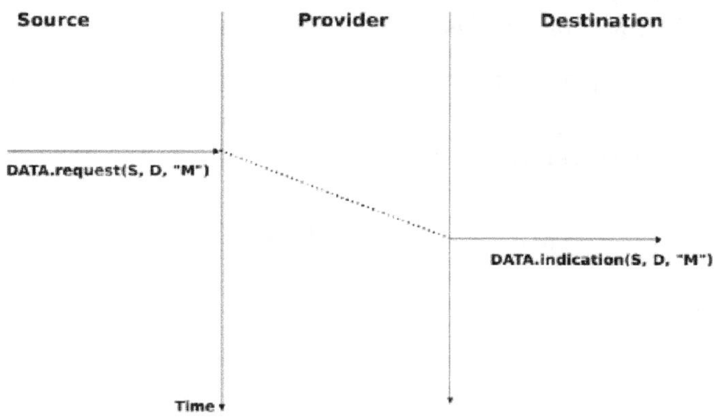

Figure 1.14: A simple connectionless service

There are several possible implementations of the connectionless service, which we will discuss later in this book. Before studying these realisations, it is useful to discuss the possible characteristics of the connectionless service. A *reliable connectionless service* is a service where the service provider guarantees that all SDUs submitted in *Data.requests* by a user will eventually be delivered to their destination. Such a service would be very useful for users, but guaranteeing perfect delivery is difficult in practice. For this reason, computer networks usually support an *unreliable connectionless service.*

An *unreliable connectionless* service may suffer from various types of problems compared to a *reliable connectionless service.* First of all, an *unreliable connectionless service* does not guarantee the delivery of all SDUs. This can be expressed graphically by using the time-sequence diagram below.

In practice, an *unreliable connectionless service* will usually deliver a large fraction of the SDUs. However, since the delivery of SDUs is not guaranteed, the user must be able to recover from the loss of any SDU.

A second imperfection that may affect an *unreliable connectionless service* is that it may duplicate SDUs. Some unreliable connectionless service providers may deliver an SDU sent by a user twice or even more. This is illustrated by the time-sequence diagram below.

Finally, some unreliable connectionless service providers may deliver to a destination a different SDU than the one that was supplied in the *Data.request*. This is illustrated in the figure below.

When a user interacts with a service provider, it must precisely know the limitations of the underlying service to be able to overcome any problem that may arise. This requires a precise definition of the characteristics of the underlying service.

Another important characteristic of the connectionless service is whether it preserves the ordering of the SDUs sent by one user. From the user's viewpoint, this is often a desirable characteristic. This is illustrated in the figure below.

However, many connectionless services, and in particular the unreliable services, do not guarantee that they will always preserve the ordering of the SDUs sent by each user. This is illustrated in the figure below.

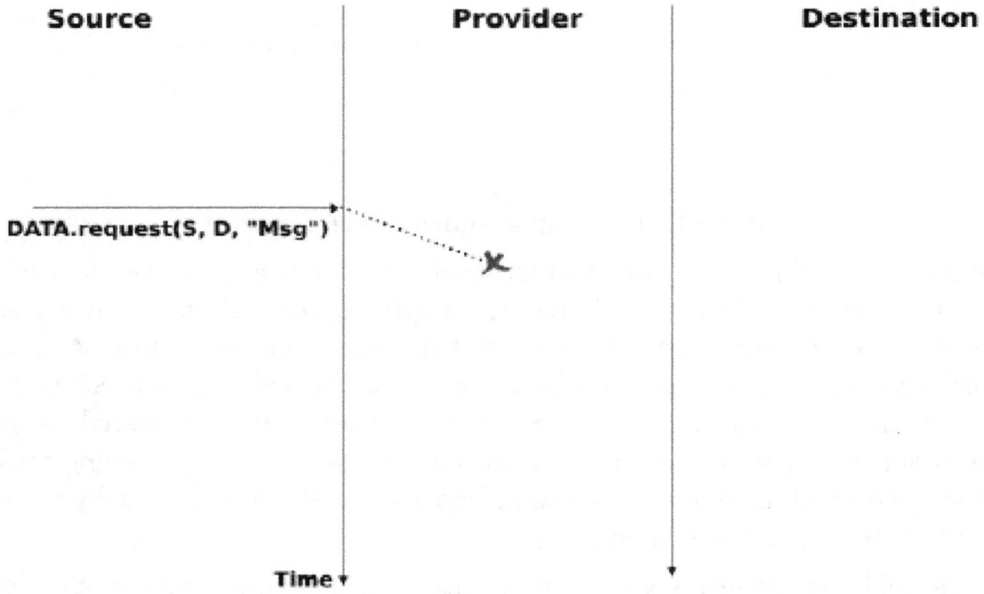

Figure 1.15: An unreliable connectionless service may loose SDUs

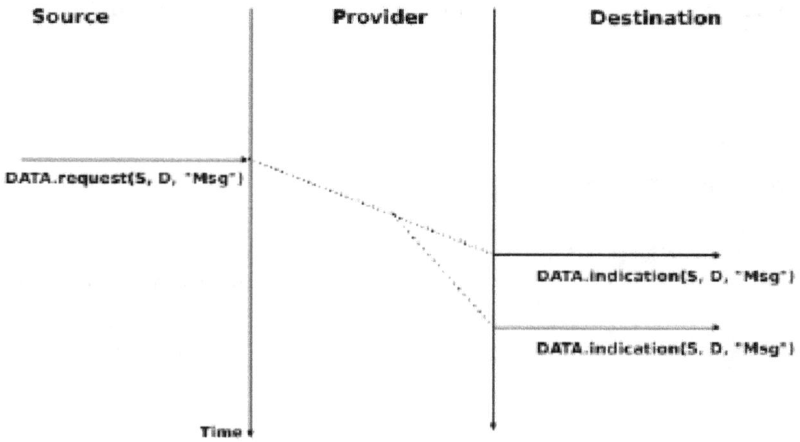

Figure 1.16: An unreliable connectionless service may duplicate SDUs

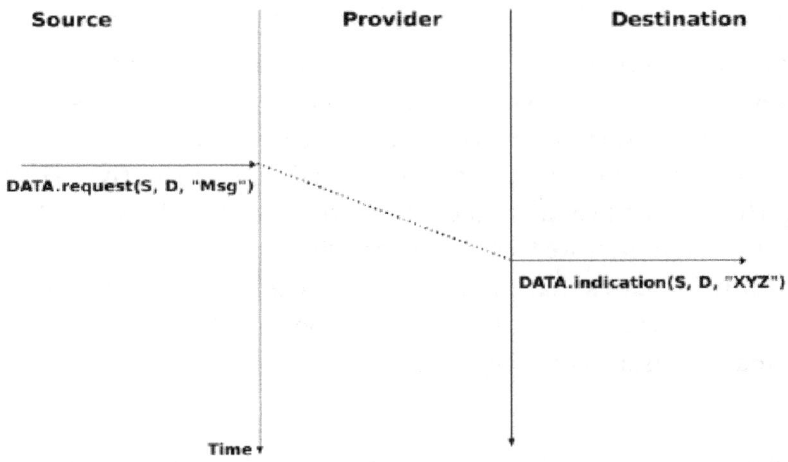

Figure 1.17: An unreliable connectionless service may deliver erroneous SDUs

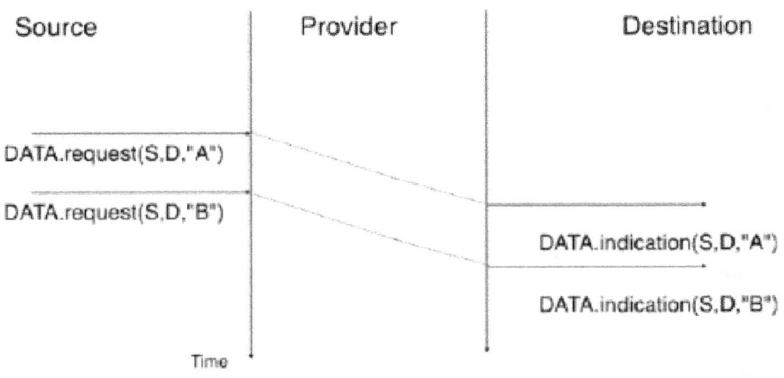

Figure 1.18: A connectionless service that preserves the ordering of SDUs sent by a given user

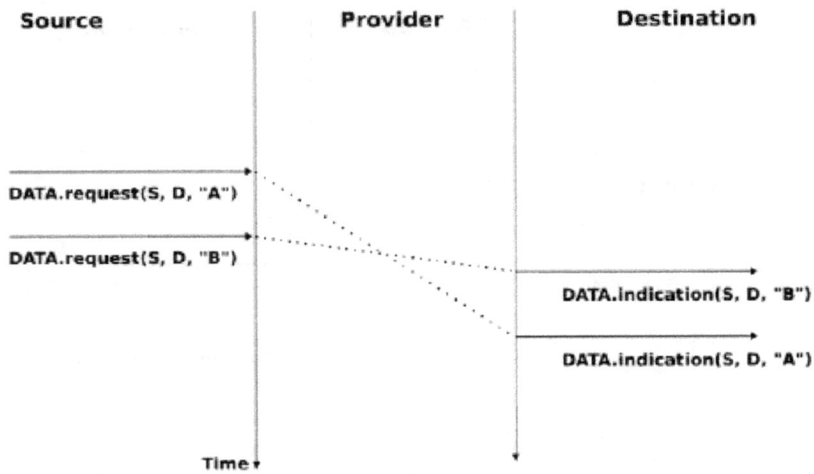

Figure 1.19: A connectionless service that does not preserve the ordering of SDUs sent by a given user

The *connectionless service* is widely used in computer networks as we will see later in this book. Several variations to this basic service have been proposed. One of these is the *confirmed connectionless service.* This service uses a *Data.confirm* primitive in addition to the classical *Data.request* and *Data.indication* primitives. This primitive is issued by the service provider to confirm to a user the delivery of a previously sent SDU to its recipient. Note that, like the registered service of the post office, the *Data.confirm* only indicates that the SDU has been delivered to the destination user. The *Data.confirm* primitive does not indicate whether the SDU has been processed by the destination user. This *confirmed connectionless service* is illustrated in the figure below.

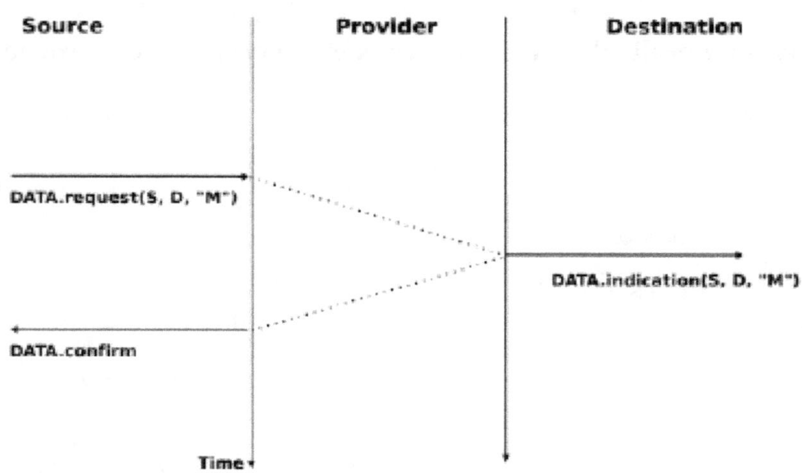

Figure 1.20: A confirmed connectionless service

The *connectionless service* we have described earlier is frequently used by users who need to exchange small SDUs. Users needing to either send or receive several different and potentially large SDUs, or who need structured exchanges often prefer the *connection-oriented service.*

An invocation of the *connection-oriented service* is divided into three phases. The first phase is the establishment of a *connection.* A *connection* is a temporary association between two users through a service provider. Several connections may exist at the same time between any pair of users. Once established, the connection is used to transfer SDUs. *Connections* usually provide one bidirectional stream supporting the exchange of SDUs between the two users that are associated through the *connection.* This stream is used to transfer data during the second phase of the connection called the *data transfer* phase. The third phase is the termination of the connection. Once the users have finished exchanging SDUs, they request to the service provider to terminate the connection. As we will see later, there are also some cases where the service provider may need to terminate a connection itself.

The establishment of a connection can be modelled by using four primitives: *Connect.request, Connect.indication, Connect.response* and *Connect.confirm.* The *Connect. request* primitive is used to request the establishment of a connection. The main parameter of this primitive is the *address* of the destination user. The service provider delivers a *Connect.indication* primitive to inform the destination user of the connection attempt. If it accepts to establish a connection, it responds with a *Connect.response* primitive. At this point, the connection is considered to be open and the destination user can start sending SDUs over the connection. The service provider processes the *Connect.response* and will deliver a *Connect.confirm* to the user who initiated the connection. The delivery of this primitive terminates the connection establishment phase. At this point, the connection is considered to be open and both users can send SDUs. A successful connection establishment is illustrated below.

The example above shows a successful connection establishment. However, in practice not all connections are successfully established. One reason is that the destination user may not agree, for policy or performance reasons, to establish a connection with the initiating user at this time. In this case, the destination user responds to the *Connect.indication* primitive by a *Disconnect.request* primitive that contains a parameter to indicate why the connection has been refused. The service provider will then deliver a *Disconnect.indication* primitive to inform the initiating user. A second reason is when the service provider is unable to reach the destination user. This might happen because the destination user is not currently attached to the network or due to congestion. In these cases, the service provider responds to the *Connect.request* with a *Disconnect.indication* primitive whose *reason* parameter contains additional information about the failure of the connection.

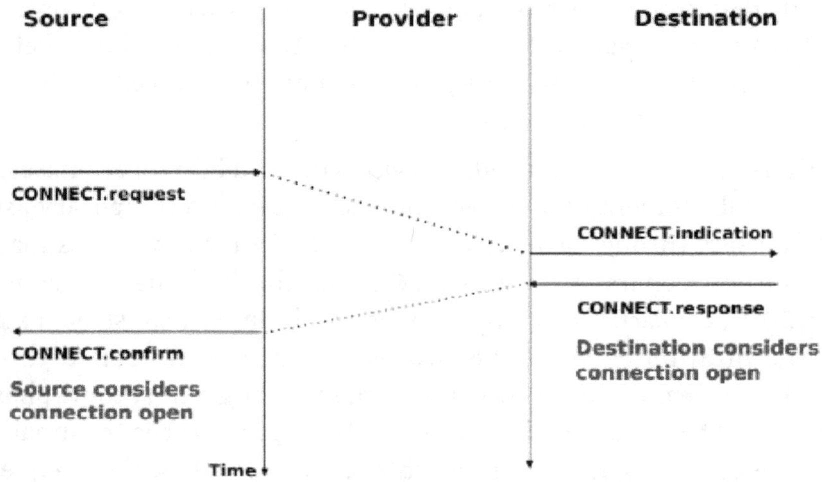

Figure 1.21: Connection establishment

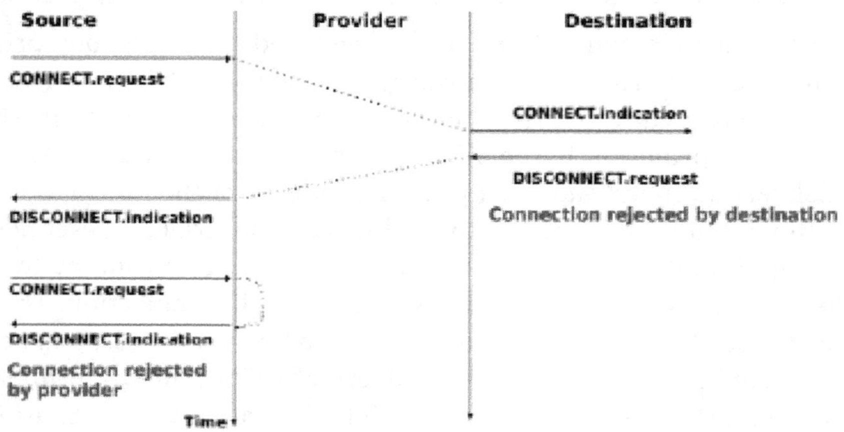

Figure 1.22: Two types of rejection for a connection establishment attempt

Once the connection has been established, the service provider supplies two data streams to the communicating users. The first data stream can be used by the initiating user to send SDUs. The second data stream allows the responding user to send SDUs to the initiating user. The data streams can be organised in different ways. A first organisation is the *message-mode* transfer. With the *message-mode* transfer, the service provider guarantees that one and only one *Data.indication* will be delivered to the endpoint of the data stream for each *Data.request* primitive issued by the other endpoint. The *message-mode* transfer is illustrated in the figure below. The main advantage of the *message-transfer* mode is that the recipient receives exactly the SDUs that were sent by the other user. If each SDU contains a command, the receiving user can process each command as soon as it receives a SDU.

Unfortunately, the *message-mode* transfer is not widely used on the Internet. On the Internet, the most popular connection-oriented service transfers SDUs in *stream-mode.* With the *stream-mode,* the service provider supplies a byte stream that links the two communicating users. The sending user sends bytes by using *Data.request* primitives that contain sequences of bytes as SDUs. The service provider delivers SDUs containing consecutive bytes to the receiving user by using *Data.indication* primitives. The service provider ensures that all the bytes sent at one end of the stream are delivered correctly in the same order at the other endpoint. However, the service provider does not attempt to preserve the boundaries of the SDUs. There is no relation enforced by the service provider between the number of *Data. request* and the number of *Data.indication* primitives. The *stream-mode* is illustrated in the figure below. In practice, a consequence of the utilisation of the *stream-mode* is that if the users want to exchange structured SDUs, they will need to provide the mechanisms that allow the receiving user to separate successive SDUs in the byte stream that it receives. As we will see in the next chapter, application layer protocols often use specific delimiters such as the end of line character to delineate SDUs in a bytestream.

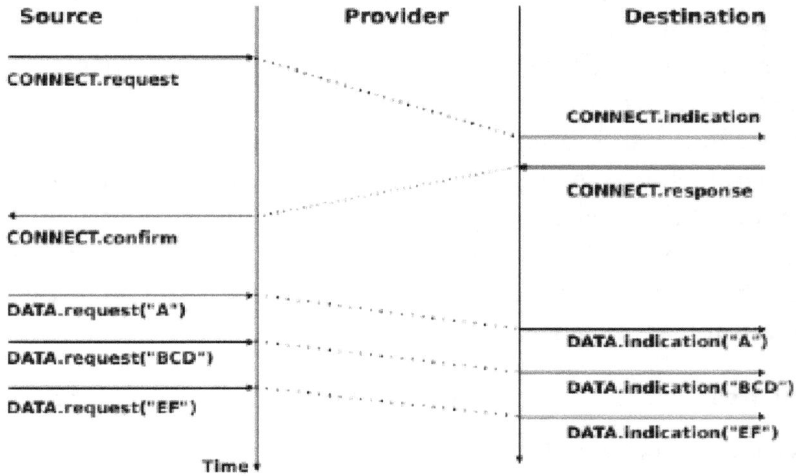

Figure 1.23: Message-mode transfer in a connection oriented service

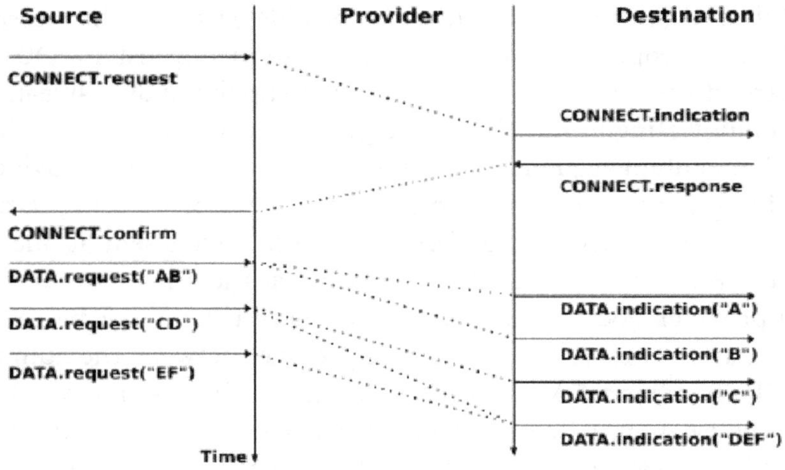

Figure 1.24: Stream-mode transfer in a connection oriented service

The third phase of a connection is when it needs to be released. As a connection involves three parties (two users and one service provider), any of them can request the termination of the connection. Usually, connections are terminated upon request of one user once the data transfer is finished. However, sometimes the service provider may be forced to terminate a connection. This can be due to lack of resources inside the service provider or because one of the users is not reachable anymore through the network. In this case, the service provider will issue Disconnect.indication primitives to both users. These primitives will contain, as parameter, some information about the reason for the termination of the connection. Unfortunately, as illustrated in the figure below, when a service provider is forced to terminate a connection it cannot guarantee that all SDUs sent by each user have been delivered to the other user. This connection release is said to be abrupt as it can cause losses of data.

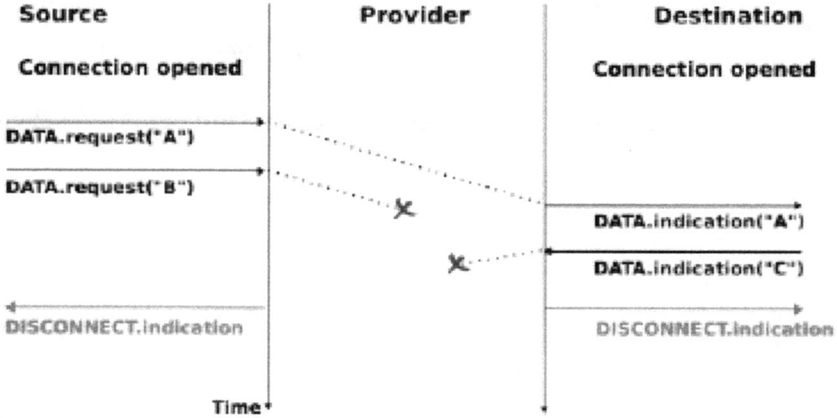

Figure 1.25: Abrupt connection release initiated by the service provider

An abrupt connection release can also be triggered by one of the users. If a user needs, for any reason, to terminate a connection quickly, it can issue a *Disconnect.request* primitive and to request an abrupt release. The service provider will process the request, stop the two data streams and deliver the *Disconnect.indication* primitive to the remote user as soon as possible. As illustrated in the figure below, this abrupt connection release may cause losses of SDUs.

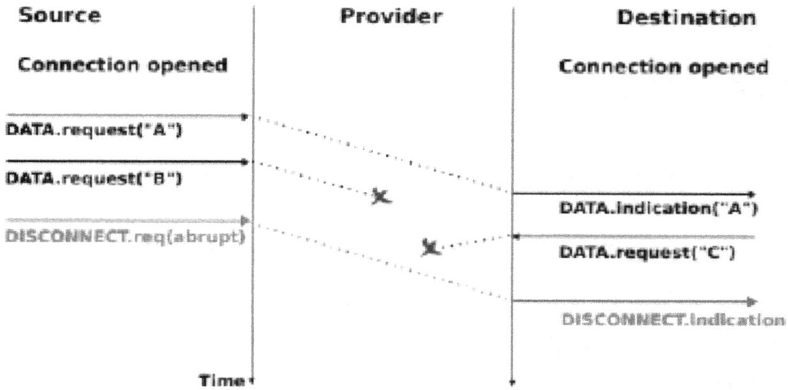

Figure 1.26: Abrupt connection release initiated by a user

To ensure a reliable delivery of the SDUs sent by each user over a connection, we need to consider the two streams that compose a connection as independent. A user should be able to release the stream that it uses to send SDUs once it has sent all the SDUs that it planned to send over this connection, but still continue to receive SDUs over the opposite stream. This *graceful* connection release is usually performed as shown in the figure below. One user issues a *Disconnect.request* primitive to its provider once it has issued all its *Data.request* primitives. The service provider will wait until all *Data.indication* primitives have been delivered to the receiving user before issuing the *Disconnnect.indication* primitive. This primitive informs the receiving user that it will no longer receive SDUs over this connection, but it is still able to issue *Data.request* primitives on the stream in the opposite direction. Once the user has issued all of its *Data.request* primitives, it issues a *Disconnnect.request* primitive to request the termination of the remaining stream. The service provider will process the request and deliver the corresponding *Disconnect.indication* to the other user once it has delivered all the pending *Data.indication* primitives. At this point, all data has been delivered and the two streams have been released successfully and the connection is completely closed.

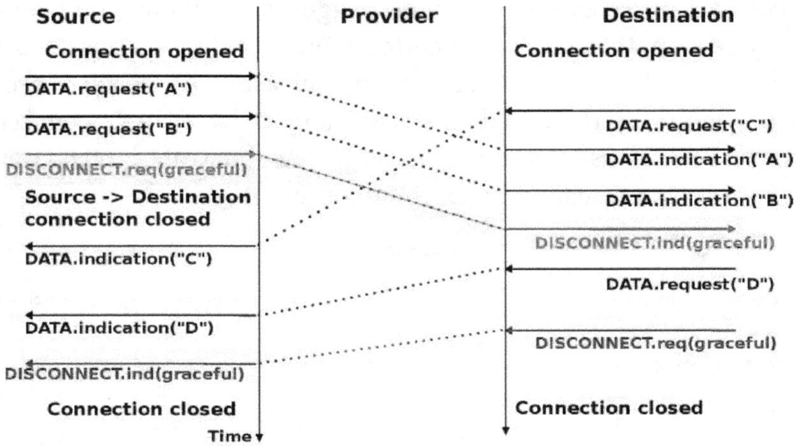

Figure 1.27: Graceful connection release

Note: Reliability of the connection-oriented service

An important point to note about the connection-oriented service is its reliability. A *connection-oriented* service can only guarantee the correct delivery of all SDUs provided that the connection has been released gracefully. This implies that while the connection is active, there is no guarantee for the actual delivery of the SDUs exchanged as the connection may need to be released abruptly at any time.

1.2 THE REFERENCE MODELS

Given the growing complexity of computer networks, during the 1970s network researchers proposed various reference models to facilitate the description of network protocols and services. Of these, the Open Systems Interconnection (OSI) model [Zimmermann80] was probably the most influential. It served as the basis for the standardisation work performed within the *ISO* to develop global computer network standards. The reference model that we use in this book can be considered as a simplified version of the OSI reference model.

1.2.1 The five layers reference model

Our reference model is divided into five layers, as shown in the figure below.

Starting from the bottom, the first layer is the Physical layer. Two communicating devices are linked through a physical medium. This physical medium is used to transfer an electrical or optical signal between two directly connected devices. Several types of physical mediums are used in practice :

- *electrical cable.* Information can be transmitted over different types of electrical cables. The most common ones are the twisted pairs that are used in the telephone network, but also in enterprise networks and coaxial cables. Coaxial cables are still used in cable TV networks, but are no longer used in enterprise networks. Some networking technologies operate over the classical electrical cable.

- *optical fiber.* Optical fibers are frequently used in public and enterprise networks when the distance between the communication devices is larger than one kilometer. There are two main types of optical fibers : multimode and monomode. Multimode is much cheaper than monomode fiber because a LED can be used to send a signal over a multimode fiber while a monomode fiber must be driven by a laser. Due to the different modes of propagation of light, monomode fibers are limited to distances of a few kilometers while multimode fibers can be used over distances greater than several tens of kilometers. In both cases, repeaters can be used to regenerate the optical signal at one endpoint of a fiber to send it over another fiber.

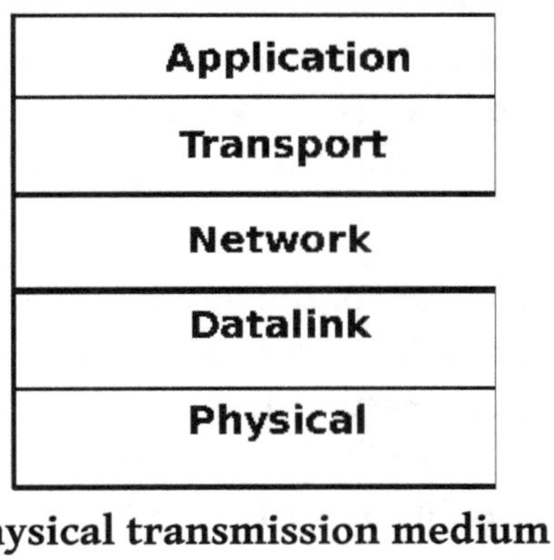

Figure 1.28: The five layers of the reference model

- *wireless.* In this case, a radio signal is used to encode the information exchanged between the communicating devices. Many types of modulation techniques are used to send information over a wireless channel and there is lot of innovation in this field with new techniques appearing every year. While most wireless networks rely on radio signals, some use a laser that sends light pulses to a remote detector. These optical techniques allow to create point-to-point links while radio-based techniques, depending on the directionality of the antennas, can be used to build networks containing devices spread over a small geographical area.

An important point to note about the Physical layer is the service that it provides. This service is usually an unreliable connection-oriented service that allows the users of the Physical layer to exchange bits. The unit of information transfer in the Physical layer is the bit. The Physical layer service is unreliable because :

- the Physical layer may change, e.g. due to electromagnetic interferences, the value of a bit being transmitted
- the Physical layer may deliver *more* bits to the receiver than the bits sent by the sender
- the Physical layer may deliver *fewer* bits to the receiver than the bits sent by the sender

The last two points may seem strange at first glance. When two devices are attached through a cable, how is it possible for bits to be created or lost on such a cable ?

This is mainly due to the fact that the communicating devices use their own clock to transmit bits at a given bit rate. Consider a sender having a clock that ticks one million times per second and sends one bit every tick. Every microsecond, the sender sends an electrical or optical signal that encodes one bit. The sender's bit rate is thus 1 Mbps. If the receiver clock ticks exactly every microsecond, it will also deliver 1 Mbps to its user. However, if the receiver's clock is slightly faster (resp. slower), than it will deliver slightly more (resp. less) than one million bits every second. This explains why the physical layer may lose or create bits.

Note: Bitrate

In computer networks, the bit rate of the physical layer is always expressed in bits per second. One Mbps is one million bits per second and one Gbps is one billion bits per second. This is in contrast with memory specifications that are usually expressed in bytes (8 bits), KiloBytes (1024 bytes) or MegaBytes (1048576 bytes). Thus transferring one MByte through a 1 Mbps link lasts 8.39 seconds.

Bit rate	Bits per second
1 Kbps	10^3
1 Mbps	10^6
1 Gbps	10^9
1 Tbps	10^{12}

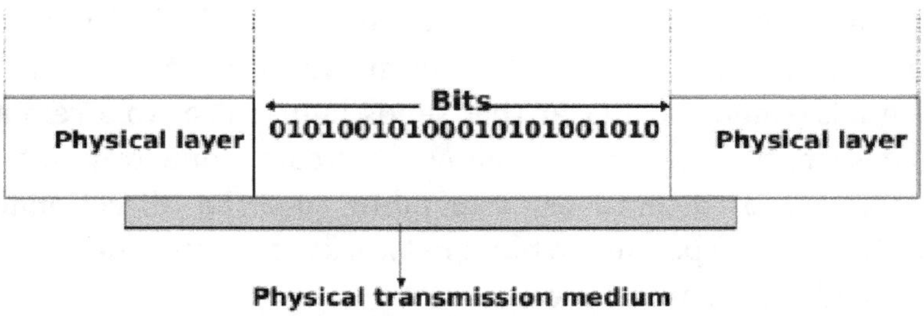

Figure 1.29: The Physical layer

The physical layer allows thus two or more entities that are directly attached to the same transmission medium to exchange bits. Being able to exchange bits is important as virtually any information can be encoded as a sequence of bits.

Electrical engineers are used to processing streams of bits, but computer scientists usually prefer to deal with higher level concepts. A similar issue arises with file storage. Storage devices such as hard-disks also store streams of bits. There are hardware devices that process the bit stream produced by a hard-disk, but computer scientists have designed filesystems to allow applications to easily access such storage devices. These filesystems are typically divided into several layers as well. Hard-disks store sectors of 512 bytes or more. Unix filesystems group sectors in larger blocks that can contain data or *inodes* representing the structure of the filesystem. Finally, applications manipulate files and directories that are translated in blocks, sectors and eventually bits by the operating system.

Computer networks use a similar approach. Each layer provides a service that is built above the underlying layer and is closer to the needs of the applications.

The *Datalink layer* builds on the service provided by the underlying physical layer. The *Datalink layer* allows two hosts that are directly connected through the physical layer to exchange information. The unit of information exchanged between two entities in the *Datalink layer* is a frame. A frame is a finite sequence of bits. Some *Datalink layers* use variable-length frames while others only use fixed-length frames. Some *Datalink layers* provide a connection-oriented service while others provide a connectionless service. Some *Datalink layers* provide reliable delivery while others do not guarantee the correct delivery of the information.

An important point to note about the *Datalink layer* is that although the figure below indicates that two entities of the *Datalink layer* exchange frames directly, in reality this is slightly different. When the *Datalink layer* entity on the left needs to transmit a frame, it issues as many *Data.request* primitives to the underlying *physical layer* as there are bits in the frame. The physical layer will then convert the sequence of bits in an electromagnetic or optical signal that will be sent over the physical medium. The *physical layer* on the right hand side of the figure will decode the received signal, recover the bits and issue the corresponding *Data.indication* primitives to its *Datalink layer* entity. If there are no transmission errors, this entity will receive the frame sent earlier.

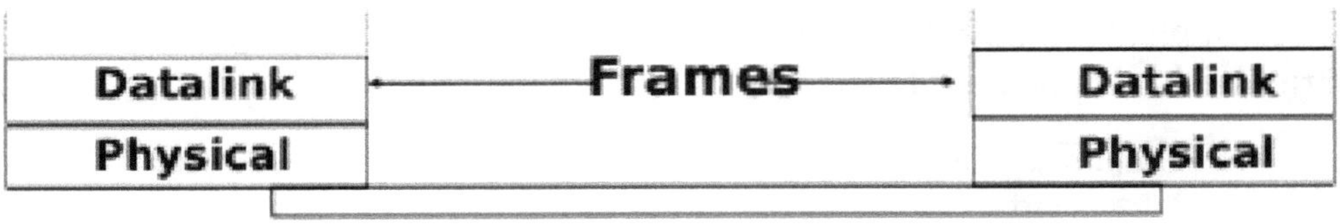

Figure 1.30: The Datalink layer

The *Datalink layer* allows directly connected hosts to exchange information, but it is often necessary to exchange information between hosts that are not attached to the same physical medium. This is the task of the *network layer*. The *network layer* is built above the *datalink layer*. Network layer entities exchange *packets*. A *packet* is a finite sequence of bytes that is transported by the datalink layer inside one or more frames. A packet usually contains information about its origin and its destination, and usually passes through several intermediate devices called routers on its way from its origin to its destination.

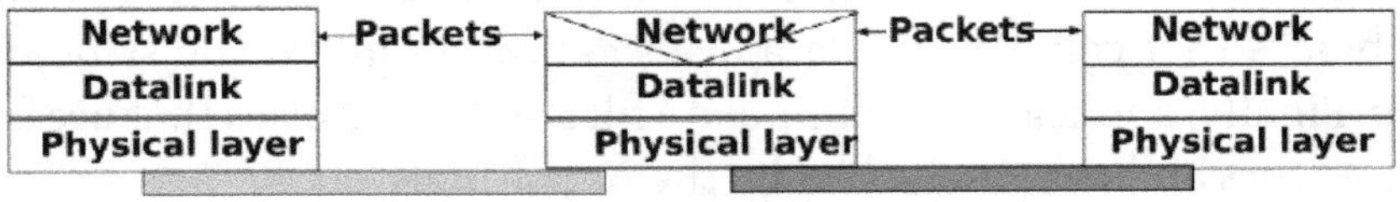

Figure 1.31: The network layer

Most realisations of the network layer, including the internet, do not provide a reliable service. However, many applications need to exchange information reliably and so using the network layer service directly would be very difficult for them. Ensuring the reliable delivery of the data produced by applications is the task of the *transport layer*. *Transport layer* entities exchange *segments*. A segment is a finite sequence of bytes that are transported inside one or more packets. A transport layer entity issues segments (or sometimes part of segments) as *Data.request* to the underlying network layer entity.

There are different types of transport layers. The most widely used transport layers on the Internet are *TCP* ,that provides a reliable connection-oriented bytestream transport service, and *UDP* ,that provides an unreliable connection-less transport service.

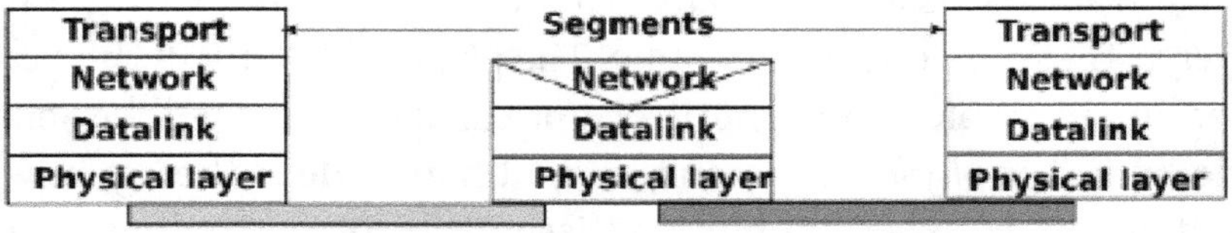

Figure 1.32: The transport layer

The upper layer of our architecture is the *Application layer*. This layer includes all the mechanisms and data structures that are necessary for the applications. We will use Application Data Unit (ADU) to indicate the data exchanged between two entities of the Application layer.

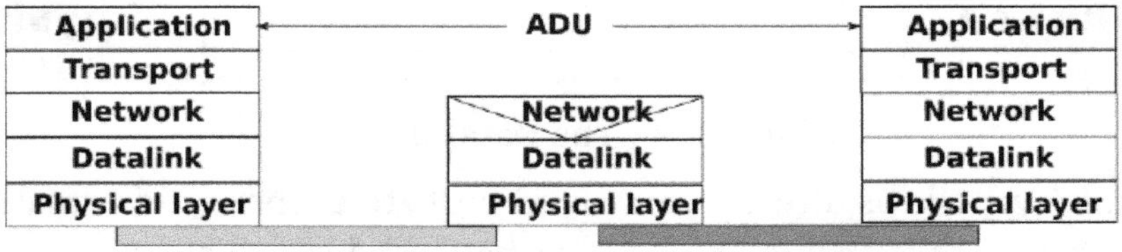

Figure 1.33: The Application layer

1.2.2. The TCP/IP reference model

In contrast with OSI, the TCP/IP community did not spend a lot of effort defining a detailed reference model; in fact, the goals of the Internet architecture were only documented after TCP/IP had been deployed [Clark88]. **RFC 1122** , which defines the requirements for Internet hosts, mentions four different layers. Starting from the top, these are :

- an Application layer
- a Transport layer
- an Internet layer which is equivalent to the network layer of our reference model
- a Link layer which combines the functionalities of the physical and datalink layers of our five-layer reference model

Besides this difference in the lower layers, the TCP/IP reference model is very close to the five layers that we use throughout this document.

1.2.3 The OSI reference model

Compared to the five layers reference model explained above, the *OSI* reference model defined in [X200] is divided in seven layers. The four lower layers are similar to the four lower layers described above. The OSI reference model refined the application layer by dividing it in three layers :

- the Session layer. The Session layer contains the protocols and mechanisms that are necessary to organize and to synchronize the dialogue and to manage the data exchange of presentation layer entities. While one of the main functions of the transport layer is to cope with the unreliability of the network layer, the session's layer objective is to hide the possible failures of transport-level connections to the upper layer higher. For this, the Session Layer provides services that allow to establish a session-connection, to support orderly data exchange (including mechanisms that allow to recover from the abrupt release of an underlying transport connection), and to release the connection in an orderly manner.
- the Presentation layer was designed to cope with the different ways of representing information on computers. There are many differences in the way computer store information. Some computers store integers as 32 bits field, others use 64 bits field and the same problem arises with floating point number. For textual information, this is even more complex with the many different character codes that have been used. The situation is even more complex when considering the exchange of

structured information such as database records. To solve this problem, the Presentation layer contains provides for a common representation of the data transferred. The *ASN.1* notation was designed for the Presentation layer and is still used today by some protocols.

- the Application layer that contains the mechanisms that do not fit in neither the Presentation nor the Session layer. The OSI Application layer was itself further divided in several generic service elements.

Note: Where are the missing layers in TCP/IP reference model ?

The TCP/IP reference places the Presentation and the Session layers implicitly in the Application layer. The main motivations for simplifying the upper layers in the TCP/IP reference model were pragmatic. Most Internet applications started as prototypes that evolved and were later standardised. Many of these applications assumed that they would be used to exchange information written in American English and for which the 7 bits US-ASCII character code was sufficient. This was the case for email, but as we'll see in the next chapter, email was able to evolve to support different character encodings. Some applications considered the different data representations explicitly. For example, *ftp* contained mechanisms to convert a file from one format to another and the HTML language was defined to represent web pages. On the other hand, many ISO specifications were developed by committees composed of people who did not all participate in actual implementations. ISO spent a lot of effort analysing the requirements and defining a solution that meets all of these requirements. Unfortunately, some of the specifications were so complex that it was difficult to implement them completely and the standardisation bodies defined recommended profiles that contained the implemented sets of options...

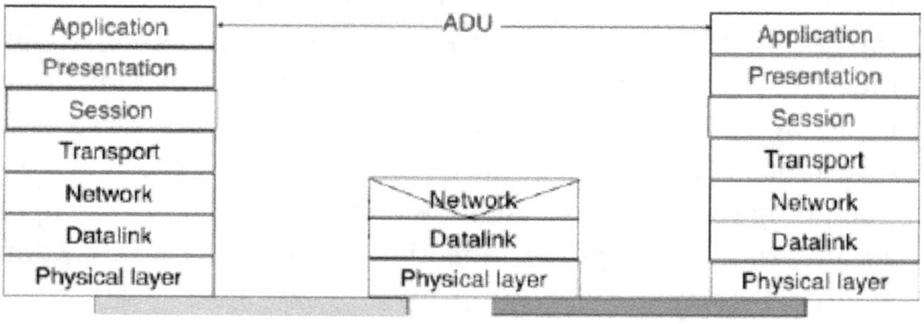

Figure 1.34: The seven layers of the OSI reference model

1.3 ORGANISATION OF THE BOOK

This document is organised according to the *TCP/IP* reference model and follows a top-down approach. Most of the classical networking textbooks chose a bottom-up approach, i.e. they first explained all the electrical and optical details of the physical layer then moved to the datalink layer. This approach worked well during the infancy of computer networks and until the late 1990s. At that time, most students were not users of computer networks and it was useful to explain computer networks by building the corresponding protocols from the simplest, in the physical layer, up to the application layer. Today, all students are active users of Internet applications, and starting to learn computer networking by looking at bits is not very motivating. Starting from [KuroseRoss09], many textbooks and teachers have chosen a top-down approach. This approach starts from applications such as email and web that students already know and explores the different layers, starting from the application layer. This approach works quite well with today's students. The traditional bottom-up approach could in fact be considered as an engineering approach as it starts from the simple network that allows the exchange of bits, and explains how to combine different protocols and mechanisms to build the most complex applications. The top-down approach could on the other hand be considered as a scientific approach. Like biologists, it starts from an existing (man- built) system and explores it layer by layer.

Besides the top-down versus bottom-up organisation, computer networking books can either aim at having an in-depth coverage of a small number of topics, or at having a limited coverage of a wide range of topics. Covering a wide range of topics is interesting for introductory courses or for students who do not need a detailed knowledge of computer networks. It allows the students to learn a *little about everything* and then start from this basic knowledge later if they need to understand computer networking in more detail. This books chose to cover, in detail, a smaller number of topics than other textbooks. This is motivated by the fact that computer networks often need to be pushed to their limits. Understanding the details of the main networking protocols is important to be able to fully grasp how a network behaves or extend it to provide innovative services.

The book is organised as follows: We first describe the application layer in chapter *The application Layer*. Given the large number of Internet-based applications, it is of course impossible to cover them all in detail. Instead we focus on three types of Internet-based applications. We first study the Domain Name System (DNS) and then explain some of the protocols involved in the exchange of electronic mail. The discussion of the application layer ends with a description of the key protocols of the world wide web.

All these applications rely on the transport layer that is explained in chapter *The transport layer*. This is a key layer in today's networks as it contains all the mechanisms necessary to provide a reliable delivery of data over an unreliable network. We cover the transport layer by first developing a simple reliable transport layer protocol and then explain the details of the TCP and UDP protocols used in TCP/IP networks.

After the transport layer, we analyse the network layer in chapter *The network layer*. This is also a very important layer as it is responsible for the delivery of packets from any source to any destination through intermediate routers. In the network layer, we describe the two possible organisations of the network layer and the routing protocols based on link-state and distance vectors. Then we explain in detail the IPv4, IPv6, RIP, OSPF and BGP protocols that are actually used in today's Internet.

The last chapter of the book is devoted to the datalink layer. In chapter *The datalink layer and the Local Area Networks*, we begin by explaining the principles of the datalink layers on point-to-point links. Then, we focus on the Local Area Networks. We first describe the Medium Access Control algorithms that allow multiple hosts to share one transmission medium. We consider both opportunistic and deterministic techniques. We then explain in detail two types of LANs that are important from a deployment viewpoint today : Ethernet and WiFi.

CHAPTER 2

The Application Layer

The Application Layer is the most important and most visible layer in computer networks. Applications reside in this layer and human users interact via those applications through the network.

In this chapter, we first briefly describe the main principles of the application layer and focus on the two most important application models : the client-server and the peer-to-peer models. Then, we review in detail two families of protocols that have proved to be very useful in the Internet : electronic mail and the protocols that allow access to information on the world wide web. We also describe the Domain Name System that allows humans to use user-friendly names while the hosts use 32 bits or 128 bits long IP addresses.

2.1 PRINCIPLES

The are two important models used to organise a networked application. The first and oldest model is the clientserver model. In this model, a server provides services to clients that exchange information with it. This model is highly asymmetrical: clients send requests and servers perform actions and return responses. It is illustrated in the figure below.

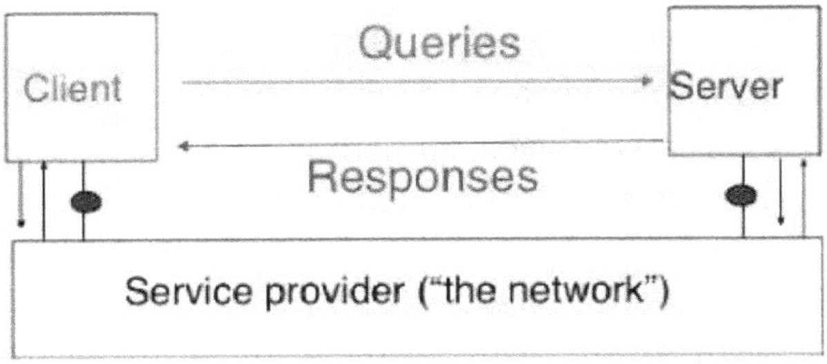

Figure 2.1: The client-server model

The client-server model was the first model to be used to develop networked applications. This model comes naturally from the mainframes and minicomputers that were the only networked computers used until the 1980s. A minicomputer is a multi-user system that is used by tens or more users at the same time. Each user interacts with the minicomputer by using a terminal. Those terminals, were mainly a screen, a keyboard and a cable directly connected to the minicomputer.

There are various types of servers as well as various types of clients. A web server provides information in response to the query sent by its clients. A print server prints documents sent as queries by the client. An email server will forward towards their recipient the email messages sent as queries while a music server will deliver the music requested by the client. From the viewpoint of the application developer, the client and the server applications directly exchange messages (the horizontal arrows labelled *Queries* and *Responses* in the above figure), but in practice these messages are exchanged thanks to the underlying layers (the vertical arrows in the above figure). In this chapter, we focus on these horizontal exchanges of messages.

Networked applications do not exchange random messages. In order to ensure that the server is able to understand the queries sent by a client, and also that the client is able to understand the responses sent by the server, they must both agree on a set of syntactical and semantic rules. These rules define the format of the messages exchanged as well as their ordering. This set of rules is called an application-level *protocol.*

An *application-level protocol* is similar to a structured conversation between humans. Assume that Alice wants to know the current time but does not have a watch. If Bob passes close by, the following conversation could take place :

- Alice: *Hello*
- Bob: *Hello*
- Alice : *What time is it ?*
- Bob: *11:55*
- Alice : *Thank you*
- Bob : *You're welcome*

Such a conversation succeeds if both Alice and Bob speak the same language. If Alice meets Tchang who only speaks Chinese, she won't be able to ask him the current time. A conversation between humans can be more complex. For example, assume that Bob is a security guard whose duty is to only allow trusted secret agents to enter a meeting room. If all agents know a secret password, the conversation between Bob and Trudy could be as follows :

- Bob : *What is the secret password ?*
- Trudy: *1234*
- Bob : *This is the correct password, you're welcome*

If Alice wants to enter the meeting room but does not know the password, her conversation could be as follows :

- Bob : *What is the secret password ?*
- Alice: *3.1415*
- Bob : *This is not the correct password.*

Human conversations can be very formal, e.g. when soldiers communicate with their hierarchy, or informal such as when friends discuss. Computers that communicate are more akin to soldiers and require well-defined rules to ensure an successful exchange of information. There are two types of rules that define how information can be exchanged between computers :

- syntactical rules that precisely define the format of the messages that are exchanged. As computers only process bits, the syntactical rules specify how information is encoded as bit strings
- organisation of the information flow. For many applications, the flow of information must be structured and there are precedence relationships between the different types of information. In the time example above, Alice must greet Bob before asking for the current time. Alice would not ask for the current time first and greet Bob afterwards. Such precedence relationships exist in networked applications as well. For example, a server must receive a username and a valid password before accepting more complex commands from its clients.

Let us first discuss the syntactical rules. We will later explain how the information flow can be organised by analysing real networked applications.

Application-layer protocols exchange two types of messages. Some protocols such as those used to support electronic mail exchange messages expressed as strings or lines of characters. As the transport layer allows hosts to exchange bytes, they need to agree on a common representation of the characters. The first and simplest method to encode characters is to use the *ASCII* table. **RFC 20** provides the ASCII table that is used by many protocols on the Internet. For example, the table defines the following binary representations :

- *A :1000011b*
- *0: 0110000b*
- *z :1111010b*
- *@ : 1000000b*
- *space : 0100000b*

In addition, the *ASCII* table also defines several non-printable or control characters. These characters were designed to allow an application to control a printer or a terminal. These control characters include *CR* and *LF*, that are used to terminate a line, and the *Bell* character which causes the terminal to emit a sound.

- *carriage return (CR): 0001101b*
- *linefeed (LF): 0001010b*
- Bell: *0000111b*

The *ASCII* characters are encoded as a seven bits field, but transmitted as an eight-bits byte whose high order bit is usually set to *0*. Bytes are always transmitted starting from the high order or most significant bit.

Most applications exchange strings that are composed of fixed or variable numbers of characters. A common solution to define the character strings that are acceptable is to define them as a grammar using a Backus-Naur Form *(BNF)* such as the Augmented BNF defined in **RFC 5234**. A BNF is a set of production rules that generate all valid character strings. For example, consider a networked application that uses two commands, where the user can supply a username and a password. The BNF for this application could be defined as shown in the figure below.

```
command          = usercommand / passworcommand
usercommand      = "user" SP username CRLF
passwordcommand  = "pass" SP password CRLF
username         = 1*8ALPHA
password         = (ALPHA) *(ALPHA/DIGIT)
ALPHA            =  %x41-5A / %x61-7A
CR               =  %x0D
CRLF             =  CR LF
DIGIT            =  "0" / "1" / "2" / "3" / "4" / "5" / "6" / "7" / "8" / "9"
LF               =  %x0A
SP               =  %x20 / %x09
```

Figure 2.2: A simple BNF specification

The example above defines several terminals and two commands : *usercommand* and *passwordcommand*. The *ALPHA* terminal contains all letters in upper and lower case. In the *ALPHA* rule, *%ox41* corresponds to ASCII character code 41 in hexadecimal, i.e. capital A. The *CR* and *LF* terminals correspond to the carriage return and linefeed control characters. The *CRLF* rule concatenates these two terminals to match the standard end of line termination. The *DIGIT* terminal contains all digits. The *SP* terminal corresponds to the white space characters. The *usercommand* is composed of two strings separated by white space. In the ABNF rules that define the messages used by Internet applications, the commands are case-insensitive. The rule *"user"* corresponds to all possible cases of the letters that compose the word between brackets, e.g. *user, uSeR, USER, usER,...* A *username* contains at least one letter and up to 8 letters. User names are case-sensitive as they are not defined as a string between brackets. The *password* rule indicates that a password starts with a letter and can contain any number of letters or digits. The white space and the control characters cannot appear in a *password* defined by the above rule.

Besides character strings, some applications also need to exchange 16 bits and 32 bits fields such as integers. A naive solution would have been to send the 16- or 32-bits field as it is encoded in the host's memory. Unfortunately, there are different methods to store 16- or 32-bits fields in memory. Some CPUs store the most significant byte of a 16-bits field in the first address of the field while others store the least significant byte at this location. When networked applications running on different CPUs exchange 16 bits fields, there are two possibilities to transfer them over the transport service :

- send the most significant byte followed by the least significant byte
- send the least significant byte followed by the most significant byte

The first possibility was named *big-endian* in a note written by Cohen [Cohen1980] while the second was named *little-endian*. Vendors of CPUs that used *big-endian* in memory insisted on using *big-endian* encoding in networked applications while vendors of CPUs that used *little-endian* recommended the opposite. Several studies were written on the relative merits of each type of encoding, but the discussion became almost a religious issue [Cohen1980]. Eventually, the Internet chose the *big-endian* encoding, i.e. multi-byte fields are always transmitted by sending the most significant byte first, **RFC 791** refers to this encoding as the *network-byte order.* Most libraries used to write networked applications contain functions to convert multi-byte fields from memory to the network byte order and vice versa.

Besides 16 and 32 bit words, some applications need to exchange data structures containing bit fields of various lengths. For example, a message may be composed of a 16 bits field followed by eight, one bit flags, a 24 bits field and two 8 bits bytes. Internet protocol specifications will define such a message by using a representation such as the one below. In this representation, each line corresponds to 32 bits and the vertical lines are used to delineate fields. The numbers above the lines indicate the bit positions in the 32-bits word, with the high order bit at position *0*.

```
 0                   1                   2                   3
 0 1 2 3 4 5 6 7 8 9 0 1 2 3 4 5 6 7 8 9 0 1 2 3 4 5 6 7 8 9 0 1
+-+-+-+-+-+-+-+-+-+-+-+-+-+-+-+-+-+-+-+-+-+-+-+-+-+-+-+-+-+-+-+-+
|        First field (16 bits)  |A|B|C|D|E|F|G|H|    Second     |
+-+-+-+-+-+-+-+-+-+-+-+-+-+-+-+-+-+-+-+-+-+-+-+-+-+-+-+-+-+-+-+-+
|        field (24 bits)        |  First Byte   |  Second Byte  |
+-+-+-+-+-+-+-+-+-+-+-+-+-+-+-+-+-+-+-+-+-+-+-+-+-+-+-+-+-+-+-+-+
```

Figure 2.3: Message format

The message mentioned above will be transmitted starting from the upper 32-bits word in network byte order. The first field is encoded in 16 bits. It is followed by eight one bit flags *(A-H),* a 24 bits field whose high order byte is shown in the first line and the two low order bytes appear in the second line followed by two one byte fields. This ASCII representation is frequently used when defining binary protocols. We will use it for all the binary protocols that are discussed in this book.

We will discuss several examples of application-level protocols in this chapter.

2.1.1 The peer-to-peer model

The peer-to-peer model emerged during the last ten years as another possible architecture for networked applications. In the traditional client-server model, hosts act either as servers or as clients and a server serves a large number of clients. In the peer-to-peer model, all hosts act as both servers and clients and they play both roles. The peer-to-peer model has been used to develop various networked applications, ranging from Internet telephony to file sharing or Internet-wide filesystems. A detailed description of peer-to-peer applications may be found in [BYL2008]. Surveys of peer-to-peer protocols and applications may be found in [AS2004] and [LCP2005].

2.1.2 The transport services

Networked applications are built on top of the transport service. As explained in the previous chapter, there are two main types of transport services :

- the *connectionless* or *datagram* service
- the *connection-oriented* or *byte-stream* service

The connectionless service allows applications to easily exchange messages or Service Data Units. On the Internet, this service is provided by the UDP protocol that will be explained in the next chapter. The connectionless transport service on the Internet is unreliable, but is able to detect transmission errors. This implies that an application will not receive an SDU that has been corrupted due to transmission errors.

The connectionless transport service allows networked application to exchange messages. Several networked applications may be running at the same time on a single host. Each of these applications must be able to exchange SDUs with remote applications. To enable these exchanges of SDUs, each networked application running on a host is identified by the following information :

- the *host* on which the application is running
- the *port number* on which the application *listens* for SDUs

On the Internet, the *port number* is an integer and the *host* is identified by its network address. As we will see in chapter *The network layer* there are two types of Internet Addresses:

- *IP version 4* addresses that are 32 bits wide
- *IP version 6* addresses that are 128 bits wide

IPv4 addresses are usually represented by using a dotted decimal representation where each decimal number corresponds to one byte of the address, e.g. *203.0.113.56.* IPv6 addresses are usually represented as a set of hexadecimal numbers separated by semicolons, e.g. *2001:db8:3080:2:217:f2ff:fed6:65c0.* Today, most Internet hosts have one IPv4 address. A small fraction of them also have an IPv6 address. In the future, we can expect that more and more hosts will have IPv6 addresses and that some of them will not have an IPv4 address anymore. A host that only has an IPv4 address cannot communicate with a host having only an IPv6 address. The figure below illustrates two that are using the datagram service provided by UDP on hosts that are using IPv4 addresses.

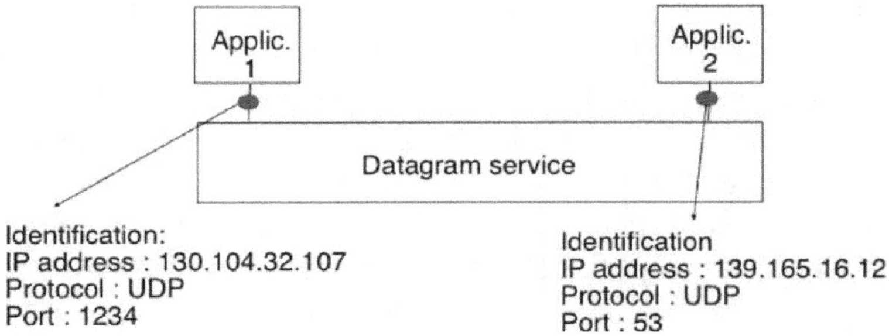

Figure 2.4: The connectionless or datagram service

The second transport service is the connection-oriented service. On the Internet, this service is often called the *byte-stream service* as it creates a reliable byte stream between the two applications that are linked by a transport connection. Like the datagram service, the networked applications that use the byte-stream service are identified by the host on which they run and a port number. These hosts can be identified by an IPv4 address, an IPv6 address or a name. The figure below illustrates two applications that are using the byte-stream service provided by the TCP protocol on IPv6 hosts. The byte stream service provided by TCP is reliable and bidirectional.

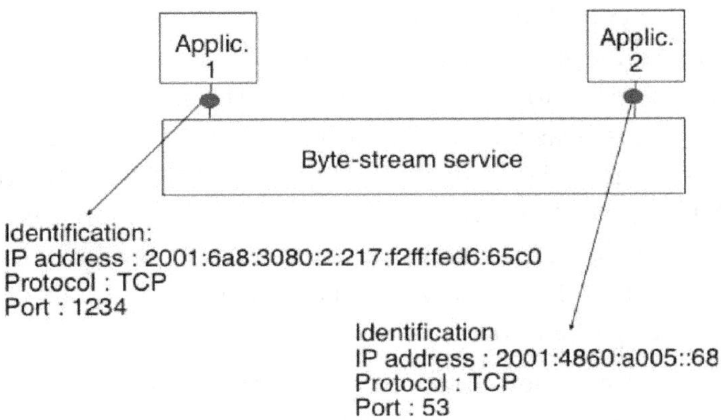

Figure 2.5: The connection-oriented or byte-stream service

2.2 APPLICATION-LEVEL PROTOCOLS

Many protocols have been defined for networked applications. In this section, we describe some of the important applications that are used on the Internet. We first explain the Domain Name System (DNS) that enables hosts to be identified by human-friendly names instead of the IPv4 or IPv6 addresses that are used by the network. Then, we describe the operation of electronic mail, one of the first killer applications on the global Internet, and the protocols used on world wide web.

2.2.1 The Domain Name System

In the early days of the Internet, there were only a few number of hosts (mainly minicomputers) connected to the network. The most popular applications were remote login and file transfer. By 1983, there were already five hundred hosts attached to the Internet. Each of these hosts were identified by a unique IPv4 address. Forcing human users to remember the IPv4 addresses of the remote hosts that they want to use was not user-friendly. Human users prefer to remember names, and use them when needed. Using names as aliases for addresses is a common technique in Computer Science. It simplifies the development of applications and allows the developer to ignore the low level details. For example, by using a programming language instead of writing machine code, a developer can write software without knowing whether the variables that it uses are stored in memory or inside registers.

Because names are at a higher level than addresses, they allow (both in the example of programming above, and on the Internet) to treat addresses as mere technical identifiers, which can change at will. Only the names are stable. On today's Internet, where switching to another ISP means changing your IP addresses, the user-friendliness of domain names is less important (they are not often typed by users) but their stability remains a very important, may be their most important property.

The first solution that allowed applications to use names was the *hosts.txt* file. This file is similar to the symbol table found in compiled code. It contains the mapping between the name of each Internet host and its associated IP address. It was maintained by SRI International that coordinated the Network Information Center (NIC). When a new host was connected to the network, the system administrator had to register its name and IP address at the NIC. The NIC updated the *hosts.txt* file on its server. All Internet hosts regularly retrieved the updated *hosts.txt* file from the server maintained by SRI. This file was stored at a well-known location on each Internet host (see **RFC 952**) and networked applications could use it to find the IP address corresponding to a name.

A *hosts.txt* file can be used when there are up to a few hundred hosts on the network. However, it is clearly not suitable for a network containing thousands or millions of hosts. A key issue in a large network is to define a suitable naming scheme. The ARPANet initially used a flat naming space, i.e. each host was assigned a unique name. To limit collisions between names, these names usually contained the name of the institution and a suffix to identify the host inside the institution (a kind of poor man's hierarchical naming scheme). On the ARPANet few institutions had several hosts connected to the network.

However, the limitations of a flat naming scheme became clear before the end of the ARPANet and **RFC 819** proposed a hierarchical naming scheme. While **RFC 819** discussed the possibility of organising the names as a directed graph, the Internet opted eventually for a tree structure capable of containing all names. In this tree, the top-level domains are those that are directly attached to the root. The first top-level domain was *.arpa*. This top-level name was initially added as a suffix to the names of the hosts attached to the ARPANet and listed in the *hosts.txt* file. In 1984, the *.gov, .edu, .com, .mil* and *.org* generic top-level domain names were added and **RFC 1032** proposed the utilisation of the two letter *ISO-3166* country codes as top-level domain names. Since *ISO-3166* defines a two letter code for each country recognised by the United Nations, this allowed all countries to automatically have a top-level domain. These domains include *.be* for Belgium, *.fr* for France, *.us* for the USA, *.ie* for Ireland or *.tv* for Tuvalu, a group of small islands in the Pacific and *.tm* for Turkmenistan. Today, the set of top-level domain-names is managed by the Internet Corporation for Assigned Names and Numbers (*ICANN*). Recently, *ICANN* added a dozen of generic top-level domains that are not related to a country and the *.cat* top-level domain has been registered for the Catalan language. There are ongoing discussions within *ICANN* to increase the number of top-level domains.

Each top-level domain is managed by an organisation that decides how sub-domain names can be registered. Most top-level domain names use a first-come first served system, and allow anyone to register domain names, but there are some exceptions. For example, *.gov* is reserved for the US government, *.int* is reserved for international organisations and names in the *.ca* are mainly reserved for companies or users who are present in Canada.

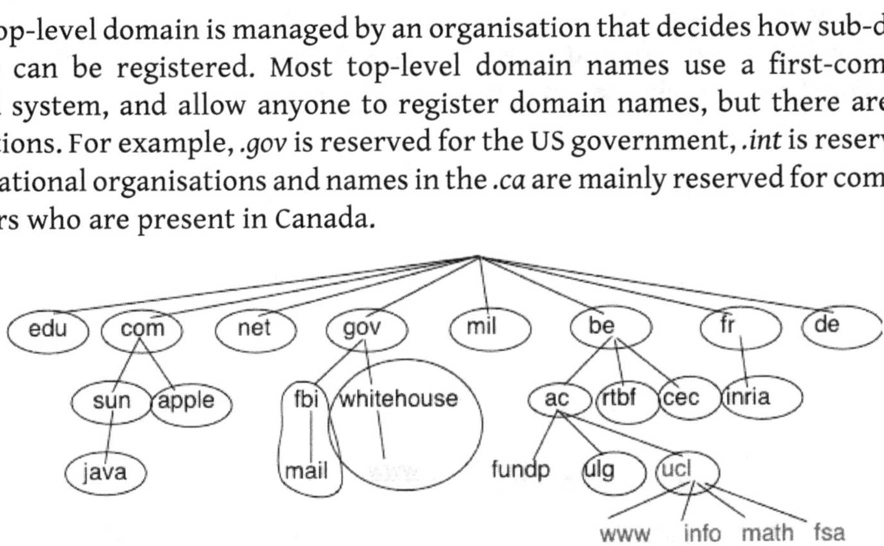

Figure 2.6: The tree of domain names

RFC 1035 recommended the following *BNF* for fully qualified domain names, to allow host names with a syntax which works with all applications (the domain names themselves have a much richer syntax).

```
domain ::= subdomain | " "
subdomain ::= label | subdomain "." label
label ::= letter [ [ ldh-str ] let-dig ]
ldh-str ::= let-dig-hyp | let-dig-hyp ldh-str
let-dig-hyp ::= let-dig | "-"
let-dig ::= letter | digit
letter ::= any one of the 52 alphabetic characters A through Z in upper case and a through z in lower case
digit ::= any one of the ten digits 0 through 9
```

Figure 2.7: BNF of the fully qualified host names

This grammar specifies that a host name is an ordered list of labels separated by the dot (.) character. Each label can contain letters, numbers and the hyphen character (-). Fully qualified domain names are read from left to right. The first label is a hostname or a domain name followed by the hierarchy of domains and ending with the root implicitly at the right. The top-level domain name must be one of the registered TLDs. For example, in the above figure, *www.whitehouse.gov* corresponds to a host named www inside the *whitehouse* domain that belongs to the *gov* top-level domain. *info.ucl.ac.be* corresponds to the *info* domain inside the *ucl* domain that is included in the *ac* sub-domain of the *be* top-level domain.

This hierarchical naming scheme is a key component of the Domain Name System (DNS). The DNS is a distributed database that contains mappings between fully qualified domain names and IP addresses. The DNS uses the client-server model. The clients are hosts that need to retrieve the mapping for a given name. Each *nameserver* stores part of the distributed database and answers the queries sent by clients. There is at least one *nameserver* that is responsible for each domain. In the figure below, domains are represented by circles and there are three hosts inside domain *dom (h1, h2* and *h3)* and three hosts inside domain *a.sdom1.dom.* As shown in the figure below, a sub-domain may contain both host names and sub-domains.

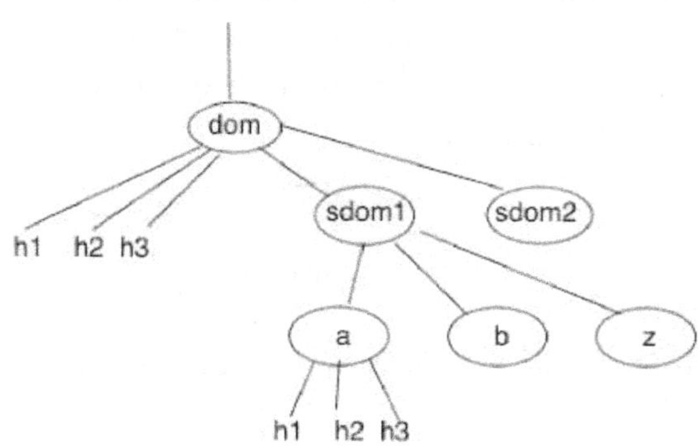

Figure 2.8: A simple tree of domain names

A *nameserver* that is responsible for domain *dom* can directly answer the following queries:

- the IP address of any host residing directly inside domain dom (e.g. *h2.dom* in the figure above)
- the nameserver(s) that are responsible for any direct sub-domain of domain dom (i.e. *sdoml.dom* and *sdom2.dom* in the figure above, but not *z.sdoml.dom)*

To retrieve the mapping for host *h2.dom*, a client sends its query to the name server that is responsible for domain *.dom.* The name server directly answers the query. To retrieve a mapping for *h3.a.sdom1.dom* a DNS client first sends a query to the name server that is responsible for the *.dom* domain. This nameserver returns the nameserver that is responsible for the *sdoml.dom* domain. This nameserver can now be contacted to obtain the nameserver that is responsible for the *a.sdoml. dom* domain. This nameserver can be contacted to retrieve the mapping for the *h3.a.sdom1.dom* name. Thanks to this organisation of the nameservers, it is possible for a DNS client to obtain the mapping of any host inside the *.dom* domain or any of its subdomains. To ensure that any DNS client will be able to resolve any fully qualified domain name, there are special nameservers that are responsible for the root of the domain name hierarchy. These nameservers are called *root nameserver.* There are currently about a dozen root nameservers.

Each root nameserver maintains the list of all the nameservers that are responsible for each of the top-level domain names and their IP addresses. All root nameservers are synchronised and provide the same answers. By querying any of the root nameservers, a DNS client can obtain the nameserver that is responsible for any top-level-domain name. From this nameserver, it is possible to resolve any domain name.

To be able to contact the root nameservers, each DNS client must know their IP addresses. This implies, that DNS clients must maintain an up-to-date list of the IP addresses of the root nameservers. Without this list, it is impossible to contact the root nameservers. Forcing all Internet hosts to maintain the most recent version of this list would be difficult from an operational point of view. To solve this problem, the designers of the DNS introduced a special type of DNS server : the DNS resolvers. A *resolver* is a server that provides the name resolution service for a set of clients. A network usually contains a few resolvers. Each host in these networks is configured to send all its DNS queries via one of its local resolvers. These queries are called *recursive queries* as the *resolver* must recurse through the hierarchy of nameservers to obtain the *answer.*

DNS resolvers have several advantages over letting each Internet host query directly nameservers. Firstly, regular Internet hosts do not need to maintain the up-to-date list of the IP addresses of the root servers. Secondly, regular Internet hosts do not need to send queries to nameservers all over the Internet. Furthermore, as a DNS resolver serves a large number of hosts, it can cache the received answers. This allows the resolver to quickly return answers for popular DNS queries and reduces the load on all DNS servers [JSBM2002].

The last component of the Domain Name System is the DNS protocol. The DNS protocol runs above both the datagram service and the bytestream services. In practice, the datagram service is used when short queries and responses are exchanged, and the bytestream service is used when longer responses are expected. In this section, we will only discuss the utilisation of the DNS protocol above the datagram service. This is the most frequent utilisation of the DNS.

DNS messages are composed of five parts that are named sections in **RFC 1035.** The first three sections are mandatory and the last two sections are optional. The first section of a DNS message is its *Header.* It contains information about the type of message and the content of the other sections. The second section contains the *Question* sent to the name server or resolver. The third section contains the *Answer* to the *Question.* When a client sends a DNS query, the *Answer* section is empty. The fourth section, named *Authority,* contains information about the servers that can provide an authoritative answer if required. The last section contains additional information that is supplied by the resolver or server but was not requested in the question.

The header of DNS messages is composed of 12 bytes and its structure is shown in the figure below.

The *ID* (identifier) is a 16-bits random value chosen by the client. When a client sends a question to a DNS server, it remembers the question and its identifier. When a server returns an answer, it returns in the *ID* field the identifier chosen by the client. Thanks to this identifier, the client can match the received answer with the question that it sent.

```
                                  1  1  1  1  1  1
    0  1  2  3  4  5  6  7  8  9  0  1  2  3  4  5
  +--+--+--+--+--+--+--+--+--+--+--+--+--+--+--+--+
  |                      ID                       |
  +--+--+--+--+--+--+--+--+--+--+--+--+--+--+--+--+
  |QR|   Opcode  |AA|TC|RD|RA|   Z    |   RCODE   |
  +--+--+--+--+--+--+--+--+--+--+--+--+--+--+--+--+
  |                    QDCOUNT                    |
  +--+--+--+--+--+--+--+--+--+--+--+--+--+--+--+--+
  |                    ANCOUNT                    |
  +--+--+--+--+--+--+--+--+--+--+--+--+--+--+--+--+
  |                    NSCOUNT                    |
  +--+--+--+--+--+--+--+--+--+--+--+--+--+--+--+--+
  |                    ARCOUNT                    |
  +--+--+--+--+--+--+--+--+--+--+--+--+--+--+--+--+
```

Figure 2.9: DNS header

The *QR* flag is set to *0* in DNS queries and *1* in DNS answers. The *Opcode* is used to specify the type of query. For instance, a *standard query* is when a client sends a *name* and the server returns the corresponding *data* and an update request is when the client sends a *name* and new *data* and the server then updates its database.

The *AA* bit is set when the server that sent the response has *authority* for the domain name found in the question section. In the original DNS deployments, two types of servers were considered : *authoritative* servers and *non- authoritative* servers. The *authoritative* servers are managed by the system administrators responsible for a given domain. They always store the most recent information about a domain. *Non-authoritative* servers are servers or resolvers that store DNS information about external domains without being managed by the owners of a domain. They may thus provide answers that are out of date. From a security point of view, the *authoritative* bit is not an absolute indication about the validity of an answer. Securing the Domain Name System is a complex problem that was only addressed satisfactorily recently by the utilisation of cryptographic signatures in the DNSSEC extensions to DNS described in **RFC 4033**. However, these extensions are outside the scope of this chapter.

The *RD* (recursion desired) bit is set by a client when it sends a query to a resolver. Such a query is said to be *recursive* because the resolver will recurse through the DNS hierarchy to retrieve the answer on behalf of the client. In the past, all resolvers were configured to perform recursive queries on behalf of any Internet host. However, this exposes the resolvers to several security risks. The simplest one is that the resolver could become overloaded by having too many recursive queries to process. As of this writing, most resolvers only allow recursive queries from clients belonging to their company or network and discard all other recursive queries. The *RA* bit indicates whether the server supports recursion. The *RCODE* is used to distinguish between different types of errors. See **RFC 1035** for additional details. The last four fields indicate the size of the *Question, Answer, Authority* and *Additional* sections of the DNS message.

The last four sections of the DNS message contain *Resource Records* (RR). All RRs have the same top level format shown in the figure below.

In a *Resource Record* (*RR*), the *Name* indicates the name of the node to which this resource record pertains. The two bytes *Type* field indicate the type of resource record. The *Class* field was used to support the utilisation of the DNS in other environments than the Internet.

The *TTL* field indicates the lifetime of the *Resource Record* in seconds. This field is set by the server that returns an answer and indicates for how long a client or a resolver can store the *Resource Record* inside its cache. A long *TTL* indicates a stable RR. Some companies use short *TTL* values for mobile hosts and also for popular servers.

```
                                1  1  1  1  1  1
  0  1  2  3  4  5  6  7  8  9  0  1  2  3  4  5
+--+--+--+--+--+--+--+--+--+--+--+--+--+--+--+--+
|                                               |
/                                               /
/                     NAME                      /
|                                               |
+--+--+--+--+--+--+--+--+--+--+--+--+--+--+--+--+
|                     TYPE                      |
+--+--+--+--+--+--+--+--+--+--+--+--+--+--+--+--+
|                    CLASS                      |
+--+--+--+--+--+--+--+--+--+--+--+--+--+--+--+--+
|                     TTL                       |
|                                               |
+--+--+--+--+--+--+--+--+--+--+--+--+--+--+--+--+
|                   RDLENGTH                    |
+--+--+--+--+--+--+--+--+--+--+--+--+--+--+--+--|
/                    RDATA                      /
/                                               /
+--+--+--+--+--+--+--+--+--+--+--+--+--+--+--+--+
```

Figure 2.10: DNS Resource Records

For example, a web hosting company that wants to spread the load over a pool of hundred servers can configure its nameservers to return different answers to different clients. If each answer has a small *TTL,* the clients will be forced to send DNS queries regularly. The nameserver will reply to these queries by supplying the address of the less loaded server.

The *RDLength* field is the length of the *RData* field that contains the information of the type specified in the *Type* field.

Several types of DNS RR are used in practice. The *A* type is used to encode the IPv4 address that corresponds to the specified name. The *AAAA* type is used to encode the IPv6 address that corresponds to the specified name. A *NS* record contains the name of the DNS server that is responsible for a given domain. For example, a query for the *A* record associated to the *www.ietf.org* name returns the following answer.

This answer contains several pieces of information. First, the name *www.ietf.org* is associated to IP address *64.170.98.32.* Second, the *ietf.org* domain is managed by six different nameservers. Three of these nameservers are reachable via IPv4 and IPv6. Two of them are not reachable via IPv6 and *ns0.ietf.org* is only reachable via IPv6. A query for the *AAAA* record associated to *www.ietf.org* returns *2001:1890:1112:1::20* and the same authority and additional sections.

CNAME (or canonical names) are used to define aliases. For example *www.example.com* could be a *CNAME* for *pc12.example.com* that is the actual name of the server on which the web server for *www.example.com* runs.

```
; <<>> DiG 9.6.0-APPLE-P2 <<>> -t A www.ietf.org
;; global options: +cmd
;; Got answer:
;; ->>HEADER<<- opcode: QUERY, status: NOERROR, id: 33431
;; flags: qr rd ra; QUERY: 1, ANSWER: 1, AUTHORITY: 6, ADDITIONAL: 9
;; QUESTION SECTION:
;www.ietf.org.                  IN      A

;; ANSWER SECTION:
www.ietf.org.           1800    IN      A       64.170.98.32

;; AUTHORITY SECTION:
ietf.org.               592     IN      NS      ns0.ietf.org.
ietf.org.               592     IN      NS      ns1.yyz1.afilias-nst.info.
ietf.org.               592     IN      NS      ns1.hkg1.afilias-nst.info.
ietf.org.               592     IN      NS      ns1.ams1.afilias-nst.info.
ietf.org.               592     IN      NS      ns1.mia1.afilias-nst.info.
ietf.org.               592     IN      NS      ns1.sea1.afilias-nst.info.

;; ADDITIONAL SECTION:
ns0.ietf.org.           1800    IN      AAAA    2001:1890:1112:1::14
ns1.ams1.afilias-nst.info. 1235         IN      A       199.19.48.79
ns1.ams1.afilias-nst.info. 3204         IN      AAAA    2001:500:6::79
ns1.hkg1.afilias-nst.info. 1428         IN      A       199.19.51.79
ns1.hkg1.afilias-nst.info. 1428         IN      AAAA    2001:500:9::79
ns1.mia1.afilias-nst.info. 2870         IN      A       199.19.52.79
ns1.sea1.afilias-nst.info. 3324         IN      A       199.19.50.79
ns1.sea1.afilias-nst.info. 3314         IN      AAAA    2001:500:8::79
ns1.yyz1.afilias-nst.info. 587 IN       A       199.19.49.79
```

Figure 2.11: Query for the A record of www.ietf.org

An important point to note regarding the Domain Name System is its extensibility. Thanks to the *Type* and *RDLength* fields, the format of the Resource Records can easily be extended. Furthermore, a DNS implementation that receives a new Resource Record that it does not understand can ignore the record while still being able to process the other parts of the message. This allows, for example, a DNS server that only supports IPv4 to ignore the IPv6 addresses listed in the DNS reply for *www.ietf.org* while still being able to correctly parse the Resource Records that it understands. This extensibility allowed the Domain Name System to evolve over the years while still preserving the backward compatibility with already deployed DNS implementations.

2.2.2 Electronic mail

Electronic mail, or email, is a very popular application in computer networks such as the Internet. Email appeared in the early 1970s and allows users to exchange text based messages. Initially, it was mainly used to exchange short messages, but over the years its usage has grown. It is now not only used to exchange small, but also long messages that can be composed of several parts as we will see later.

Before looking at the details of Internet email, let us consider a simple scenario illustrated in the figure below, where Alice sends an email to Bob. Alice prepares her email by using an email clients and sends it to her email server. Alice's email server extracts Bob's address from the email and delivers the message to Bob's server. Bob retrieves Alice's message on his server and reads it by using his favourite email client or through his webmail interface.

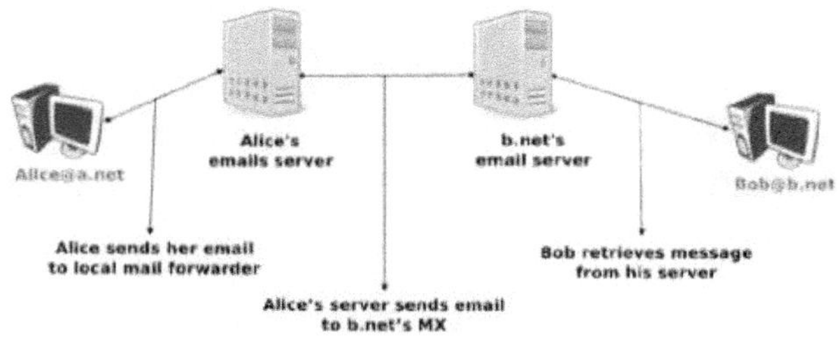

Figure 2.12

The email system that we consider in this book is composed of four components:

- a message format, that defines how valid email messages are encoded
- protocols, that allow hosts and servers to exchange email messages
- client software, that allows users to easily create and read email messages
- software, that allows servers to efficiently exchange email messages

We will first discuss the format of email messages followed by the protocols that are used on today's Internet to exchange and retrieve emails. Other email systems have been developed in the past [Bush1993] [Genilloud1990] [GC2000], but today most email solutions have migrated to the Internet email. Information about the software that is used to compose and deliver emails may be found on wikipedia among others, for both email clients and email servers. More detailed information about the full Internet Mail Architecture may be found in **RFC 5598.**

Email messages, like postal mail, are composed of two parts:

- a *header* that plays the same role as the letterhead in regular mail. It contains metadata about the message.
- the *body* that contains the message itself.

Email messages are entirely composed of lines of ASCII characters. Each line can contain up to 998 characters and is terminated by the *CR* and *LF* control characters **RFC 5322.** The lines that compose the *header* appear before the message *body.* An empty line, containing only the CR and *LF* characters, marks the end of the *header.* This is illustrated in the figure below.

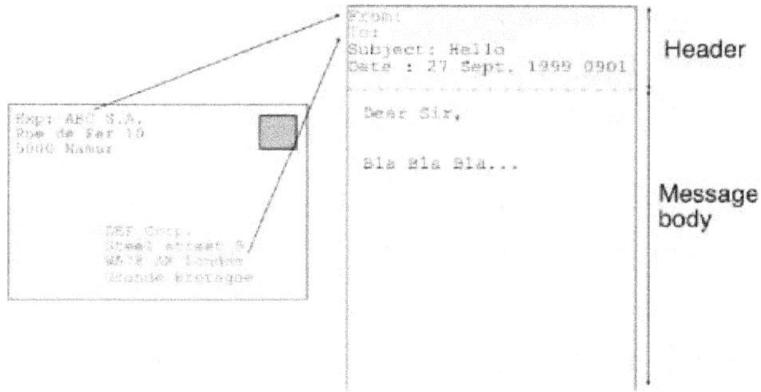

Figure 2.13: The structure of email messages

The email header contains several lines that all begin with a keyword followed by a colon and additional information. The format of email messages and the different types of header lines are defined in **RFC 5322.** Two of these header lines are mandatory and must appear in all email messages :

- The sender address. This header line starts with *From:*. This contains the (optional) name of the sender followed by its email address between < and >. Email addresses are always composed of a username followed by the @ sign and a domain name.
- The date. This header line starts with *Date:*. **RFC 5322** precisely defines the format used to encode a date.

Other header lines appear in most email messages. The *Subject:* header line allows the sender to indicate the topic discussed in the email. Three types of header lines can be used to specify the recipients of a message :

- the *To:* header line contains the email addresses of the primary recipients of the message. Several addresses can be separated by using commas.
- the *cc:* header line is used by the sender to provide a list of email addresses that must receive a carbon copy of the message. Several addresses can be listed in this header line, separated by commas. All recipients of the email message receive the *To:* and *cc:* header lines.
- the *bcc:* header line is used by the sender to provide a list of comma separated email addresses that must receive a blind carbon copy of the message. The *bcc:* header line is not delivered to the recipients of the email message.

A simple email message containing the *From:*, *To:*, *Subject:* and *Date:* header lines and two lines of body is shown below.

From: Bob Smith <Bob@machine.example>
To: Alice Doe <alice@example.net>, Alice Smith <Alice@machine.example>
Subject: Hello

Date: Mon, 8 Mar 2010 19:55:06 -0600
This is the "Hello world" of email messages.
This is the second line of the body

Note the empty line after the *Date:* header line; this empty line contains only the *CR* and *LF* characters, and marks the boundary between the header and the body of the message.

Several other optional header lines are defined in **RFC 5322** and elsewhere. Furthermore, many email clients and servers define their own header lines starting from *X-*. Several of the optional header lines defined in **RFC 5322** are worth being discussed here :

- the *Message-Id:* header line is used to associate a "unique" identifier to each email. Email identifiers are usually structured like *string@domain* where *string* is a unique character string or sequence number chosen by the sender of the email and *domain* the domain name of the sender. Since domain names are unique, a host can generate globally unique message identifiers concatenating a locally unique identifier with its domain name.
- the *In-reply-to:* is used when a message was created in reply to a previous message. In this case, the end of the *In-reply-to:* line contains the identifier of the original message.
- the *Received:* header line is used when an email message is processed by several servers before reaching its destination. Each intermediate email server adds a *Received:* header line. These header lines are useful to debug problems in delivering email messages.

The figure below shows the header lines of one email message. The message originated at a host named *wira.firstpr.com.au* and was received by *smtp3.sgsi.ucl.ac.be*. The *Received:* lines have been wrapped for readability.

Received: from smtp3.sgsi.ucl.ac.be (Unknown [10.1.5.3])
by mmp.sipr-dc.ucl.ac.be
(Sun Java(tm) System Messaging Server 7u3-15.01 64bit (built Feb 12 2010)) with ESMTP
id <0KYY00L85LI5JLE0@mmp.sipr-dc.ucl.ac.be>; Mon,
08 Mar 2010 11:37:17 +0100 (CET)
Received: from mail.ietf.org (mail.ietf.org [64.170.98.32])
by smtp3.sgsi.ucl.ac.be (Postfix) with ESMTP id B92351C60D7; Mon,
08 Mar 2010 11:36:51 +0100 (CET)
Received: from [127.0.0.1] (localhost [127.0.0.1]) by core3.amsl.com (Postfix)
with ESMTP id F066A3A68B9; Mon, 08 Mar 2010 02:36:38 -0800 (PST)

Received: from localhost (localhost [127.0.0.1]) by core3.amsl.com (Postfix)
with ESMTP id A1E6C3A681B for <rrg@core3.amsl.com>; Mon,
08 Mar 2010 02:36:37 -0800 (PST)
Received: from mail.ietf.org ([64.170.98.32])
by localhost (core3.amsl.com [127.0.0.1]) (amavisd-new, port 10024)
with ESMTP id erw8ih2v8VQa for <rrg@core3.amsl.com>; Mon,
08 Mar 2010 02:36:36 -0800 (PST)
Received: from gair.firstpr.com.au (gair.firstpr.com.au [150.101.162.123])
by core3.amsl.com (Postfix) with ESMTP id 03E893A67ED for <rrg@irtf.org>; Mon,
08 Mar 2010 02:36:35 -0800 (PST)
Received: from [10.0.0.6] (wira.firstpr.com.au [10.0.0.6])
by gair.firstpr.com.au (Postfix) with ESMTP id D0A49175B63; Mon,
08 Mar 2010 21:36:37 +1100 (EST)
Date: Mon, 08 Mar 2010 21:36:38 +1100
From: Robin Whittle <rw@firstpr.com.au>
Subject: Re: [rrg] Recommendation and what happens next
In-reply-to: <C7B9C21A.4FAB%tony.li@tony.li>
To: RRG <rrg@irtf.org>
Message-id: <4B94D336.7030504@firstpr.com.au>
Message content removed

Initially, email was used to exchange small messages of ASCII text between computer scientists. However, with the growth of the Internet, supporting only ASCII text became a severe limitation for two reasons. First of all, non-English speakers wanted to write emails in their native language that often required more characters than those of the ASCII character table. Second, many users wanted to send other content than just ASCII text by email such as binary files, images or sound.

To solve this problem, the IETF developed the Multipurpose Internet Mail Extensions *(MIME)*. These extensions were carefully designed to allow Internet email to carry non-ASCII characters and binary files without breaking the email servers that were deployed at that time. This requirement for backward compatibility forced the MIME designers to develop extensions to the existing email message format **RFC 822** instead of defining a completely new format that would have been better suited to support the new types of emails.

RFC 2045 defines three new types of header lines to support MIME :

- The *MIME-Version:* header indicates the version of the MIME specification that was used to encode the email message. The current version of MIME is 1.0. Other versions of MIME may be defined in the future. Thanks to this header line, the software that processes email messages will be able to adapt to the MIME version used to encode the message. Messages that do not contain this header are supposed to be formatted according to the original **RFC 822** specification.

- The *Content-Type:* header line indicates the type of data that is carried inside the message (see below)
- The *Content-Transfer-Encoding:* header line is used to specify how the message has been encoded. When MIME was designed, some email servers were only able to process messages containing characters encoded using the 7 bits ASCII character set. MIME allows the utilisation of other character encodings.

Inside the email header, the *Content-Type:* header line indicates how the MIME email message is structured. **RFC 2046** defines the utilisation of this header line. The two most common structures for MIME messages are :

- *Content-Type: multipart/mixed.* This header line indicates that the MIME message contains several independent parts. For example, such a message may contain a part in plain text and a binary file.
- *Content-Type: multipart/alternative.* This header line indicates that the MIME message contains several representations of the same information. For example, a *multipart/alternative* message may contain both a plain text and an HTML version of the same text.

To support these two types of MIME messages, the recipient of a message must be able to extract the different parts from the message. In **RFC 822**, an empty line was used to separate the header lines from the body. Using an empty line to separate the different parts of an email body would be difficult as the body of email messages often contains one or more empty lines. Another possible option would be to define a special line, e.g. *-*LAST_LINE-** to mark the boundary between two parts of a MIME message. Unfortunately, this is not possible as some emails may contain this string in their body (e.g. emails sent to students to explain the format of MIME messages). To solve this problem, the *Content-Type:* header line contains a second parameter that specifies the string that has been used by the sender of the MIME message to delineate the different parts. In practice, this string is often chosen randomly by the mail client.

The email message below, copied from **RFC 2046** shows a MIME message containing two parts that are both in plain text and encoded using the ASCII character set. The string *simple boundary* is defined in the *Content-Type:* header as the marker for the boundary between two successive parts. Another example of MIME messages may be found in **RFC 2046**.

```
Date: Mon, 20 Sep 1999 16:33:16 +0200
From: Nathaniel Borenstein <nsb@bellcore.com>
To: Ned Freed <ned@innosoft.com>
Subject: Test
MIME-Version: 1.0
Content-Type: multipart/mixed; boundary="simple boundary"
preamble, to be ignored
--simple boundary
Content-Type: text/plain; charset=us-ascii
First part
—simple boundary
Content-Type: text/plain; charset=us-ascii
Second part
--simple boundary
```

The *Content-Type:* header can also be used inside a MIME part. In this case, it indicates the type of data placed in this part. Each data type is specified as a type followed by a subtype. A detailed description may be found in **RFC 2046**. Some of the most popular *Content-Type:* header lines are :

- text. The message part contains information in textual format. There are several subtypes : *text/plain* for regular ASCII text, *text/html* defined in **RFC 2854** for documents in *HTML* format or the *text/enriched* format defined in **RFC 1896.** The *Content-Type:* header line may contain a second parameter that specifies the character set used to encode the text. *charset=us-ascii* is the standard ASCII character table. Other frequent character sets include *charset=UTF8* or *charset=iso-8859-1.* The list of standard character sets is maintained by *IANA*
- *image.* The message part contains a binary representation of an image. The subtype indicates the format of the image such as gif, jpg or png.
- *audio.* The message part contains an audio clip. The subtype indicates the format of the audio clip like wav or mp3
- *video.* The message part contains a video clip. The subtype indicates the format of the video clip like avi or mp4
- *application.* The message part contains binary information that was produced by the particular application listed as the subtype. Email clients use the subtype to launch the application that is able to decode the received binary information.

Note: From ASCII to Unicode

The first computers used different techniques to represent characters in memory and on disk. During the 1960s, computers began to exchange information via tape or telephone lines. Unfortunately, each vendor had its own proprietary character set and exchanging data between computers from different vendors was often difficult. The 7 bits ASCII character table **RFC 20** set was adopted by several vendors and by many Internet protocols. However, ASCII became a problem with the internationalisation of the Internet and the desire of more and more users to use character sets that support their own written language. A first attempt at solving this problem was the definition of the ISO-8859 character sets by ISO. This family of standards specified various character sets that allowed the representation of many European written languages by using 8 bits characters. Unfortunately, an 8-bits character set is not sufficient to support some widely used languages, such as those used in Asian countries. Fortunately, at the end of the 1980s, several computer scientists proposed to develop a standard that supports all written languages used on Earth today. The Unicode standard [Unicode] has now been adopted by most computer and software vendors. For example, Java uses Unicode natively to manipulate characters, Python can handle both ASCII and Unicode characters. Internet applications are slowly moving towards complete support for the Unicode character sets, but moving from ASCII to Unicode is an important change that can have a huge impact on current deployed implementations. See for example, the work to completely internationalise email **RFC 4952** and domain names **RFC 5890**.

The last MIME header line is *Content-Transfer-Encoding:*. This header line is used after the *Content-Type:* header line, within a message part, and specifies how the message part has been encoded. The default encoding is to use 7 bits ASCII. The most frequent encodings are *quoted-printable* and *Base64.* Both support encoding a sequence of bytes into a set of ASCII lines that can be safely transmitted by email servers. *quoted-printable* is defined in **RFC 2045**. We briefly describe *base64* which is defined in **RFC 2045** and **RFC 4648**.

Base64 divides the sequence of bytes to be encoded into groups of three bytes (with the last group possibly being partially filled). Each group of three bytes is then divided into four six-bit fields and each six bit field is encoded as a character from the table below.

Value	Encoding	Value	Encoding	Value	Encoding	Value	Encoding
0	A	17	R	34	i	51	z
1	B	18	S	35	j	52	0
2	C	19	T	36	k	53	1
3	D	20	U	37	l	54	2

Value	Encoding	Value	Encoding	Value	Encoding	Value	Encoding
4	E	21	V	38	m	55	3
5	F	22	W	39	n	56	4
6	G	23	X	40	o	57	5
7	H	24	Y	41	p	58	6
8	I	25	Z	42	q	59	7
9	J	26	a	43	r	60	8
10	K	27	b	44	s	61	9
11	L	28	c	45	t	62	+
12	M	29	d	46	u	63	/
13	N	30	e	47	v		
14	O	31	f	48	w		
15	P	32	g	49	x		
16	Q	33	h	50	y		

The example below, from RFC 4648, illustrates the Base64 encoding.

Input data 8-bit 6-bit Decimal Encoding	0x14fb9c03d97e 00010100 11111011 10011100 00000011 1101100101111110 000101 001111 101110 011100 000000 111101 100101 111110 5 15 46 28 0 61 37 62 FPucA9l +

The last point to be discussed about *base64* is what happens when the length of the sequence of bytes to be encoded is not a multiple of three. In this case, the last group of bytes may contain one or two bytes instead of three. *Base64* reserves the = character as a padding character. This character is used twice when the last group contains two bytes and once when it contains one byte as illustrated by the two examples below.

Input data	0x14
8-bit	00010100
6-bit	000101 000000
Decimal	50
Encoding	FA = =

Input data	0x14b9

8-bit	00010100 11111011
6-bit	000101 001111 101100
Decimal	5 15 44
Encoding	FPs =

Now that we have explained the format of the email messages, we can discuss how these messages can be exchanged through the Internet. The figure below illustrates the protocols that are used when *Alice* sends an email message to Bob. *Alice* prepares her email with an email client or on a webmail interface. To send her email to Bob, *Alice's* client will use the Simple Mail Transfer Protocol *(SMTP)* to deliver her message to her SMTP server. *Alice's* email client is configured with the name of the default SMTP server for her domain. There is usually at least one SMTP server per domain. To deliver the message, *Alice's* SMTP server must find the SMTP server that contains *Bob's* mailbox. This can be done by using the Mail eXchange (MX) records of the DNS. A set of MX records can be associated to each domain. Each MX record contains a numerical preference and the fully qualified domain name of a SMTP server that is able to deliver email messages destined to all valid email addresses of this domain. The DNS can return several MX records for a given domain. In this case, the server with the lowest preference is used first. If this server is not reachable, the second most preferred server is used etc. *Bob's* SMTP server will store the message sent by *Alice* until *Bob* retrieves it using a webmail interface or protocols such as the Post Office Protocol *(POP)* or the Internet Message Access Protocol *(IMAP)*.

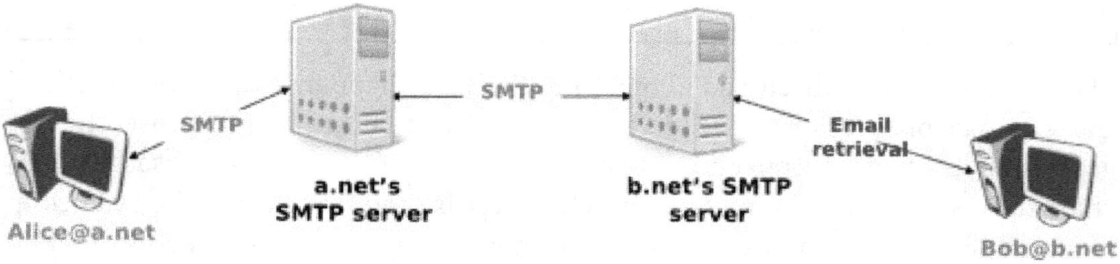

Figure 2.14: Email delivery protocols

The Simple Mail Transfer Protocol

The Simple Mail Transfer Protocol *(SMTP)* defined in **RFC 5321** is a client-server protocol. The SMTP specification distinguishes between five types of processes involved in the delivery of email messages. Email messages are composed on a Mail User Agent (MUA). The MUA is usually either an email client or a webmail. The MUA sends the email message to a Mail Submission Agent (MSA). The MSA processes the received email and forwards it to the Mail Transmission Agent (MTA). The MTA is responsible for the transmission of the email, directly or via intermediate MTAs to the MTA of the destination domain. This destination MTA will then forward the message to the Mail Delivery Agent (MDA) where it will be accessed by the recipient's MUA. SMTP is used for the interactions between MUA and MSA , MSA-MTA and MTA-MTA.

SMTP is a text-based protocol like many other application-layer protocols on the Internet. It relies on the bytestream service. Servers listen on port 25. Clients send commands that are each composed of one line of ASCII text terminated by *CR+LF.* Servers reply by sending ASCII lines that contain a three digit numerical error/ success code and optional comments.

The SMTP protocol, like most text-based protocols, is specified as a *BNF.* The full BNF is defined in **RFC 5321**. The main SMTP commands are defined by the BNF rules shown in the figure below.

```
helo = "HELO" SP Domain CRLF
mail = "MAIL FROM:" Path CRLF
rcpt = "RCPT TO:" ( "<Postmaster@" Domain ">" / "<Postmaster>" / Path ) CRLF
data = "DATA" CRLF
quit = "QUIT" CRLF
Path            = "<" Mailbox ">"
Domain          = sub-domain *("." sub-domain)
sub-domain      = Let-dig [Ldh-str]
Let-dig         = ALPHA / DIGIT
Ldh-str         = *( ALPHA / DIGIT / "-" ) Let-dig
Mailbox         = Local-part "@" Domain
Local-part      = Dot-string
Dot-string      = Atom *("."  Atom)
Atom            = 1*atext
```

Figure 2.15: BNF specification of the SMTP commands

In this BNF, *atext* corresponds to printable ASCII characters. This BNF rule is defined in **RFC 5322.** The five main commands are *EHLO, MAIL FROM:, RCPT TO:, DATA* and *QUIT*. *Postmaster* is the alias of the system administrator who is responsible for a given domain or SMTP server. All domains must have a *Postmaster* alias.

The SMTP responses are defined by the BNF shown in the figure below.

```
Greeting        = "220 " Domain [ SP textstring ] CRLF
textstring      = 1*atext
Reply-line      = *( Reply-code "-" [ textstring ] CRLF )
                  Reply-code [ SP textstring ] CRLF
Reply-code      = %x32-35 %x30-35 %x30-39
```

Figure 2.16: BNF specification of the SMTP responses

SMTP servers use structured reply codes containing three digits and an optional comment. The first digit of the reply code indicates whether the command was successful or not. A reply code of *2xy* indicates that the command has been accepted. A reply code of *3xy* indicates that the command has been accepted, but additional information from the client is expected. A reply code of *4xy* indicates a transient negative reply. This means that for some reason, which is indicated by either the other digits or the comment, the command cannot be processed immediately, but there is some hope that the problem will only be transient. This is basically telling the client to try the same command again later. In contrast, a reply code of 5xy indicates a permanent failure or error. In this case, it is useless for the client to retry the same command later. Other application layer protocols such as FTP **RFC 959** or HTTP **RFC 2616** use a similar structure for their reply codes. Additional details about the other reply codes may be found in **RFC 5321.**

Examples of SMTP reply codes include the following :

Syntax error, command unrecognized
Syntax error in parameters or arguments
Command not implemented
Bad sequence of commands
<domain> Service ready
<domain> Service closing transmission channel
421 <domain> Service not available, closing transmission channel
250 Requested mail action okay, completed
450 Requested mail action not taken: mailbox unavailable
452 Requested action not taken: insufficient system storage
550 Requested action not taken: mailbox unavailable
354 Start mail input; end with <CRLF>.<CRLF>

The first four reply codes correspond to errors in the commands sent by the client. The fourth reply code would be sent by the server when the client sends commands in an incorrect order (e.g. the client tries to send an email before providing the destination address of the message). Reply code *220* is used by the server as the first message when it agrees to interact with the client. Reply code *221* is sent by the server before closing the underlying transport connection. Reply code *421* is returned when there is a problem (e.g. lack of memory/disk resources) that prevents the server from accepting the transport connection. Reply code *250* is the standard positive reply that indicates the success of the previous command. Reply codes 450 and 452 indicate that the destination mailbox is temporarily unavailable, for various reasons, while reply code *550* indicates that the mailbox does not exist or cannot be used for policy reasons. Reply code *354* indicates that the client can start transmitting its email message.

The transfer of an email message is performed in three phases. During the first phase, the client opens a transport connection with the server. Once the connection has been established, the client and the server exchange greetings messages *(EHLO* command). Most servers insist on receiving valid greeting messages and some of them drop the underlying transport connection if they do not receive a valid greeting. Once the greetings have been exchanged, the email transfer phase can start. During this phase, the client transfers one or more email messages by indicating the email address of the sender (*MAIL FROM:* command), the email address of the recipient (*RCPT TO:* command) followed by the headers and the body of the email message (DATA command). Once the client has finished sending all its queued email messages to the SMTP server, it terminates the SMTP association (*QUIT* command).

A successful transfer of an email message is shown below

```
S: 220 smtp.example.com ESMTP MTA information
C: EHLO mta.example.org
S: 250 Hello mta.example.org, glad to meet you
C: MAIL FROM:<alice@example.org>
S: 250 Ok
C: RCPT TO:<bob@example.com>
S: 250 Ok
C: DATA
S: 354 End data with <CR><LF>.<CR><LF>
C: From: "Alice Doe" <alice@example.org>
C: To: Bob Smith <bob@example.com>
C: Date: Mon, 9 Mar 2010 18:22:32 +0100
C: Subject: Hello
C:
C: Hello Bob
C: This is a small message containing 4 lines of text.
C: Best regards,
C: Alice
C: .
S: 250 Ok: queued as 12345
C: QUIT
S: 221 Bye
```

In the example above, the MTA running on *mta.example.org* opens a TCP connection to the SMTP server on host *smtp.example.com.* The lines prefixed with S: (resp. C:) are the responses sent by the server (resp. the commands sent by the client). The server sends its greetings as soon as the TCP connection has been established. The client then sends the *EHLO* command with its fully qualified domain name. The server replies with reply-code *250* and sends its greetings. The SMTP association can now be used to exchange an email.

To send an email, the client must first provide the address of the recipient with *RCPT TO:*. Then it uses the *MAIL FROM:* with the address of the sender. Both the recipient and the sender are accepted by the server. The client can now issue the *DATA* command to start the transfer of the email message. After having received the *354* reply code, the client sends the headers and the body of its email message. The client indicates the end of the message by sending a line containing only the. (dot) character. The server confirms that the email message has been queued for delivery or transmission with a reply code of *250*. The client issues the *QUIT* command to close the session and the server confirms with reply-code 221, before closing the TCP connection.

Note: Open SMTP relays and spam

Since its creation in 1971, email has been a very useful tool that is used by many users to exchange lots of information. In the early days, all SMTP servers were open and anyone could use them to forward emails towards their final destination. Unfortunately, over the years, some unscrupulous users have found ways to use email for marketing purposes or to send malware. The first documented abuse of email for marketing purposes occurred in 1978 when a marketer who worked for a computer vendor sent a marketing email to many ARPANET users. At that time, the ARPANET could only be used for research purposes and this was an abuse of the acceptable use policy. Unfortunately, given the extremely low cost of sending emails, the problem of unsolicited emails has not stopped. Unsolicited emails are now called spam and a study carried out by ENISA in 2009 reveals that 95% of email was spam and this number seems to continue to grow. This places a burden on the email infrastructure of Internet Service Providers and large companies that need to process many useless messages.

Given the amount of spam messages, SMTP servers are no longer open **RFC 5068.** Several extensions to SMTP have been developed in recent years to deal with this problem. For example, the SMTP authentication scheme defined in **RFC 4954** can be used by an SMTP server to authenticate a client. Several techniques have also been proposed to allow SMTP servers to *authenticate* the messages sent by their users **RFC 4870 RFC 4871.**

The Post Office Protocol

When the first versions of SMTP were designed, the Internet was composed of minicomputers that were used by an entire university department or research lab. These minicomputers were used by many users at the same time. Email was mainly used to send messages from a user on a given host to another user on a remote host. At that time, SMTP was the only protocol involved in the delivery of the emails as all hosts attached to the network were running an SMTP server. On such hosts, an email destined to local users was delivered by placing the email in a special directory or file owned by the user. However, the introduction of personal computers in the 1980s, changed this environment. Initially, users of these personal computers used applications such as *telnet* to open a remote session on the local *minicomputer* to read their email. This was not user-friendly. A better solution appeared with the development of user friendly email client applications on personal computers. Several protocols were designed to allow these client applications to retrieve the email messages destined to a user from his/her server. Two of these protocols became popular and are still used today. The Post Office Protocol (POP), defined in **RFC 1939**, is the simplest one. It allows a client to download all the messages destined to a given user from his/her email server. We describe POP briefly in this section. The second protocol is the Internet Message Access Protocol (IMAP), defined in **RFC 3501**. IMAP is more powerful, but also more complex than POP. IMAP was designed to allow client applications to efficiently access in real-time to messages stored in various folders on servers. IMAP assumes that all the messages of a given user are stored on a server and provides the functions that are necessary to search, download, delete or filter messages.

POP is another example of a simple line-based protocol. POP runs above the bytestream service. A POP server usually listens to port 110. A POP session is composed of three parts : an *authorisation* phase during which the server verifies the client's credential, a *transaction* phase during which the client downloads messages and an *update* phase that concludes the session. The client sends commands and the server replies are prefixed by *+OK* to indicate a successful command or by *-ERR* to indicate errors.

When a client opens a transport connection with the POP server, the latter sends as banner an ASCII-line starting with +OK. The POP session is at that time in the *authorisation* phase. In this phase, the client can send its username (resp. password) with the *USER* (resp. *PASS)* command. The server replies with *+OK* if the username (resp. password) is valid and *-ERR* otherwise.

Once the username and password have been validated, the POP session enters in the *transaction* phase. In this phase, the client can issue several commands. The *STAT* command is used to retrieve the status of the server. Upon reception of this command, the server replies with a line that contains *+OK* followed by the number of messages in the mailbox and the total size of the mailbox in bytes. The *RETR* command, followed by a space and an integer, is used to retrieve the nth message of the mailbox. The *DELE* command is used to mark for deletion the nth message of the mailbox.

Once the client has retrieved and possibly deleted the emails contained in the mailbox, it must issue the *QUIT* command. This command terminates the POP session and allows the server to delete all the messages that have been marked for deletion by using the *DELE* command.

The figure below provides a simple POP session. All lines prefixed with *C:* (resp. *S:*) are sent by the client (resp. server).

S: +OK POP3 server ready
C: USER alice
S: +OK
C PASS 12345pass
S: +OK alice's maildrop has 2 messages (620 octets)
C: STAT
S: +OK 2 620
C: LIST
S: +OK 2 messages (620 octets)
S: 1 120
S: 2 500
S: .
C: RETR 1
S: +OK 120 octets
S: <the POP3 server sends message 1>
S: .
C: DELE 1
S: +OK message 1 deleted
C: QUIT
S: +OK POP3 server signing off (1 message left)

In this example, a POP client contacts a POP server on behalf of the user named *alice*. Note that in this example, Alice's password is sent in clear by the client. This implies that if someone is able to capture the packets sent by Alice, he will know Alice's password. Then Alice's client issues the *STAT* command to know the number of messages that are stored in her mailbox. It then retrieves and deletes the first message of the mailbox.

2.2.3 The HyperText Transfer Protocol

In the early days of the Internet was mainly used for remote terminal access with telnet, email and file transfer. The default file transfer protocol, FTP, defined in **RFC 959** was widely used and *FTP* clients and servers are still included in most operating systems.

Many *FTP* clients offer a user interface similar to a Unix shell and allow the client to browse the file system on the server and to send and retrieve files. FTP servers can be configured in two modes:

- authenticated : in this mode, the ftp server only accepts users with a valid user name and password. Once authenticated, they can access the files and directories according to their permissions
- anonymous: in this mode, clients supply the *anonymous* userid and their email address as password. These clients are granted access to a special zone of the file system that only contains public files.

ftp was very popular in the 1990s and early 2000s, but today it has mostly been superseded by more recent protocols. Authenticated access to files is mainly done by using the Secure Shell (ssh) protocol defined in **RFC 4251** and supported by clients such as scp or sftp. Nowadays, anonymous access is mainly provided by web protocols.

In the late 1980s, high energy physicists working at CERN had to efficiently exchange documents about their ongoing and planned experiments. Tim Berners-Lee evaluated several of the documents sharing techniques that were available at that time [B1989]. As none of the existing solutions met CERN's requirements, they choose to develop a completely new document sharing system. This system was initially called the *mesh*, but was quickly renamed the *world wide web*. The starting point for the *world wide web* are hypertext documents. An hypertext document is a document that contains references (hyperlinks) to other documents that the reader can immediately access. Hypertext was not invented for the world wide web. The idea of hypertext documents was proposed in 1945 [Bush1945] and the first experiments were done during the 1960s [Nelson1965] [Myers1998]. Compared to the hypertext documents that were used in the late 1980s, the main innovation introduced by the *world wide web* was to allow hyperlinks to reference documents stored on remote machines.

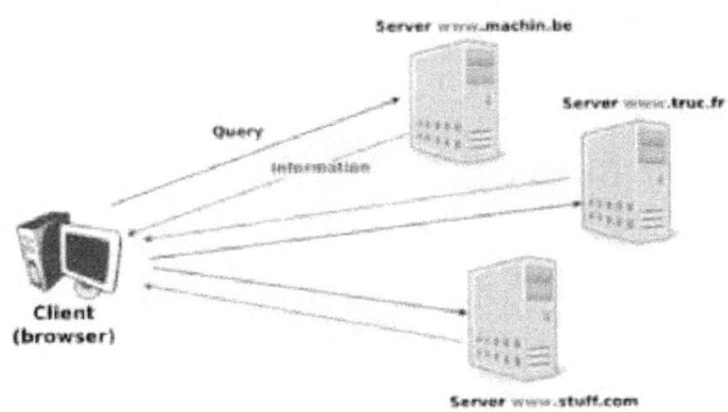

Figure 2.17: World-wide web clients and servers

A document sharing system such as the *world wide web* is composed of three important parts.

1. A standardised addressing scheme that allows unambiguous identification of documents
2. A standard document format : the HyperText Markup Language
3. A standardised protocol that facilitates efficient retrieval of documents stored on a server

Note: Open standards and open implementations

Open standards have, and are still playing a key role in the success of the world wide web as we know it today. Without open standards, the world wide web would never have reached its current size. In addition to open standards, another important factor for the success of the web was the availability of open and efficient implementations of these standards. When CERN started to work on the web, their objective was to build a running system that could be used by physicists. They developed open-source implementations of the first web servers and web clients. These open-source implementations were powerful and could be used as is, by institutions willing to share information on the web. They were also extended by other developers who contributed to new features. For example, NCSA added support for images in their Mosaic browser that was eventually used to create Netscape Communications.

The first components of the *world wide web* are the Uniform Resource Identifiers (URI), defined in **RFC 3986.** A URI is a character string that unambiguously identifies a resource on the world wide web. Here is a subset of the BNF for URIs

URI = scheme ":" "//" authority path ["?" query] ["#" fragment]
scheme = ALPHA *(ALPHA / DIGIT / "+" / "-" / ".")
authority = [userinfo "@"] host [":" port]
query = *(pchar / "/" / "?")
fragment = *(pchar / "/" / "?")
pchar = unreserved / pct-encoded / sub-delims / ":" / "@"
query = *(pchar / "/" / "?")
fragment = *(pchar / "/" / "?")
pct-encoded = "%" HEXDIG HEXDIG
unreserved = ALPHA / DIGIT / "-" / "." / "_" / "~"
reserved = gen-delims / sub-delims
gen-delims = ":" / "/" / "?" / "#" / "[" / "]" / "@"
sub-delims = "!" / "$" / "&" / "'" / "(" / ")" / "*" / "+" / "," / ";" / "="

The first component of a URI is its scheme. A scheme can be seen as a selector, indicating the meaning of the fields after it. In practice, the scheme often identifies the application-layer protocol that must be used by the client to retrieve the document, but it is not always the case. Some schemes do not imply a protocol at all and some do not indicate a retrievable document 17. The most frequent scheme is http that will be described later. A URI scheme can be defined for almost any application layer protocol [#furilist]_. The characters ': and // follow the scheme of any URI.

The second part of the URI is the *authority*. With retrievable URI, this includes the DNS name or the IP address of the server where the document can be retrieved using the protocol specified via the *scheme*. This name can be preceded by some information about the user (e.g. a user name) who is requesting the information. Earlier definitions of the URI allowed the specification of a user name and a password before the @ character (**RFC 1738**), but this is now deprecated as placing a password inside a URI is insecure. The host name can be followed by the semicolon character and a port number. A default port number is defined for some protocols and the port number should only be included in the URI if a non-default port number is used (for other protocols, techniques like service DNS records are used).

The third part of the URI is the path to the document. This path is structured as filenames on a Unix host (but it does not imply that the files are indeed stored this way on the server). If the path is not specified, the server will return a default document. The last two optional parts of the URI are used to provide a query and indicate a specific part (e.g. a section in an article) of the requested document. Sample URIs are shown below.

http://tools.ietf.org/html/rfc3986.htmlmailto:infobot@example.com?subject=current-issue
http://docs.python.org/library/basehttpserver.html?highlight=http#BaseHTTPServer.BaseHTTPRequestH<
telnet://[2001:6a8:3080:3::2]:80/
ftp://cnn.example.com&story=breaking_news@10.0.0.1/top_story.htm

The first URI corresponds to a document named *rfc3986.html* that is stored on the server named *tools.ietf.org* and can be accessed by using the *http* protocol on its default port. The second URI corresponds to an email message, with subject *current-issue*, that will be sent to user *infobot* in domain *example.com*. The *mailto:* URI scheme is defined in **RFC 6068**. The third URI references the portion *BaseHTTPServer.BaseHTTPRequestHandler* of the document *basehttpserver.html* that is stored in the *library* directory on server *docs.python.org*. This document can be retrieved by using the *http* protocol. The query *highlight=http* is associated to this URI. The fourth example is a server that operates the telnet protocol, uses IPv6 address *2001:6a8:3080:3::2* and is reachable on port 80. The last URI is somewhat special. Most users will assume that it corresponds to a document stored on the *cnn.example.com* server. However, to parse this URI, it is important to remember that the @ character is used to separate the user name from the host name in the authorisation part of a URI. This implies that the URI points to a document named *top_story.htm* on host having IPv4 address *10.0.0.1.* The document will be retrieved by using the *ftp* protocol with the user name set to *cnn.example.com&story=breaking_news.*

The second component of the *word wide web* is the HyperText Markup Language (HTML). HTML defines the format of the documents that are exchanged on the web. The first version of HTML was derived from the Standard Generalized Markup Language (SGML) that was standardised in 1986 by ISO. SGML was designed to allow large project documents in industries such as government, law or aerospace to be shared efficiently in a machine- readable manner. These industries require documents to remain readable and editable for tens of years and insisted on a standardised format supported by multiple vendors. Today, SGML is no longer widely used beyond specific applications, but its descendants including *HTML* and *XML* are now widespread.

A markup language is a structured way of adding annotations about the formatting of the document within the document itself. Example markup languages include troff, which is used to write the Unix man pages or Latex. HTML uses markers to annotate text and a document is composed of *HTML elements.* Each element is usually composed of three items: a start tag that potentially includes some specific attributes, some text (often including other elements), and an end tag. A HTML tag is a keyword enclosed in angle brackets. The generic form of a HTML element is

<tag>Some text to be displayed</tag>

More complex HTML elements can also include optional attributes in the start tag

<tag attribute1="value1" attribute2="value2">some text to be displayed</tag>

The HTML document shown below is composed of two parts : a header, delineated by the *<head>* and *</head>* markers, and a body (between the *<body>* and *</body>* markers). In the example below, the header only contains a title, but other types of information can be included in the header. The body contains an image, some text and a list with three hyperlinks. The image is included in the web page by indicating its URI between brackets inside the *<img src="...">* marker. The image can, of course, reside on any server and the client will automatically download it when rendering the web page. The *<h1>...</h1>* marker is used to specify the first level of headings. The *<ul>* marker indicates an unnumbered list while the *<li>* marker indicates a list item. The *<a href="URI">text</a>* indicates a hyperlink. The *text* will be underlined in the rendered web page and the client will fetch the specified URI when the user clicks on the link.

Figure 2.18: A simple HTML page

Additional details about the various extensions to HTML may be found in the official specifications maintained by W3C.

The third component of the *world wide web* is the HyperText Transport Protocol (HTTP). HTTP is a text-based protocol, in which the client sends a request and the server returns a response. HTTP runs above the bytestream service and HTTP servers listen by default on port 80. The design of HTTP has largely been inspired by the Internet email protocols. Each HTTP request contains three parts :

- a *method*, that indicates the type of request, a URI, and the version of the HTTP protocol used by the client
- a *header* , that is used by the client to specify optional parameters for the request. An empty line is used to mark the end of the header
- an optional MIME document attached to the request

The response sent by the server also contains three parts :

- a *status line* , that indicates whether the request was successful or not
- a *header*, that contains additional information about the response. The response header ends with an empty line.
- a MIME document

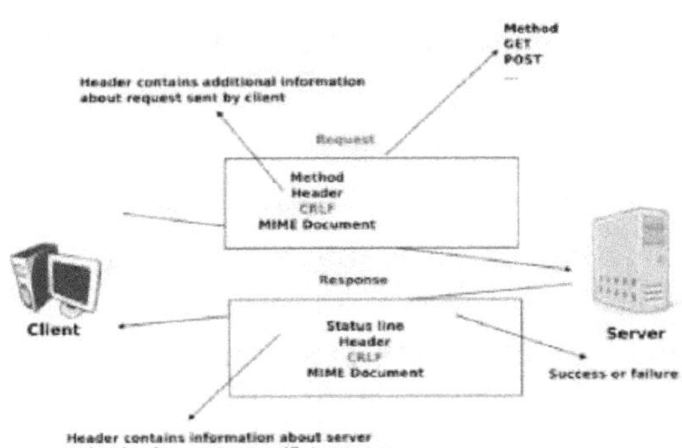

Figure 2.19: HTTP requests and responses

Several types of method can be used in HTTP requests. The three most important ones are :

- the *GET* method is the most popular one. It is used to retrieve a document from a server. The *GET* method is encoded as *GET* followed by the path of the URI of the requested document and the version of HTTP used by the client. For example, to retrieve the http://www.w3.org/MarkUp/ URI, a client must open a TCP on port *80* with host *www.w3.org* and send a HTTP request containing the following line

  GET /MarkUp/ HTTP/1.0
- - the *HEAD* method is a variant of the *GET* method that allows the retrieval of the header lines for a given URI without retrieving the entire document. It can be used by a client to verify if a document exists, for instance.
- the *POST* method can be used by a client to send a document to a server. The sent document is attached to the HTTP request as a MIME document.

HTTP clients and servers can include many different HTTP headers in HTTP requests and responses. Each HTTP header is encoded as a single ASCII-line terminated by *CR* and *LF*. Several of these headers are briefly described below. A detailed discussion of all standard headers may be found in **RFC 1945**. The MIME headers can appear in both HTTP requests and HTTP responses.

- the *Content-Length:* header is the *MIME* header that indicates the length of the MIME document in bytes.
- the *Content-Type:* header is the *MIME* header that indicates the type of the attached MIME document. HTML pages use the *text/html* type.
- the *Content-Encoding:* header indicates how the *MIME document* has been encoded. For example, this header would be set to *x-gzip* for a document compressed using the gzip software.

RFC 1945 and **RFC 2616** define headers that are specific to HTTP responses. These server headers include :

- the *Server:* header indicates the version of the web server that has generated the HTTP response. Some servers provide information about their software release and optional modules that they use. For security reasons, some system administrators disable these headers to avoid revealing too much information about their server to potential attackers.
- the *Date:* header indicates when the HTTP response has been produced by the server.

- the *Last-Modified:* header indicates the date and time of the last modification of the document attached to the HTTP response.

Similarly, the following header lines can only appear inside HTTP requests sent by a client :

- the *User-Agent:* header provides information about the client that has generated the HTTP request. Some servers analyse this header line and return different headers and sometimes different documents for different user agents.
- the *If-Modified-Since:* header is followed by a date. It enables clients to cache in memory or on disk the recent or most frequently used documents. When a client needs to request a URI from a server, it first checks whether the document is already in its cache. If it is, the client sends a HTTP request with the *If-Modified- Since:* header indicating the date of the cached document. The server will only return the document attached to the HTTP response if it is newer than the version stored in the client's cache.
- the *Referrer:* header is followed by a URI. It indicates the URI of the document that the client visited before sending this HTTP request. Thanks to this header, the server can know the URI of the document containing the hyperlink followed by the client, if any. This information is very useful to measure the impact of advertisements containing hyperlinks placed on websites.
- the *Host:* header contains the fully qualified domain name of the URI being requested.

Note: The importance of the *Host:* header line

The first version of HTTP did not include the *Host:* header line. This was a severe limitation for web hosting companies. For example consider a web hosting company that wants to serve both *web.example.com* and

www.example.net on the same physical server. Both web sites contain a */index.html* document. When a client sends a request for either *http://web.example.com/index.html* or *http://www.example.net/index.html,* the HTTP 1.0 request contains the following line :

GET /index.html HTTP/1.0

By parsing this line, a server cannot determine which *index.html* file is requested. Thanks to the *Host:* header line, the server knows whether the request is for *http://web.example.com/index.html* or *http://www.dummy.net/index.html.* Without the *Host:* header, this is impossible. The *Host:* header line allowed web hosting companies to develop their business by supporting a large number of independent web servers on the same physical server.

The status line of the HTTP response begins with the version of HTTP used by the server (usually *HTTP/1.0* defined in **RFC 1945** or *HTTP/1.1* defined in **RFC 2616**) followed by a three digit status code and additional information in English. HTTP status codes have a similar structure as the reply codes used by SMTP.

- All status codes starting with digit *2* indicate a valid response. *200 Ok* indicates that the HTTP request was successfully processed by the server and that the response is valid.
- All status codes starting with digit *3* indicate that the requested document is no longer available on the server. *301 Moved Permanently* indicates that the requested document is no longer available on this server. A *Location:* header containing the new URI of the requested document is inserted in the HTTP response. *304 Not Modified* is used in response to an HTTP request containing the *If-Modified-Since:* header. This status line is used by the server if the document stored on the server is not more recent than the date indicated in the *If-Modified-Since:* header.
- All status codes starting with digit *4* indicate that the server has detected an error in the HTTP request sent by the client. *400 Bad Request* indicates a syntax error in the HTTP request. *404 Not Found* indicates that the requested document does not exist on the server.
- All status codes starting with digit 5 indicate an error on the server. *500 Internal Server Error* indicates that the server could not process the request due to an error on the server itself.

In both the HTTP request and the HTTP response, the MIME document refers to a representation of the document with the MIME headers indicating the type of document and its size.

As an illustration of HTTP/1.0, the transcript below shows a HTTP request for http://www.ietf.org and the corresponding HTTP response. The HTTP request was sent using the curl command line tool. The *User-Agent:* header line contains more information about this client software. There is no MIME document attached to this HTTP request, and it ends with a blank line.

GET / HTTP/1.0
User-Agent: curl/7.19.4 (universal-apple-darwin10.0) libcurl/7.19.4 OpenSSL/0.9.8l zlib/1.2.3 Host: www.ietf.org

The HTTP response indicates the version of the server software used with the modules included. The *Last- Modified:* header indicates that the requested document was modified about one week before the request. A HTML document (not shown) is attached to the response. Note the blank line between the header of the HTTP response and the attached MIME document. The *Server:* header line has been truncated in this output.

```
HTTP/1.1 200 OK
Date: Mon, 15 Mar 2010 13:40:38 GMT
Server: Apache/2.2.4 (Linux/SUSE) mod_ssl/2.2.4 OpenSSL/0.9.8e (truncated)
Last-Modified: Tue, 09 Mar 2010 21:26:53 GMT
Content-Length: 17019
Content-Type: text/html
<!DOCTYPE HTML PUBLIC .../HTML>
```

HTTP was initially designed to share self-contained text documents. For this reason, and to ease the implementation of clients and servers, the designers of HTTP chose to open a TCP connection for each HTTP request. This implies that a client must open one TCP connection for each URI that it wants to retrieve from a server as illustrated on the figure below. For a web page containing only text documents this was a reasonable design choice as the client usually remains idle while the (human) user is reading the retrieved document.

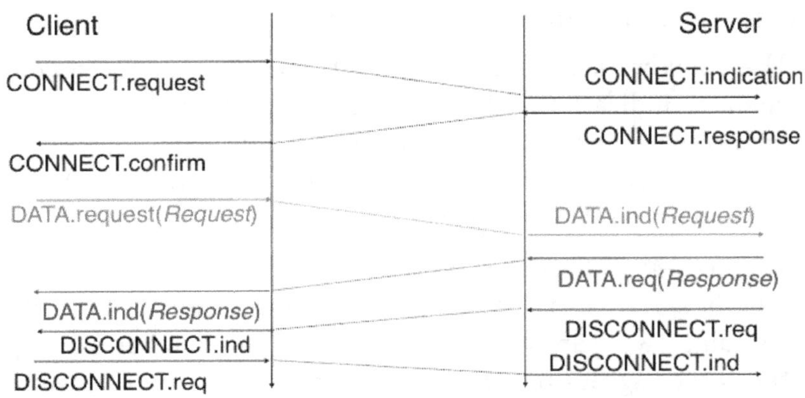

Figure 2.20: HTTP 1.0 and the underlying TCP connection

However, as the web evolved to support richer documents containing images, opening a TCP connection for each URI became a performance problem [Mogul1995]. Indeed, besides its HTML part, a web page may include dozens of images or more. Forcing the client to open a TCP connection for each component of a web page has two important drawbacks. First, the client and the server must exchange packets to open and close a TCP connection as we will see later. This increases the network overhead and the total delay of completely retrieving all the components of a web page. Second, a large number of established TCP connections may be a performance bottleneck on servers.

This problem was solved by extending HTTP to support persistent TCP connections **RFC 2616.** A persistent connection is a TCP connection over which a client may send several HTTP requests. This is illustrated in the figure below.

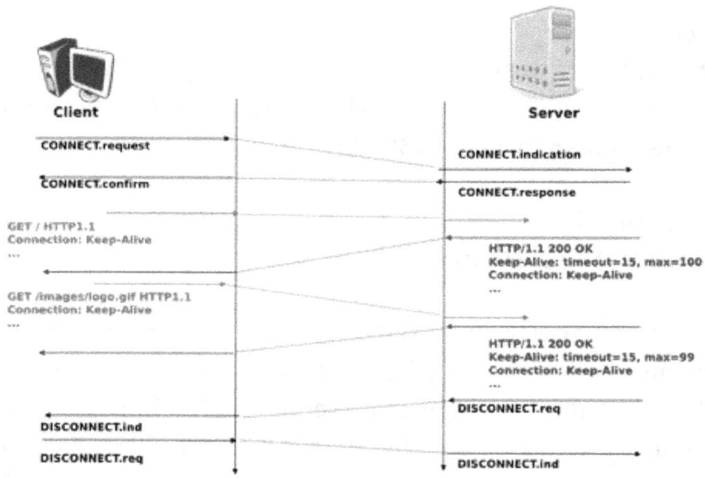

Figure 2.21: HTTP 1.1 persistent connections

To allow the clients and servers to control the utilisation of these persistent TCP connections, HTTP 1.1 **RFC 2616** defines several new HTTP headers:

- The *Connection:* header is used with the *Keep-Alive* argument by the client to indicate that it expects the underlying TCP connection to be persistent. When this header is used with the *Close* argument, it indicates that the entity that sent it will close the underlying TCP connection at the end of the HTTP response.
- The *Keep-Alive:* header is used by the server to inform the client about how it agrees to use the persistent connection. A typical *Keep-Alive:* contains two parameters : the maximum number of requests that the server agrees to serve on the underlying TCP connection and the timeout (in seconds) after which the server will close an idle connection

The example below shows the operation of HTTP/1.1 over a persistent TCP connection to retrieve three URIs stored on the same server. Once the connection has been established, the client sends its first request with the *Connection: keep-alive* header to request a persistent connection.

GET / HTTP/1.1

Host: www.kame.net

User-Agent: Mozilla/5.0 (Macintosh; U; Intel Mac OS X 10_6_2; en-us) Connection: keep-alive

The server replies with the *Connection: Keep-Alive* header and indicates that it accepts a maximum of 100 HTTP requests over this connection and that it will close the connection if it remains idle for 15 seconds.

```
HTTP/1.1 200 OK
Date: Fri, 19 Mar 2010 09:23:37 GMT
Server: Apache/2.0.63 (FreeBSD) PHP/5.2.12 with Suhosin-Patch
Keep-Alive: timeout=15, max=100
Connection: Keep-Alive
Content-Length: 3462
Content-Type: text/html
<html>... </html>
```

The client sends a second request for the style sheet of the retrieved web page.

```
GET /style.css HTTP/1.1
Host: www.kame.net
Referer: http://www.kame.net/
User-Agent: Mozilla/5.0 (Macintosh; U; Intel Mac OS X 10_6_2; en-us) Connection:
keep-alive
```

The server replies with the requested style sheet and maintains the persistent connection. Note that the server only accepts 99 remaining HTTP requests over this persistent connection.

```
HTTP/1.1 200 OK
Date: Fri, 19 Mar 2010 09:23:37 GMT
Server: Apache/2.0.63 (FreeBSD) PHP/5.2.12 with Suhosin-Patch
Last-Modified: Mon, 10 Apr 2006 05:06:39 GMT
Content-Length: 2235
Keep-Alive: timeout=15, max=99
Connection: Keep-Alive
Content-Type: text/css
...
```

Then the client automatically requests the web server's icon, that could be displayed by the browser. This server does not contain such URI and thus replies with a *404* HTTP status. However, the underlying TCP connection is not closed immediately.

```
GET /favicon.ico HTTP/1.1
Host: www.kame.net
Referer: http://www.kame.net/
User-Agent: Mozilla/5.0 (Macintosh; U; Intel Mac OS X 10_6_2; en-us)
```

Connection: keep-alive
HTTP/1.1 404 Not Found
Date: Fri, 19 Mar 2010 09:23:40 GMT
Server: Apache/2.0.63 (FreeBSD) PHP/5.2.12 with Suhosin-Patch
Content-Length: 318
Keep-Alive: timeout=15, max=98
Connection: Keep-Alive
Content-Type: text/html; charset=iso-8859-1
<!DOCTYPE HTML PUBLIC "-//IETF//DTD HTML 2.0//EN"> ...

As illustrated above, a client can send several HTTP requests over the same persistent TCP connection. However, it is important to note that all of these HTTP requests are considered to be independent by the server. Each HTTP request must be self-contained. This implies that each request must include all the header lines that are required by the server to understand the request. The independence of these requests is one of the important design choices of HTTP. As a consequence of this design choice, when a server processes a HTTP request, it doesn't' use any other information than what is contained in the request itself. This explains why the client adds its *User-Agent:* header in all of the HTTP requests it sends over the persistent TCP connection.

However, in practice, some servers want to provide content tuned for each user. For example, some servers can provide information in several languages or other servers want to provide advertisements that are targeted to different types of users. To do this, servers need to maintain some information about the preferences of each user and use this information to produce content matching the user's preferences. HTTP contains several mechanisms that enable to solve this problem. We discuss three of them below.

A first solution is to force the users to be authenticated. This was the solution used by *FTP* to control the files that each user could access. Initially, user names and passwords could be included inside URIs **RFC 1738**. However, placing passwords in the clear in a potentially publicly visible URI is completely insecure and this usage has now been deprecated **RFC 3986**. HTTP supports several extension headers **RFC 2617** that can be used by a server to request the authentication of the client by providing his/her credentials. However, user names and passwords have not been popular on web servers as they force human users to remember one user name and one password per server. Remembering a password is acceptable when a user needs to access protected content, but users will not accept the need for a user name and password only to receive targeted advertisements from the web sites that they visit.

A second solution to allow servers to tune that content to the needs and capabilities of the user is to rely on the different types of *Accept-** HTTP headers. For example, the *Accept-Language:* can be used by the client to indicate its preferred languages. Unfortunately, in practice this header is usually set based on the default language of the browser and it is not possible for a user to indicate the language it prefers to use by selecting options on each visited web server.

The third, and widely adopted, solution are HTTP cookies. HTTP cookies were initially developed as a private extension by Netscape. They are now part of the standard **RFC 6265**. In a nutshell, a cookie is a short string that is chosen by a server to represent a given client. Two HTTP headers are used : *Cookie:* and *Set-Cookie:*. When a server receives an HTTP request from a new client (i.e. an HTTP request that does not contain the *Cookie:* header), it generates a cookie for the client and includes it in the *Set-Cookie:* header of the returned HTTP response. The *Set-Cookie:* header contains several additional parameters including the domain names for which the cookie is valid. The client stores all received cookies on disk and every time it sends a HTTP request, it verifies whether it already knows a cookie for this domain. If so, it attaches the *Cookie:* header to the HTTP request. This is illustrated in the figure below with HTTP 1.1, but cookies also work with HTTP 1.0.

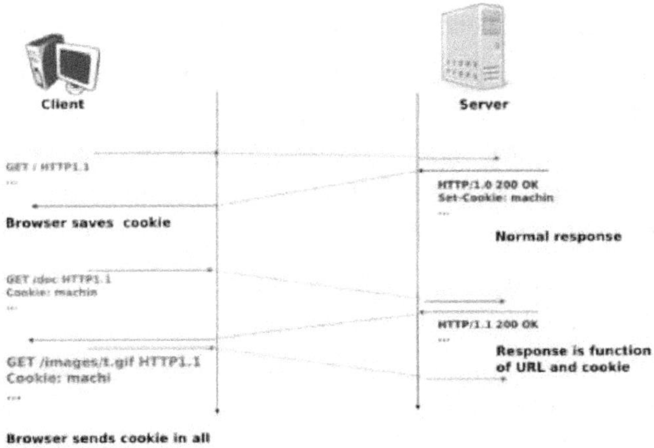

Figure 2.22: HTTP cookies

Note: Privacy issues with HTTP cookies

The HTTP cookies introduced by Netscape are key for large e-commerce websites. However, they have also raised many discussions concerning their potential misuses. Consider *ad.com*, a company that delivers lots of advertisements on web sites. A web site that wishes to include *ad.com's* advertisements next to its content will add links to *ad.com* inside its HTML pages. If *ad.com* is used by many web sites, *ad.com* could be able to track the interests of all the users that visit its client websites and use this information to provide targeted advertisements. Privacy advocates have even sued online advertisement companies to force them to comply with the privacy regulations. More recent related technologies also raise privacy concerns.

2.3 WRITING SIMPLE NETWORKED APPLICATIONS

Networked applications were usually implemented by using the *socket API.* This API was designed when TCP/IP was first implemented in the Unix BSD operating system [Sechrest] [LFJLMT], and has served as the model for many APIs between applications and the networking stack in an operating system. Although the socket API is very popular, other APIs have also been developed. For example, the STREAMS API has been added to several Unix System V variants [Rago1993]. The socket API is supported by most programming languages and several textbooks have been devoted to it. Users of the C language can consult [DC2009], [Stevens1998], [SFR2004] or [Kerrisk2010]. The Java implementation of the socket API is described in [CD2008] and in the Java tutorial. In this section, we will use the python implementation of the socket API to illustrate the key concepts. Additional information about this API may be found in the socket section of the python documentation .

The socket API is quite low-level and should be used only when you need a complete control of the network access. If your application simply needs, for instance, to retrieve data with HTTP, there are much simpler and higher-level APIs.

A detailed discussion of the socket API is outside the scope of this section and the references cited above provide a detailed discussion of all the details of the socket API. As a starting point, it is interesting to compare the socket API with the service primitives that we have discussed in the previous chapter. Let us first consider the connectionless service that consists of the following two primitives :

- *DATA.request(destination,message)* is used to send a message to a specified destination. In this socket API, this corresponds to the send method.
- *DATA.indication(message)* is issued by the transport service to deliver a message to the application. In the socket API, this corresponds to the return of the recv method that is called by the application.

The *DATA* primitives are exchanged through a service access point. In the socket API, the equivalent to the service access point is the *socket.* A *socket* is a data structure which is maintained by the networking stack and is used by the application every time it needs to send or receive data through the networking stack. The *socket* method in the python API takes two main arguments :

- an *address family* that specifies the type of address family and thus the underlying networking stack that will be used with the socket. This parameter can be either socket.AF_INET or socket.AF_INET6. socket.

AF_INET, which corresponds to the TCP/IPv4 protocol stack is the default. socket.AF_INET6 corresponds to the TCP/IPv6 protocol stack.

- a *type* indicates the type of service which is expected from the networking stack. socket.STREAM (the default) corresponds to the reliable bytestream connection-oriented service. socket.DGRAM corresponds to the connectionless service.

A simple client that sends a request to a server is often written as follows in descriptions of the socket API.

```
# A simple client of the connectionless service
import socket
import sys
HOSTIP=sys.argv[1]
PORT=int(sys.argv[2])
MSG="Hello, World!"
s = socket.socket( socket.AF_INET, socket.SOCK_DGRAM )
s.sendto( MSG, (HOSTIP, PORT) )
```

A typical usage of this application would be

python client.py 127.0.0.1 12345

where 127.0.0.1 is the IPv4 address of the host (in this case the localhost) where the server is running and 12 34 5 the port of the server.

The first operation is the creation of the socket. Two parameters must be specified while creating a socket. The first parameter indicates the address family and the second the socket type. The second operation is the transmission of the message by using sendto to the server. It should be noted that sendto takes as arguments the message to be transmitted and a tuple that contains the IPv4 address of the server and its port number.

The code shown above supports only the TCP/IPv4 protocol stack. To use the TCP/IPv6 protocol stack the socket must be created by using the socket.AF_INET6 address family. Forcing the application developer to select TCP/IPv4 or TCP/IPv6 when creating a socket is a major hurdle for the deployment and usage of TCP/IPv6 in the global Internet [Cheshire2010]. While most operating systems support both TCP/IPv4 and TCP/IPv6, many applications still only use TCP/IPv4 by default. In the long term, the socket API should be able to handle TCP/IPv4 and TCP/IPv6 transparently and should not force the application developer to always specify whether it uses TCP/IPv4 or TCP/IPv6.

Another important issue with the socket API as supported by python is that it forces the application to deal with IP addresses instead of dealing directly with domain names. This limitation dates from the early days of the socket API in Unix 4.2BSD. At that time, the DNS was not widely available and only IP addresses could be used. Most applications rely on DNS names to interact with servers and this utilisation of the DNS plays a very important role to scale web servers and content distribution networks. To use domain names, the application needs to perform the DNS resolution by using the getaddrinfo method. This method queries the DNS and builds the sockaddr data structure which is used by other methods of the socket API. In python, getaddrinfo takes several arguments :

- a *name* that is the domain name for which the DNS will be queried
- an optional *port number* which is the port number of the remote server
- an optional *address family* which indicates the address family used for the DNS request. socket.AF_lNET (resp. socket.AF_INET6) indicates that an IPv4 (IPv6) address is expected. Furthermore, the python socket API allows an application to use socket.AF_UNSPEC to indicate that it is able to use either IPv4 or IPv6 addresses.
- an optional *socket type* which can be either socket.SOCK_DGRAM or socket.SOCK_STREAM

In today's Internet hosts that are capable of supporting both IPv4 and IPv6, all applications should be able to handle both IPv4 and IPv6 addresses. When used with the socket.AF_UNSPEC parameter, the socket.getaddrinfo method returns a list of tuples containing all the information to create a socket.

```
import socket
socket.getaddrinfo('www.example.net',80,socket.AF_UNSPEC,socket.SOCK_STREAM)
[ (30, 1, 6, '', ('2001:db8:3080:3::2', 80, 0, 0)),
(2, 1, 6, '', ('203.0.113.225', 80))]
```

In the example above, socket.getaddrinfo returns two tuples. The first one corresponds to the sockaddr containing the IPv6 address of the remote server and the second corresponds to the IPv4 information. Due to some peculiarities of IPv6 and IPv4, the format of the two tuples is not exactly the same, but the key information in both cases are the network layer address (2001 :db8:3080:3::2 and 2 03.0.113.225) and the port number (80). The other parameters are seldom used.

socket.getaddrinfo can be used to build a simple client that queries the DNS and contact the server by using either IPv4 or IPv6 depending on the addresses returned by the socket.getaddrinfo method. The client below iterates over the list of addresses returned by the DNS and sends its request to the first destination address for which it can create a socket. Other strategies are of course possible. For example, a host running in an IPv6 network might prefer to always use IPv6 when

IPv6 is available. Another example is the happy eyeballs approach which is being discussed within the IETF [WY2011]. For example, [WY2011] mentions that some web browsers try to use the first address returned by socket.getaddrinfo. If there is no answer within some small delay (e.g. 300 milliseconds), the second address is tried.

```
import socket
import sys
HOSTNAME=sys.argv[1]
PORT=int(sys.argv[2])
MSG="Hello, World!"
for a in socket.getaddrinfo(HOSTNAME, PORT, socket.AF_UNSPEC,socket.SOCK_
DGRAM,0, socket.AI address_family,sock_type,protocol,canonicalname, sockaddr=a
try:
s = socket.socket(address_family, sock_type)
except socket.error:
s = None
print "Could not create socket"
continue
if s is not None:
s.sendto(MSG, sockaddr)
break
```

Now that we have described the utilisation of the socket API to write a simple client using the connectionless transport service, let us have a closer look at the reliable byte stream transport service. As explained above, this service is invoked by creating a socket of type socket.SOCK_STREAM. Once a socket has been created, a client will typically connect to the remote server, send some data, wait for an answer and eventually close the connection. These operations are performed by calling the following methods :

- socket.connect : this method takes a sockaddr data structure, typically returned by socket.getaddrinfo, as argument. It may fail and raise an exception if the remote server cannot be reached.
- socket.send : this method takes a string as argument and returns the number of bytes that were actually sent. The string will be transmitted as a sequence of consecutive bytes to the remote server. Applications are expected to check the value returned by this method and should resend the bytes that were not send.
- socket.recv : this method takes an integer as argument that indicates the size of the buffer that has been allocated to receive the data. An

important point to note about the utilisation of the socket.recv method is that as it runs above a bytestream service, it may return any amount of bytes (up to the size of the buffer provided by the application). The application needs to collect all the received data and there is no guarantee that some data sent by the remote host by using a single call to the socket.send method will be received by the destination with a single call to the socket.recv method.

- socket.shutdown : this method is used to release the underlying connection. On some platforms, it is possible to specify the direction of transfer to be released (e.g. socket.SHUT_WR to release the outgoing direction or socket.SHUT_RDWR to release both directions).
- socket.close: this method is used to close the socket. It calls socket.shutdown if the underlying connection is still open.

With these methods, it is now possible to write a simple HTTP client. This client operates over both IPv6 and IPv4 and writes the homepage of the remote server on the standard output. It also reports the number of socket.recv calls that were used to retrieve the homepage.

```
#!/usr/bin/python
# A simple http client that retrieves the first page of a web site
import socket, sys
if len(sys.argv)!=3 and len(sys.argv)!=2:
print "Usage : ",sys.argv[0]," hostname [port]"
hostname = sys.argv[1]
if len(sys.argv)==3 :
port=int(sys.argv[2])
else:
port = 80
READBUF=16384 # size of data read from web server
s=None
for res in socket.getaddrinfo(hostname, port, socket.AF_UNSPEC, socket.SOCK_
STREAM):
af, socktype, proto, canonname, sa = res
create socket
try:
s = socket.socket(af, socktype, proto)
except socket.error:
s = None
continue
connect to remote host
```

```
try:
print "Trying "+sa[0]
s.connect(sa)
except socket.error, msg:
# socket failed
s.close()
s = None
continue
if s :
print "Connected to "+sa[0]
s.send('GET / HTTP/1.1\r\nHost:'+hostname+'\r\n\r\n')
finished=False
count=0
while not finished:
data=s.recv(READBUF)
count=count+1
if len(data)!=0:
print repr(data)
else:
finished=True
s.shutdown(socket.SHUT_WR)
s.close()
print "Data was received in ",count," recv calls"
break
```

As mentioned above, the socket API is very low-level. This is the interface to the transport service. For a common and simple task, like retrieving a document from the Web, there are much simpler solutions. For example, the python standard library includes several high-level APIs to implementations of various application layer protocols including HTTP. For example, the httplib module can be used to easily access documents via HTTP.

```
#!/usr/bin/python
A simple http client that retrieves the first page of a web site, using
the standard httplib library
import httplib, sys
if len(sys.argv)!=3 and len(sys.argv)!=2:
print "Usage : ",sys.argv[0]," hostname [port]"
sys.exit(1)
path = '/'
hostname = sys.argv[1]
```

```
if len(sys.argv)==3 :
port = int(sys.argv[2])
else:
port = 80
conn = httplib.HTTPConnection(hostname, port)
conn.request("GET", path)
r = conn.getresponse()
print "Response is %i (%s)" % (r.status, r.reason)
print r.read()
```

Another module, urllib2 allows the programmer to directly use URLs. This is much more simpler than directly using sockets.

But simplicity is not the only advantage of using high-level libraries. They allow the programmer to manipulate higher-level concepts (e.g. *I want the content pointed by this URL)* but also include many features such as transparent support for the utilisation of *TLS* or IPv6.

The second type of applications that can be written by using the socket API are the servers. A server is typically runs forever waiting to process requests coming from remote clients. A server using the connectionless will typically start with the creation of a *socket* with the socket.socket. This socket can be created above the TCP/IPv4 networking stack (socket.AF_INET) or the TCP/IPv6 networking stack (socket.AF_INET6), but not both by default. If a server is willing to use the two networking stacks, it must create two threads, one to handle the TCP/IPv4 socket and the other to handle the TCP/IPv6 socket. It is unfortunately impossible to define a socket that can receive data from both networking stacks at the same time with the python socket API.

A server using the connectionless service will typically use two methods from the socket API in addition to those that we have already discussed.

- socket.bind is used to bind a socket to a port number and optionally an IP address. Most servers will bind their socket to all available interfaces on the servers, but there are some situations where the server may prefer to be bound only to specific IP addresses. For example, a server running on a smartphone might want to be bound to the IP address of the WiFi interface but not on the 3G interface that is more expensive.
- socket.recvfrom is used to receive data from the underlying networking stack. This method returns both the sender's address and the received data.

The code below illustrates a very simple server running above the connectionless transport service that simply prints on the standard output all the received messages. This server uses the TCP/IPv6 networking stack.

```
import socket, sys
PORT=int(sys.argv[1])
BUFF_LEN=8192
s=socket.socket(socket.AF_INET6, socket.SOCK_DGRAM)
s.bind((‘’,PORT,0,0))
while True:
data, addr = s.recvfrom( BUFF_LEN )
if data==”STOP” :
print “Stopping server”
sys.exit(0)
print “received from “, addr, “ message:”, data
```

A server that uses the reliable byte stream service can also be built above the socket API. Such a server starts by creating a socket that is bound to the port that has been chosen for the server. Then the server calls the socket.listen method. This informs the underlying networking stack of the number of transport connection attempts that can be queued in the underlying networking stack waiting to be accepted and processed by the server. The server typically has a thread waiting on the socket. accept method. This method returns as soon as a connection attempt is received by the underlying stack. It returns a socket that is bound to the established connection and the address of the remote host. With these methods, it is possible to write a very simple web server that always returns a *404* error to all *GET* requests and a *501* errors to all other requests.

```
An extremely simple HTTP server
import socket, sys, time
Server runs on all IP addresses by default
HOST=”
8080 can be used without root priviledges
PORT=8080
BUFLEN=8192 # buffer size
s = socket.socket(socket.AF_INET6, socket.SOCK_STREAM)
try:
print “Starting HTTP server on port “, PORT
s.bind((HOST,PORT,0,0))
except socket.error :
print “Cannot bind to port :”,PORT
```

```
sys.exit(-1)
s.listen(10) # maximum 10 queued connections
while True:
# a real server would be multithreaded and would catch exceptions
conn, addr = s.accept()
print "Connection from ", addr
data=''
while not '\n' in data : # wait until first line has been received
data = data+conn.recv(BUFLEN)
if data.startswith('GET'):
GET request
conn.send('HTTP/1.0 404 Not Found\r\n')
a real server should serve files
else:
# other type of HTTP request
conn.send('HTTP/1.0 501 Not implemented\r\n')
now = time.strftime("%a, %d %b %Y %H:%M:%S", time.localtime())
conn.send('Date: ' + now +' \r\n'
conn.send('Server: Dummy-HTTP-Server\r\n')
conn.send (      )
conn.shutdown(socket.SHUT_RDWR)
conn.close()
```

This server is far from a production-quality web server. A real web server would use multiple threads and/or non-blocking IO to process a large number of concurrent requests. Furthermore, it would also need to handle all the errors that could happen while receiving data over a transport connection. These are outside the scope of this section and additional information on more complex networked applications may be found elsewhere. For example, [RG2010] provides an in-depth discussion of the utilisation of the socket API with python while [SFR2004] remains an excellent source of information on the socket API in C.

2.4 SUMMARY

In this chapter, we began by describing the client-server and peer-to-peer models. We then described, in detail, three important families of protocols in the application layer. The Internet identifies hosts by using 32 bits IPv4 or 128 bits IPv6. However, using these addresses directly inside applications would be difficult for the humans that use them. We have explained how the Domain Name System allows the mapping of names to corresponding addresses. We have described both the DNS protocol that runs above UDP and the naming hierarchy. We have then discussed one of the oldest applications on the Internet : electronic mail. We have described the format of email messages and described the SMTP protocol that is used to send email messages as well as the POP protocol that is used by email recipients to retrieve their email messages from their server. Finally, we have explained the protocols that are used in the world wide web and the HyperText Transfer Protocol in particular.

2.5 EXERCISES

This section contains several exercises and small challenges about the application layer protocols.

2.5.1 The Domain Name System

The Domain Name System (DNS) plays a key role in the Internet today as it allows applications to use fully qualified domain names (FQDN) instead of IPv4 or IPv6 addresses. Many tools allow to perform queries through DNS servers. For this exercise, we will use dig which is installed on most Unix systems.

A typical usage of dig is as follows

dig @server -t type fqdn

where

- *server* is the IP address or the name of a DNS server or resolver
- *type* is the type of DNS record that is requested by the query such as *NS* for a nameserver, *A* for an IPv4 address, *AAAA* for an IPv6 address, *MX* for a mail relay,...
- *fqdn* is the fully qualified domain name being queried

1. What are the IP addresses of the resolvers that the *dig* implementation you are using relies on?
2. What is the IP address that corresponds to *inl.info.ucl.ac.be* ? Which type of DNS query does *dig* send to obtain this information ?
3. Which type of DNS request do you need to send to obtain the nameservers that are responsible for a given domain ?
4. What are the nameservers that are responsible for the *be* top-level domain ? Where are they located ? Is it possible to use IPv6 to query them ?
5. When run without any parameter, *dig* queries one of the root DNS servers and retrieves the list of the the names of all root DNS servers. For technical reasons, there are only 13 different root DNS servers. This information is also available as a text file from http://www.internic.net/zones/named.root What are the IP addresses of all these servers. Can they be queried by using IPv6 ?
6. Assume now that you are residing in a network where there is no DNS resolver and that you need to start your query from the DNS root.

- Use *dig* to send a query to one of these root servers to find the IP address of the DNS server(s) (NS record) responsible for the *org* top-level domain
- Use *dig* to send a query to one of these DNS servers to find the IP address of the DNS server(s) (NS record) responsible for root-servers.org‘
- Continue until you find the server responsible for *www.root-servers.org*
- What is the lifetime associated to this IP address ?

7. Perform the same analysis for a popular website such as *www.google.com.* What is the lifetime associated to this IP address ? If you perform the same request several times, do you always receive the same answer ? Can you explain why a lifetime is associated to the DNS replies ?
8. Use *dig* to find the mail relays used by the *uclouvain.be* and *gmail.com* domains. What is the *TTL* of these records (use the *+ttlid* option when using dig) ? Can you explain the preferences used by the *MX* records. You can find more information about the MX records in **RFC 974**
9. Use *dig* to query the IPv6 address (DNS record AAAA) of the following hosts
   - *www.sixxs.net*
   - *www.google.com*
   - *ipv6.google.com*
10. When *dig* is run, the header section in its output indicates the *id* the DNS identifier used to send the query. Does your implementation of *dig* generates random identifiers ?

```
dig -t MX gmail.com
; <<>> DiG 9.4.3-P3 <<>> -t MX gmail.com
;; global options: printcmd
;; Got answer:
;; ->>HEADER<<- opcode: QUERY, status: NOERROR, id: 25718
```

A DNS implementation such as *dig* and more importantly a name resolver such as bind or unbound, always checks that the received DNS reply contains the same identifier as the DNS request that it sent. Why is this so important ?

- Imagine an attacker who is able to send forged DNS replies to, for example, associate *www.bigbank.com* to his own IP address. How could he attack a DNS implementation that
  - sends DNS requests containing always the same identifier
  - sends DNS requests containing identifiers that are incremented by one after each request
  - sends DNS requests containing random identifiers

11. The DNS protocol can run over UDP and over TCP. Most DNS servers prefer to use UDP because it consumes fewer resources on the server. However, TCP is useful when a large answer is expected or when a large answer must. You can force the utilisation of TCP by using *dig +tcp.* Use TCP and UDP to query a root DNS server. Is it faster to receive an answer via TCP or via UDP ?

2.5.2 Internet email protocols

Many Internet protocols are ASCII-based protocols where the client sends requests as one line of ASCII text terminated by *CRLF* and the server replies with one of more lines of ASCII text. Using such ASCII messages has several advantages compared to protocols that rely on binary encoded messages

- the messages exchanged by the client and the server can be easily understood by a developer or network engineer by simply reading the messages
- it is often easy to write a small prototype that implements a part of the protocol
- it is possible to test a server manually by using telnet Telnet is a protocol that allows to obtain a terminal on a remote server. For this, telnet opens a TCP connection with the remote server on port 23. However, most *telnet* implementations allow the user to specify an alternate port as *telnet hosts port* When used with a port number as parameter, *telnet* opens a TCP connection to the remote host on the specified port. *telnet* can thus be used to test any server using an ASCII-based protocol on top of TCP. Note that if you need to stop a running *telnet* session, Ctrl-C will not work as it will be sent by *telnet* to the remote host over the TCP connection. On many *telnet* implementations you can type *Ctrl-]* to freeze the TCP connection and return to the telnet interface.

1. Assume that Alice sends an email from her *alice@yahoo.com* account to *Bob* who uses *bob@yahoo.com.* Which protocols are involved in the transmission of this email ?
2. Same question when Alice sends an email to her friend Trudy, *trudy@gmail.com.*
3. Before the advent of webmail and feature rich mailers, email was written and read by using command line tools on servers. Using your account on *sirius.info.ucl.ac.be* use the */bin/mail* command line tool to send an email to yourself *on this host.* This server stores local emails in the */var/mail* directory with one file per user. Check with */bin/more* the content of your mail file and try to understand which lines have been added by the server in the header of your email.
4. Use your preferred email tool to send an email message to yourself containing a single line of text. Most email tools have the ability to show the *source* of the message, use this function to look at the message that you sent and the message

that you received. Can you find an explanation for all the lines that have been added to your single line email ?

5. The first version of the SMTP protocol was defined in **RFC 821**. The current standard for SMTP is defined in **RFC 5321** Considering only **RFC 821** what are the main commands of the *SMTP* protocol?
6. When using SMTP, how do you recognise a positive reply from a negative one ?
7. A SMTP server is a daemon process that can fail due to a bug or lack of resources (e.g. memory). Network administrators often install tools that regularly connect to their servers to check that they are operating correctly. A simple solution is to open a TCP connection on port 25 to the SMTP server's host. If the connection is established, this implies that there is a process listening. What is the reply sent by the SMTP server when you type the following command? telnet cnp3.info.ucl.ac.be 25

Warning : Do *not* try this on a random SMTP server. The exercises proposed in this section should only be run on the SMTP server dedicated for these exercises : *cnp3.info.ucl.ac.be.* If you try them on a production SMTP server, the administrator of this server may become angry.

1. Continue the SMTP session that you started above by sending the greetings command *(HELO* followed by the fully qualified domain name of your host) and terminate the session by sending the *QUIT* command.
2. The minimum SMTP session above allows to verify that the SMTP is running. However, this does not always imply that mail can be delivered. For example, large SMTP servers often use a database to store all the email addresses that they serve. To verify the correct operation of such a server, one possibility is to use the *VRFY* command. Open a SMTP session on the lab's SMTP server *(cnp3.info.ucl.ac.be)* and use this command to verify that your account is active.
3. Now that you know the basics of opening and closing an SMTP session, you can now send email manually by using the *MAIL FROM:*, *RCPT TO:* and *DATA* commands. Use these commands to *manually* send an email to *INGI2141@cnp3.info.ucl.ac.be*. Do not forget to include the *From:*, *To:* and *Subject:* lines in your header.

By using SMTP, is it possible to send an email that contains exactly the following ASCII art ?

1. Most email agents allow you to send email in carbon-copy (cc:) and also in blind-carbon-copy *(bcc:)* to a recipient. How does a SMTP server supports these two types of recipients ?
2. In the early days, email was read by using tools such as */bin/mail* or more advanced text-based mail readers such as pine or elm. Today, emails are stored on dedicated servers and retrieved by using protocols such as **POP_** or IMAP. From the user's viewpoint, can you list the advantages and drawbacks of these two protocols ?

3. The TCP protocol supports 65536 different ports numbers. Many of these port numbers have been reserved for some applications. The official repository of the reserved port numbers is maintained by the Internet Assigned Numbers Authority (IANA) on http://www.iana.org/assignments/port-numbers. Using this information, what is the default port number for the POP3 protocol ? Does it run on top of UDP or TCP
4. The Post Office Protocol (POP) is a rather simple protocol described in **RFC 1939.** POP operates in three phases. The first phase is the authorization phase where the client provides a username and a password. The second phase is the transaction phase where the client can retrieve emails. The last phase is the update phase where the client finalises the transaction. What are the main POP commands and their parameters ? When a POP server returns an answer, how can you easily determine whether the answer is positive or negative ?
5. On smartphones, users often want to avoid downloading large emails over a slow wireless connection. How could a POP client only download emails that are smaller than 5 KBytes ?
6. Open a POP session with the lab's POP server *(nostromo.info.ucl.ac.be)* by using the username and password that you received. Verify that your username and password are accepted by the server.
7. The lab's POP server contains a script that runs every minute and sends two email messages to your account if your email folder is empty. Use POP to retrieve these two emails and provide the secret message to your teaching assistant.

2.5.3 The HyperText Transfer Protocol

1. What are the main methods supported by the first version of the HyperText Transfer Protocol (HTTP) defined in **RFC 1945**? What are the main types of replies sent by a http server?
2. System administrators who are responsible for web servers often want to monitor these servers and check that they are running correctly. As a HTTP server uses TCP on port 80, the simplest solution is to open a TCP connection on port 80 and check that the TCP connection is accepted by the remote host. However, as HTTP is an ASCII-based protocol, it is also very easy to write a small script that downloads a web page on the server and compares its content with the expected one. Use *telnet* to verify that a web server is running on host *rembrandt.info.ucl.ac.be*
3. Instead of using *telnet* on port 80, it is also possible to use a command-line tool such as curl Use curl with the *-trace-ascii tracefile* option to store in *tracefile* all the information exchanged by curl when accessing the server.
    - what is the version of HTTP used by curl ?
    - can you explain the different headers placed by curl in the request ?
    - can you explain the different headers found in the response ?

4. HTTP 1.1, specified in **RFC 2616** forces the client to use the *Host:* in all its requests. HTTP 1.0 does not define the *Host:* header, by most implementations support it. By using *telnet* and *curl* retrieve the first page of the http://totem.info.ucl.ac.be webserver by sending http requests with and without the *Host:* header. Explain the difference between the two.
5. By using dig and curl , determine on which physical host the http://www.info.ucl.ac.be, http://inl.info.ucl.ac.be and http://totem.info.ucl.ac.be are hosted
6. Use curl with the *-trace-ascii filename* to retrieve http://www.google.com. Explain what a browser such as firefox would do when retrieving this URL.
7. The headers sent in a HTTP request allow the client to provide additional information to the server. One of these headers is the Language header that allows to indicate the preferred language of the client . For example, *curl -HAccept-Language:en http://www.google.be' will send to 'http://www.google.be* a HTTP request indicating English (en) as the preferred language. Does google provide a different page in French (fr) and Walloon (wa) ? Same question for http://www.uclouvain.be (given the size of the homepage, use diff to compare the different pages retrieved from www.uclouvain.be)
8. Compare the size of the http://www.yahoo.com and http://www.google.com web pages by downloading them with curl
9. What is a http cookie ? List some advantages and drawbacks of using cookies on web servers.
10. You are now responsible for the *http://www.belgium.be.* The government has built two datacenters containing 1000 servers each in Antwerp and Namur. This website contains static information and your objective is to balance the load between the different servers and ensures that the service remains up even if one of the datacenters is disconnected from the Internet due to flooding or other natural disasters. What are the techniques that you can use to achieve this goal ?

CHAPTER 3

The Transport Layer

As the transport layer is built on top of the network layer, it is important to know the key features of the network layer service. There are two types of network layer services : connectionless and connection-oriented. The connectionless network layer service is the most widespread. Its main characteristics are :

- the connectionless network layer service can only transfer SDUs of *limited size* [1]
- the connectionless network layer service may discard SDUs
- the connectionless network layer service may corrupt SDUs
- the connectionless network layer service may delay, reorder or even duplicate SDUs

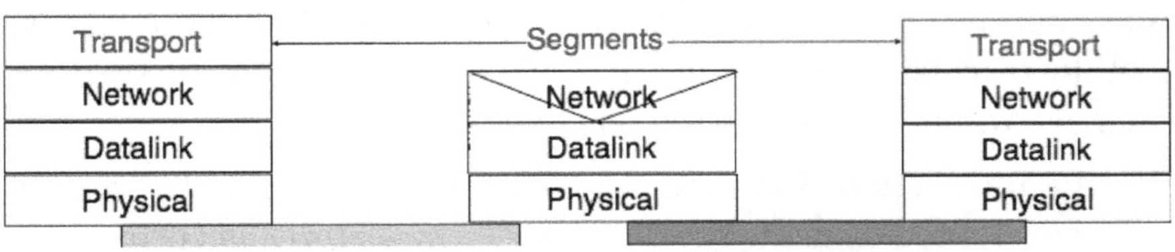

Figure 3.1: The transport layer in the reference model

These imperfections of the connectionless network layer service will become much clearer once we have explained the network layer in the next chapter. At this point, let us simply assume that these imperfections occur without trying to understand why they occur.

Some transport protocols can be used on top of a connection-oriented network service, such as class 0 of the ISO Transport Protocol (TP0) defined in [X224] , but they have not been widely used. We do not discuss in further detail such utilisation of a connection-oriented network service in this book.

This chapter is organised as follows. We will first explain how it is possible to provide a reliable transport service on top of an unreliable connectionless network service. For this, we explain the main mechanisms found in such protocols. Then, we will study in detail the two transport protocols that are used in the Internet. We begin with the User Datagram Protocol (UDP) which provides a simple connectionless transport service. Then, we will describe in detail the Transmission Control Protocol (TCP), including its congestion control mechanism.

3.1 PRINCIPLES OF A RELIABLE TRANSPORT PROTOCOL

In this section, we depict a reliable transport protocol running above a connectionless network layer service. For this, we first assume that the network layer provides a perfect service, i.e. :

- the connectionless network layer service never corrupts SDUs
- the connectionless network layer service never discards SDUs
- the connectionless network layer service never delays, reorders nor duplicate SDUs
- the connectionless network layer service can support SDUs of *any size*

We will then remove each of these assumptions one after the other in order to better understand the mechanisms used to solve each imperfection.

3.1.1 Reliable data transfer on top of a perfect network service

The transport layer entity interacts with both a user in the application layer and an entity in the network layer. According to the reference model, these interactions will be performed using *DATA.req* and *DATA.ind* primitives. However, to simplify the presentation and to avoid confusion between a *DATA.req* primitive issued by the user of the transport layer entity, and a *DATA.req* issued by the transport layer entity itself, we will use the following terminology :

- the interactions between the user and the transport layer entity are represented by using the classical *DATA.req, DATA.ind* primitives
- the interactions between the transport layer entity and the network layer service are represented by using *send* instead of *DATA.req* and *recvd* instead of *DATA.ind*

This is illustrated in the figure below.

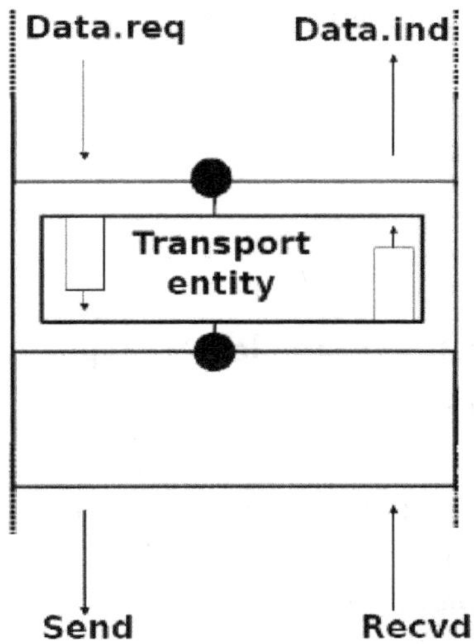

Figure 3.2: Interactions between the transport layer, its user, and its network layer provider

When running on top of a perfect connectionless network service, a transport level entity can simply issue a *send(SDU)* upon arrival of a *DATA.req(SDU)*. Similarly, the receiver issues a *DATA.ind(SDU)* upon receipt of a *recvd(SDU)*. Such a simple protocol is sufficient when a single SDU is sent.

Unfortunately, this is not always sufficient to ensure a reliable delivery of the SDUs. Consider the case where a client sends tens of SDUs to a server. If the server is faster that the client, it will be able to receive and process all the segments sent by the client and deliver their content to its user. However, if the server is slower than the client, problems may arise. The transport layer entity contains buffers to store SDUs that have been received as a *Data.request* from the application but have not yet been sent via the network service. If the application is faster than the network layer, the buffer becomes full and the operating system suspends the application to let the transport entity empty its transmission queue. The transport entity also uses a buffer to store the segments received from the network layer that have not yet been processed by the application. If the application is slow to process the data, this buffer becomes full and the transport entity is not able to accept anymore the segments from the network layer. The buffers of the transport entity have a limited size and if they overflow, the transport entity is forced to discard received segments.

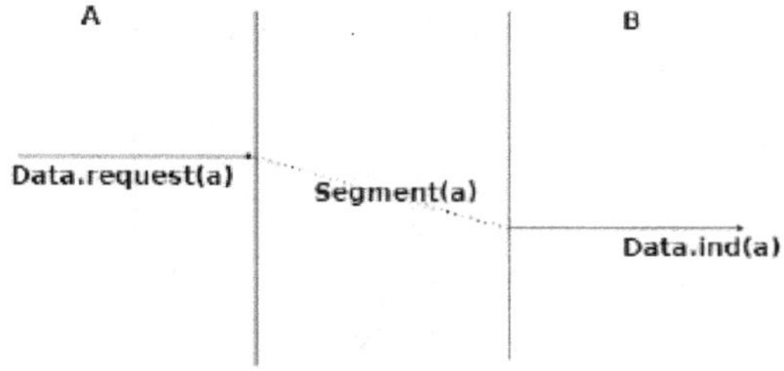

Figure 3.3: The simplest transport protocol

To solve this problem, our transport protocol must include a feedback mechanism that allows the receiver to inform the sender that it has processed a segment and that another one can be sent. This feedback is required even though the network layer provides a perfect service. To include such a feedback, our transport protocol must process two types of segments :

- data segments carrying a SDU
- control segments carrying an acknowledgment indicating that the previous segment was processed correctly

These two types of segments can be distinguished using a segment composed of two parts:

- the *header* that contains one bit set to *0* in data segments and set to *1* in control segments
- the payload that contains the SDU supplied by the user application

The transport entity can then be modelled as a finite state machine, containing two states for the receiver and two states for the sender. The figure below provides a graphical representation of this state machine with the sender above and the receiver below.

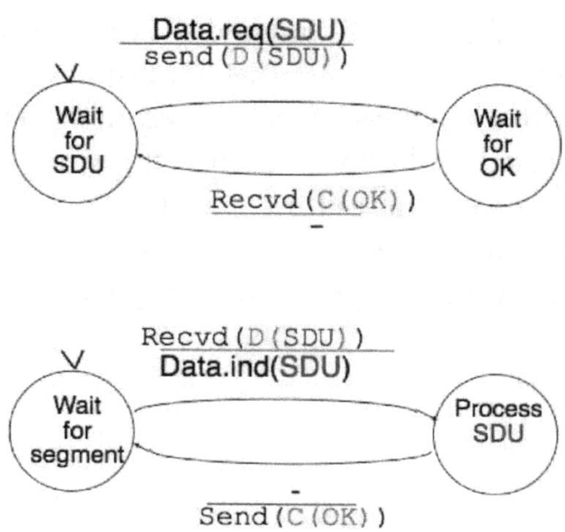

Figure 3.4: Finite state machine of the simplest transport protocol

The above FSM shows that the sender has to wait for an acknowledgement from the receiver before being able to transmit the next SDU. The figure below illustrates the exchange of a few segments between two hosts.

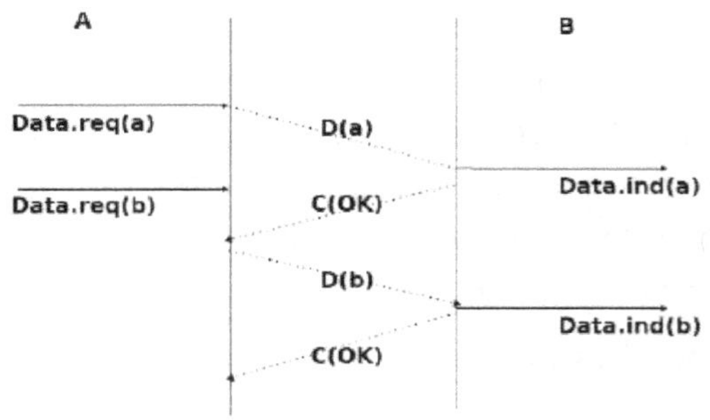

Figure 3.5: Time sequence diagram illustrating the operation of the simplest transport protocol

3.1.2 Reliable data transfer on top of an imperfect network service

The transport layer must deal with the imperfections of the network layer service. There are three types of imperfections that must be considered by the transport layer :

1. Segments can be corrupted by transmission errors
2. Segments can be lost
3. Segments can be reordered or duplicated

To deal with these types of imperfections, transport protocols rely on different types of mechanisms. The first problem is transmission errors. The segments sent by a transport entity is processed by the network and datalink layers and finally transmitted by the physical layer. All of these layers are imperfect. For example, the physical layer may be affected by different types of errors :

- random isolated errors where the value of a single bit has been modified due to a transmission error
- random burst errors where the values of *n* consecutive bits have been changed due to transmission errors
- random bit creations and random bit removals where bits have been added or removed due to transmission errors

The only solution to protect against transmission errors is to add redundancy to the segments that are sent. *Information Theory* defines two mechanisms that can be used to transmit information over a transmission channel affected by random errors. These two mechanisms add redundancy to the information sent, to allow the receiver to detect or sometimes even correct transmission errors. A detailed discussion of these mechanisms is outside the scope of this chapter, but it is useful to consider a simple mechanism to understand its operation and its limitations. *Information theory* defines *coding schemes.* There are different types of coding schemes, but let us focus on coding schemes that operate on binary strings. A coding scheme is a function that maps information encoded as a string of m bits into a string of n bits. The simplest coding scheme is the even parity coding. This coding scheme takes an m bits source string and produces an $m+1$ bits coded string where the first m bits of the coded string are the bits of the source string and the last bit of the coded string is chosen such that the coded string will always contain an even number of bits set to 1. For example :

- *1001* is encoded as *10010*
- *1101* is encoded as *11011*

This parity scheme has been used in some RAMs as well as to encode characters sent over a serial line. It is easy to show that this coding scheme allows the receiver to detect a single transmission error, but it cannot correct it. However, if two or more bits are in error, the receiver may not always be able to detect the error.

Some coding schemes allow the receiver to correct some transmission errors. For example, consider the coding scheme that encodes each source bit as follows :

- *1* is encoded as *111*
- *0* is encoded as *000*

For example, consider a sender that sends 111. If there is one bit in error, the receiver could receive 011 or 101 or 110. In these three cases, the receiver will decode the received bit pattern as a 1 since it contains a majority of bits set to 1. If there are two bits in error, the receiver will not be able anymore to recover from the transmission error. This simple coding scheme forces the sender to transmit three bits for each source bit. However, it allows the receiver to correct single bit errors. More advanced coding systems that allow to recover from errors are used in several types of physical layers.

Transport protocols use error detection schemes, but none of the widely used transport protocols rely on error correction schemes. To detect errors, a segment is usually divided into two parts :

- a *header* that contains the fields used by the transport protocol to ensure reliable delivery. The header contains a checksum or Cyclical Redundancy Check (CRC) [Williams1993] that is used to detect transmission errors
- a *payload* that contains the user data passed by the application layer.

Some segment headers also include a *length* , which indicates the total length of the segment or the length of the payload.

The simplest error detection scheme is the checksum. A checksum is basically an arithmetic sum of all the bytes that a segment is composed of. There are different types of checksums. For example, an eight bit checksum can be computed as the arithmetic sum of all the bytes of (both the header and trailer of) the segment. The checksum is computed by the sender before sending the segment and the receiver verifies the checksum upon reception of each segment. The receiver discards segments received with an invalid checksum. Checksums can be easily implemented in software, but their error detection capabilities are limited. Cyclical Redundancy Checks (CRC) have better error detection capabilities [SGP98], but require more CPU when implemented in software.

Note: Checksums, CRCs,...

Most of the protocols in the TCP/IP protocol suite rely on the simple Internet checksum in order to verify that the received segment has not been affected by transmission errors. Despite its popularity and ease of implementation, the Internet checksum is not the only available checksum mechanism. Cyclical Redundancy Checks (CRC) are very powerful error detection schemes that are used notably on disks, by many datalink layer protocols and file formats such as zip or png. They can easily be implemented efficiently in hardware and have better error-detection capabilities than the Internet checksum [SGP98]. However, when the first transport protocols were designed, CRCs were considered to be too CPU-intensive for software implementations and other checksum mechanisms were used instead. The TCP/IP community chose the Internet checksum, the OSI community chose the Fletcher checksum [Sklower89]. Now, there are efficient techniques to quickly compute CRCs in software [Feldmeier95] , the SCTP protocol initially chose the Adler-32 checksum but replaced it recently with a CRC (see **RFC 3309**).

The second imperfection of the network layer is that segments may be lost. As we will see later, the main cause of packet losses in the network layer is the lack of buffers in intermediate routers. Since the receiver sends an acknowledgement segment after having received each data segment, the simplest solution to deal with losses is to use a retransmission timer. When the sender sends a segment, it starts a retransmission timer. The value of this retransmission timer should be larger than the *round-trip-time,* i.e. the delay between the transmission of a data segment and the reception of the corresponding acknowledgement. When the retransmission timer expires, the sender assumes that the data segment has been lost and retransmits it. This is illustrated in the figure below.

Unfortunately, retransmission timers alone are not sufficient to recover from segment losses. Let us consider, as an example, the situation depicted below where an acknowledgement is lost. In this case, the sender retransmits the data segment that has not been acknowledged. Unfortunately, as illustrated in the figure below, the receiver considers the retransmission as a new segment whose payload must be delivered to its user.

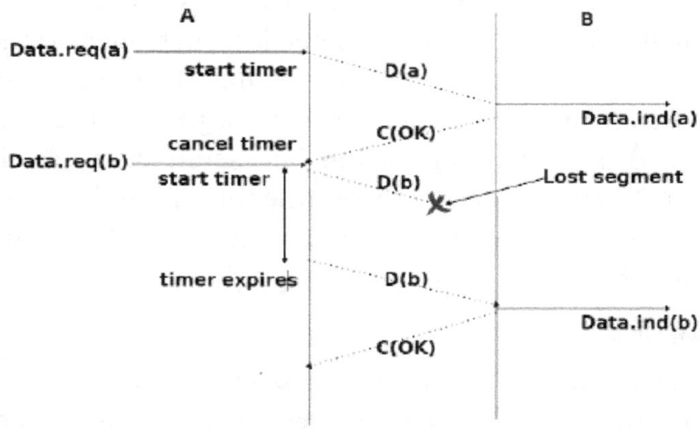

Figure 3.6: Using retransmission timers to recover from segment losses

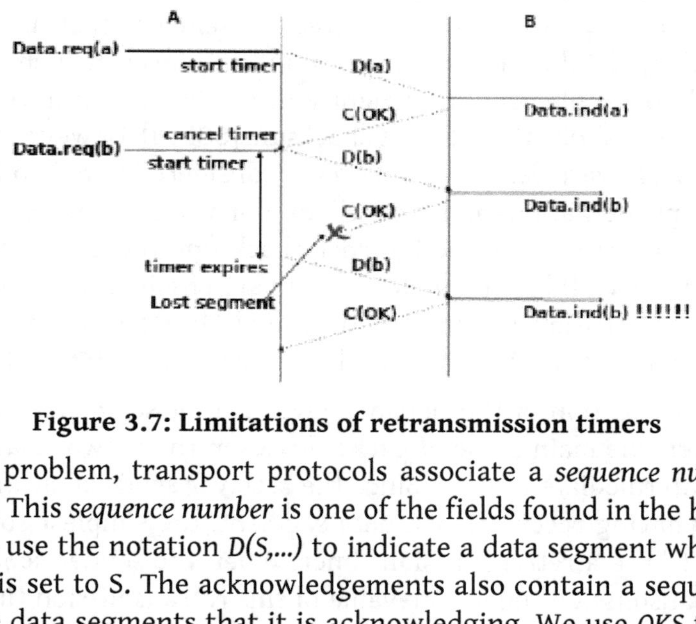

Figure 3.7: Limitations of retransmission timers

To solve this problem, transport protocols associate a *sequence number* to each data segment. This *sequence number* is one of the fields found in the header of data segments. We use the notation *D(S,...)* to indicate a data segment whose sequence number field is set to S. The acknowledgements also contain a sequence number indicating the data segments that it is acknowledging. We use *OKS* to indicate an acknowledgement segment that confirms the reception of *D(S,...)*. The sequence number is encoded as a bit string of fixed length. The simplest transport protocol is the Alternating Bit Protocol (ABP).

The Alternating Bit Protocol uses a single bit to encode the sequence number. It can be implemented easily. The sender and the receivers only require a four states Finite State Machine.

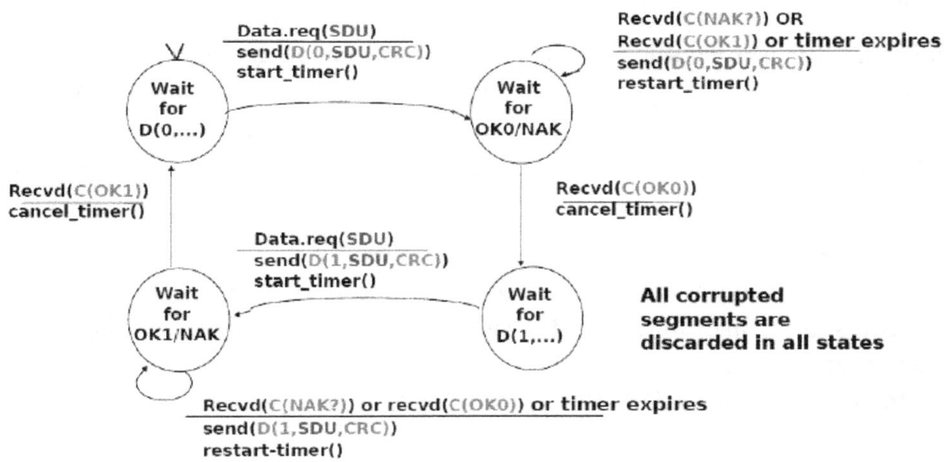

Figure 3.8: Alternating bit protocol: Sender FSM

The initial state of the sender is *Wait for D(0,...)*. In this state, the sender waits for a *Data.request.* The first data segment that it sends uses sequence number 0. After having sent this segment, the sender waits for an *OK0* acknowledgement. A segment is retransmitted upon expiration of the retransmission timer or if an acknowledgement with an incorrect sequence number has been received.

The receiver first waits for *D(0,...)*. If the segment contains a correct *CRC,* it passes the SDU to its user and sends OK0. If the segment contains an invalid CRC, it is immediately discarded. Then, the receiver waits for *D(1,...)*. In this state, it may receive a duplicate *D(0,...)* or a data segment with an invalid CRC. In both cases, it returns an *OK0* segment to allow the sender to recover from the possible loss of the previous *OK0* segment.

Note: Dealing with corrupted segments

The receiver FSM of the Alternating bit protocol discards all segments that contain an invalid CRC. This is the safest approach since the received segment can be completely different from the segment sent by the remote host. A receiver should not attempt at extracting information from a corrupted segment because it cannot know which portion of the segment has been affected by the error.

The figure below illustrates the operation of the alternating bit protocol.

The Alternating Bit Protocol can recover from transmission errors and segment losses. However, it has one important drawback. Consider two hosts that are directly connected by a 50 Kbits/sec satellite link that has a 250 milliseconds propagation delay. If these hosts send 1000 bits segments, then the maximum throughput that can be achieved by the alternating bit protocol is one segment every 20 + 250 + 250 = 520 milliseconds if we ignore the transmission time of the acknowledgement. This is less than 2 Kbits/sec !

Go-back-n and selective repeat

To overcome the performance limitations of the alternating bit protocol, transport protocols rely on *pipelining*. This technique allows a sender to transmit several consecutive segments without being forced to wait for an acknowledgement after each segment. Each data segment contains a sequence number encoded in an *n* bits field.

Pipelining allows the sender to transmit segments at a higher rate, but we need to ensure that the receiver does not become overloaded. Otherwise, the segments sent by the sender are not correctly received by the destination. The transport protocols that rely on pipelining allow the sender to transmit W unacknowledged segments before being forced to wait for an acknowledgement from the receiving entity.

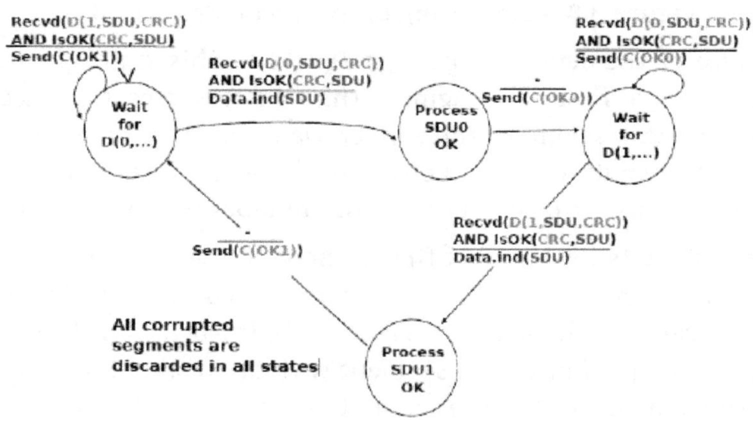

Figure 3.9: Alternating bit protocol : Receiver FSM

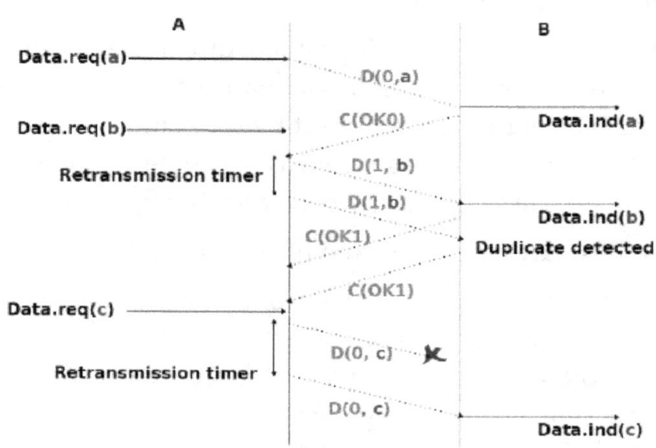

Figure 3.10: Operation of the alternating bit protocol

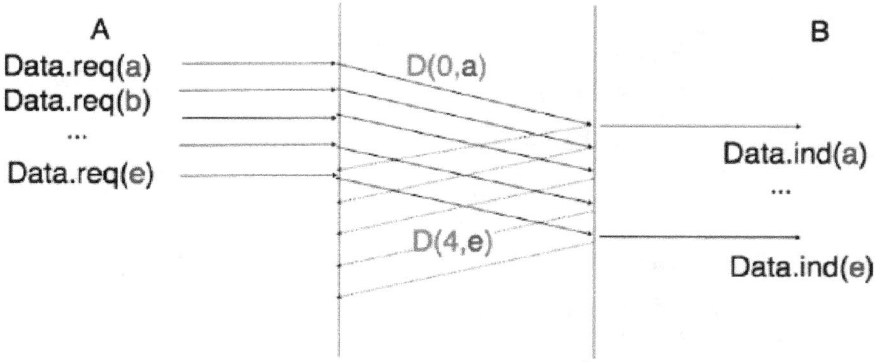

Figure 3.11: Pipelining to improve the performance of transport protocols

This is implemented by using a *sliding window.* The sliding window is the set of consecutive sequence numbers that the sender can use when transmitting segments without being forced to wait for an acknowledgement. The figure below shows a sliding window containing five segments *(6,7,8,9* and *10).* Two of these sequence numbers *(6* and *7)* have been used to send segments and only three sequence numbers (8, 9 and 10) remain in the sliding window. The sliding window is said to be closed once all sequence numbers contained in the sliding window have been used.

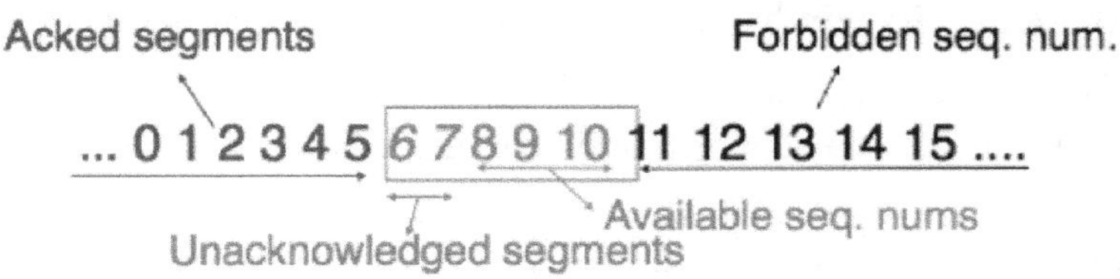

Figure 3.12: The sliding window

The figure below illustrates the operation of the sliding window. The sliding window shown contains three segments. The sender can thus transmit three segments before being forced to wait for an acknowledgement. The sliding window moves to the higher sequence numbers upon reception of acknowledgements. When the first acknowledgement *(OK0)* is received, it allows the sender to move its sliding window to the right and sequence number *3* becomes available. This sequence number is used later to transmit SDU d.

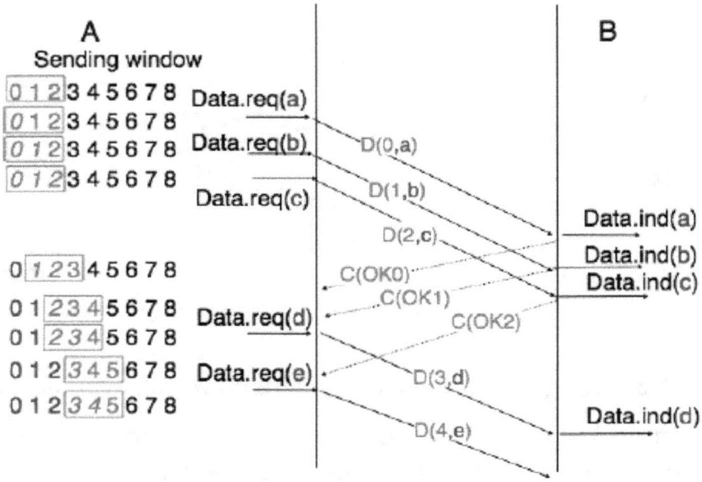

Figure 3.13: Sliding window example

In practice, as the segment header encodes the sequence number in an *n* bits string, only the sequence numbers between 0 and 2^n - 1 can be used. This implies that the same sequence number is used for different segments and that the sliding window will wrap. This is illustrated in the figure below assuming that 2 bits are used to encode the sequence number in the segment header. Note that upon reception of OKI, the sender slides its window and can use sequence number *0* again.

Unfortunately, segment losses do not disappear because a transport protocol is using a sliding window. To recover from segment losses, a sliding window protocol must define :

- a heuristic to detect segment losses
- a *retransmission strategy* to retransmit the lost segments.

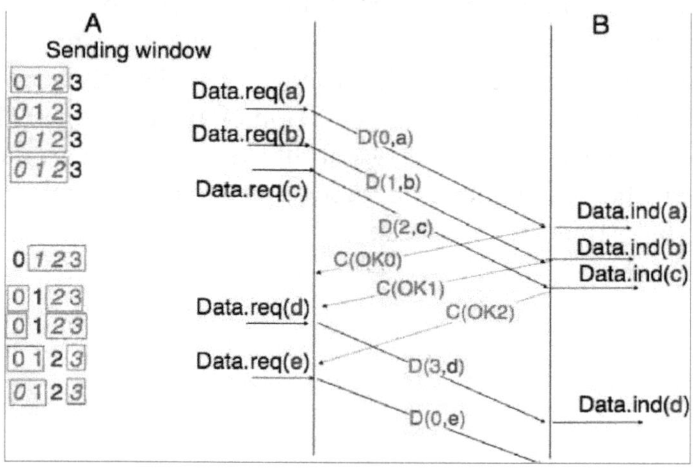

Figure 3.14: Utilisation of the sliding window with modulo arithmetic

The simplest sliding window protocol uses *go-back-n* recovery. Intuitively, *go-back-n* operates as follows. A *go-back-n* receiver is as simple as possible. It only accepts the segments that arrive in-sequence. A *go-back- n* receiver discards any out-of-sequence segment that it receives. When *go-back-n* receives a data segment, it always returns an acknowledgement containing the sequence number of the last in-sequence segment that it has received. This acknowledgement is said to be *cumulative.* When a *go-back-n* receiver sends an acknowledgement for sequence number *x,* it implicitly acknowledges the reception of all segments whose sequence number is earlier than x. A key advantage of these cumulative acknowledgements is that it is easy to recover from the loss of an acknowledgement. Consider for example a *go-back-n* receiver that received segments *1, 2* and *3.* It sent *OKI, OK2* and OK3. Unfortunately, *OK1* and *OK2* were lost. Thanks to the cumulative acknowledgements, when the receiver receives *OK3,* it knows that all three segments have been correctly received.

The figure below shows the FSM of a simple *go-back-n* receiver. This receiver uses two variables : *lastack* and *next. next* is the next expected sequence number and *lastack* the sequence number of the last data segment that has been acknowledged. The receiver only accepts the segments that are received in sequence. *maxseq* is the number of different sequence numbers (2^n).

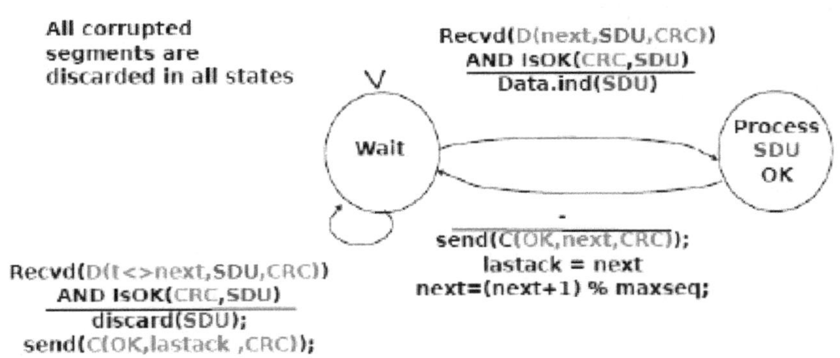

Figure 3.15: Go-back-n : receiver FSM

A *go-back-n* sender is also very simple. It uses a sending buffer that can store an entire sliding window of segments. The segments are sent with increasing sequence number (modulo *maxseq).* The sender must wait for an acknowledgement once its sending buffer is full. When a *go-back-n* sender receives an acknowledgement, it removes from the sending buffer all the acknowledged segments and uses a retransmission timer to detect segment losses. A simple *go-back-n* sender maintains one retransmission timer per connection. This timer is started when the first segment is sent. When the *go-back-n sender* receives an acknowledgement, it restarts the retransmission timer only if there are still unacknowledged segments in its sending buffer. When the retransmission timer expires, the *go-back-n* sender assumes that all the unacknowledged segments currently stored in its sending buffer have been lost. It thus retransmits all the unacknowledged segments in the buffer and restarts its retransmission timer.

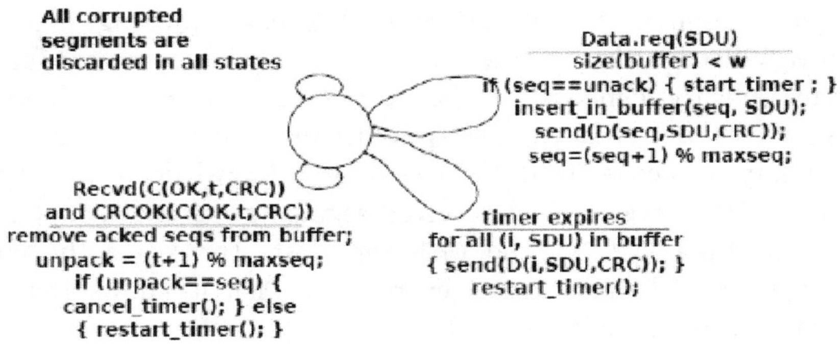

Figure 3.16: Go-back-n : sender FSM

The operation of *go-back-n* is illustrated in the figure below. In this figure, note that upon reception of the out- of-sequence segment *D(2,c)*, the receiver returns a cumulative acknowledgement *C(OK,0)* that acknowledges all the segments that have been received in sequence. The lost segment is retransmitted upon the expiration of the retransmission timer.

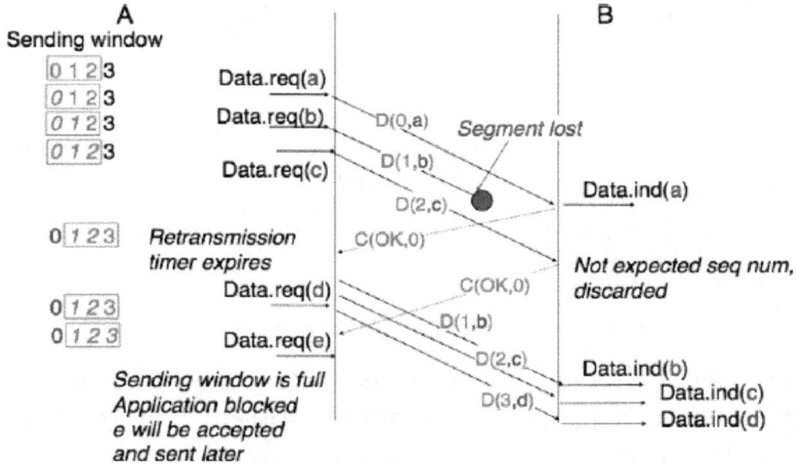

Figure 3.17: Go-back-n : example

The main advantage of *go-back-n* is that it can be easily implemented, and it can also provide good performance when only a few segments are lost. However, when there are many losses, the performance of *go-back-n* quickly drops for two reasons :

- the *go-back-n* receiver does not accept out-of-sequence segments

- the *go-back-n* sender retransmits all unacknowledged segments once its has detected a loss

Selective repeat is a better strategy to recover from segment losses. Intuitively, *selective repeat* allows the receiver to accept out-of-sequence segments. Furthermore, when a *selective repeat* sender detects losses, it only retransmits the segments that have been lost and not the segments that have already been correctly received.

A *selective repeat* receiver maintains a sliding window of W segments and stores in a buffer the out-of-sequence segments that it receives. The figure below shows a five segment receive window on a receiver that has already received segments 7 and 9.

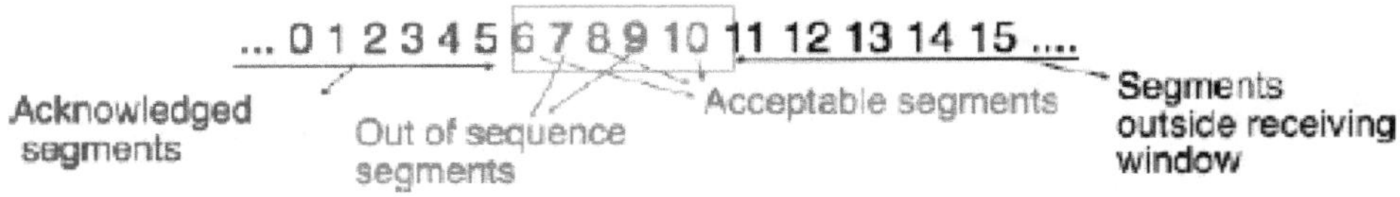

Figure 3.18: The receiving window with selective repeat

A *selective repeat* receiver discards all segments having an invalid CRC, and maintains the variable *lastack* as the sequence number of the last in-sequence segment that it has received. The receiver always includes the value of *lastack* in the acknowledgements that it sends. Some protocols also allow the *selective repeat* receiver to acknowledge the out-of-sequence segments that it has received. This can be done for example by placing the list of the sequence numbers of the correctly received, but out-of-sequence segments in the acknowledgements together with the *lastack* value.

When a *selective repeat* receiver receives a data segment, it first verifies whether the segment is inside its receiving window. If yes, the segment is placed in the receive buffer. If not, the received segment is discarded and an acknowledgement containing *lastack* is sent to the sender. The receiver then removes all consecutive segments starting at *lastack* (if any) from the receive buffer. The payloads of these segments are delivered to the user, *lastack* and the receiving window are updated, and an acknowledgement acknowledging the last segment received in sequence is sent.

The *selective repeat* sender maintains a sending buffer that can store up to W unacknowledged segments. These segments are sent as long as the sending buffer is not full. Several implementations of a *selective repeat* sender are possible. A simple implementation is to associate a retransmission timer to each segment. The timer is started when the segment is sent and cancelled upon reception of an acknowledgement that covers this segment. When a retransmission timer expires, the corresponding segment is retransmitted and this retransmission timer is restarted. When an acknowledgement is received, all the segments that are covered by this acknowledgement are removed from the sending buffer and the sliding window is updated.

The figure below illustrates the operation of *selective repeat* when segments are lost. In this figure, *C(OK,x)* is used to indicate that all segments, up to and including sequence number *x* have been received correctly.

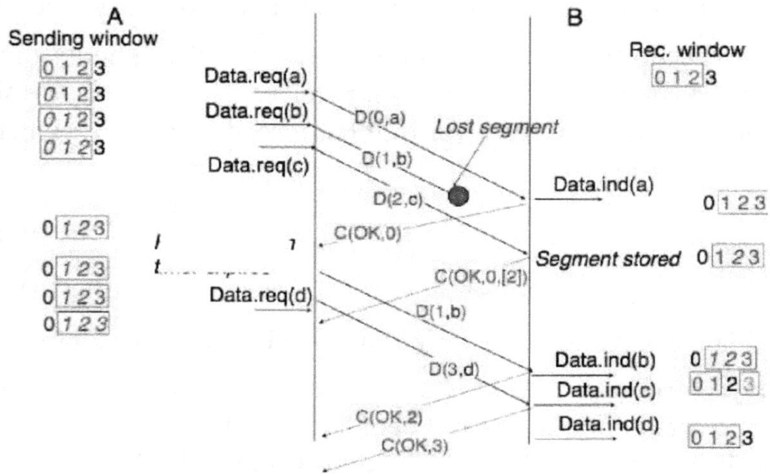

Figure 3.19: Selective repeat : example

Pure cumulative acknowledgements work well with the *go-back-n* strategy. However, with only cumulative acknowledgements a *selective repeat* sender cannot easily determine which data segments have been correctly received after a data segment has been lost. For example, in the figure above, the second *C(OK,0)* does not inform explicitly the sender of the reception of *D(2,c)* and the sender could retransmit this segment although it has already been received. A possible solution to improve the performance of *selective repeat* is to provide additional information about the received segments in the acknowledgements that are returned by the receiver. For example, the receiver could add in the returned acknowledgement the list of the sequence numbers of all segments that have already been received. Such acknowledgements are sometimes called *selective acknowledgements.* This is illustrated in the figure below.

In the figure above, when the sender receives *C(OK,0,[2]),* it knows that all segments up to and including *D(0,...)* have been correctly received. It also knows that segment *D(2,...)* has been received and can cancel the retransmission timer associated to this segment. However, this segment should not be removed from the sending buffer before the reception of a cumulative acknowledgement *(C(OK,2)* in the figure above) that covers this segment.

Note: Maximum window size with *go-back-n* and *selective repeat*

A transport protocol that uses *n* bits to encode its sequence number can send up to 2^n different segments. However, to ensure a reliable delivery of the segments, *go-back-n* and *selective repeat* cannot use a sending window of 2^n segments. Consider first *go-back-n* and assume that a sender sends 2^n segments. These segments are received in-sequence by the destination, but all the returned acknowledgements are lost. The sender will retransmit all segments and they will all be accepted by the receiver and delivered a second time to the user. It is easy to see that this problem can be avoided if the maximum size of the sending window is $2^n - 1$ segments. A similar problem occurs with *selective repeat*. However, as the receiver accepts out-of-sequence segments, a sending window of $2^n - 1$ segments is not sufficient to ensure a reliable delivery of all segments. It can be easily shown that to avoid this problem, a *selective repeat* sender cannot use a window that is larger than 2^ segments.

Go-back-n or *selective repeat* are used by transport protocols to provide a reliable data transfer above an unreliable network layer service. Until now, we have assumed that the size of the sliding window was fixed for the entire lifetime of the connection. In practice a transport layer entity is usually implemented in the operating system and shares memory with other parts of the system. Furthermore, a transport layer entity must support several (possibly hundreds or thousands) of transport connections at the same time. This implies that the memory which can be used to support the sending or the receiving buffer of a transport connection may change during the lifetime of the connection . Thus, a transport protocol must allow the sender and the receiver to adjust their window sizes.

To deal with this issue, transport protocols allow the receiver to advertise the current size of its receiving window in all the acknowledgements that it sends. The receiving window advertised by the receiver bounds the size of the sending buffer used by the sender. In practice, the sender maintains two state variables : *swin*, the size of its sending window (that may be adjusted by the system) and *rwin*, the size of the receiving window advertised by the receiver. At any time, the number of unacknowledged segments cannot be larger than *min(swin,rwin)*. The utilisation of dynamic windows is illustrated in the figure below.

The receiver may adjust its advertised receive window based on its current memory consumption, but also to limit the bandwidth used by the sender. In practice, the receive buffer can also shrink as the application may not able to process the received data quickly enough. In this case, the receive buffer may be completely full and the advertised receive window may shrink to *0*. When the sender receives an acknowledgement with a receive window set to *0*, it is blocked until it receives an acknowledgement with a positive receive window. Unfortunately, as shown in the figure below, the loss of this acknowledgement could cause a deadlock as the sender waits for an acknowledgement while the receiver is waiting for a data segment.

To solve this problem, transport protocols rely on a special timer : the *persistence timer*. This timer is started by the sender whenever it receives an acknowledgement advertising a receive window set to *0*. When the timer expires, the sender retransmits an old segment in order to force the receiver to send a new acknowledgement, and hence send the current receive window size.

To conclude our description of the basic mechanisms found in transport protocols, we still need to discuss the impact of segments arriving in the wrong order. If two consecutive segments are reordered, the receiver relies on their sequence numbers to reorder them in its receive buffer. Unfortunately, as transport protocols reuse the same sequence number for different segments, if a segment is delayed for a prolonged period of time, it might still be accepted by the receiver. This is illustrated in the figure below where segment *D(1,b)* is delayed.

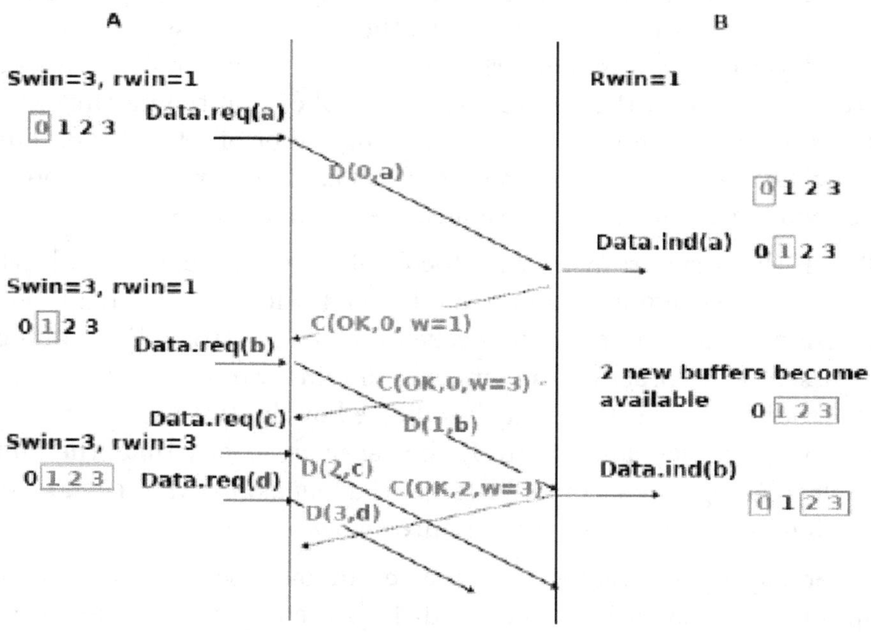

Figure 3.20: Dynamic receiving window

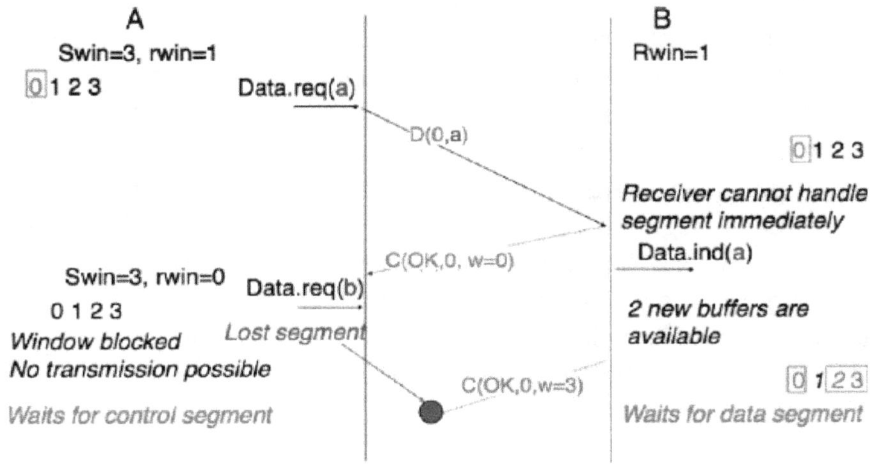

Figure 3.21: Risk of deadlock with dynamic windows

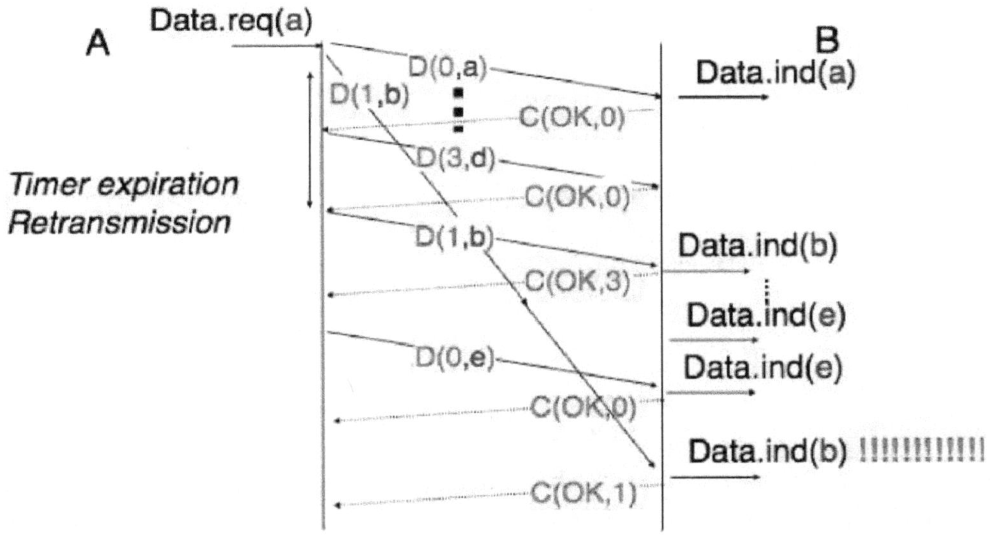

Figure 3.22: Ambiguities caused by excessive delays

To deal with this problem, transport protocols combine two solutions. First, they use 32 bits or more to encode the sequence number in the segment header. This increases the overhead, but also increases the delay between the transmission of two different segments having the same sequence number. Second, transport protocols require the network layer to enforce a *Maximum Segment Lifetime (MSL)*. The network layer must ensure that no packet remains in the network for more than MSL seconds. In the Internet the MSL is assumed to be 2 minutes **RFC 793**. Note that this limits the maximum bandwidth of a transport protocol. If it uses *n* bits to encode its sequence numbers, then it cannot send more than 2^n segments every MSL seconds.

Transport protocols often need to send data in both directions. To reduce the overhead caused by the acknowledgements, most transport protocols use *piggybacking.* Thanks to this technique, a transport entity can place inside the header of the data segments that it sends, the acknowledgements and the receive window that it advertises for the opposite direction of the data flow. The main advantage of piggybacking is that it reduces the overhead as it is not necessary to send a complete segment to carry an acknowledgement. This is illustrated in the figure below where the acknowledgement number is underlined in the data segments. Piggybacking is only used when data flows in both directions. A receiver will generate a pure acknowledgement when it does not send data in the opposite direction as shown in the bottom of the figure.

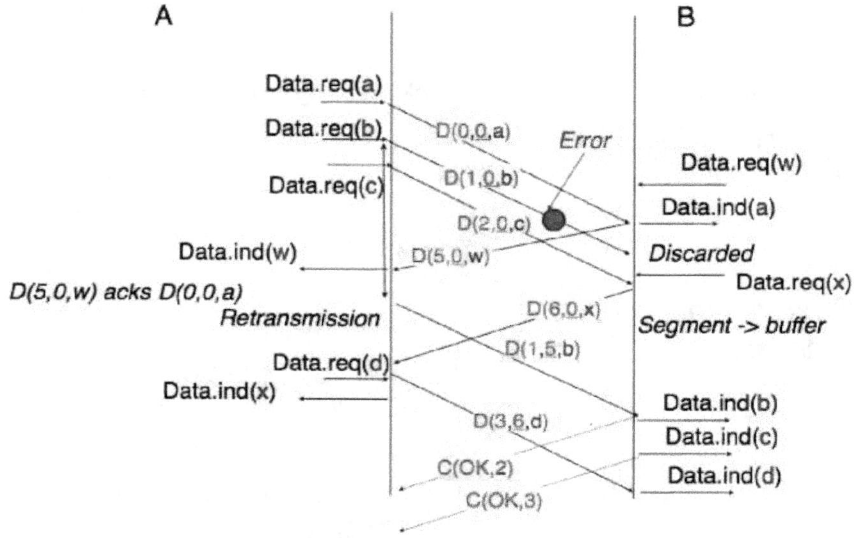

Figure 3.23: Piggybacking

The last point to be discussed about the data transfer mechanisms used by transport protocols is the provision of a byte stream service. As indicated in the first chapter, the byte stream service is widely used in the transport layer. The transport protocols that provide a byte stream service associate a sequence number to all the bytes that are sent and place the sequence number of the first byte of the segment in the segment's header. This is illustrated in the figure below. In this example, the sender chooses to put two bytes in each of the first three segments. This is due to graphical reasons, a real transport protocol would use larger segments in practice. However, the division of the byte stream into segments combined with the losses and retransmissions explain why the byte stream service does not preserve the SDU boundaries.

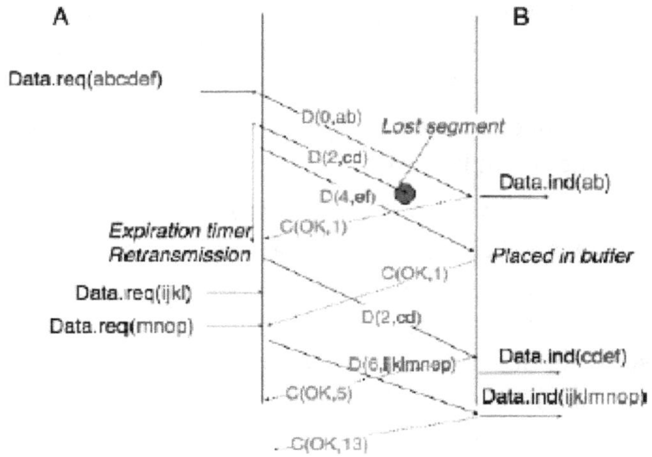

Figure 3.24: Provision of the byte stream service

Connection establishment and release

The last points to be discussed about the transport protocol are the mechanisms used to establish and release a transport connection.

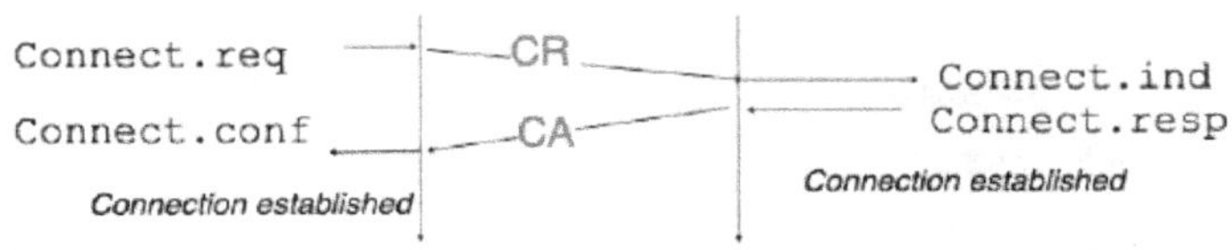

Figure 3.25: Naive transport connection establishment

We explained in the first chapters the service primitives used to establish a connection. The simplest approach to establish a transport connection would be to define two special control segments: *CR* and *CA*. The *CR* segment is sent by the transport entity that wishes to initiate a connection. If the remote entity wishes to accept the connection, it replies by sending a *CA* segment. The transport connection is considered to be established once the *CA* segment has been received and data segments can be sent in both directions.

Unfortunately, this scheme is not sufficient for several reasons. First, a transport entity usually needs to maintain several transport connections with remote entities. Sometimes, different users (i.e. processes) running above a given transport entity request the establishment of several transport connections to different users attached to the same remote transport entity. These different transport connections must be clearly separated to ensure that data from one connection is not passed to the other connections. This can be achieved by using a connection identifier, chosen by the transport entities and placed inside each segment to allow the entity which receives a segment to easily associate it to one established connection.

Second, as the network layer is imperfect, the *CR* or *CA* segment can be lost, delayed, or suffer from transmission errors. To deal with these problems, the control segments must be protected by using a CRC or checksum to detect transmission errors. Furthermore, since the CA segment acknowledges the reception of the CR segment, the CR segment can be protected by using a retransmission timer.

Unfortunately, this scheme is not sufficient to ensure the reliability of the transport service. Consider for example a short-lived transport connection where a single, but important transfer (e.g. money transfer from a bank account) is sent. Such a short-lived connection starts with a CR segment acknowledged by a CA segment, then the data segment is sent, acknowledged and the connection terminates. Unfortunately, as the network layer service is unreliable, delays combined to retransmissions may lead to the situation depicted in the figure below, where a delayed CR and data segments from a former connection are accepted by the receiving entity as valid segments, and the corresponding data is delivered to the user. Duplicating SDUs is not acceptable, and the transport protocol must solve this problem.

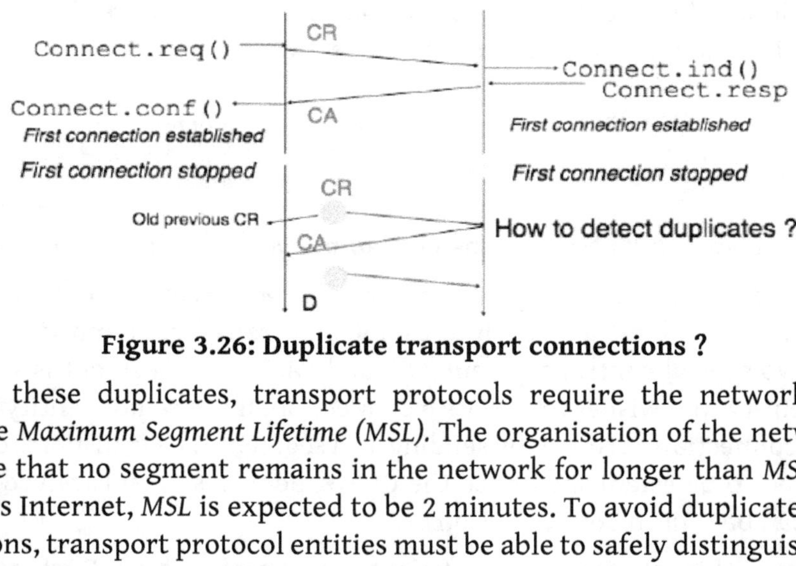

Figure 3.26: Duplicate transport connections ?

To avoid these duplicates, transport protocols require the network layer to bound the *Maximum Segment Lifetime (MSL)*. The organisation of the network must guarantee that no segment remains in the network for longer than *MSL* seconds. On today's Internet, *MSL* is expected to be 2 minutes. To avoid duplicate transport connections, transport protocol entities must be able to safely distinguish between a duplicate *CR* segment and a new *CR* segment, without forcing each transport entity to remember all the transport connections that it has established in the past.

A classical solution to avoid remembering the previous transport connections to detect duplicates is to use a clock inside each transport entity. This *transport clock* has the following characteristics:

- the *transport clock* is implemented as a *k* bits counter and its clock cycle is such that 2^k x *cycle* >> *MSL*. Furthermore, the *transport clock* counter is incremented every clock cycle and after each connection establishment. This clock is illustrated in the figure below.

- the *transport clock* must continue to be incremented even if the transport entity stops or reboots

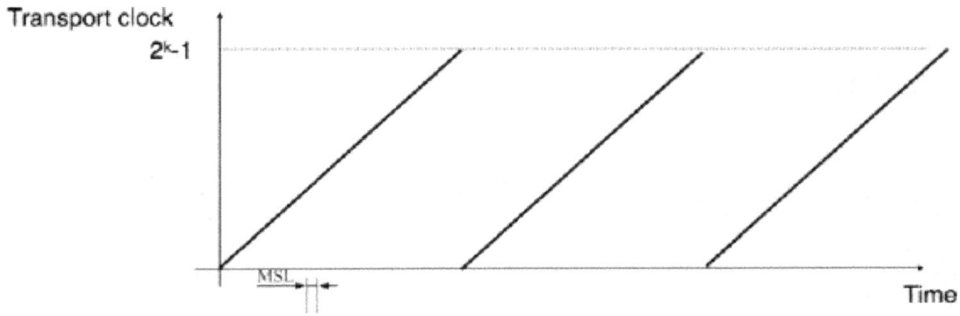

Figure 3.27: Transport clock

It should be noted that *transport clocks* do not need and usually are not synchronised to the real-time clock. Precisely synchronising real-time clocks is an interesting problem, but it is outside the scope of this document. See [Mills2006] for a detailed discussion on synchronising the real-time clock.

The *transport clock* is combined with an exchange of three segments, called the *three way handshake,* to detect duplicates. This *three way handshake* occurs as follows:

1. The initiating transport entity sends a *CR* segment. This segment requests the establishment of a transport connection. It contains a connection identifier (not shown in the figure) and a sequence number *(seq=x* in the figure below) whose value is extracted from the *transport clock.* The transmission of the *CR* segment is protected by a retransmission timer.
2. The remote transport entity processes the *CR* segment and creates state for the connection attempt. At this stage, the remote entity does not yet know whether this is a new connection attempt or a duplicate segment. It returns a *CA* segment that contains an acknowledgement number to confirm the reception of the *CR* segment *(ack=x* in the figure below) and a sequence number *(seq=y* in the figure below) whose value is extracted from its transport clock. At this stage, the connection is not yet established.
3. The initiating entity receives the *CA* segment. The acknowledgement number of this segment confirms that the remote entity has correctly received the *CA* segment. The transport connection is considered to be established by the initiating entity and the numbering of the data segments starts at sequence number *x.* Before sending data segments, the initiating entity must acknowledge the received *CA* segments by sending another *CA* segment.
4. The remote entity considers the transport connection to be established after having received the segment that acknowledges its *CA* segment. The numbering of the data segments sent by the remote entity starts at sequence number *y.*

The three way handshake is illustrated in the figure below.

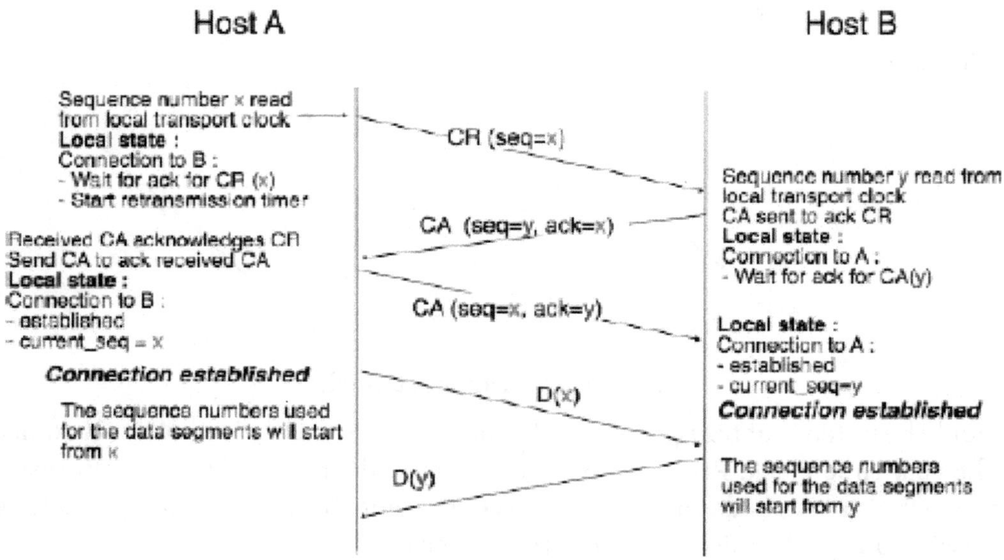

Figure 3.28: Three-way handshake

Thanks to the three way handshake, transport entities avoid duplicate transport connections. This is illustrated by the three scenarios below.

The first scenario is when the remote entity receives an old *CR* segment. It considers this *CR* segment as a connection establishment attempt and replies by sending a *CA* segment. However, the initiating host cannot match the received *CA* segment with a previous connection attempt. It sends a control segment *(REJECT* in the figure below) to cancel the spurious connection attempt. The remote entity cancels the connection attempt upon reception of this control segment.

A second scenario is when the initiating entity sends a *CR* segment that does not reach the remote entity and receives a duplicate *CA* segment from a previous connection attempt. This duplicate *CA* segment cannot contain a valid acknowledgement for the *CR* segment as the sequence number of the *CR* segment was extracted from the transport clock of the initiating entity. The *CA* segment is thus rejected and the *CR* segment is retransmitted upon expiration of the retransmission timer.

The last scenario is less likely, but it it important to consider it as well. The remote entity receives an old *CR* segment. It notes the connection attempt and acknowledges it by sending a *CA* segment. The initiating entity does not have a matching connection attempt and replies by sending a *REJECT*. Unfortunately, this segment never reaches the remote entity. Instead, the remote entity receives a retransmission of an older *CA* segment that contains the same sequence number as the first CR segment. This CA segment cannot be accepted by the remote entity as a confirmation of the transport connection as its acknowledgement number cannot have the same value as the sequence number of the first *CA* segment.

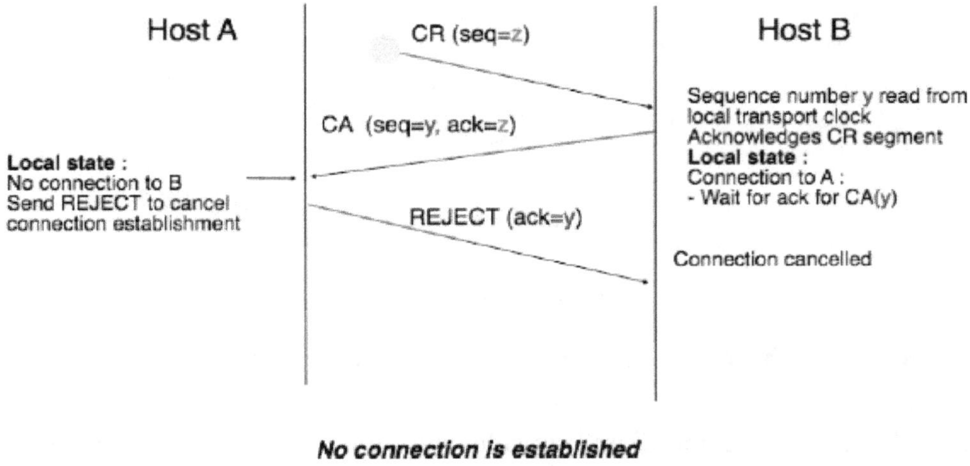

Figure 3.29: Three-way handshake : recovery from a duplicate CR

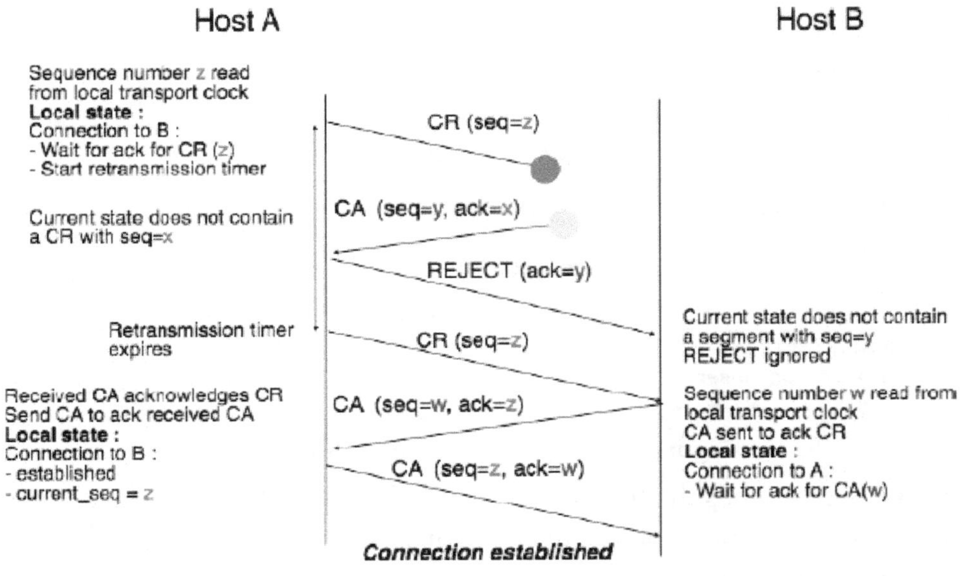

Figure 3.30: Three-way handshake : recovery from a duplicate *CA*

When we discussed the connection-oriented service, we mentioned that there are two types of connection releases : *abrupt release* and *graceful release.*

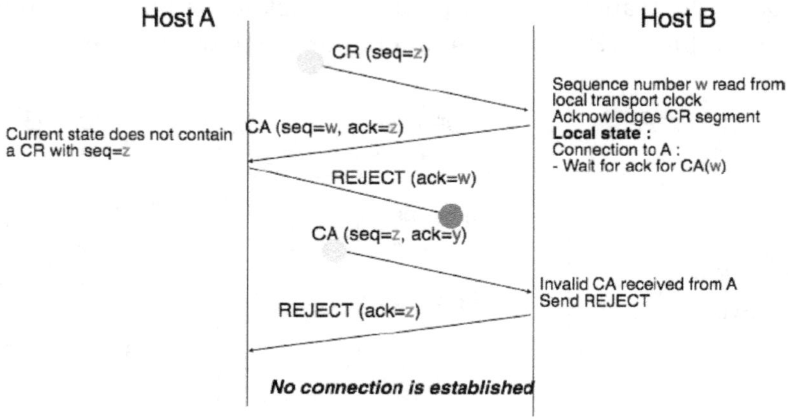

Figure 3.31: Three-way handshake : recovery from duplicates CR and CA

The first solution to release a transport connection is to define a new control segment (e.g. the *DR* segment) and consider the connection to be released once this segment has been sent or received. This is illustrated in the figure below.

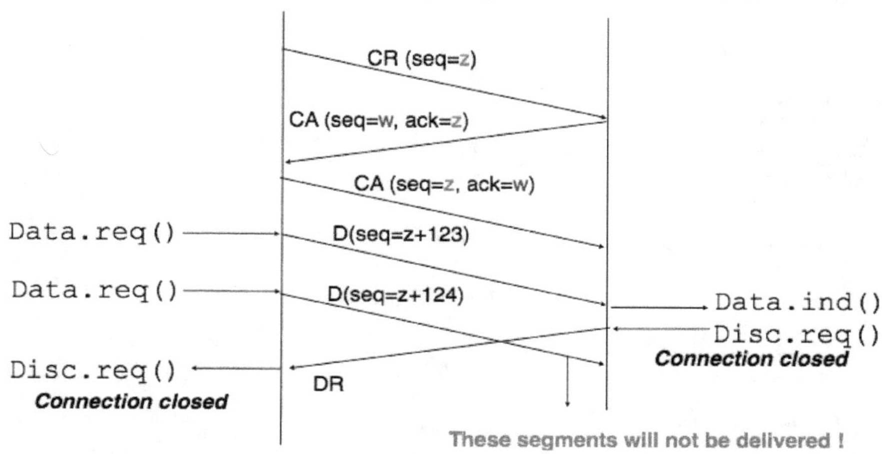

Figure 3.32: Abrupt connection release

As the entity that sends the *DR* segment cannot know whether the other entity has already sent all its data on the connection, SDUs can be lost during such an *abrupt connection release.*

The second method to release a transport connection is to release independently the two directions of data transfer. Once a user of the transport service has sent all its SDUs, it performs a *DISCONNECT.req* for its direction of data transfer. The transport entity sends a control segment to request the release of the connection *after* the delivery of all previous SDUs to the remote user. This is usually done by placing in the *DR* the next sequence number and by delivering the *DISCONNECT.ind* only after all previous *DATA.ind.* The remote entity confirms the reception of the *DR* segment and the release of the corresponding direction of data transfer by returning an acknowledgement. This is illustrated in the figure below.

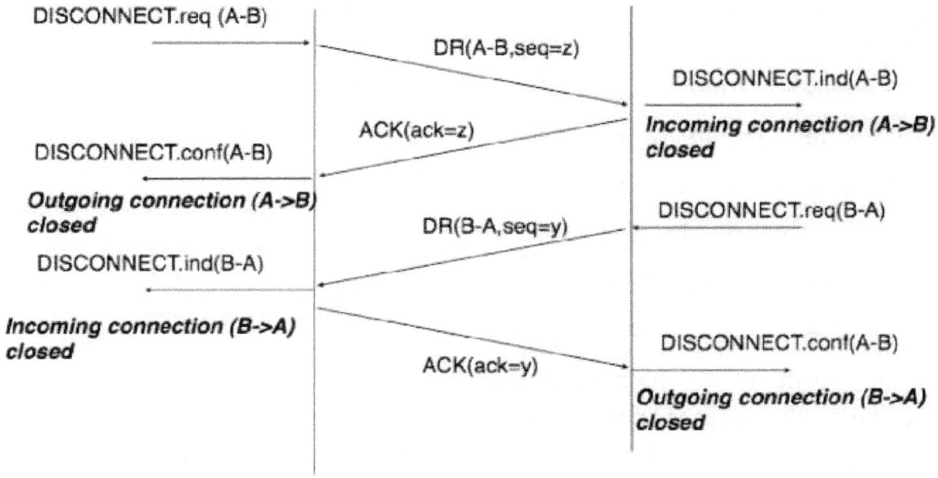

Figure 3.33: Graceful connection release

3.2 THE USER DATAGRAM PROTOCOL

The User Datagram Protocol (UDP) is defined in **RFC 768.** It provides an unreliable connectionless transport service on top of the unreliable network layer connectionless service. The main characteristics of the UDP service are :

- the UDP service cannot deliver SDUs that are larger than 65507 bytes
- the UDP service does not guarantee the delivery of SDUs (losses and desquencing can occur)
- the UDP service will not deliver a corrupted SDU to the destination

Compared to the connectionless network layer service, the main advantage of the UDP service is that it allows several applications running on a host to exchange SDUs with several other applications running on remote hosts. Let us consider two hosts, e.g. a client and a server. The network layer service allows the client to send information to the server, but if an application running on the client wants to contact a particular application running on the server, then an additional addressing mechanism is required other than the IP address that identifies a host, in order to differentiate the application running on a host. This additional addressing is provided by *port numbers.* When a server using UDP is enabled on a host, this server registers a *port number.* This *port number* will be used by the clients to contact the server process via UDP.

The figure below shows a typical usage of the UDP port numbers. The client process uses port number *1234* while the server process uses port number *5678.* When the client sends a request, it is identified as originating from port number *1234* on the client host and destined to port number *5678* on the server host. When the server process replies to this request, the server's UDP implementation will send the reply as originating from port *5678* on the server host and destined to port *1234* on the client host.

UDP uses a single segment format shown in the figure below.

The UDP header contains four fields :

- a 16 bits source port
- a 16 bits destination port
- a 16 bits length field
- a 16 bits checksum

As the port numbers are encoded as a 16 bits field, there can be up to only 65535 different server processes that are bound to a different UDP port at the same time on a given server. In practice, this limit is never reached. However, it is worth noticing that most implementations divide the range of allowed UDP port numbers into three different ranges :

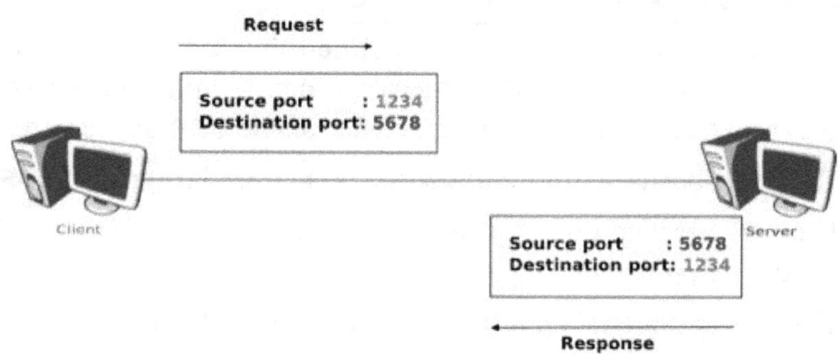

Figure 3.34: Usage of the UDP port numbers

```
 0                   1                   2                   3
 0 1 2 3 4 5 6 7 8 9 0 1 2 3 4 5 6 7 8 9 0 1 2 3 4 5 6 7 8 9 0 1
+-+-+-+-+-+-+-+-+-+-+-+-+-+-+-+-+-+-+-+-+-+-+-+-+-+-+-+-+-+-+-+-+
|          Source Port          |       Destination Port        |
+-+-+-+-+-+-+-+-+-+-+-+-+-+-+-+-+-+-+-+-+-+-+-+-+-+-+-+-+-+-+-+-+
|            Length             |           Checksum            |
+-+-+-+-+-+-+-+-+-+-+-+-+-+-+-+-+-+-+-+-+-+-+-+-+-+-+-+-+-+-+-+-+
```

Figure 3.35: UDP Header Format

- the privileged port numbers (1 < port < 1024)
- the ephemeral port numbers (officially 49152 <= port <= 65535)
- the registered port numbers (officially 1024 <= port < 49152)

In most Unix variants, only processes having system administrator privileges can be bound to port numbers smaller than *1024.* Well-known servers such as *DNS, NTP* or *RPC* use privileged port numbers. When a client needs to use UDP, it usually does not require a specific port number. In this case, the UDP implementation will allocate the first available port number in the ephemeral range. The range of registered port numbers should be used by servers. In theory, developers of network servers should register their port number officially through IANA, but few developers do this.

Note: Computation of the UDP checksum

The checksum of the UDP segment is computed over :

- a pseudo header containing the source IP address, the destination IP address and a 32 bits bit field containing the most significant byte set to 0, the second set to 17 and the length of the UDP segment in the lower two bytes
- the entire UDP segment, including its header

This pseudo-header allows the receiver to detect errors affecting the IP source or destination addresses placed in the IP layer below. This is a violation of the layering principle that dates from the time when UDP and IP were elements of a single protocol. It should be noted that if the checksum algorithm computes value '0x0000', then value '0xffff' is transmitted. A UDP segment whose checksum is set to '0x0000' is a segment for which the transmitter did not compute a checksum upon transmission. Some *NFS* servers chose to disable UDP checksums for performance reasons, but this caused problems that were difficult to diagnose. In practice, there are rarely good reasons to disable UDP checksums. A detailed discussion of the implementation of the Internet checksum may be found in **RFC 1071.**

Several types of applications rely on UDP. As a rule of thumb, UDP is used for applications where delay must be minimised or losses can be recovered by the application itself. A first class of the UDP-based applications are applications where the client sends a short request and expects a quick and short answer. The DNS is an example of a UDP application that is often used in the wide area. However, in local area networks, many distributed systems rely on Remote Procedure Call *(RPC)* that is often used on top of UDP. In Unix environments, the Network File System *(NFS)* is built on top of RPC and runs frequently on top of UDP. A second class of UDP-based applications are the interactive computer games that need to frequently exchange small messages, such as the player's location or their recent actions. Many of these games use UDP to minimise the delay and can recover from losses. A third class of applications are multimedia applications such as interactive Voice over IP or interactive Video over IP. These interactive applications expect a delay shorter than about 200 milliseconds between the sender and the receiver and can recover from losses directly inside the application.

3.3 THE TRANSMISSION CONTROL PROTOCOL

The Transmission Control Protocol (TCP) was initially defined in **RFC 793.** Several parts of the protocol have been improved since the publication of the original protocol specification. However, the basics of the protocol remain and an implementation that only supports **RFC 793** should inter-operate with today's implementation.

TCP provides a reliable bytestream, connection-oriented transport service on top of the unreliable connectionless network service provided by *IP*. TCP is used by a large number of applications, including :

- Email *(SMTP, POP, IMAP)*
- World wide web (*HTTP,...*)
- Most file transfer protocols (*ftp,* peer-to-peer file sharing applications,...) remote computer access: *telnet, ssh, X11, VNC,...*
- non-interactive multimedia applications: flash

On the global Internet, most of the applications used in the wide area rely on TCP. Many studies have reported that TCP was responsible for more than 90% of the data exchanged in the global Internet.

To provide this service, TCP relies on a simple segment format that is shown in the figure below. Each TCP segment contains a header described below and, optionally, a payload. The default length of the TCP header is twenty bytes, but some TCP headers contain options.

```
 0                   1                   2                   3
 0 1 2 3 4 5 6 7 8 9 0 1 2 3 4 5 6 7 8 9 0 1 2 3 4 5 6 7 8 9 0 1
+-+-+-+-+-+-+-+-+-+-+-+-+-+-+-+-+-+-+-+-+-+-+-+-+-+-+-+-+-+-+-+-+
|          Source Port          |       Destination Port        |
+-+-+-+-+-+-+-+-+-+-+-+-+-+-+-+-+-+-+-+-+-+-+-+-+-+-+-+-+-+-+-+-+
|                        Sequence Number                        |
+-+-+-+-+-+-+-+-+-+-+-+-+-+-+-+-+-+-+-+-+-+-+-+-+-+-+-+-+-+-+-+-+
|                    Acknowledgment Number                      |
+-+-+-+-+-+-+-+-+-+-+-+-+-+-+-+-+-+-+-+-+-+-+-+-+-+-+-+-+-+-+-+-+
|  Data |       |C|E|U|A|P|R|S|F|                               |
| Offset| Res.  |W|C|R|C|S|S|Y|I|            Window             |
|       |       |R|E|G|K|H|T|N|N|                               |
+-+-+-+-+-+-+-+-+-+-+-+-+-+-+-+-+-+-+-+-+-+-+-+-+-+-+-+-+-+-+-+-+
|           Checksum            |         Urgent Pointer        |
+-+-+-+-+-+-+-+-+-+-+-+-+-+-+-+-+-+-+-+-+-+-+-+-+-+-+-+-+-+-+-+-+
```

Figure 3.36: TCP header format

A TCP header contains the following fields :

- Source and destination ports. The source and destination ports play an important role in TCP, as they allow the identification of the connection to which a TCP segment belongs. When a client opens a TCP connection, it typically selects an ephemeral TCP port number as its source port and contacts the server by using the server's port number. All the segments that are sent by the client on this connection have the same source and destination ports. The server sends segments that contain as source (resp. destination port, the destination (resp. source) port of the segments sent by the client (see figure *Utilization of the TCP source and destination ports)*. A TCP connection is always identified by five pieces of information :

  - the IP address of the client
  - the IP address of the server
  - the port chosen by the client
  - the port chosen by the server
  - TCP

- the *sequence number* (32 bits), *acknowledgement number* (32 bits) and *window* (16 bits) fields are used to provide a reliable data transfer, using a window-based protocol. In a TCP bytestream, each byte of the stream consumes one sequence number. Their utilisation will be described in more detail in section *TCP reliable data transfer*
- the *Urgent pointer* is used to indicate that some data should be considered as urgent in a TCP bytestream. However, it is rarely used in practice and will not be described here. Additional details about the utilisation of this pointer may be found in **RFC 793, RFC 1122** or [Stevens1994]
- the flags field contains a set of bit flags that indicate how a segment should be interpreted by the TCP entity receiving it :
  - the *SYN* flag is used during connection establishment
  - the *FIN* flag is used during connection release
  - the *RST* is used in case of problems or when an invalid segment has been received
  - when the *ACK* flag is set, it indicates that the *acknowledgment* field contains a valid number. Otherwise, the content of the *acknowledgment* field must be ignored by the receiver
  - the *URG* flag is used together with the *Urgent pointer*
  - the *PSH* flag is used as a notification from the sender to indicate to the receiver that it should pass all the data it has received to the receiving process. However, in practice TCP implementations do not allow TCP users to indicate when the *PSH* flag should be set and thus there are few real utilizations of this flag.
- the *checksum* field contains the value of the Internet checksum computed over the entire TCP segment and a pseudo-header as with UDP

- the *Reserved* field was initially reserved for future utilization. It is now used by **RFC 3168**.
- the *TCP Header Length* (THL) or *Data Offset* field is a four bits field that indicates the size of the TCP header in 32 bit words. The maximum size of the TCP header is thus 64 bytes.
- the *Optional header extension* is used to add optional information to the TCP header. Thanks to this header extension, it is possible to add new fields to the TCP header that were not planned in the original specification. This allowed TCP to evolve since the early eighties. The details of the TCP header extension are explained in sections *TCP connection establishment* and *TCP reliable data transfer*.

The rest of this section is organised as follows. We first explain the establishment and the release of a TCP connection, then we discuss the mechanisms that are used by TCP to provide a reliable bytestream service. We end the section with a discussion of network congestion and explain the mechanisms that TCP uses to avoid congestion collapse.

3.3.1 TCP connection establishment

A TCP connection is established by using a three-way handshake. The connection establishment phase uses the *sequence number*, the *acknowledgment number* and the *SYN* flag. When a TCP connection is established, the two communicating hosts negotiate the initial sequence number to be used in both directions of the connection. For this, each TCP entity maintains a 32 bits counter, which is supposed to be incremented by one at least every 4 microseconds and after each connection establishment[11]. When a client host wants to open a TCP connection with a server host, it creates a TCP segment with :

- the *SYN* flag set
- the *sequence number* set to the current value of the 32 bits counter of the client host's TCP entity

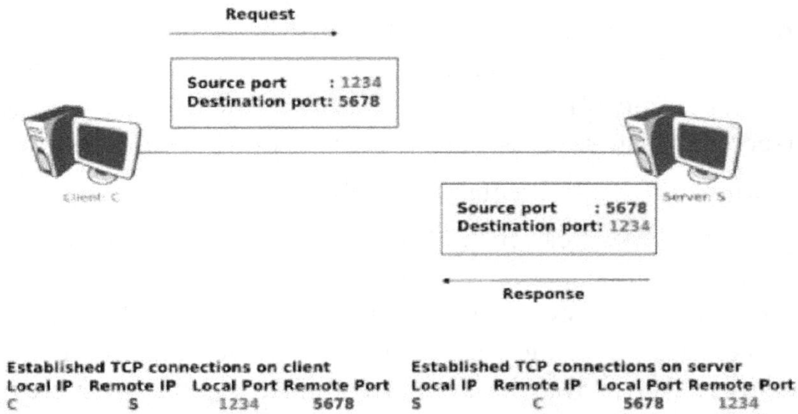

Figure 3.37: Utilization of the TCP source and destination ports

Upon reception of this segment (which is often called a SYN *segment),* the server host replies with a segment containing :

- the *SYN* flag set
- the *sequence number* set to the current value of the 32 bits counter of the server host's TCP entity
- the *ACK* flag set
- the *acknowledgment number* set to the *sequence number* of the received *SYN* segment incremented by 1 (*mod* 2^{32}). When a TCP entity sends a segment having *x+1* as acknowledgment number, this indicates that it has received all data up to and including sequence number *x* and that it is expecting data having sequence number x+1. As the *SYN* flag was set in a segment having sequence number x, this implies that setting the *SYN* flag in a segment consumes one sequence number.

This segment is often called a *SYN+ACK* segment. The acknowledgment confirms to the client that the server has correctly received the *SYN* segment. The *sequence number* of the *SYN+ACK* segment is used by the server host to verify that the *client* has received the segment. Upon reception of the *SYN+ACK* segment, the client host replies with a segment containing :

- the *ACK* flag set
- the *acknowledgment number* set to the *sequence number* of the received *SYN+ACK* segment incremented by 1 (*mod* 2^{32})

At this point, the TCP connection is open and both the client and the server are allowed to send TCP segments containing data.

In the figure above, the connection is considered to be established by the client once it has received the *SYN+ACK* segment, while the server considers the connection to be established upon reception of the *ACK* segment. The first data segment sent by the client (server) has its *sequence number* set to *x+1* (resp. *y+1).*

Note: Computing TCP's initial sequence number

In the original TCP specification **RFC 793**, each TCP entity maintained a clock to compute the initial sequence number *(ISN)* placed in the *SYN* and *SYN+ACK* segments. This made the ISN predictable and caused a security issue. The typical security problem was the following. Consider a server that trusts a host based on its IP address and allows the system administrator to login from this host without giving a password. Consider now an attacker who knows this particular configuration and is able to send IP packets having the client's address as source. He can send fake TCP segments to the server, but does not receive the server's answers. If he can predict the *ISN* that is chosen by the server, he can send a fake *SYN* segment and shortly after the fake *ACK* segment confirming the reception of the *SYN+ACK* segment sent by the server. Once the TCP connection is open, he can use it to send any command to the server. To counter this attack, current TCP implementations add randomness to the *ISN*. One of the solutions, proposed in **RFC 1948** is to compute the ISN as

ISN = M + H(localhost, localport, remotehost, remoteport, secret).

where *M* is the current value of the TCP clock and *H'is a cryptographic hash function. 'localhost* and *remotehost* (resp. *localport* and *remoteport*) are the IP addresses (port numbers) of the local and remote host and *secret* is a random number only known by the server. This method allows the server to use different ISNs for different clients at the same time. Measurements performed with the first implementations of this technique showed that it was difficult to implement it correctly, but today's TCP implementation now generate good ISNs.

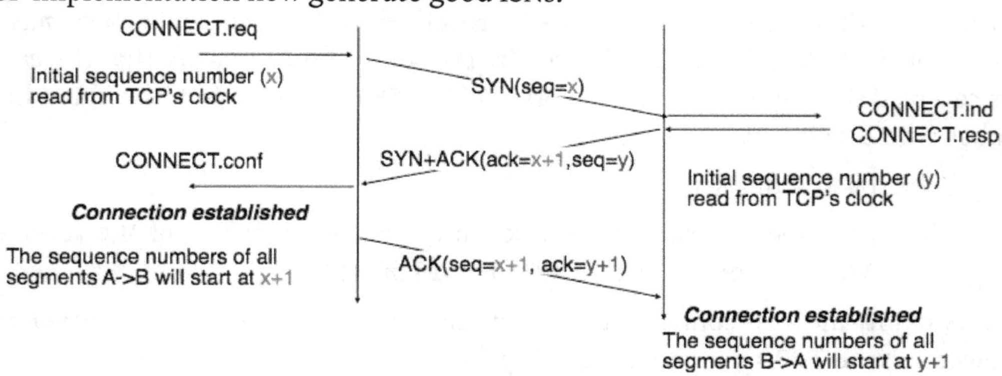

Figure 3.38: Establishment of a TCP connection

A server could, of course, refuse to open a TCP connection upon reception of a *SYN* segment. This refusal may be due to various reasons. There may be no server process that is listening on the destination port of the *SYN* segment. The server could always refuse connection establishments from this particular client (e.g. due to security reasons) or the server may not have enough resources to accept a new TCP connection at that time. In this case, the server would reply with a TCP segment having its *RST* flag set and containing the *sequence number* of the received *SYN* segment as its *acknowledgment number*. This is illustrated in the figure below. We discuss the other utilizations of the TCP *RST* flag later (see *TCP connection release*).

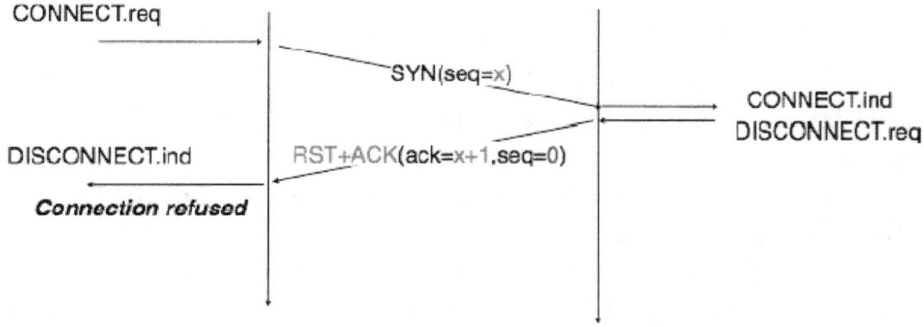

Figure 4.39: TCP connection establishment rejected by peer

TCP connection establishment can be described as the four state Finite State Machine shown below. In this FSM, *!X* (resp. *?Y)* indicates the transmission of segment X (resp. reception of segment Y) during the corresponding transition. *Init* is the initial state.

A client host starts in the *Init* state. It then sends a *SYN* segment and enters the *SYN Sent* state where it waits for a *SYN+ACK* segment. Then, it replies with an *ACK* segment and enters the *Established* state where data can be exchanged. On the other hand, a server host starts in the *Init* state. When a server process starts to listen to a destination port, the underlying TCP entity creates a TCP control block and a queue to process incoming *SYN* segments. Upon reception of a SYN segment, the server's TCP entity replies with a *SYN+ACK* and enters the SYN *RCVD* state. It remains in this state until it receives an ACK segment that acknowledges its *SYN+ACK* segment, with this it then enters the Established state.

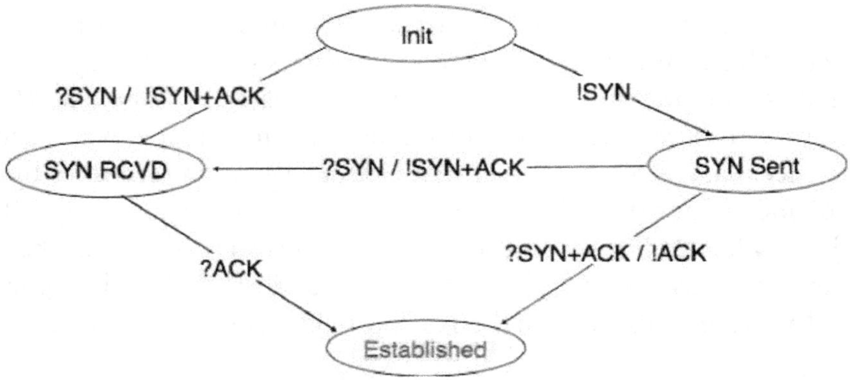

Figure 3.40: TCP FSM for connection establishment

Apart from these two paths in the TCP connection establishment FSM, there is a third path that corresponds to the case when both the client and the server send a SYN segment to open a TCP connection. In this case, the client and the server send a SYN segment and enter the SYN *Sent* state. Upon reception of the SYN segment sent by the other host, they reply by sending a *SYN+ACK* segment and enter the SYN *RCVD* state. The *SYN+ACK* that arrives from the other host allows it to transition to the *Established* state. The figure below illustrates such a simultaneous establishment of a TCP connection.

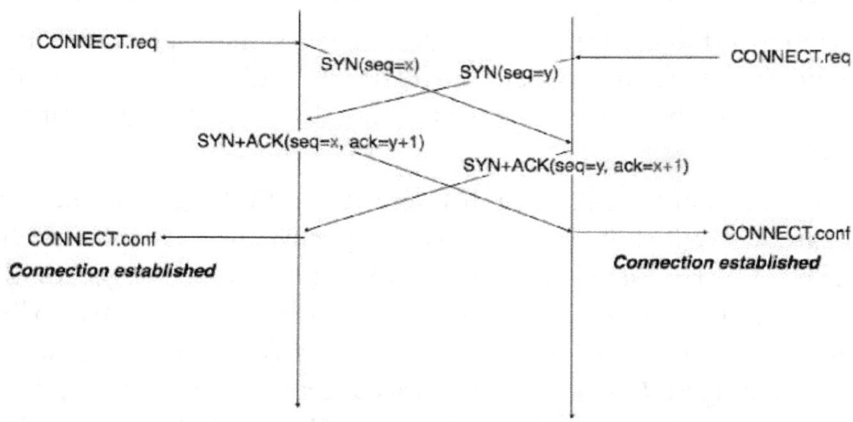

Figure 3.41: Simultaneous establishment of a TCP connection

Denial of Service attacks

When a TCP entity opens a TCP connection, it creates a Transmission Control Block *(TCB).* The TCB contains the entire state that is maintained by the TCP entity for each TCP connection. During connection establishment, the TCB contains the local IP address, the remote IP address, the local port number, the remote port number, the current local sequence number, the last sequence number received from the remote entity. Until the mid 1990s, TCP implementations had a limit on the number of TCP connections that could be in the *SYNRCVD* state at a given time. Many implementations set this limit to about 100 TCBs. This limit was considered sufficient even for heavily load http servers given the small delay between the reception of a SYN segment and the reception of the *ACK* segment that terminates the establishment of the TCP connection. When the limit of 100 TCBs in the SYN*Rcvd* state is reached, the TCP entity discards all received TCP SYN segments that do not correspond to an existing TCB.

This limit of 100 TCBs in the SYN *Rcvd* state was chosen to protect the TCP entity from the risk of overloading its memory with too many TCBs in the SYN Rcvd state. However, it was also the reason for a new type of Denial of Service (DoS) attack **RFC 4987**. A DoS attack is defined as an attack where an attacker can render a resource unavailable in the network. For example, an attacker may cause a DoS attack on a 2 Mbps link used by a company by sending more than 2 Mbps of packets through this link. In this case, the DoS attack was more subtle. As a TCP entity discards all received SYN segments as soon as it has 100 TCBs in the SYN *Rcvd* state, an attacker simply had to send a few 100 SYN segments every second to a server and never reply to the received *SYN+ACK* segments. To avoid being caught, attackers were of course sending these SYN segments with a different address than their own IP address [a]. On most TCP implementations, once a TCB entered the SYN Rcvd state, it remained in this state for several seconds, waiting for a retransmission of the initial SYN segment. This attack was later called a SYN *flood* attack and the servers of the ISP named panix were among the first to be affected by this attack.

To avoid the SYN *flood* attacks, recent TCP implementations no longer enter the SYN *Rcvd* state upon reception of a SYN *segment.* Instead, they reply directly with a *SYN+ACK* segment and wait until the reception of a valid *ACK*. This implementation trick is only possible if the TCP implementation is able to verify that the received ACK segment acknowledges the *SYN+ACK* segment sent earlier without storing the initial sequence number of this *SYN+ACK* segment in a TCB. The solution to solve this problem, which is known as SYN cookies is to compute the 32 bits of the ISN as follows:

- the high order bits contain the low order bits of a counter that is incremented slowly
- the low order bits contain a hash value computed over the local and remote IP addresses and ports and a random secret only known to the server

The advantage of the SYN cookies is that by using them, the server does not need to create a *TCB* upon reception of the SYN segment and can still check the returned ACK segment by recomputing the SYN *cookie.*

Retransmitting the first SYN segment

As IP provides an unreliable connectionless service, the SYN and SYN+ACK segments sent to open a TCP connection could be lost. Current TCP implementations start a retransmission timer when they send the first SYN segment. This timer is often set to three seconds for the first retransmission and then doubles after each retransmission RFC 2988. TCP implementations also enforce a maximum number of retransmissions for the initial SYN segment.

As explained earlier, TCP segments may contain an optional header extension. In the *SYN* and *SYN+ACK* segments, these options are used to negotiate some parameters and the utilisation of extensions to the basic TCP specification.

The first parameter which is negotiated during the establishment of a TCP connection is the Maximum Segment Size (*MSS*). The MSS is the size of the largest segment that a TCP entity is able to process. According to RFC 879, all TCP implementations must be able to receive TCP segments containing 536 bytes of payload. However, most TCP implementations are able to process larger segments. Such TCP implementations use the TCP MSS Option in the *SYN/SYN+ACK* segment to indicate the largest segment they are able to process. The MSS value indicates the maximum size of the payload of the TCP segments. The client (resp. server) stores in its TCB the MSS value announced by the server (resp. the client).

Another utilisation of TCP options during connection establishment is to enable TCP extensions. For example, consider **RFC 1323** (which is discussed in *TCP reliable data transfer*). **RFC 1323** defines TCP extensions to support timestamps and larger windows. If the client supports **RFC 1323**, it adds a **RFC 1323** option to its *SYN* segment. If the server understands this **RFC 1323** option and wishes to use it, it replies with an **RFC 1323** option in the *SYN+ACK* segment and the extension defined in **RFC 1323** is used throughout the TCP connection. Otherwise, if the server's *SYN+ACK* does not contain the **RFC 1323** option, the client is not allowed to use this extension and the corresponding TCP header options throughout the TCP connection. TCP's option mechanism is flexible and it allows the extension of TCP while maintaining compatibility with older implementations.

The TCP options are encoded by using a Type Length Value format where :

- the first byte indicates the *type* of the option.
- the second byte indicates the total length of the option (including the first two bytes) in bytes
- the last bytes are specific for each type of option

RFC 793 defines the Maximum Segment Size (MSS) TCP option that must be understood by all TCP implementations. This option (type 2) has a length of 4 bytes and contains a 16 bits word that indicates the MSS supported by the sender of the

SYN segment. The MSS option can only be used in TCP segments having the *SYN* flag set.

RFC 793 also defines two special options that must be supported by all TCP implementations. The first option is *End of option.* It is encoded as a single byte having value *0x00* and can be used to ensure that the TCP header extension ends on a 32 bits boundary. The *No-Operation* option, encoded as a single byte having value *0x01,* can be used when the TCP header extension contains several TCP options that should be aligned on 32 bit boundaries. All other options are encoded by using the TLV format.

Note: The robustness principle

The handling of the TCP options by TCP implementations is one of the many applications of the *robustness principle* which is usually attributed to Jon Postel and is often quoted as *"Be liberal in what you accept, and conservative in what you send"* **RFC 1122**

Concerning the TCP options, the robustness principle implies that a TCP implementation should be able to accept TCP options that it does not understand, in particular in received *SYN* segments, and that it should be able to parse any received segment without crashing, even if the segment contains an unknown TCP option. Furthermore, a server should not send in the *SYN+ACK* segment or later, options that have not been proposed by the client in the *SYN* segment.

3.3.2 TCP connection release

TCP, like most connection-oriented transport protocols, supports two types of connection release :

- graceful connection release, where each TCP user can release its own direction of data transfer
- abrupt connection release, where either one user closes both directions of data transfer or one TCP entity is forced to close the connection (e.g. because the remote host does not reply anymore or due to lack of resources)

The abrupt connection release mechanism is very simple and relies on a single segment having the *RST* bit set. A TCP segment containing the *RST* bit can be sent for the following reasons :

- a non-SYN segment was received for a non-existing TCP connection **RFC 793**
- by extension, some implementations respond with an *RST* segment to a segment that is received on an existing connection but with an

invalid header **RFC 3360**. This causes the corresponding connection to be closed and has caused security attacks **RFC 4953**

- by extension, some implementations send an *RST* segment when they need to close an existing TCP connection (e.g. because there are not enough resources to support this connection or because the remote host is considered to be unreachable). Measurements have shown that this usage of TCP *RST* was widespread [AW05]

When an *RST* segment is sent by a TCP entity, it should contain the current value of the *sequence number* for the connection (or 0 if it does not belong to any existing connection) and the *acknowledgement number* should be set to the next expected in-sequence *sequence number* on this connection.

Note: TCP *RST* wars

TCP implementers should ensure that two TCP entities never enter a TCP *RST* war where host *A* is sending a *RST* segment in response to a previous *RST* segment that was sent by host *B* in response to a TCP *RST* segment sent by host *A* ... To avoid such an infinite exchange of *RST* segments that do not carry data, a TCP entity is *never* allowed to send a *RST* segment in response to another *RST* segment.

The normal way of terminating a TCP connection is by using the graceful TCP connection release. This mechanism uses the *FIN* flag of the TCP header and allows each host to release its own direction of data transfer. As for the *SYN* flag, the utilisation of the *FIN* flag in the TCP header consumes one sequence number. The figure *FSM for TCP connection release* shows the part of the TCP FSM used when a TCP connection is released.

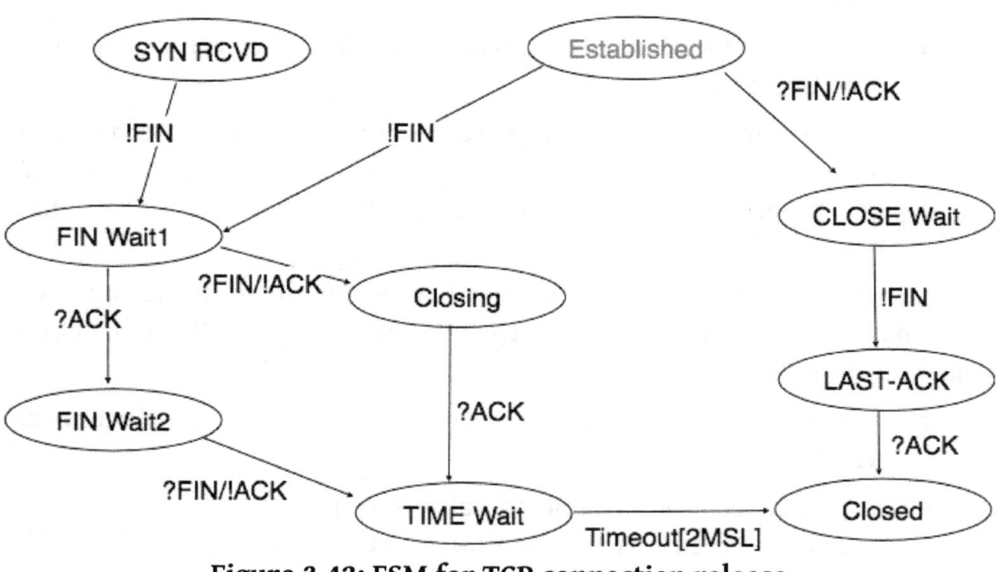

Figure 3.42: FSM for TCP connection release

Starting from the *Established* state, there are two main paths through this FSM.

The first path is when the host receives a segment with sequence number *x* and the *FIN* flag set. The utilisation of the *FIN* flag indicates that the byte before *sequence number x* was the last byte of the byte stream sent by the remote host. Once all of the data has been delivered to the user, the TCP entity sends an *ACK* segment whose *ack* field is set to (x +1) *mod* 2^{32} to acknowledge the *FIN* segment. The *FIN* segment is subject to the same retransmission mechanisms as a normal TCP segment. In particular, its transmission is protected by the retransmission timer. At this point, the TCP connection enters the *CLOSE_WAIT* state. In this state, the host can still send data to the remote host. Once all its data have been sent, it sends a *FIN* segment and enter the *LAST_ACK* state. In this state, the TCP entity waits for the acknowledgement of its *FIN* segment. It may still retransmit unacknowledged data segments e.g. if the retransmission timer expires. Upon reception of the acknowledgement for the *FIN* segment, the TCP connection is completely closed and its *TCB* can be discarded.

The second path is when the host decides first to send a *FIN* segment. In this case, it enters the *FIN_WAIT1* state. It this state, it can retransmit unacknowledged segments but cannot send new data segments. It waits for an acknowledgement of its *FIN* segment, but may receive a *FIN* segment sent by the remote host. In the first case, the TCP connection enters the *FIN_WAIT2* state. In this state, new data segments from the remote host are still accepted until the reception of the *FIN* segment. The acknowledgement for this *FIN* segment is sent once all data received before the *FIN* segment have been delivered to the user and the connection enters the *TIME_WAIT* state. In the second case, a *FIN* segment is received and the connection enters the *Closing* state once all data received from the remote host have been delivered to the user. In this state, no new data segments can be sent and the host waits for an acknowledgement of its *FIN* segment before entering the *TIME_WAIT* state.

The *TIME_WAIT* state is different from the other states of the TCP FSM. A TCP entity enters this state after having sent the last *ACK* segment on a TCP connection. This segment indicates to the remote host that all the data that it has sent have been correctly received and that it can safely release the TCP connection and discard the corresponding *TCB*. After having sent the last *ACK* segment, a TCP connection enters the *TIME_WAIT* and remains in this state for 2 * *MSL* seconds. During this period, the TCB of the connection is maintained. This ensures that the TCP entity that sent the last *ACK* maintains enough state to be able to retransmit this segment if this ACK segment is lost and the remote host retransmits its last *FIN* segment or another one. The delay of 2 * *MSL* seconds ensures that any duplicate segments on the connection would be handled correctly without causing the transmission of an *RST* segment. Without the *TIME_WAIT* state and the 2 * *MSL* seconds delay, the connection release would not be graceful when the last *ACK* segment is lost.

Note: TIME_WAIT on busy TCP servers

The 2 * *MSL* seconds delay in the *TIME_WAIT* state is an important operational problem on servers having thousands of simultaneously opened TCP connections [FTY99]. Consider for example a busy web server that processes 10.000 TCP connections every second. If each of these connections remain in the *TIME_WAIT* state for 4 minutes, this implies that the server would have to maintain more than 2 million TCBs at any time. For this reason, some TCP implementations prefer to perform an abrupt connection release by sending a *RST* segment to close the connection [AW05] and immediately discard the corresponding TCB. However, if the *RST* segment is lost, the remote host continues to maintain a *TCB* for a connection no longer exists. This optimisation reduces the number of TCBs maintained by the host sending the *RST* segment but at the potential cost of increased processing on the remote host when the *RST* segment is lost.

3.3.3 TCP reliable data transfer

The original TCP data transfer mechanisms were defined in **RFC 793**. Based on the experience of using TCP on the growing global Internet, this part of the TCP specification has been updated and improved several times, always while preserving the backward compatibility with older TCP implementations. In this section, we review the main data transfer mechanisms used by TCP.

TCP is a window-based transport protocol that provides a bi-directional byte stream service. This has several implications on the fields of the TCP header and the mechanisms used by TCP. The three fields of the TCP header are:

- *sequence number.* TCP uses a 32 bits sequence number. The *sequence number* placed in the header of a TCP segment containing data is the sequence number of the first byte of the payload of the TCP segment.
- *acknowledgement number.* TCP uses cumulative positive acknowledgements. Each TCP segment contains the *sequence number* of the next byte that the sender of the acknowledgement expects to receive from the remote host. In theory, the *acknowledgement number* is only valid if the *ACK* flag of the TCP header is set. In practice almost all TCP segments have their *ACK* flag set.
- *window.* a TCP receiver uses this 16 bits field to indicate the current size of its receive window expressed in bytes.

Note: The Transmission Control Block

For each established TCP connection, a TCP implementation must maintain a Transmission Control Block (TCB). A TCB contains all the information required to send and receive segments on this connection **RFC 793**. This includes :

- the local IP address
- the remote IP address
- the local TCP port number
- the remote TCP port number
- the current state of the TCP FSM
- the *maximum segment size* (MSS)
- *snd.nxt*: the sequence number of the next byte in the byte stream (the first byte of a new data segment that you send uses this sequence number)
- *snd.una* : the earliest sequence number that has been sent but has not yet been acknowledged
- *snd.wnd* : the current size of the sending window (in bytes)
- *rcv.nxt*: the sequence number of the next byte that is expected to be received from the remote host
- *rcv.wnd* : the current size of the receive window advertised by the remote host
- *sending buffer* : a buffer used to store all unacknowledged data
- *receiving buffer* : a buffer to store all data received from the remote host that has not yet been delivered to the user. Data may be stored in the *receiving buffer* because either it was not received in sequence or because the user is too slow to process it

The original TCP specification can be categorised as a transport protocol that provides a byte stream service and uses *go-back-n.*

To send new data on an established connection, a TCP entity performs the following operations on the corresponding TCB. It first checks that the *sending buffer* does not contain more data than the receive window advertised by the remote host *(rcv.wnd).* If the window is not full, up to *MSS* bytes of data are placed in the payload of a TCP segment. The *sequence number* of this segment is the sequence number of the first byte of the payload. It is set to the first available sequence number : *snd.nxt* and *snd.nxt* is incremented by the length of the payload of the TCP segment. The *acknowledgement number* of this segment is set to the current value of *rcv.nxt* and the *window* field of the TCP segment is computed based on the current occupancy of the *receiving buffer*. The data is kept in the *sending buffer* in case it needs to be retransmitted later.

When a TCP segment with the *ACK* flag set is received, the following operations are performed. *rcv.wnd* is set to the value of the *window* field of the received segment.

The *acknowledgement number* is compared to *snd.una.* The newly acknowledged data is remove from the *sending buffer* and *snd.una* is updated. If the TCP segment contained data, the *sequence number* is compared to *rcv.nxt.* If they are equal, the segment was received in sequence and the data can be delivered to the user and *rcv.nxt* is updated. The contents of the *receiving buffer* is checked to see whether other data already present in this buffer can be delivered in sequence to the user. If so, *rcv.nxt* is updated again. Otherwise, the segment's payload is placed in the *receiving buffer*.

Segment transmission strategies

In a transport protocol such as TCP that offers a bytestream, a practical issue that was left as an implementation choice in **RFC 793** is to decide when a new TCP segment containing data must be sent. There are two simple and extreme implementation choices. The first implementation choice is to send a TCP segment as soon as the user has requested the transmission of some data. This allows TCP to provide a low delay service. However, if the user is sending data one byte at a time, TCP would place each user byte in a segment containing 20 bytes of TCP header. This is a huge overhead that is not acceptable in wide area networks. A second simple solution would be to only transmit a new TCP segment once the user has produced MSS bytes of data. This solution reduces the overhead, but at the cost of a potentially very high delay.

An elegant solution to this problem was proposed by John Nagle in **RFC 896.** John Nagle observed that the overhead caused by the TCP header was a problem in wide area connections, but less in local area connections where the available bandwidth is usually higher. He proposed the following rules to decide to send a new data segment when a new data has been produced by the user or a new ack segment has been received

```
if rcv.wnd>= MSS and len(data) >= MSS :
send one MSS-sized segment
else
if there are unacknowledged data:
place data in buffer until acknowledgement has been received
else
send one TCP segment containing all buffered data
```

The first rule ensures that a TCP connection used for bulk data transfer always sends full TCP segments. The second rule sends one partially filled TCP segment every round-trip-time.

This algorithm, called the Nagle algorithm, takes a few lines of code in all TCP implementations. These lines of code have a huge impact on the packets that are exchanged in TCP/IP networks. Researchers have analysed the distribution of the packet sizes by capturing and analysing all the packets passing through a given link. These studies have shown several important results :

- in TCP/IPv4 networks, a large fraction of the packets are TCP segments that contain only an acknowledgement. These packets usually account for 40-50% of the packets passing through the studied link
- in TCP/IPv4 networks, most of the bytes are exchanged in long packets, usually packets containing up to 1460 bytes of payload which is the default MSS for hosts attached to an Ethernet network, the most popular type of LAN

The figure below provides a distribution of the packet sizes measured on a link. It shows a three-modal distribution of the packet size. 50% of the packets contain pure TCP acknowledgements and occupy 40 bytes. About 20% of the packets contain about 500 bytes of user data and 12% of the packets contain 1460 bytes of user data. However, most of the user data is transported in large packets. This packet size distribution has implications on the design of routers as we discuss in the next chapter.

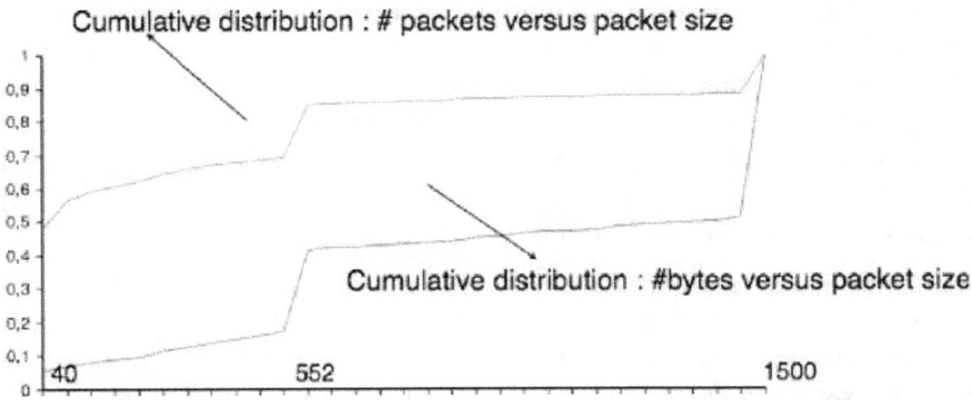

Figure 3.43: Packet size distribution in the Internet

Recent measurements indicate that these packet size distributions are still valid in today's Internet, although the packet distribution tends to become bimodal with small packets corresponding to TCP pure acks (40-64 bytes depending on the utilisation of TCP options) and large 1460-bytes packets carrying most of the user data.

TCP windows

From a performance point of view, one of the main limitations of the original TCP specification is the 16 bits *window* field in the TCP header. As this field indicates the current size of the receive window in bytes, it limits the TCP receive window at 65535 bytes. This limitation was not a severe problem when TCP was designed since at that time high-speed wide area networks offered a maximum bandwidth of 56 kbps. However, in today's network, this limitation is not acceptable anymore. The table below provides the rough maximum throughput that can be achieved by a TCP connection with a 64 KBytes window in function of the connection's round-trip-time

RTT	Maximum Throughput
1 msec	524 Mbps
10 msec	52.4 Mbps
100 msec	5.24 Mbps
500 msec	1.05 Mbps

To solve this problem, a backward compatible extension that allows TCP to use larger receive windows was proposed in **RFC 1323**. Today, most TCP implementations support this option. The basic idea is that instead of storing *snd.wnd* and *rcv.wnd* as 16 bits integers in the *TCB,* they should be stored as 32 bits integers. As the TCP segment header only contains 16 bits to place the window field, it is impossible to copy the value of *snd.wnd* in each sent TCP segment. Instead the header contains *snd.wnd* >> *S* where *S* is the scaling factor ($0 < S < 14$) negotiated during connection establishment. The client adds its proposed scaling factor as a TCP option in the *SYN* segment. If the server supports **RFC 1323**, it places in the *SYN+ACK* segment the scaling factor that it uses when advertising its own receive window. The local and remote scaling factors are included in the *TCB*. If the server does not support **RFC 1323**, it ignores the received option and no scaling is applied.

By using the window scaling extensions defined in **RFC 1323**, TCP implementations can use a receive buffer of up to 1 GByte. With such a receive buffer, the maximum throughput that can be achieved by a single TCP connection becomes :

RTT	Maximum Throughput
1 msec	8590 Gbps
10 msec	859 Gbps
100 msec	86 Gbps
500 msec	17 Gbps

These throughputs are acceptable in today's networks. However, there are already servers having 10 Gbps interfaces... Early TCP implementations had fixed receiving and sending buffers. Today's high performance implementations are able to automatically adjust the size of the sending and receiving buffer to better support high bandwidth flows [SMM1998]

TCP's retransmission timeout

In a go-back-n transport protocol such as TCP, the retransmission timeout must be correctly set in order to achieve good performance. If the retransmission timeout expires too early, then bandwidth is wasted by retransmitting segments that have already been correctly received; whereas if the retransmission timeout expires too late, then bandwidth is wasted because the sender is idle waiting for the expiration of its retransmission timeout.

A good setting of the retransmission timeout clearly depends on an accurate estimation of the round-trip-time of each TCP connection. The round-trip-time differs between TCP connections, but may also change during the lifetime of a single connection. For example, the figure below shows the evolution of the round-trip-time between two hosts during a period of 45 seconds.

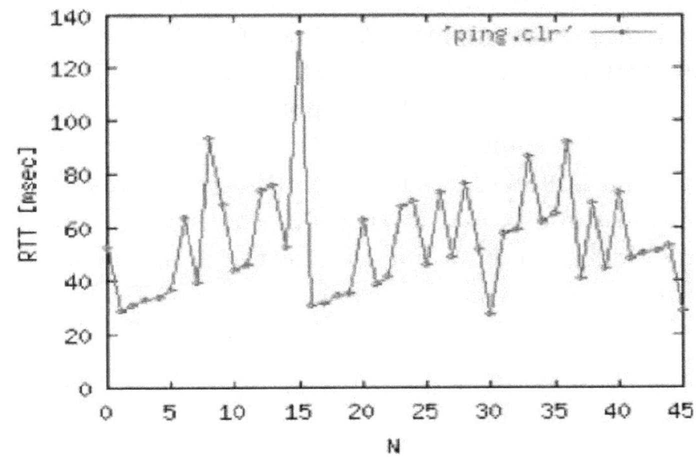

Figure 3.44: Evolution of the round-trip-time between two hosts

The easiest solution to measure the round-trip-time on a TCP connection is to measure the delay between the transmission of a data segment and the reception of a corresponding acknowledgement. As illustrated in the figure below, this measurement works well when there are no segment losses.

However, when a data segment is lost, as illustrated in the bottom part of the figure, the measurement is ambiguous as the sender cannot determine whether the received acknowledgement was triggered by the first transmission of segment *123* or its retransmission. Using incorrect round-trip-time estimations could lead to incorrect values of the retransmission timeout. For this reason, Phil Karn and Craig Partridge proposed, in [KP91], to ignore the round-trip-time measurements performed during retransmissions.

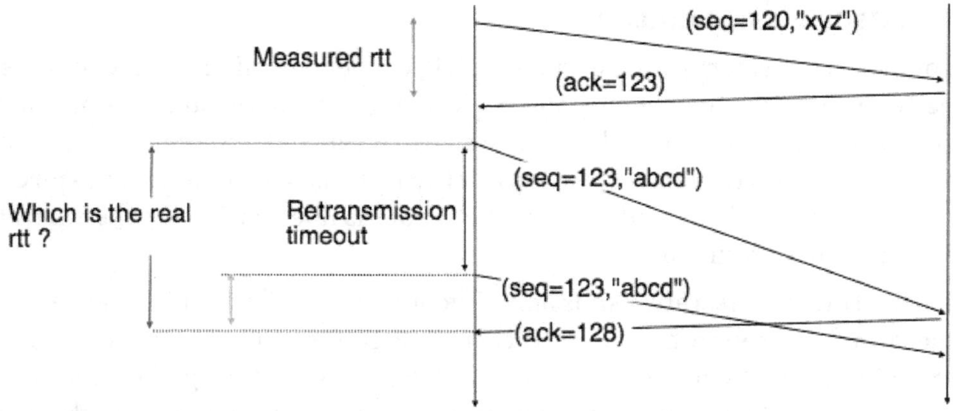

Figure 3.45: How to measure the round-trip-time ?

To avoid this ambiguity in the estimation of the round-trip-time when segments are retransmitted, recent TCP implementations rely on the *timestamp option* defined in **RFC 1323.** This option allows a TCP sender to place two 32 bit timestamps in each TCP segment that it sends. The first timestamp, TS Value *(TSval)* is chosen by the sender of the segment. It could for example be the current value of its real-time clock . The second value, TS Echo Reply *(TSecr),* is the last *TSval* that was received from the remote host and stored in the *TCB.* The figure below shows how the utilization of this timestamp option allows for the disambiguation of the round-trip-time measurement when there are retransmissions.

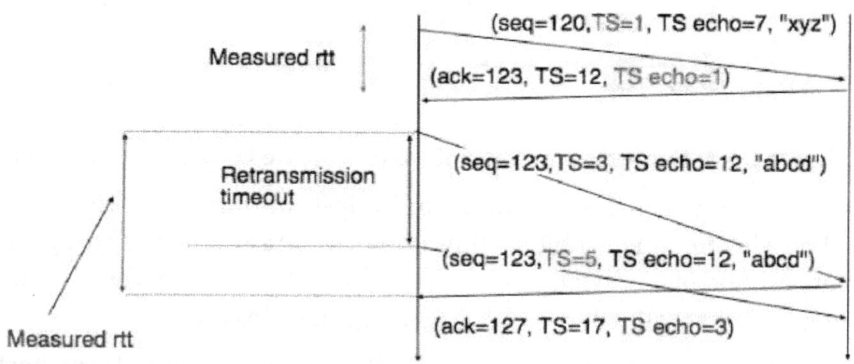

Figure 3.46: Disambiguating round-trip-time measurements with the RFC 1323 timestamp option

Once the round-trip-time measurements have been collected for a given TCP connection, the TCP entity must compute the retransmission timeout. As the round-trip-time measurements may change during the lifetime of a connection, the retransmission timeout may also change. At the beginning of a connection, the TCP entity that sends a *SYN* segment does not know the round-trip-time to reach the remote host and the initial retransmission timeout is usually set to 3 seconds **RFC 2988.**

The original TCP specification proposed in **RFC 793** to include two additional variables in the TCB :

- *srtt* : the smoothed round-trip-time computed as *srrt* = (*a* x *srtt*) + ((1 - *a*) x rtt) where *rtt* is the round-trip-time measured according to the above procedure and *a* a smoothing factor (e.g. 0.8 or 0.9)
- *rto* : the retransmission timeout is computed as *rto* = *min*(60, *max*(1, *ft* x srtt)) where *ft* is used to take into account the delay variance (value : 1.3 to 2.0). The *60* and *1* constants are used to ensure that the rto is not larger than one minute nor smaller than 1 second.

However, in practice, this computation for the retransmission timeout did not work well. The main problem was that the computed rto did not correctly take into account the variations in the measured round-trip-time. *Van Jacobson* proposed in his seminal paper [Jacobson1988] an improved algorithm to compute the rto and implemented it in the BSD Unix distribution. This algorithm is now part of the TCP standard **RFC 2988.**

Jacobson's algorithm uses two state variables, srtt the smoothed rtt and *rttvar* the estimation of the variance of the rtt and two parameters: *a* and ft. When a TCP connection starts, the first rto is set to 3 seconds. When a first estimation of the rtt is available, the srtt, *rttvar* and rto are computed as

srtt=rtt
rttvar=rtt/2
rto=srtt+4*rttvar

Then, when other rtt measurements are collected, srtt and rttvar are updated as follows :

rttvar = (1 — ft) x *rttvar* + ft x |srtt — rtt|
srtt = (1 — *a*) x *srtt* + *a* x *rtt*
rto = *srtt* + 4 x *rttvar*

The proposed values for the parameters are *a* = 8 and *ft* = |. This allows a TCP implementation, implemented in the kernel, to perform the rtt computation by using shift operations instead of the more costly floating point operations [Jacobson1988]. The figure below illustrates the computation of the rto upon rtt changes.

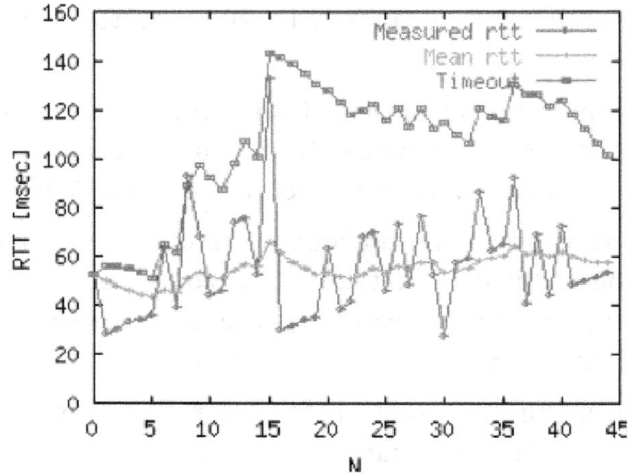

Figure 3.47: Example computation of the rto

Advanced retransmission strategies

The default go-back-n retransmission strategy was defined in **RFC 793.** When the retransmission timer expires, TCP retransmits the first unacknowledged segment (i.e. the one having sequence number *snd.una).* After each expiration of the retransmission timeout, **RFC 2988** recommends to double the value of the retransmission timeout. This is called an *exponential backoff.* This doubling of the retransmission timeout after a retransmission was included in TCP to deal with issues such as network/receiver overload and incorrect initial estimations of the retransmission timeout. If the same segment is retransmitted several times, the retransmission timeout is doubled after every retransmission until it reaches a configured maximum. **RFC 2988** suggests a maximum retransmission timeout of at least 60 seconds. Once the retransmission timeout reaches this configured maximum, the remote host is considered to be unreachable and the TCP connection is closed.

This retransmission strategy has been refined based on the experience of using TCP on the Internet. The first refinement was a clarification of the strategy used to send acknowledgements. As TCP uses piggybacking, the easiest and less costly method to send acknowledgements is to place them in the data segments sent in the other direction. However, few application layer protocols exchange data in both directions at the same time and thus this method rarely works. For an application that is sending data segments in one direction only, the remote TCP entity returns empty TCP segments whose only useful information is their acknowledgement number. This may cause a large overhead in wide area network if a pure *ACK* segment is sent in response to each received data segment. Most TCP implementations use a *delayed acknowledgement* strategy. This strategy ensures that piggybacking is used whenever possible, otherwise pure *ACK* segments are sent for every second received data segments when there are no losses. When there are losses or reordering, *ACK* segments are more important for the sender and they are sent immediately **RFC 813 RFC 1122.** This strategy relies on a new timer with a short delay (e.g. 50 milliseconds) and one additional flag in the TCB. It can be implemented as follows

```
reception of a data segment:
if pkt.seq==rcv.nxt:      # segment received in sequence
if delayedack :
send pure ack segment
cancel acktimer
delayedack=False
else:
delayedack=True
start acktimer
else:    # out of sequence segment
send pure ack segment
if delayedack:
delayedack=False
cancel acktimer
transmission of a data segment: # piggyback ack
if delayedack:
delayedack=False
cancel acktimer
acktimer expiration:
send pure ack segment
delayedack=False
```

Due to this delayed acknowledgement strategy, during a bulk transfer, a TCP implementation usually acknowledges every second TCP segment received.

The default go-back-n retransmission strategy used by TCP has the advantage of being simple to implement, in particular on the receiver side, but when there are losses, a go-back-n strategy provides a lower performance than a selective repeat strategy. The TCP developers have designed several extensions to TCP to allow it to use a selective repeat strategy while maintaining backward compatibility with older TCP implementations. These TCP extensions assume that the receiver is able to buffer the segments that it receives out-of-sequence.

The first extension that was proposed is the fast retransmit heuristic. This extension can be implemented on TCP senders and thus does not require any change to the protocol. It only assumes that the TCP receiver is able to buffer out-of-sequence segments.

From a performance point of view, one issue with TCP's *retransmission timeout* is that when there are isolated segment losses, the TCP sender often remains idle waiting for the expiration of its retransmission timeouts. Such isolated losses are frequent in the global Internet [Paxson99]. A heuristic to deal with isolated losses without waiting for the expiration of the retransmission timeout has been included in many TCP implementations since the early 1990s. To understand this heuristic, let us consider the figure below that shows the segments exchanged over a TCP connection when an isolated segment is lost.

As shown above, when an isolated segment is lost the sender receives several *duplicate acknowledgements* since the TCP receiver immediately sends a pure acknowledgement when it receives an out-of-sequence segment. A duplicate acknowledgement is an acknowledgement that contains the same *acknowledgement number* as a previous segment. A single duplicate acknowledgement does not necessarily imply that a segment was lost, as a simple reordering of the segments may cause duplicate acknowledgements as well. Measurements [Paxson99] have shown that segment reordering is frequent in the Internet. Based on these observations, the *fast retransmit* heuristic has been included in most TCP implementations. It can be implemented as follows

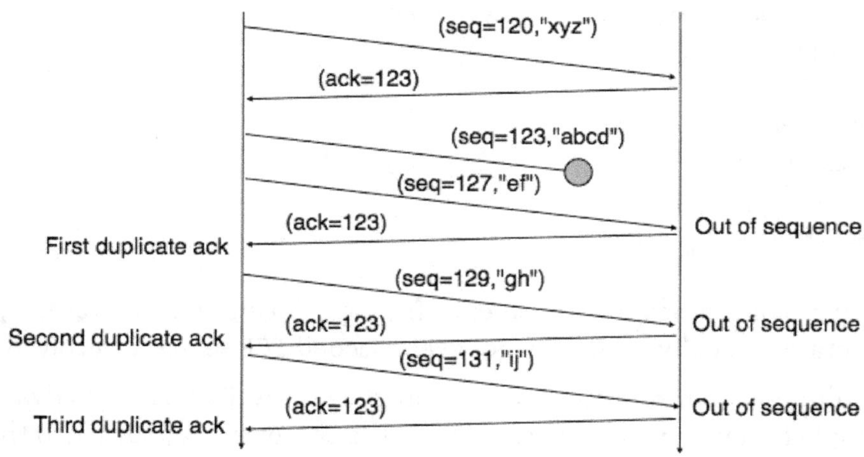

Figure 3.48: Detecting isolated segment losses

```
ack arrival:
if tcp.ack==snd.una:    # duplicate acknowledgement
dupacks++
if dupacks==3:
retransmit segment(snd.una)
else:
dupacks=0
# process acknowledgement
```

This heuristic requires an additional variable in the TCB *(dupacks).* Most implementations set the default number of duplicate acknowledgements that trigger a retransmission to 3. It is now part of the standard TCP specification **RFC 2581.** The *fast retransmit* heuristic improves the TCP performance provided that isolated segments are lost and the current window is large enough to allow the sender to send three duplicate acknowledgements.

The figure below illustrates the operation of the *fast retransmit* heuristic.

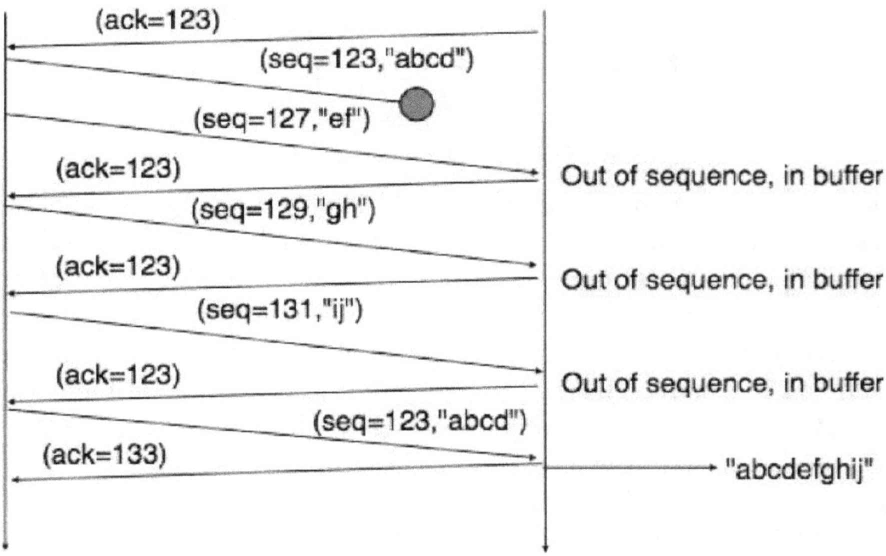

Figure 3.49: TCP fast retransmit heuristics

When losses are not isolated or when the windows are small, the performance of the *fast retransmit* heuristic decreases. In such environments, it is necessary to allow a TCP sender to use a selective repeat strategy instead of the default go-back-n strategy. Implementing selective-repeat requires a change to the TCP protocol as the receiver needs to be able to inform the sender of the out-of-order segments that it has already received. This can be done by using the Selective Acknowledgements (SACK) option defined in **RFC 2018.** This TCP option is negotiated during the establishment of a TCP connection. If both TCP hosts support the option, SACK blocks can be attached by the receiver to the segments that it sends. SACK blocks allow a TCP receiver to indicate the blocks of data that it has received correctly but out of sequence. The figure below illustrates the utilisation of the SACK blocks.

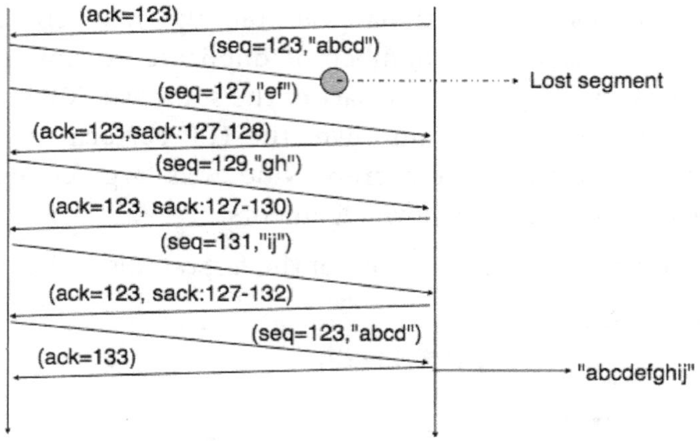

Figure 3.50: TCP selective acknowledgements

An SACK option contains one or more blocks. A block corresponds to all the sequence numbers between the *left edge* and the *right edge* of the block. The two edges of the block are encoded as 32 bit numbers (the same size as the TCP sequence number) in an SACK option. As the SACK option contains one byte to encode its type and one byte for its length, a SACK option containing *b* blocks is encoded as a sequence of 2 + 8 x *b* bytes. In practice, the size of the SACK option can be problematic as the optional TCP header extension cannot be longer than 44 bytes. As the SACK option is usually combined with the **RFC 1323** timestamp extension, this implies that a TCP segment cannot usually contain more than three SACK blocks. This limitation implies that a TCP receiver cannot always place in the SACK option that it sends, information about all the received blocks.

To deal with the limited size of the SACK option, a TCP receiver currently having more than 3 blocks inside its receiving buffer must select the blocks to place in the SACK option. A good heuristic is to put in the SACK option the blocks that have most recently changed, as the sender is likely to be already aware of the older blocks.

When a sender receives an SACK option indicating a new block and thus a new possible segment loss, it usually does not retransmit the missing segment(s immediately. To deal with reordering, a TCP sender can use a heuristic similar to *fast retransmit* by retransmitting a gap only once it has received three SACK options indicating this gap. It should be noted that the SACK option does not supersede the *acknowledgement number* of the TCP header. A TCP sender can only remove data from its sending buffer once they have been acknowledged by TCP's cumulative acknowledgements. This design was chosen for two reasons. First, it allows the receiver to discard parts of its receiving buffer when it is running out of memory without loosing data. Second, as the SACK option is not transmitted reliably, the cumulative acknowledgements are still required to deal with losses of *ACK* segments carrying only SACK information. Thus, the SACK option only serves as a hint to allow the sender to optimise its retransmissions.

TCP congestion control

In the previous sections, we have explained the mechanisms that TCP uses to deal with transmission errors and segment losses. In a heterogeneous network such as the Internet or enterprise IP networks, endsystems have very different levels of performance. Some endsystems are high-end servers attached to 10 Gbps links while others are mobile devices attached to a very low bandwidth wireless link. Despite these huge differences in performance, a mobile device should be able to efficiently exchange segments with a high-end server.

To understand this problem better, let us consider the scenario shown in the figure below, where a server (*A*) attached to a *10 Mbps* link is sending TCP segments to another computer (*C*) through a path that contains a 2 *Mbps* link.

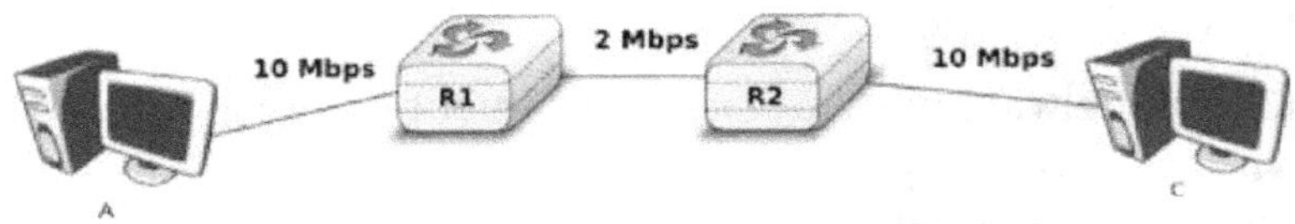

Figure 3.51: TCP over heterogeneous links

In this network, the TCP segments sent by the server reach router *R1*. *R1* forwards the segments towards router *R2*. Router R2 can potentially receive segments at 10 *Mbps,* but it can only forward them at 2 *Mbps* to router R2 and then to host *C*. Router *R2* contains buffers that allow it to store the packets that cannot immediately be forwarded to their destination. To understand the operation of TCP in this environment, let us consider a simplified model of this network where host *A* is attached to a 10 *Mbps* link to a queue that represents the buffers of router R2. This queue is emptied at a rate of *2 Mbps.*

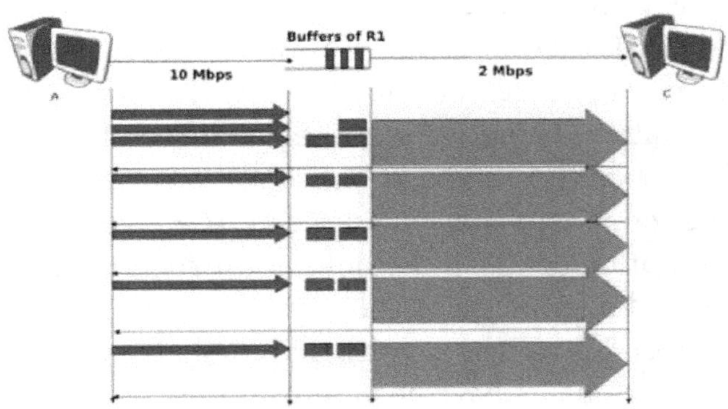

Figure 3.52: TCP self clocking

Let us consider that host *A* uses a window of three segments. It thus sends three back-to-back segments at *10 Mbps* and then waits for an acknowledgement. Host *A* stops sending segments when its window is full. These segments reach the buffers of router *R2*. The first segment stored in this buffer is sent by router *R2* at a rate of *2 Mbps* to the destination host. Upon reception of this segment, the destination sends an acknowledgement. This acknowledgement allows host *A* to transmit a new segment. This segment is stored in the buffers of router *R2* while it is transmitting the second segment that was sent by host *A*... Thus, after the transmission of the first window of segments, TCP sends one data segment after the reception of each acknowledgement returned by the destination. In practice, the acknowledgements sent by the destination serve as a kind of *clock* that allows the sending host to adapt its transmission rate to the rate at which segments are received by the destination. This *TCP self-clocking* is the first mechanism that allows TCP to adapt to heterogeneous networks [Jacobson1988]. It depends on the availability of buffers to store the segments that have been sent by the sender but have not yet been transmitted to the destination.

However, TCP is not always used in this environment. In the global Internet, TCP is used in networks where a large number of hosts send segments to a large number of receivers. For example, let us consider the network depicted below which is similar to the one discussed in [Jacobson1988] and **RFC 896**. In this network, we assume that the buffers of the router are infinite to ensure that no packet is lost.

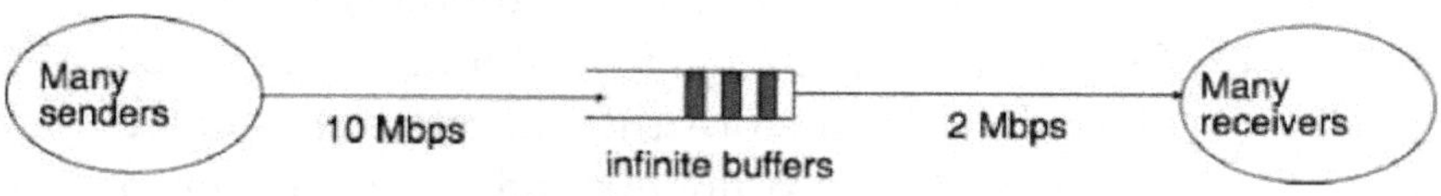

Figure 3.53: The congestion collapse problem

If many TCP senders are attached to the left part of the network above, they all send a window full of segments. These segments are stored in the buffers of the router before being transmitted towards their destination. If there are many senders on the left part of the network, the occupancy of the buffers quickly grows. A consequence of the buffer occupancy is that the round-trip-time, measured by TCP, between the sender and the receiver increases. Consider a network where 10,000 bits segments are sent. When the buffer is empty, such a segment requires 1 millisecond to be transmitted on the *10 Mbps* link and 5 milliseconds to be the transmitted on the 2 *Mbps* link. Thus, the round-trip-time measured by TCP is roughly 6 milliseconds if we ignore the propagation delay on the links. Most routers manage their buffers as a FIFO queue . If the buffer contains 100 segments, the round-triptime becomes 1 + 100 x 5 + 5 milliseconds as new segments are only transmitted on the 2 *Mbps* link once all previous segments have been transmitted. Unfortunately, TCP uses a retransmission timer and performs *go-back-n* to recover from transmission errors.

If the buffer occupancy is high, TCP assumes that some segments have been lost and retransmits a full window of segments. This increases the occupancy of the buffer and the delay through the buffer... Furthermore, the buffer may store and send on the low bandwidth links several retransmissions of the same segment. This problem is called *congestion collapse.* It occurred several times in the late 1980s. For example, [Jacobson1988] notes that in 1986, the usable bandwidth of a 32 Kbits link dropped to 40 bits per second due to congestion collapse!

The *congestion collapse* is a problem that all heterogeneous networks face. Different mechanisms have been proposed in the scientific literature to avoid or control network congestion. Some of them have been implemented and deployed in real networks. To understand this problem in more detail, let us first consider a simple network with two hosts attached to a high bandwidth link that are sending segments to destination *C* attached to a low bandwidth link as depicted below.

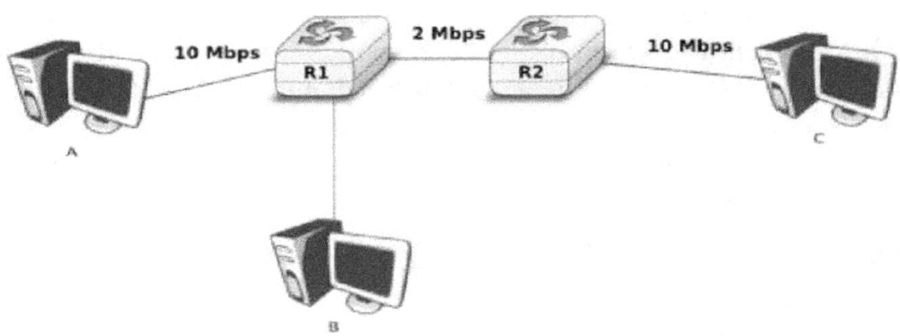

Figure 3.54: The congestion problem

To avoid *congestion collapse,* the hosts must regulate their transmission rate by using a *congestion control* mechanism. Such a mechanism can be implemented in the transport layer or in the network layer. In TCP/IP networks, it is implemented in the transport layer, but other technologies such as *Asynchronous Transfer Mode (ATM)* or *Frame Relay* include congestion control mechanisms in lower layers.

Let us first consider the simple problem of a set of *i* hosts that share a single bottleneck link as shown in the example above. In this network, the congestion control scheme must achieve the following objectives [CJ1989] :

1. The congestion control scheme must *avoid congestion.* In practice, this means that the bottleneck link cannot be overloaded. If $r_i(t)$ is the transmission rate allocated to host *i* at time *t* and *R* the bandwidth of the bottleneck link, then the congestion control scheme should ensure that, on average, $\forall t \sum r_i(t) \leq R$.
2. The congestion control scheme must be *efficient.* The bottleneck link is usually both a shared and an expensive resource. Usually, bottleneck links are wide area links that are much more expensive to upgrade than the local area networks. The congestion control scheme should ensure that such links are efficiently

used. Mathematically, the control scheme should ensure that $\forall t \sum r_i(t) \approx R$.

3. The congestion control scheme should be *fair.* Most congestion schemes aim at achieving *max- min fairness.* An allocation of transmission rates to sources is said to be *max-minfair* if:
    - no link in the network is congested
    - the rate allocated to source *j* cannot be increased without decreasing the rate allocated to a source i whose allocation is smaller than the rate allocated to source j [Leboudec2008] .

Depending on the network, a *max-minfair allocation* may not always exist. In practice, *max-min fairness* is an ideal objective that cannot necessarily be achieved. When there is a single bottleneck link as in the example above, *max-min fairness* implies that each source should be allocated the same transmission rate.

To visualise the different rate allocations, it is useful to consider the graph shown below. In this graph, we plot on the *x-axis* (resp. *y-axis)* the rate allocated to host *B* (resp. A). A point in the graph (r_B, r_A) corresponds to a possible allocation of the transmission rates. Since there is a *2 Mbps* bottleneck link in this network, the graph can be divided into two regions. The lower left part of the graph contains all allocations (r_B, r_A) such that the bottleneck link is not congested $(r_A + r_B < 2)$. The right border of this region is the *efficiency line,* i.e. the set of allocations that completely utilise the bottleneck link $(r_A + r_B = 2)$. Finally, the *fairness line* is the set of fair allocations.

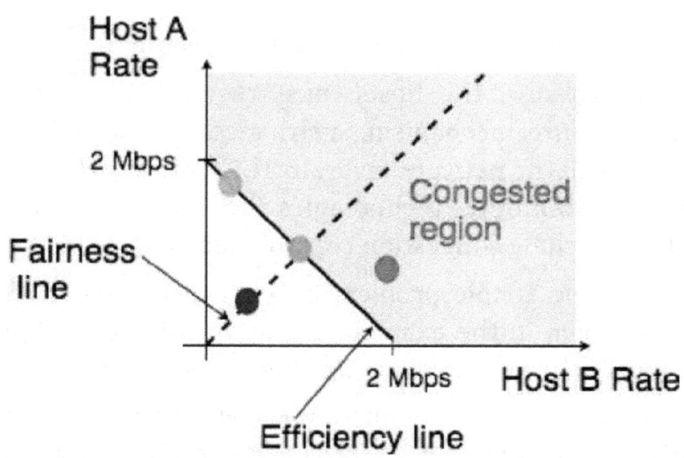

Figure 3.55: Possible allocated transmission rates

As shown in the graph above, a rate allocation may be fair but not efficient (e.g. $r_A = 0.7$, $r_B = 0.7$), fair and efficient (e.g. $r_A = 1, r_B = 1$) or efficient but not fair (e.g. $r_A = 1.5$, $r_B = 0.5$). Ideally, the allocation should be both fair and efficient. Unfortunately, maintaining such an allocation with fluctuations in the number of flows that use the network is a challenging problem. Furthermore, there might be several thousands of TCP connections or more that pass through the same link.

To deal with these fluctuations in demand, which result in fluctuations in the available bandwidth, computer networks use a congestion control scheme. This congestion control scheme should achieve the three objectives listed above. Some congestion control schemes rely on a close cooperation between the endhosts and the routers, while others are mainly implemented on the endhosts with limited support from the routers.

A congestion control scheme can be modelled as an algorithm that adapts the transmission rate of host i based on the feedback received from the network. Different types of feedbacks are possible. The simplest scheme is a binary feedback [CJ1989] [Jacobson1988] where the hosts simply learn whether the network is congested or not. Some congestion control schemes allow the network to regularly send an allocated transmission rate in Mbps to each host [BF1995].

Let us focus on the binary feedback scheme which is the most widely used today. Intuitively, the congestion control scheme should decrease the transmission rate of a host when congestion has been detected in the network, in order to avoid congestion collapse. Furthermore, the hosts should increase their transmission rate when the network is not congested. Otherwise, the hosts would not be able to efficiently utilise the network. The rate allocated to each host fluctuates with time, depending on the feedback received from the network. The figure below illustrates the evolution of the transmission rates allocated to two hosts in our simple network. Initially, two hosts have a low allocation, but this is not efficient. The allocations increase until the network becomes congested. At this point, the hosts decrease their transmission rate to avoid congestion collapse. If the congestion control scheme works well, after some time the allocations should become both fair and efficient.

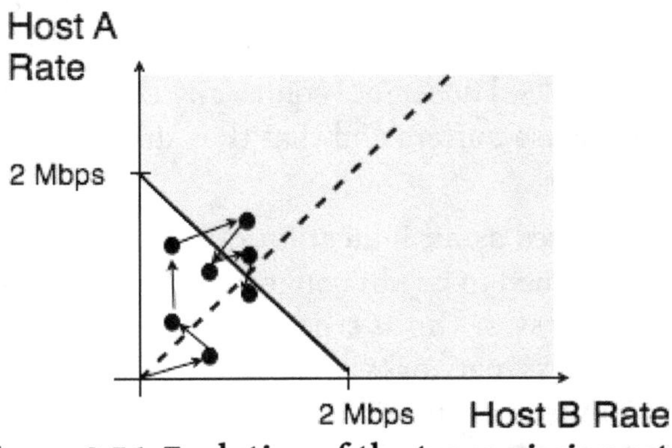

Figure 3.56: Evolution of the transmission rates

Various types of rate adaption algorithms are possible. Dah Ming Chiu and Raj Jain have analysed, in [CJ1989], different types of algorithms that can be used by a source to adapt its transmission rate to the feedback received from the network. Intuitively, such a rate adaptation algorithm increases the transmission rate when the network is not congested (ensure that the network is efficiently used) and decrease the transmission rate when the network is congested (to avoid congestion collapse).

The simplest form of feedback that the network can send to a source is a binary feedback (the network is congested or not congested). In this case, a *linear* rate adaptation algorithm can be expressed as:

- $rate(t+1) = \alpha_C + \beta_C rate(t)$ when the network is congested
- $rate(t+1) = \alpha_C + \beta_C rate(t)$ when the network is *not* congested

With a linear adaption algorithm, a_c, a_N, β_c and β_N are constants. The analysis of [CJ1989] shows that to be fair and efficient, such a binary rate adaption mechanism must rely on *Additive Increase and Multiplicative Decrease.* When the network is not congested, the hosts should slowly increase their transmission rate ($\beta_N = 1$ *and* $a_N > 0$). When the network is congested, the hosts must multiplicatively decrease their transmission rate ($\beta_c < 1$ and $a_c = 0$). Such an AIMD rate adaptation algorithm can be implemented by the pseudo-code below

```
# Additive Increase Multiplicative Decrease
if congestion :
rate=rate*betaC # multiplicative decrease, betaC<1
else
rate=rate+alphaN # additive increase, v0>0
```

Note: Which binary feedback ?

Two types of binary feedback are possible in computer networks. A first solution is to rely on implicit feedback. This is the solution chosen for TCP. TCP's congestion control scheme [Jacobson1988] does not require any cooperation from the router. It only assumes that they use buffers and that they discard packets when there is congestion.

TCP uses the segment losses as an indication of congestion. When there are no losses, the network is assumed to be not congested. This implies that congestion is the main cause of packet losses. This is true in wired networks, but unfortunately not always true in wireless networks. Another solution is to rely on explicit feedback. This is the solution proposed in the DECBit congestion control scheme [RJ1995] and used in Frame Relay and ATM networks. This explicit feedback can be implemented in two ways. A first solution would be to define a special message that could be sent by routers to hosts when they are congested. Unfortunately, generating such messages may increase the amount of congestion in the network. Such a congestion indication packet is thus discouraged **RFC 1812.** A better approach is to allow the intermediate routers to indicate, in the packets that they forward, their current congestion status. Binary feedback can be encoded by using one bit in the packet header. With such a scheme, congested routers set a special bit in the packets that they forward while non-congested routers leave this bit unmodified. The destination host returns the congestion status of the network in the acknowledgements that it sends. Details about such a solution in IP networks may be found in **RFC 3168.** Unfortunately, as of this writing, this solution is still not deployed despite its potential benefits.

The TCP congestion control scheme was initially proposed by Van Jacobson in [Jacobson1988]. The current specification may be found in RFC 5681. TCP relies on Additive Increase and Multiplicative Decrease (AIMD). To implement AIMD, a TCP host must be able to control its transmission rate. A first approach would be to use timers and adjust their expiration times in function of the rate imposed by AIMD. Unfortunately, maintaining such timers for a large number of TCP connections can be difficult. Instead, Van Jacobson noted that the rate of TCP congestion can be artificially controlled by constraining its sending window. A TCP connection cannot send data faster than $\frac{window}{rtt}$ where window is the maximum between the host's sending window and the window advertised by the receiver.

TCP's congestion control scheme is based on a congestion window. The current value of the congestion window (*cwnd*) is stored in the TCB of each TCP connection and the window that can be used by the sender is constrained by min(*cwnd; rwin; swin*) where swin is the current sending window and *rwin* the last received receive window. The Additive Increase part of the TCP congestion control increments the congestion window by MSS bytes every round-trip-time. In the TCP literature, this phase is often called the congestion avoidance phase. The Multiplicative Decrease part of the TCP congestion control divides the current value of the congestion window once congestion has been detected. When a TCP connection begins, the sending host does not know whether the part of the network that it uses to reach the destination is congested or not. To avoid causing too much congestion, it must start with a small congestion window. [Jacobson1988] recommends an initial window of MSS bytes. As the additive increase part of the TCP congestion control scheme increments the congestion window by MSS bytes every round-trip-time, the TCP connection may have to wait many round-trip-times before being able to efficiently use the available bandwidth. This is especially important in environments where the *bandwidth X rtt* product is high. To avoid waiting too many round-trip-times before reaching a congestion window that is large enough to efficiently utilise the network, the TCP congestion control scheme includes the slow-start algorithm. The objective of the TCP slow-start is to quickly reach an acceptable value for the cwnd. During slow-start, the congestion window is doubled every round-trip-time. The slow-start algorithm uses an additional variable in the TCB : sshtresh (slowstart threshold). The ssthresh is an estimation of the last value of the cwnd that did not cause congestion. It is initialised at the sending window and is updated after each congestion event.

In practice, a TCP implementation considers the network to be congested once its needs to retransmit a segment. The TCP congestion control scheme distinguishes between two types of congestion :

- mild congestion. TCP considers that the network is lightly congested if it receives three duplicate acknowledgements and performs a fast retransmit. If the fast retransmit is successful, this implies that only one segment has been lost. In this case, TCP performs multiplicative decrease and the congestion window is divided by 2. The slow-start threshold is set to the new value of the congestion window.
- severe congestion. TCP considers that the network is severely congested when its retransmission timer expires. In this case, TCP retransmits the first segment, sets the slow-start threshold to 50% of the congestion window. The congestion window is reset to its initial value and TCP performs a slow-start.

The figure below illustrates the evolution of the congestion window when there is severe congestion. At the beginning of the connection, the sender performs slow-start until the first segments are lost and the retransmission timer expires. At this time, the ssthresh is set to half of the current congestion window and the congestion window is reset at one segment. The lost segments are retransmitted as the sender again performs slow-start until the congestion window reaches the sshtresh. It then switches to congestion avoidance and the congestion window increases linearly until segments are lost and the retransmission timer expires.

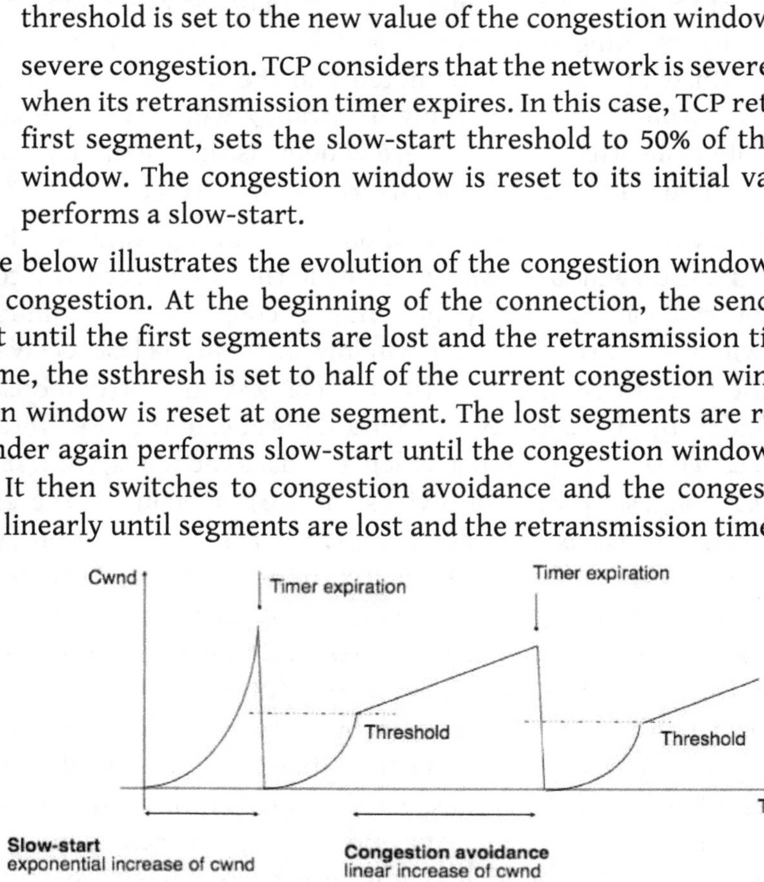

Figure 3.57: Evaluation of the TCP congestion window with severe congestion

The figure below illustrates the evolution of the congestion window when the network is lightly congested and all lost segments can be retransmitted using fast retransmit. The sender begins with a slow-start. A segment is lost but successfully retransmitted by a fast retransmit. The congestion window is divided by 2 and the sender immediately enters congestion avoidance as this was a mild congestion.

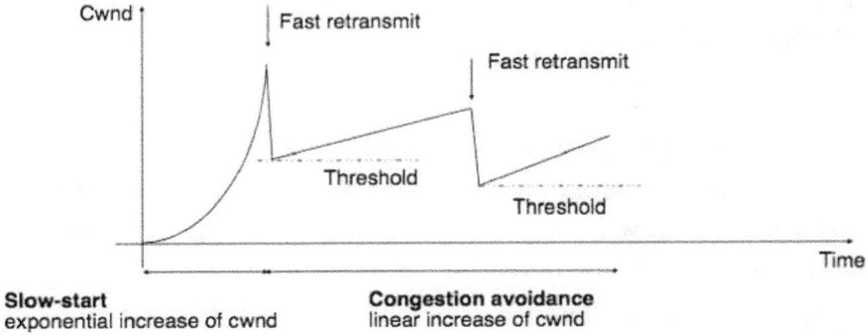

Figure 3.58: Evaluation of the TCP congestion window when the network is lightly congested

Most TCP implementations update the congestion window when they receive an acknowledgement. If we assume that the receiver acknowledges each received segment and the sender only sends MSS sized segments, the TCP congestion control scheme can be implemented using the simplified pseudo-code below

```
# Initialisation
cwnd = MSS;
ssthresh= swin;
# Ack arrival
if tcp.ack > snd.una :     # new ack, no congestion
if cwnd < ssthresh :
# slow-start : increase quickly cwnd
# double cwnd every rtt
cwnd = cwnd + MSS
else:
# congestion avoidance : increase slowly cwnd
# increase cwnd by one mss every rtt
cwnd = cwnd+ mss*(mss/cwnd)
else: # duplicate or old ack
if tcp.ack==snd.una:     # duplicate acknowledgement
dupacks++
if dupacks==3:
retransmitsegment(snd.una)
ssthresh=max(cwnd/2,2 *MSS)
```

```
cwnd=ssthresh
else:
dupacks=0
# ack for old segment, ignored
Expiration of the retransmission timer:
send(snd.una)  # retransmit first lost segment
sshtresh=max(cwnd/2,2*MSS)
cwnd=MSS
```

Furthermore when a TCP connection has been idle for more than its current retransmission timer, it should reset its congestion window to the congestion window size that it uses when the connection begins, as it no longer knows the current congestion state of the network.

Note: Initial congestion window

The original TCP congestion control mechanism proposed in [Jacobson1988] recommended that each TCP connection should begin by setting *cwnd* = *MSS*. However, in today's higher bandwidth networks, using such a small initial congestion window severely affects the performance for short TCP connections, such as those used by web servers. Since the publication of **RFC 3390**, TCP hosts are allowed to use an initial congestion window of about 4 KBytes, which corresponds to 3 segments in many environments.

Thanks to its congestion control scheme, TCP adapts its transmission rate to the losses that occur in the network. Intuitively, the TCP transmission rate decreases when the percentage of losses increases. Researchers have proposed detailed models that allow the prediction of the throughput of a TCP connection when losses occur [MSMO1997]. To have some intuition about the factors that affect the performance of TCP, let us consider a very simple model. Its assumptions are not completely realistic, but it gives us good intuition without requiring complex mathematics.

This model considers a hypothetical TCP connection that suffers from equally spaced segment losses. If p is the segment loss ratio, then the TCP connection successfully transfers p - 1 segments and the next segment is lost. If we ignore the slow-start at the beginning of the connection, TCP in this environment is always in congestion avoidance as there are only isolated losses that can be recovered by using fast retransmit. The evolution of the congestion window is thus as shown in the figure below. Note the that *x-axis* of this figure represents time measured in units of one round-trip-time, which is supposed to be constant in the model, and the *y-axis* represents the size of the congestion window measured in MSS-sized segments.

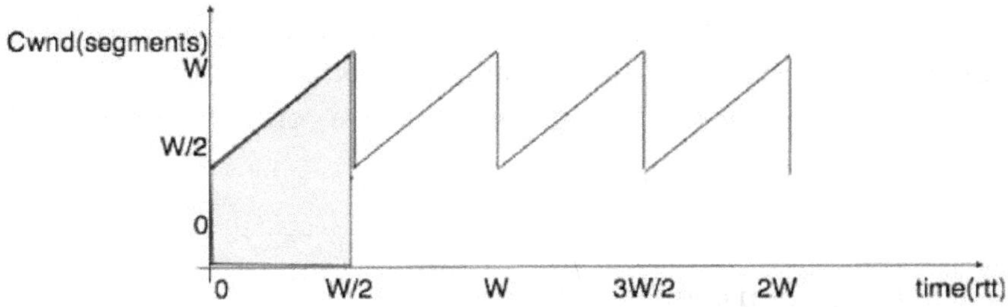

Figure 3.59: Evolution of the congestion window with regular losses

As the losses are equally spaced, the congestion window always starts at some value (W), and is incremented by one MSS every round-trip-time until it reaches twice this value (W). At this point, a segment is retransmitted and the cycle starts again. If the congestion window is measured in MSS-sized segments, a cycle lasts W round-triptimes. The bandwidth of the TCP connection is the number of bytes that have been transmitted during a given period of time. During a cycle, the number of segments that are sent on the TCP connection is equal to the area of the yellow trapeze in the figure. Its area is thus :

$$area = (\frac{W}{2})^2 + \frac{1}{2} \times (\frac{W}{2})^2 = \frac{3 \times W^2}{8}$$

However, given the regular losses that we consider, the number of segments that are sent between two losses (i.e. during a cycle) is by definition equal to 1/p. Thus, $W = \sqrt{\frac{8}{3 \times p}} = \frac{k}{\sqrt{p}}$. The throughput (in bytes per second) of the TCP connection is equal to the number of segments transmitted divided by the duration of the cycle : *Throughput* = $\frac{area \times MSS}{time} = \frac{\frac{3 \times W^2}{8}}{\frac{W}{2} \times rtt}$ or, after having eliminated *W*, *Throughput* = $\sqrt{\frac{3}{2}} \times \frac{MSS}{rtt \times \sqrt{p}}$

More detailed models and the analysis of simulations have shown that a first order model of the TCP throughput when losses occur was *Throughput* $\approx \frac{k \times MSS}{rtt \times \sqrt{p}}$. This is an important result which shows that:

- TCP connections with a small round-trip-time can achieve a higher throughput than TCP connections having a longer round-trip-time when losses occur. This implies that the TCP congestion control scheme is not completely fair since it favors the connections that have the shorter round-trip-time
- TCP connections that use a large MSS can achieve a higher throughput that the TCP connections that use a shorter MSS. This creates another source of unfairness between TCP connections. However, it should be noted that today most hosts are using almost the same MSS, roughly 1460 bytes.

In general, the maximum throughput that can be achieved by a TCP connection depends on its maximum window size and the round-trip-time if there are no losses. If there are losses, it depends on the MSS, the round-trip-time and the loss ratio.

$$Throughput < min(\frac{window}{rtt}, \frac{k \times MSS}{rtt \times \sqrt{p}})$$

Note: The TCP congestion control zoo

The first TCP congestion control scheme was proposed by Van Jacobson in [Jacobson1988]. In addition to writing the scientific paper, Van Jacobson also implemented the slow-start and congestion avoidance schemes in release 4.3 *Tahoe* of the BSD Unix distributed by the University of Berkeley. Later, he improved the congestion control by adding the fast retransmit and the fast recovery mechanisms in the *Reno* release of 4.3 BSD Unix. Since then, many researchers have proposed, simulated and implemented modifications to the TCP congestion control scheme. Some of these modifications are still used today, e.g. :

- *NewReno* (**RFC 3782**), which was proposed as an improvement of the fast recovery mechanism in the Reno implementation
- *TCP Vegas,* which uses changes in the round-trip-time to estimate congestion in order to avoid it [BOP1994]
- *CUBIC,* which was designed for high bandwidth links and is the default congestion control scheme in the Linux 2.6.19 kernel [HRX2008]
- *Compound TCP,* which was designed for high bandwidth links is the default congestion control scheme in several Microsoft operating systems [STBT2009]

A search of the scientific literature will probably reveal more than 100 different variants of the TCP congestion control scheme. Most of them have only been evaluated by simulations. However, the TCP implementation in the recent Linux kernels supports several congestion control schemes and new ones can be easily added. We can expect that new TCP congestion control schemes will always continue to appear.

3.4 SUMMARY

In this chapter, we have studied the transport layer. This layer provides two types of services to the application layer. The unreliable connectionless service is the simplest service offered to applications. On the Internet, this is the service offered by UDP. However, most applications prefer to use a reliable and connection-oriented transport service. We have shown that providing this service was much more complex than providing an unreliable service as the transport layer needs to recover from the errors that occur in the network layer. For this, transport layer protocols rely on several mechanisms. First, they use a handshake mechanism, such as the three-way handshake mechanism, to correctly establish a transport connection. Once the connection has been established, transport entities exchange segments. Each segment contains a sequence number, and the transport layer uses acknowledgements to confirm the segments that have been correctly received. In addition, timers are used to recover from segment losses and sliding windows are used to avoid overflowing the buffers of the transport entities. Finally, we explained how a transport connection can be safely released. We then discussed the mechanisms that are used in TCP, the reliable transport protocol, used by most applications on the Internet. Most notably, we described the congestion control mechanism that has been included in TCP since the late 1980s and explained how the reliability mechanisms used by TCP have been tuned over the years.

3.5 EXERCISES

This section is divided in two parts. The first part contains exercises on the principles of transport protocols, including TCP. The second part contains programming challenges packet analysis tools to observe the behaviour of transport protocols.

3.5.1 Principles

1. Consider the Alternating Bit Protocol as described in this chapter
    - How does the protocol recover from the loss of a data segment ?
    - How does the protocol recovers from the loss of an acknowledgement ?
2. A student proposed to optimise the Alternating Bit Protocol by adding a negative acknowledgment, i.e. the receiver sends a *NAK* control segment when it receives a corrupted data segment. What kind of information should be placed in this control segment and how should the sender react when receiving such a NAK ?
3. Transport protocols rely on different types of checksums to verify whether segments have been affected by transmission errors. The most frequently used checksums are :
    - the Internet checksum used by UDP, TCP and other Internet protocols which is defined in **RFC 1071** and implemented in various modules, e.g. http://ilab.cs.byu.edu/cs460/code/ftp/ichecksum.py for a python implementation
    - the 16 bits or the 32 bits Cyclical Redundancy Checks (CRC) that are often used on disks, in zip archives and in datalink layer protocols. See http://docs.python.org/library/binascii.html for a python module that contains the 32 bits CRC

- the Alder checksum defined in **RFC 2920** for the SCTP protocol but replaced by a CRC later **RFC 3309**
- the Fletcher checksum [Fletcher1982], see http://drdobbs.com/database/184408761 for implementation details

By using your knowledge of the Internet checksum, can you find a transmission error that will not be detected by the Internet checksum ?

4. The CRCs are efficient error detection codes that are able to detect :
    - all errors that affect an odd number of bits
    - all errors that affect a sequence of bits which is shorter than the length of the CRC

Carry experiments with one implementation of CRC-32 to verify that this is indeed the case.

5. Checksums and CRCs should not be confused with secure hash functions such as MD5 defined in **RFC 1321** or SHA-1 described in **RFC 4634.** Secure hash functions are used to ensure that files or sometimes packets/segments have not been modified. Secure hash functions aim at detecting malicious changes while checksums and CRCs only detect random transmission errors. Perform some experiments with hash functions such as those defined in the http://docs.python.org/library/hashlib.html python hashlib module to verify that this is indeed the case.
6. A version of the Alternating Bit Protocol supporting variable length segments uses a header that contains the following fields :
    - a *number* (0 or 1)
    - a *length* field that indicates the length of the data
    - a *CRC*

To speedup the transmission of the segments, a student proposes to compute the CRC over the data part of the segment but not over the header. What do you think of this optimisation ?

7. On Unix hosts, the *ping(8)* command can be used to measure the round-trip-time to send and receive packets from a remote host. Use *ping(8)* to measure the round-trip to a remote host. Chose a remote destination which is far from your current location, e.g. a small web server in a distant country. There are implementations of ping in various languages, see e.g. http://pypi.python.org/pypi/ping/0.2 for a python implementation of "ping"
8. How would you set the retransmission timer if you were implementing the Alternating Bit Protocol to exchange files with a server such as the one that you measured above ?

9. What are the factors that affect the performance of the Alternating Bit Protocol?
10. Links are often considered as symmetrical, i.e. they offer the same bandwidth in both directions. Symmetrical links are widely used in Local Area Networks and in the core of the Internet, but there are many asymmetrical link technologies. The most common example are the various types of ADSL and CATV technologies. Consider an implementation of the Alternating Bit Protocol that is used between two hosts that are directly connected by using an asymmetric link. Assume that a host is sending segments containing 10 bytes of control information and 90 bytes of data and that the acknowledgements are 10 bytes long. If the round-trip-time is negligible, what is the minimum bandwidth required on the return link to ensure that the transmission of acknowledgements is not a bottleneck ?
11. Derive a mathematical expression that provides the *goodput* achieved by the Alternating Bit Protocol assuming that :
    - Each segment contains D bytes of data and c bytes of control information
    - Each acknowledgement contains c bytes of control information
    - The bandwidth of the two directions of the link is set to B bits per second
    - The delay between the two hosts is s seconds in both directions

The *goodput* is defined as the amount of SDUs (measured in bytes) that is successfully transferred during a period of time

12. Consider an Alternating Bit Protocol that is used over a link that suffers from deterministic errors. When the error ratio is set to p, this means that $p - 1$ bits are transmitted correctly and the pth bit is corrupted. Discuss the factors that affect the performance of the Alternating Bit Protocol over such a link.
13. Amazon provides the S3 storage service where companies and researchers can store lots of information and perform computations on the stored information. Amazon allows users to send files through the Internet, but also by sending hard-disks. Assume that a 1 Terabyte hard-disk can be delivered within 24 hours to Amazon by courier service. What is the minimum bandwidth required to match the bandwidth of this courier service
14. Several large data centers operators (e.g. Microsoft and google) have announced that they install servers as containers with each container hosting up to 2000 servers. Assuming a container with 2000 servers and each storing 500 GBytes of data, what is the time required to move all the data stored in one container over one 10 Gbps link ? What is the bandwidth of a truck that needs 10 hours to move one container from one data center to another.
15. What are the techniques used by a go-back-n sender to recover from :
    - transmission errors
    - losses of data segments
    - losses of acknowledgements

16. Consider a b bits per second link between two hosts that has a propagation delay of t seconds. Derive a formula that computes the time elapsed between the transmission of the first bit of a d bytes segment from a sending host and the reception of the last bit of this segment on the receiving host.
17. Consider a go-back-n sender and a go-back receiver that are directly connected with a 10 Mbps link that has a propagation delay of 100 milliseconds. Assume that the retransmission timer is set to three seconds. If the window has a length of 4 segments, draw a time-sequence diagram showing the transmission of 10 segments (each segment contains 10000 bits):
    - when there are no losses
    - when the third and seventh segments are lost
    - when the second, fourth, sixth, eighth,... acknowledgements are lost
    - when the third and fourth data segments are reordered (i.e. the fourth arrives before the third)
18. Same question when using selective repeat instead of go-back-n. Note that the answer is not necessarily the same.
19. Consider two high-end servers connected back-to-back by using a 10 Gbps interface. If the delay between the two servers is one millisecond, what is the throughput that can be achieved by a transport protocol that is using 10,000 bits segments and a window of
    - one segment
    - ten segments
    - hundred segments
20. Consider two servers are directly connected by using a b bits per second link with a round-trip-time of r seconds. The two servers are using a transport protocol that sends segments containing s bytes and acknowledgements composed of a bytes. Can you derive a formula that computes the smallest window (measured in segments) that is required to ensure that the servers will be able to completely utilise the link ?
21. Same question as above if the two servers are connected through an asymmetrical link that transmits bu bits per second in the direction used to send data segments and bd bits per second in the direction used to send acknowledgements.
22. The Trivial File Transfer Protocol is a very simple file transfer protocol that is often used by disk-less hosts when booting from a server. Read the TFTP specification in **RFC 1350** and explain how TFTP recovers from transmission errors and losses.
23. Is it possible for a go-back-n receiver to inter-operate with a selective-repeat sender ? Justify your answer.

24. Is it possible for a selective-repeat receiver to inter-operate with a go-back-n sender ? Justify your answer.
25. The go-back-n and selective repeat mechanisms that are described in the book exclusively rely on cumulative acknowledgements. This implies that a receiver always returns to the sender information about the last segment that was received in-sequence. If there are frequent losses or reordering, a selective repeat receiver could return several times the same cumulative acknowledgment. Can you think of other types of acknowledgements that could be used by a selective repeat receiver to provide additional information about the out-of-sequence segments that it has received. Design such acknowledgements and explain how the sender should react upon reception of this information.
26. The *goodput* achieved by a transport protocol is usually defined as the number of application layer bytes that are exchanged per unit of time. What are the factors that can influence the *goodput* achieved by a given transport protocol ?
27. When used with IPv4, Transmission Control Protocol (TCP) attaches 40 bytes of control information to each segment sent. Assuming an infinite window and no losses nor transmission errors, derive a formula that computes the maximum TCP goodput in function of the size of the segments that are sent.
28. A go-back-n sender uses a window size encoded in a n bits field. How many segments can it send without receiving an acknowledgement ?
29. Consider the following situation. A go-back-n receiver has sent a full window of data segments. All the segments have been received correctly and in-order by the receiver, but all the returned acknowledgements have been lost. Show by using a time sequence diagram (e.g. by considering a window of four segments) what happens in this case. Can you fix the problem on the go-back-n sender ?
30. Same question as above, but assume now that both the sender and the receiver implement selective repeat. Note the the answer will be different from the above question.
31. Consider a transport that supports window of one hundred 1250 Bytes segments. What is the maximum bandwidth that this protocol can achieve if the round-trip-time is set to one second ? What happens if, instead of advertising a window of one hundred segments, the receiver decides to advertise a window of 10 segments ?
32. Explain under which circumstances a transport entity could advertise a window of 0 segments ?
33. To understand the operation of the TCP congestion control mechanism, it is useful to draw some time sequence diagrams. Let us consider a simple scenario of a web client connected to the Internet that wishes to retrieve a simple web page from a remote web server. For simplicity, we will assume that the delay between the client and the server is 0.5 seconds and that the packet transmission

times on the client and the servers are negligible (e.g. they are both connected to a 1 Gbps network). We will also assume that the client and the server use 1 KBytes segments.

   1. Compute the time required to open a TCP connection, send an HTTP request and retrieve a 16 KBytes web page. This page size is typical of the results returned by search engines like **google_** or bing. An important factor in this delay is the initial size of the TCP congestion window on the server. Assume first that the initial window is set to 1 segment as defined in **RFC 2001**, 4 KBytes (i.e. 4 segments in this case) as proposed in **RFC 3390** or 16 KBytes as proposed in a recent paper.
   2. Perform the same analysis with an initial window of one segment is the third segment sent by the server is lost and the retransmission timeout is fixed and set to 2 seconds.
   3. Same question as above but assume now that the 6th segment is lost.
   4. Same question as above, but consider now the loss of the second and seventh acknowledgements sent by the client.
   5. Does the analysis above changes if the initial window is set to 16 KBytes instead of one segment ?

34. Several MBytes have been sent on a TCP connection and it becomes idle for several minutes. Discuss which values should be used for the congestion window, slow start threshold and retransmission timers.
35. To operate reliably, a transport protocol that uses Go-back-n (resp. selective repeat) cannot use a window that is larger than $2^n - 1$ (resp. 2^{n-1}) segments. Does this limitation affects TCP ? Explain your answer.
36. Consider the simple network shown in the figure below. In this network, the router between the client and the server can only store on each outgoing interface one packet in addition to the packet that it is currently transmitting. It discards all the packets that arrive while its buffer is full. Assuming that you can neglect the transmission time of acknowledgements and that the server uses an initial window of one segment and has a retransmission timer set to 500 milliseconds, what is the time required to transmit 10 segments from the client to the server. Does the performance increases if the server uses an initial window of 16 segments instead ?

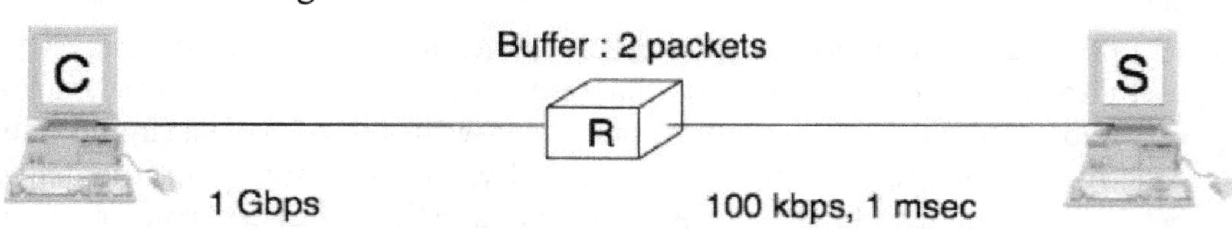

Figure 3.60: Simple network

37. The figure below describes the evolution of the congestion window of a TCP connection. Can you find the reasons for the three events that are marked in the figure ?
38. The figure below describes the evolution of the congestion window of a TCP connection. Can you find the reasons for the three events that are marked in the figure ?

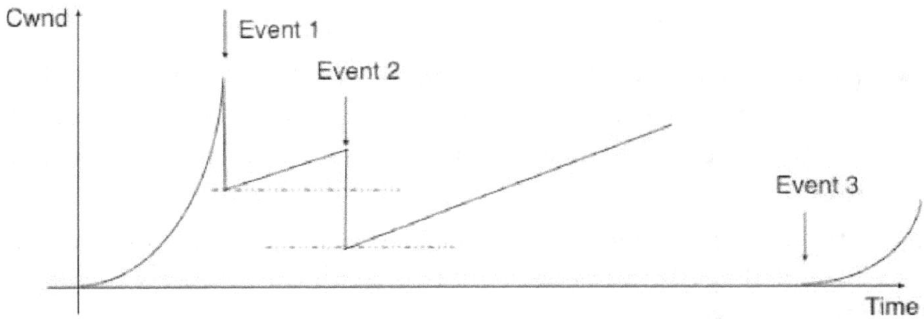

Figure 3.61: Evolution of the congestion window

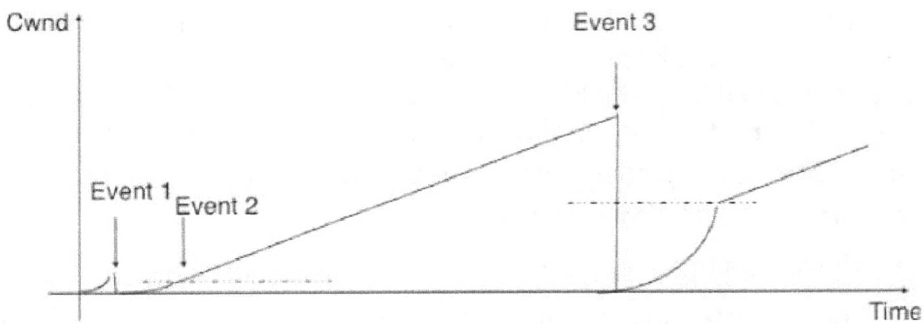

Figure 3.62: Evolution of the congestion window

39. A web server serves mainly HTML pages that fit inside 10 TCP segments. Assuming that the transmission time of each segment can be neglected, compute the total transfer time of such a page (in round-trip-times) assuming that :
    - the TCP stack uses an initial window size of 1 segment
    - the TCP stack uses an initial window size of three segments
40. **RFC 3168** defines mechanism that allow routers to mark packets by setting one bit in the packet header when they are congested. When a TCP destination receives such a marking in a packet, it returns the congestion marking to the source that reacts by halving its congestion window and performs congestion avoidance. Consider a TCP connection where the fourth data segment experiences congestion. Compare the delay to transmit 8 segments in a network where routers discards packets during congestion and a network where routers mark packets during congestion.

3.5.2 Practice

1. The socket interface allows you to use the UDP protocol on a Unix host. UDP provides a connectionless unreliable service that in theory allows you to send SDUs of up to 64 KBytes.
    - Implement a small UDP client and a small UDP server (in python, you can start from the example provided in http://docs.python.org/library/socket.html but you can also use C or java)
    - run the client and the servers on different workstations to determine experimentally the largest SDU that is supported by your language and OS. If possible, use different languages and Operating Systems in each group.
2. By using the socket interface, implement on top of the connectionless unreliable service provided by UDP a simple client that sends the following message shown in the figure below.

    In this message, the bit flags should be set to *01010011b,* the value of the 16 bits field must be the square root of the value contained in the 32 bits field, the character string must be an ASCII representation (without any trailing *0*) of the number contained in the 32 bits character field. The last 16 bits of the message contain an Internet checksum that has been computed over the entire message.

    Upon reception of a message, the server verifies that :
    - the flag has the correct value
    - the 32 bits integer is the square of the 16 bits integer
    - the character string is an ASCII representation of the 32 bits integer
    - the Internet checksum is correct

    If the verification succeeds, the server returns a SDU containing *11111111b.* Otherwise it returns *01010101b*

    Your implementation must be able to run on both low endian and big endian machines. If you have access to different types of machines (e.g. x86 laptops and SPARC servers), try to run your implementation on both types of machines.

```
 0                   1                   2                   3
 0 1 2 3 4 5 6 7 8 9 0 1 2 3 4 5 6 7 8 9 0 1 2 3 4 5 6 7 8 9 0 1
+-+-+-+-+-+-+-+-+-+-+-+-+-+-+-+-+-+-+-+-+-+-+-+-+-+-+-+-+-+-+-+-+
|   Bit flags   |          16 bits field        |      Zero     |
+-+-+-+-+-+-+-+-+-+-+-+-+-+-+-+-+-+-+-+-+-+-+-+-+-+-+-+-+-+-+-+-+
|                        32 bits field                          |
+-+-+-+-+-+-+-+-+-+-+-+-+-+-+-+-+-+-+-+-+-+-+-+-+-+-+-+-+-+-+-+-+
| Type=1        |Len (8 bits)   |   Character string ...        |
+-+-+-+-+-+-+-+-+-+-+-+-+-+-+-+-+-+-+-+-+-+-+-+-+-+-+-+-+-+-+-+-+
|                   Character string (cont.)                    |
+-+-+-+-+-+-+-+-+-+-+-+-+-+-+-+-+-+-+-+-+-+-+-+-+-+-+-+-+-+-+-+-+
|   16 bits Internet checksum   |
+-+-+-+-+-+-+-+-+-+-+-+-+-+-+-+-+
```

Figure 3.63: Simple SDU format

3. The socket library is also used to develop applications above the reliable bytestream service provided by TCP. We have installed on the *cnp3.info.ucl.ac.be* server a simple server that provides a simple client-server service. The service operates as follows :
    - the server listens on port *62141* for a TCP connection
    - upon the establishment of a TCP connection, the server sends an integer by using the following TLV format :
        - the first two bits indicate the type of information (01 for ASCII, 10 for boolean)
        - the next six bits indicate the length of the information (in bytes)
        - An ASCII TLV has a variable length and the next bytes contain one ASCII character per byte. A boolean TLV has a length of one byte. The byte is set to *00000000b* for *true* and *00000001b* for false.
    - the client replies by sending the received integer encoded as a 32 bits integer in *network byte order*
    - the server returns a TLV containing *true* if the integer was correct and a TLV containing *false* otherwise and closes the TCP connection

    Implement a client to interact with this server in C, Java or python.
4. It is now time to implement a small transport protocol. The protocol uses a sliding window to transmit more than one segment without being forced to wait for an acknowledgment. Your implementation must support variable size sliding window as the other end of the flow can send its maximum window size. The window size is encoded as a three bits unsigned integer.

    The protocol identifies the DATA segments by using sequence numbers. The sequence number of the first segment must be 0. It is incremented by one for each new segment. The receiver must acknowledge the delivered segments by sending an ACK segment. The sequence number field in the ACK segment always contains the sequence number of the next expected in-sequence segment at the receiver. The flow of data is unidirectional, meaning that the sender only sends DATA segments and the receiver only sends ACK segments.

    To deal with segments losses, the protocol must implement a recovery technique such as go-back-n or selective repeat and use retransmission timers. You can select the technique that best suite your needs and start from a simple technique that you improve later.

```
 0                   1                   2                   3
 0 1 2 3 4 5 6 7 8 9 0 1 2 3 4 5 6 7 8 9 0 1 2 3 4 5 6 7 8 9 0 1
+-+-+-+-+-+-+-+-+-+-+-+-+-+-+-+-+-+-+-+-+-+-+-+-+-+-+-+-+-+-+-+-+
|   Type    | WIN |    Sequence     |          Length           |
+-+-+-+-+-+-+-+-+-+-+-+-+-+-+-+-+-+-+-+-+-+-+-+-+-+-+-+-+-+-+-+-+
|                                                               |
.                           Payload                             .
.                                                               .
+-+-+-+-+-+-+-+-+-+-+-+-+-+-+-+-+-+-+-+-+-+-+-+-+-+-+-+-+-+-+-+-+
```

Figure 3.64: Segment format

This segment format contains the following fields:

- *Type:* segment type
  - 0x1 DATA segment.
  - 0x2 ACK segment
- *WIN*: the size of the current window (an integer encoded as a 3 bits field). In DATA segments, this field indicates the size of the sending window of the sender. In ACK segments, this field indicates the current value of the receiving window.
- *Sequence:* Sequence number (8 bits unsigned integer), starts at 0. The sequence number is incremented by 1 for each new DATA segment sent by the sender. Inside an ACK segment, the sequence field carries the sequence number of the next in-sequence segment that is expected by the receiver.
- *Length:* length of the payload in multiple of one byte. All DATA segments contain a payload with 512 bytes of data, except the last DATA segment of a transfer that can be shorter. The reception of a DATA segment whose length is different than 512 indicates the end of the data transit.
- *Payload:* the data to send

The client and the server exchange UDP datagrams that contain the DATA and ACK segments. They must provide a command-line interface that allows to transmit one binary file and support the following parameters :
sender <destination_DNS_name> <destination_port_number> <window_size> <input_file> receiver <listening port number> <window_size> <output_file>
In order to test the reactions of your protocol against errors and losses, you you can use a random number generator to probabilistically drop received segments and introduce random delays upon the arrival of a segment.

Packet trace analysis

When debugging networking problems or to analyse performance problems, it is sometimes useful to capture the segments that are exchanged between two hosts and to analyse them.

Several packet trace analysis tools are available, either as commercial or open-source tools. These tools are able to capture all the packets exchanged on a link. Of course, capturing packets require administrator privileges. They can also analyse the content of the captured packets and display information about them. The captured packets can be stored in a file for offline analysis.

tcpdump is probably one of the most well known packet capture software. It is able to both capture packets and display their content. tcpdump is a text-based tool that can display the value of the most important fields of the captured packets. Additional information about tcpdump may be found in *tcpdump(l)*. The text below is an example of the output of tcpdump for the first TCP segments exchanged on an scp transfer between two hosts.

21:05:56.230737 IP 192.168.1.101.54150 > 130.104.78.8.22: S 1385328972:1385328972(0) win 65535 <mss

21:05:56.251468 IP 130.104.78.8.22 > 192.168.1.101.54150: S 3627767479:3627767479(0) ack 1385328973

21:05:56.251560 IP 192.168.1.101.54150 > 130.104.78.8.22: . ack 1 win 65535 <nop,nop,timestamp 274527749

21:05:56.279137 IP 130.104.78.8.22 > 192.168.1.101.54150: P 1:21(20) ack 1 win 49248 <nop,nop,timestamp

21:05:56.279241 IP 192.168.1.101.54150 > 130.104.78.8.22: . ack 21 win 65535 <nop,nop,timestamp 274527749

21:05:56.279534 IP 192.168.1.101.54150 > 130.104.78.8.22: P 1:22(21) ack 21 win 65535 <nop,nop,timestamp

21:05:56.303527 IP 130.104.78.8.22 > 192.168.1.101.54150: . ack 22 win 49248 <nop,nop,timestamp 1212093357

21:05:56.303623 IP 192.168.1.101.54150 > 130.104.78.8.22: P 22:814(792) ack 21 win 65535 <nop,nop,

You can easily recognise in the output above the *SYN* segment containing the *MSS, window scale, timestamp* and *sackOK* options, the *SYN+ACK* segment whose *wscale* option indicates that the server uses window scaling for this connection and then the first few segments exchanged on the connection.

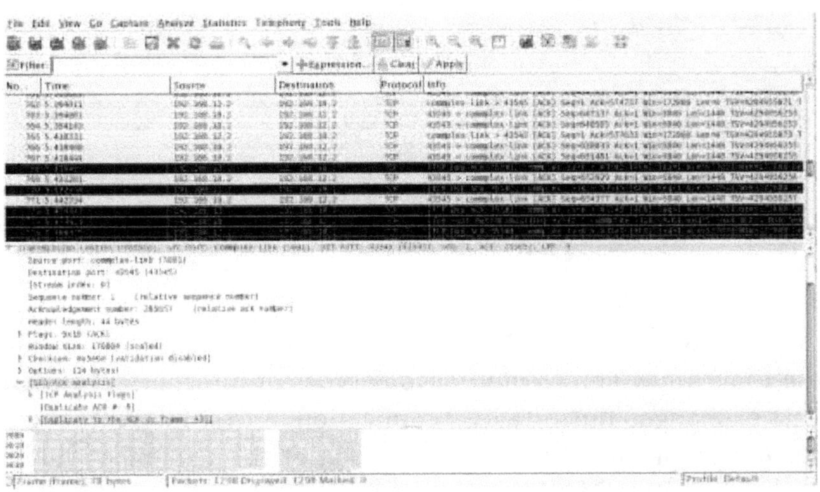

Figure 3.65: Wireshark : default window

wireshark is more recent than tcpdump. It evolved from the ethereal packet trace analysis software. It can be used as a text tool like tcpdump. For a TCP connection, wireshark would provide almost the same output as tcpdump. The main advantage of wireshark is that it also includes a graphical user interface that allows to perform various types of analysis on a packet trace.

The wireshark window is divided in three parts. The top part of the window is a summary of the first packets from the trace. By clicking on one of the lines, you can show the detailed content of this packet in the middle part of the window. The middle of the window allows you to inspect all the fields of the captured packet. The bottom part of the window is the hexadecimal representation of the packet, with the field selected in the middle window being highlighted.

wireshark is very good at displaying packets, but it also contains several analysis tools that can be very useful. The first tool is *Follow TCP stream*. It is part of the *Analyze* menu and allows you to reassemble and display all the payload exchanged during a TCP connection. This tool can be useful if you need to analyse for example the commands exchanged during a SMTP session.

The second tool is the flow graph that is part of the *Statistics* menu. It provides a time sequence diagram of the packets exchanged with some comments about the packet contents. See blow for an example.

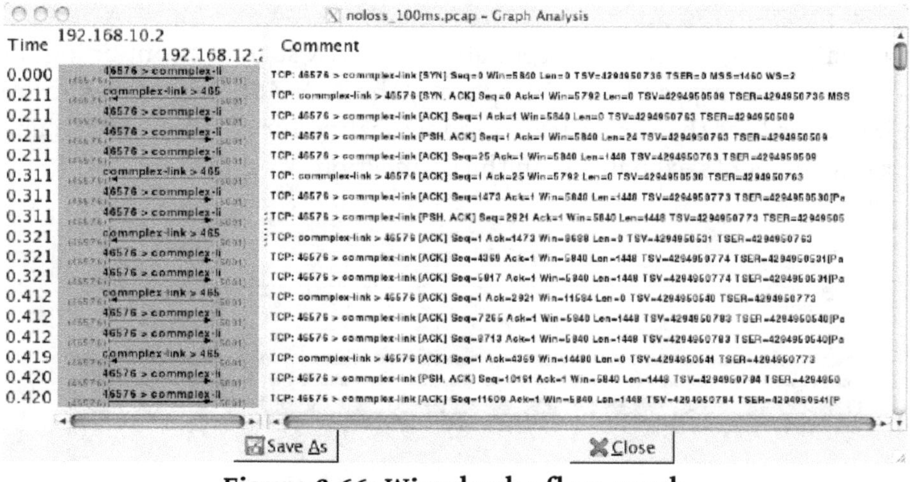

Figure 3.66: Wireshark : flow graph

The third set of tools are the *TCP stream graph* tools that are part of the *Statistics menu*. These tools allow you to plot various types of information extracted from the segments exchanged during a TCP connection. A first interesting graph is the *sequence number graph* that shows the evolution of the sequence number field of the captured segments with time. This graph can be used to detect graphically retransmissions.

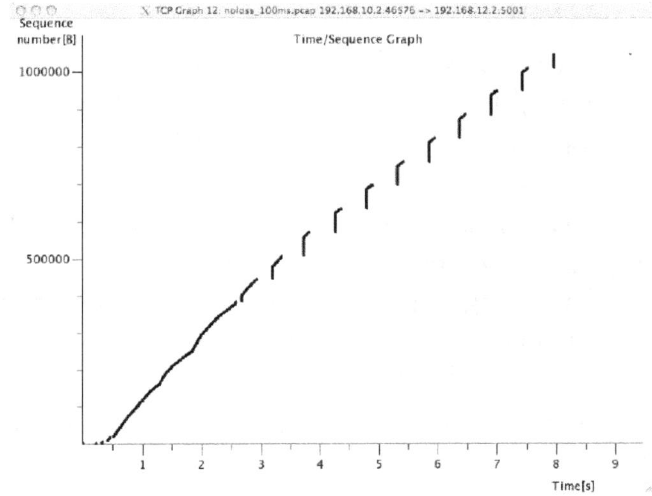

Figure 3.67: Wireshark : sequence number graph

A second interesting graph is the round-trip-time graph that shows the evolution of the round-trip-time in function of time. This graph can be used to check whether the round-trip-time remains stable or not. Note that from a packet trace, wireshark can plot two round-trip-time graphs, One for the flow from the client to the server and the other one. wireshark will plot the round-trip-time graph that corresponds to the selected packet in the top wireshark window.

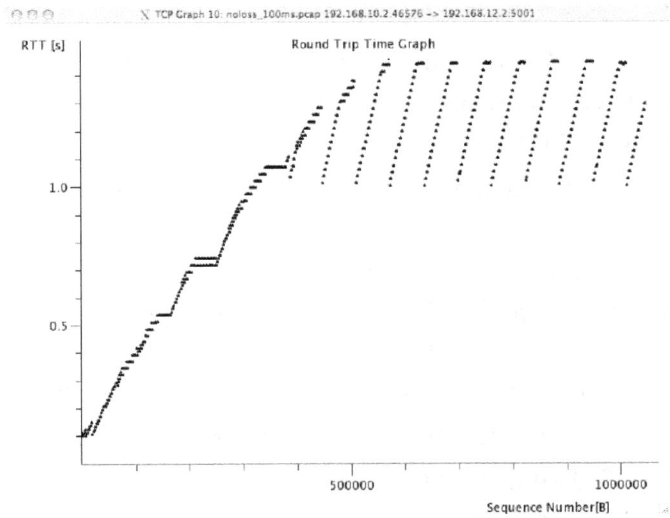

Figure 3.68: Wireshark : round-trip-time graph

Emulating a network with netkit

Netkit is network emulator based on User Mode Linux. machines, that can act as end-host or routers.

Note: Where can I find Netkit?

Netkit is available at http://www.netkit.org. Files can be downloaded from http://wiki.netkit.org/index.php/Download_Official, and instructions for the installations are available here : http://wiki.netkit.org/download/netkit/INSTALL.

There are two ways to use Netkit : The manual way, and by using pre-configured labs. In the first case, you boot and control each machine individually, using the commands starting with a "v" (for virtual machine). In the second case, you can start a whole network in a single operation. The commands for controlling the lab start with a "l". The man pages of those commands is available from http://wiki.netkit.org/man/man7/netkiL7.html

You must be careful not to forgot to stop your virtual machines and labs, using either *vhalt* or *lhalt.*

A netkit lab is simply a directory containing at least a configuration file called *lab.conf,* and one directory for each virtual machine. In the case the lab available on iCampus, the network is composed of two pcs, *pci* and *pc2,* both of them being connected to a router *ri.* The lab.conf file contains the following lines:

pc1[0]=A
pc2[0]=B
r1[0]=A
r1[1]=B

This means that *pci* and *ri* are connected to a "virtual LAN" named *A* via their interface *eth0,* while *pc2* and *ri* are connected to the "virtual LAN" *B* via respectively their interfaces *eth0* and *ethi.*

The directory of each device is initially empty, but will be used by Netkit to store their filesystem.

The lab directory can contain optional files. In the lab provided to you, the "pc1.startup" file contains the shell instructions to be executed on startup of the virtual machine. In this specific case, the script configures the interface *eth0* to allow traffic exchanges between *pci* and *ri,* as well as the routing table entry to join *pc2.*

Starting a lab consists thus simply in unpacking the provided archive, going into the lab directory and typing *lstart* to start the network.

Note: File sharing between virtual machines and host

Virtual machines can access to the directory of the lab they belong to. This repertory is mounted in their filesystem at the path */hostlab.*

In the netkit lab (exercises/netkit/netkit_lab_2hosts_1rtr_ipv4.tar.tar.gz, you can find a simple python client/server application that establishes TCP connections. Feel free to re-use this code to perform your analysis.

Note: netkit tools

As the virtual machines run Linux, standard networking tools such as hping, tcpdump, netstat etc. are available as usual.

Note that capturing network traces can be facilitated by using the *uml_dump* extension available at http://kartoch.msi.unilim.fr/blog/?p=19. This extension is already installed in the Netkit installation on the student lab. In order to capture the traffic exchanged on a given 'virtual LAN', you simply need to issue the command *vdump <LAN name>* on the host. If you want to pipe the trace to wireshark, you can use *vdump A | wireshark -i - -k*

1. A TCP/IP stack receives a SYN segment with the sequence number set to 1234. What will be the value of the acknowledgement number in the returned SYN+ACK segment ?
2. Is it possible for a TCP/IP stack to return a SYN+ACK segment with the acknowledgement number set to *0* ? If no, explain why. If yes, what was the content of the received SYN segment.
3. Open the tcpdump packet trace exercises/traces/trace.5connections_opening_closing.pcap and identify the number of different TCP connections that are established and closed. For each connection, explain by which mechanism they are closed. Analyse the initial sequence numbers that are used in the SYN and SYN+ACK segments. How do these initial sequence numbers evolve ? Are they increased every 4 microseconds ?
4. The tcpdump packet trace exercises/traces/trace.5connections.pcap contains several connection attempts. Can you explain what is happening with these connection attempts ?
5. The tcpdump packet trace exercises/traces/trace.ipv6.google.com.pcap was collected from a popular website that is accessible by using IPv6. Explain the TCP options that are supported by the client and the server.
6. The tcpdump packet trace exercises/traces/trace.sirius.info.ucl.ac.be.pcap Was collected on the departmental server. What are the TCP options supported by this server ?
7. A TCP implementation maintains a Transmission Control Block (TCB) for each TCP connection. This TCB is a data structure that contains the complete "*state*" of each TCP connection. The TCB is described in **RFC 793**. It contains first the identification of the TCP connection :
    - *localip* : the IP address of the local host
    - *remoteip* : the IP address of the remote host
    - *remoteport*: the TCP port used for this connection on the remote host
    - *localport* : the TCP port used for this connection on the local host. Note that when a client opens a TCP connection, the local port will often be

chosen in the ephemeral port range (49152 <= localport <= 65535).

- *sndnxt*: the sequence number of the next byte in the byte stream (the first byte of a new data segment that you send will use this sequence number)
- *snduna* : the earliest sequence number that has been sent but has not yet been acknowledged
- *rcvnxt* : the sequence number of the next byte that your implementation expects to receive from the remote host. For this exercise, you do not need to maintain a receive buffer and your implementation can discard the out-of-sequence segments that it receives
- *sndwnd* : the current sending window
- *rcvwnd* : the current window advertised by the receiver

Using the exercises/traces/trace.sirius.info.ucl.ac.be.pcap packet trace, what is the TCB of the connection on host *130.104.78.8* when it sends the third segment of the trace ?

8. The tcpdump packet trace exercises/traces/trace.maps.google.com was collected by containing a popular web site that provides mapping information. How many TCP connections were used to retrieve the information from this server ?
9. Some network monitoring tools such as ntop collect all the TCP segments sent and received by a host or a group of hosts and provide interesting statistics such as the number of TCP connections, the number of bytes exchanged over each TCP connection, ... Assuming that you can capture all the TCP segments sent by a host, propose the pseudo-code of an application that would list all the TCP connections established and accepted by this host and the number of bytes exchanged over each connection. Do you need to count the number of bytes contained inside each segment to report the number of bytes exchanged over each TCP connection ?
10. There are two types of firewal: special devices that are placed at the border of campus or enterprise networks and software that runs on endhosts. Software firewalls typically analyse all the packets that are received by a host and decide based on the packet's header and contents whether it can be processed by the host's network stack or must be discarded. System administrators often configure firewalls on laptop or student machines to prevent students from installing servers on their machines. How would you design a simple firewall that blocks all incoming TCP connections but still allows the host to establish TCP connections to any remote server ?
11. Using the netkit lab explained above, perform some tests by using *hping3(8)*. *hping3(8)* is a command line tool that allows anyone (having system administrator privileges) to send special IP packets and TCP segments. *hping3(8)* can be used

to verify the configuration of firewalls[33] or diagnose problems. We will use it to test the operation of the Linux TCP stack running inside netkit.

1. On the server host, launch *tcpdump(l)* with *-vv* as parameter to collect all packets received from the client and display them. Using *hping3(8)* on the client host, send a valid SYN segment to one unused port on the server host (e.g. *12345*). What are the contents of the segment returned by the server ?

2. Perform the same experiment, but now send a SYN segment towards port 7. This port is the default port for the discard service (see *services(5)*) launched by *xinetd(8)*). What segment does the server sends in reply ? What happens upon reception of this segment ? Explain your answer.

12. The Linux TCP/IP stack can be easily configured by using *sysctl(8)* to change kernel configuration variables. See http://fasterdata.es.net/TCP-tuning/ip-sysctl-2.6.txt for a recent list of the sysctl variables on the Linux TCP/IP stack. Try to disable the selective acknowledgements and the RFC1323 timestamp and large window options and open a TCP connection on port 7 on the server by using :manpage:telnet'(1)'. Check by using *tcpdump(l)* the effect of these kernel variables on the segments sent by the Linux stack in netkit.
13. Network administrators sometimes need to verify which networking daemons are active on a server. When logged on the server, several tools can be used to verify this. A first solution is to use the *netstat(8)* command. This command allows you to extract various statistics from the networking stack on the Linux kernel. For TCP, *netstat* can list all the active TCP connections with the state of their FSM. *netstat* supports the following options that could be useful during this exercises :

   - *-t* requests information about the TCP connections
   - -n requests numeric output (by default, *netstat* sends DNS queries to resolve IP addresses in hosts and uses */etc/services* to convert port number in service names, -n is recommended on netkit machines)
   - *-e* provides more information about the state of the TCP connections
   - *-o* provides information about the timers
   - *-a* provides information about all TCP connections, not only those in the Established state

   On the netkit lab, launch a daemon and start a TCP connection by using *telnet(l)* and use *netstat(8)* to verify the state of these connections.

   A second solution to determine which network daemons are running on a server is to use a tool like *nmap(l)*. *nmap(l)* can be run remotely and thus can provide information about a host on which the system administrator cannot login. Use *tcpdump(l)* to collect the segments sent by *nmap(l)* running on the client and explain how *nmap(l)* operates.

14. Long lived TCP connections are susceptible to the so-called *RST attacks.* Try to find additional information about this attack and explain how a TCP stack could mitigate such attacks.
15. For the exercises below, we have performed measurements in an emulated network similar to the one shown below.

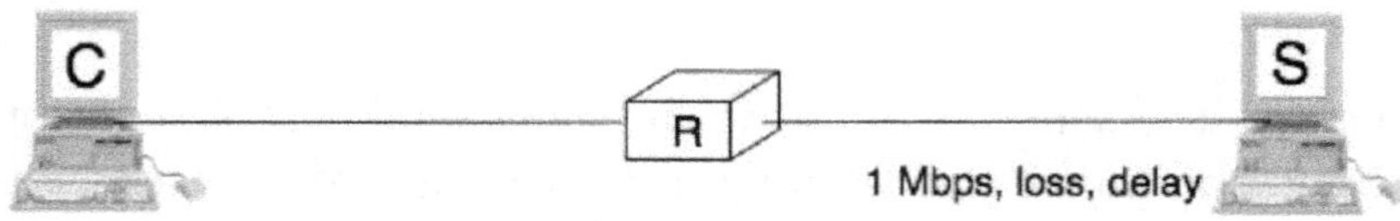

Figure 3.69: Emulated network

The emulated network is composed of three UML machines: a client, a server and a router. The client and the server are connected via the router. The client sends data to the server. The link between the router and the client is controlled by using the netem Linux kernel module. This module allows us to insert additional delays, reduce the link bandwidth and insert random packet losses.

We used netem to collect several traces:

- exercises/traces/trace0.pcap
- exercises/traces/trace1.pcap
- exercises/traces/trace2.pcap
- exercises/traces/trace3.pcap

Using wireshark or tcpdump, carry out the following analyses:

- Identify the TCP options that have been used on the TCP connection
- Try to find explanations for the evolution of the round-trip-time on each of these TCP connections. For this, you can use the *round-trip-time* graph of wireshark, but be careful with their estimation as some versions of wireshark are buggy
- Verify whether the TCP implementation used implemented *delayed acknowledgements*
- Inside each packet trace, find :
  - one segment that has been retransmitted by using *fast retransmit.* Explain this retransmission in details.
  - one segment that has been retransmitted thanks to the expiration of TCP's retransmission timeout. Explain why this segment could not have been retransmitted by using *fast retransmit.*
  - wireshark contains several two useful graphs: the *round-trip-time* graph and the *time sequence* graph. Explain how you would compute the same graph from such a trace .

  - When displaying TCP segments, recent versions of wireshark contain *expert analysis* heuristics that indicate whether the segment has been retransmitted, whether it is a duplicate ack or whether the retransmission timeout has expired. Explain how you would implement the same heuristics as wireshark.
- Can you find which file has been exchanged during the transfer ?

16. You have been hired as an networking expert by a company. In this company, users of a networked application complain that the network is very slow. The developers of the application argue that any delays are caused by packet losses and a buggy network. The network administrator argues that the network works perfectly and that the delays perceived by the users are caused by the applications or the servers where the application is running. To resolve the case and determine whether the problem is due to the network or the server on which the application is running. The network administrator has collected a representative packet trace that you can download from exercises/traces/trace9.pcap. By looking at the trace, can you resolve this case and indicate whether the network or the application is the culprit ?

CHAPTER

The Network Layer

4

The transport layer enables the applications to efficiently and reliably exchange data. Transport layer entities expect to be able to send segment to any destination without having to understand anything about the underlying subnetwork technologies. Many subnetwork technologies exist. Most of them differ in subtle details (frame size, addressing, ...). The network layer is the glue between these subnetworks and the transport layer. It hides to the transport layer all the complexity of the underlying subnetworks and ensures that information can be exchanged between hosts connected to different types of subnetworks.

In this chapter, we first explain the principles of the network layer. These principles include the datagram and virtual circuit modes, the separation between the data plane and the control plane and the algorithms used by routing protocols. Then, we explain, in more detail, the network layer in the Internet, starting with IPv4 and IPv6 and then moving to the routing protocols (RIP, OSPF and BGP).

4.1 PRINCIPLES

The main objective of the network layer is to allow endsystems, connected to different networks, to exchange information through intermediate systems called *router*. The unit of information in the network layer is called a *packet*.

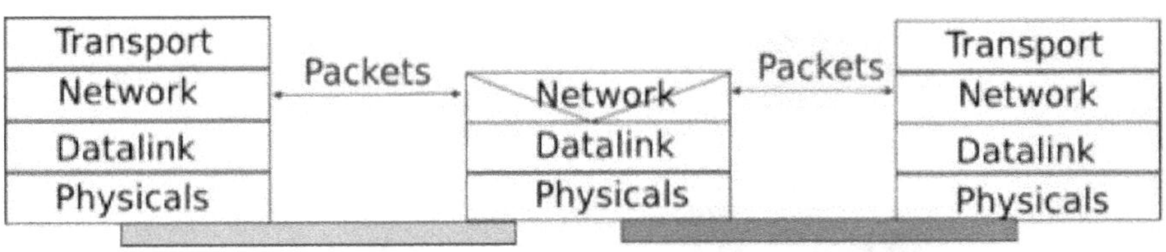

Figure 4.1: The network layer in the reference model

Before explaining the network layer in detail, it is useful to begin by analysing the service provided by the *datalink* layer. There are many variants of the datalink layer. Some provide a connection-oriented service while others provide a connectionless service. In this section, we focus on connectionless datalink layer services as they are the most widely used. Using a connection-oriented datalink layer causes some problems that are beyond the scope of this chapter. See **RFC 3819** for a discussion on this topic.

There are three main types of datalink layers. The simplest datalink layer is when there are only two communicating systems that are directly connected through the physical layer. Such a datalink layer is used when there is a point-to-point link between the two communicating systems. The two systems can be endsystems or routers. PPP (Point-to-Point Protocol), defined in **RFC 1661**, is an example of such a point-to-point datalink layer. Datalink layers exchange *frames* and a datalink *frame* sent by a datalink layer entity on the left is transmitted through the physical layer, so that it can reach the datalink layer entity on the right. Point-to-point datalink layers can either provide an unreliable service (frames can be corrupted or lost) or a reliable service (in this case, the datalink layer includes retransmission mechanisms similar to the ones used in the transport layer). The unreliable service is frequently used above physical layers (e.g. optical fiber, twisted pairs) having a low bit error ratio while reliability mechanisms are often used in wireless networks to recover locally from transmission errors.

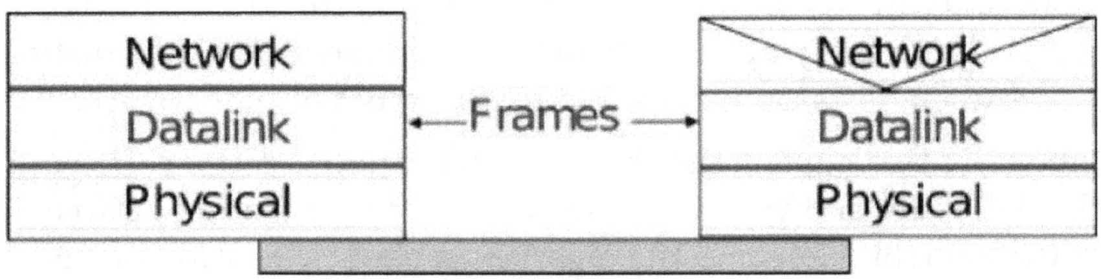

Figure 4.2: The point-to-point datalink layer

The second type of datalink layer is the one used in Local Area Networks (LAN). Conceptually, a LAN is a set of communicating devices such that any two devices can directly exchange frames through the datalink layer. Both endsystems and routers can be connected to a LAN. Some LANs only connect a few devices, but there are LANs that can connect hundreds or even thousands of devices.

Figure 4.3: A local area network

In the next chapter, we describe the organisation and the operation of Local Area Networks. An important difference between the point-to-point datalink layers and the datalink layers used in LANs is that in a LAN, each communicating device is identified by a unique *datalink layer address.* This address is usually embedded in the hardware of the device and different types of LANs use different types of datalink layer addresses. A communicating device attached to a LAN can send a datalink frame to any other communicating device that is attached to the same LAN. Most LANs also support special broadcast and multicast datalink layer addresses. A frame sent to the broadcast address of the LAN is delivered to all communicating devices that are attached to the LAN. The multicast addresses are used to identify groups of communicating devices. When a frame is sent towards a multicast datalink layer address, it is delivered by the LAN to all communicating devices that belong to the corresponding group.

The third type of datalink layers are used in Non-Broadcast Multi-Access (NBMA) networks. These networks are used to interconnect devices like a LAN. All devices attached to an NBMA network are identified by a unique datalink layer address. However, and this is the main difference between an NBMA network and a traditional LAN, the NBMA service only supports unicast. The datalink layer service provided by an NBMA network supports neither broadcast nor multicast.

Unfortunately no datalink layer is able to send frames of unlimited side. Each datalink layer is characterised by a maximum frame size. There are more than a dozen different datalink layers and unfortunately most of them use a different maximum frame size. The network layer must cope with the heterogeneity of the datalink layer.

The network layer itself relies on the following principles :

1. Each network layer entity is identified by a *network layer address.* This address is independent of the datalink layer addresses that it may use.
2. The service provided by the network layer does not depend on the service or the internal organisation of the underlying datalink layers.
3. The network layer is conceptually divided into two planes: the *data plane* and the *control plane.* The *data plane* contains the protocols and mechanisms that allow hosts and routers to exchange packets carrying user data. The *control plane* contains the protocols and mechanisms that enable routers to efficiently learn how to forward packets towards their final destination.

The independence of the network layer from the underlying datalink layer is a key principle of the network layer. It ensures that the network layer can be used to allow hosts attached to different types of datalink layers to exchange packets through intermediate routers. Furthermore, this allows the datalink layers and the network layer to evolve independently from each other. This enables the network layer to be easily adapted to a new datalink layer every time a new datalink layer is invented.

There are two types of service that can be provided by the network layer :

- an *unreliable connectionless* service
- a *connection-oriented,* reliable or unreliable, service

Connection-oriented services have been popular with technologies such as *X.25* and *ATM* or *frame-relay,* but nowadays most networks use an *unreliable connectionless* service. This is our main focus in this chapter.

4.1.1 Organisation of the network layer

There are two possible internal organisations of the network layer :

- datagram
- virtual circuits

The internal organisation of the network is orthogonal to the service that it provides, but most of the time a datagram organisation is used to provide a connectionless service while a virtual circuit organisation is used in networks that provide a connection-oriented service.

Datagram organisation

The first and most popular organisation of the network layer is the datagram organisation. This organisation is inspired by the organisation of the postal service. Each host is identified by a *network layer address.* To send information to a remote host, a host creates a packet that contains :

- the network layer address of the destination host
- its own network layer address
- the information to be sent

The network layer limits the maximum packet size. Thus, the information must have been divided in packets by the transport layer before being passed to the network layer.

To understand the datagram organisation, let us consider the figure below. A network layer address, represented by a letter, has been assigned to each host and router. To send some information to host *J*, host *A* creates a packet containing its own address, the destination address and the information to be exchanged.

With the datagram organisation, routers use *hop-by-hop forwarding.* This means that when a router receives a packet that is not destined to itself, it looks up the destination address of the packet in its *routing table.* A *routing table* is a data structure that maps each destination address (or set of destination addresses) to the outgoing interface over which a packet destined to this address must be forwarded to reach its final destination.

The main constraint imposed on the routing tables is that they must allow any host in the network to reach any other host. This implies that each router must know a route towards each destination, but also that the paths composed from the information stored in the routing tables must not contain loops. Otherwise, some destinations would be unreachable.

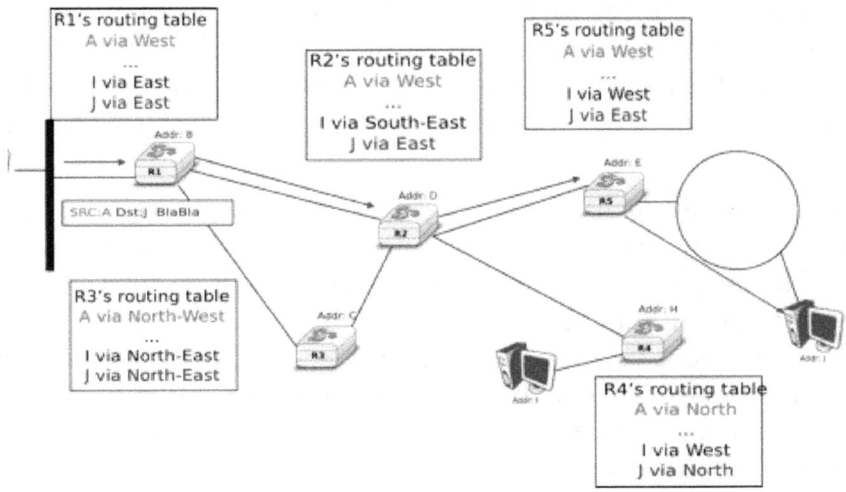

Figure 4.4: A simple internetwork

In the example above, host *A* sends its packet to router *R1*. *R1* consults its routing table and forwards the packet towards R2. Based on its own routing table, R2 decides to forward the packet to R5 that can deliver it to its destination.

To allow hosts to exchange packets, a network relies on two different types of protocols and mechanisms. First, there must be a precise definition of the format of the packets that are sent by hosts and processed by routers. Second, the algorithm used by the routers to forward these packets must be defined. This protocol and this algorithm are part of the *data plane* of the network layer. The *data plane* contains all the protocols and algorithms that are used by hosts and routers to create and process the packets that contain user data.

The *data plane*, and in particular the forwarding algorithm used by the routers, depends on the routing tables that are maintained on reach router. These routing tables can be maintained by using various techniques (manual configuration, distributed protocols, centralised computation, etc). These techniques are part of the *control plane* of the network layer. The *control plane* contains all the protocols and mechanisms that are used to compute and install routing tables on the routers.

The datagram organisation has been very popular in computer networks. Datagram based network layers include IPv4 and IPv6 in the global Internet, CLNP defined by the ISO, IPX defined by Novell or XNS defined by Xerox [Perlman2000].

Virtual circuit organisation

The main advantage of the datagram organisation is its simplicity. The principles of this organisation can easily be understood. Furthermore, it allows a host to easily send a packet towards any destination at any time. However, as each packet is forwarded independently by intermediate routers, packets sent by a host may not follow the same path to reach a given destination. This may cause packet reordering, which may be annoying for transport protocols. Furthermore, as a router using *hop-by-hop forwarding* always forwards packets sent towards the same destination over the same outgoing interface, this may cause congestion over some links.

The second organisation of the network layer, called *virtual circuits,* has been inspired by the organisation of telephone networks. Telephone networks have been designed to carry phone calls that usually last a few minutes. Each phone is identified by a telephone number and is attached to a telephone switch. To initiate a phone call, a telephone first needs to send the destination's phone number to its local switch. The switch cooperates with the other switches in the network to create a bi-directional channel between the two telephones through the network. This channel will be used by the two telephones during the lifetime of the call and will be released at the end of the call. Until the 1960s, most of these channels were created manually, by telephone operators, upon request of the caller. Today's telephone networks use automated switches and allow several channels to be carried over the same physical link, but the principles remain roughly the same.

In a network using virtual circuits, all hosts are identified with a network layer address. However, a host must explicitly request the establishment of a *virtual circuit* before being able to send packets to a destination host. The request to establish a virtual circuit is processed by the *control plane,* which installs state to create the virtual circuit between the source and the destination through intermediate routers. All the packets that are sent on the virtual circuit contain a virtual circuit identifier that allows the routers to determine to which virtual circuit each packet belongs. This is illustrated in the figure below with one virtual circuit between host *A* and host *I* and another one between host *A* and host *J*.

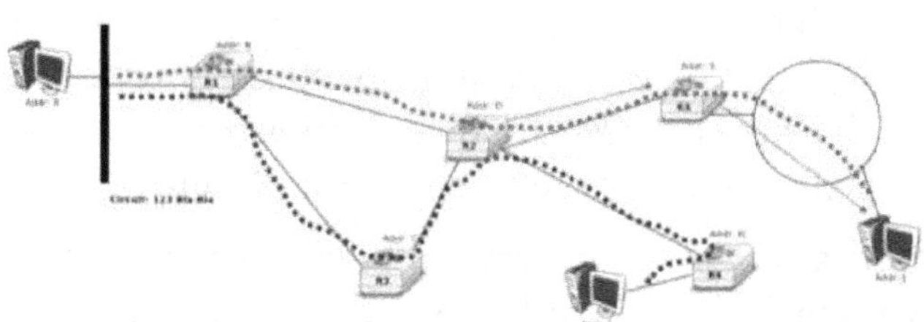

Figure 4.5: A simple internetwork using virtual-circuits

The establishment of a virtual circuit is performed using a *signalling protocol* in the *control plane.* Usually, the source host sends a signalling message to indicate to its router the address of the destination and possibly some performance characteristics of the virtual circuit to be established. The first router can process the signalling message in two different ways.

A first solution is for the router to consult its routing table, remember the characteristics of the requested virtual circuit and forward it over its outgoing interface towards the destination. The signalling message is thus forwarded hop-by-hop until it reaches the destination and the virtual circuit is opened along the path followed by the signalling message. This is illustrated with the red virtual circuit in the figure below.

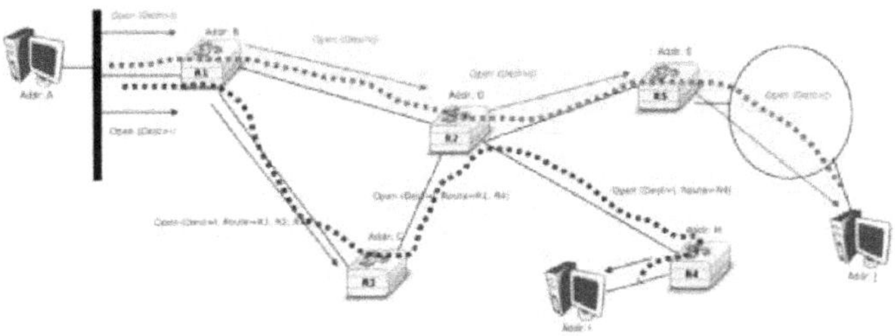

Figure 4.6: Virtual circuit establishment

A second solution can be used if the routers know the entire topology of the network. In this case, the first router can use a technique called *source routing.* Upon reception of the signalling message, the first router chooses the path of the virtual circuit in the network. This path is encoded as the list of the addresses of all intermediate routers to reach the destination. It is included in the signalling message and intermediate routers can remove their address from the signalling message before forwarding it. This technique enables routers to spread the virtual circuits throughout the network better. If the routers know the load of remote links, they can also select the least loaded path when establishing a virtual circuit. This solution is illustrated with the blue circuit in the figure above.

The last point to be discussed about the virtual circuit organisation is its *data plane.* The *data plane* mainly defines the format of the data packets and the algorithm used by routers to forward packets. The data packets contain a virtual circuit identifier, encoded as a fixed number of bits. These virtual circuit identifiers are usually called *labels.*

Each host maintains a flow table that associates a label with each virtual circuit that is has established. When a router receives a packet containing a label, it extracts the label and consults its *label forwarding table.* This table is a data structure that maps each couple *(incoming interface, label)* to the outgoing interface to be used to forward the packet as well as the label that must be placed in the outgoing packets. In practice, the label forwarding table can be implemented as a vector and the couple *(incoming interface, label)* is the index of the entry in the vector that contains the outgoing interface and the outgoing label. Thus a single memory access is sufficient to consult the label forwarding table. The utilisation of the label forwarding table is illustrated in the figure below.

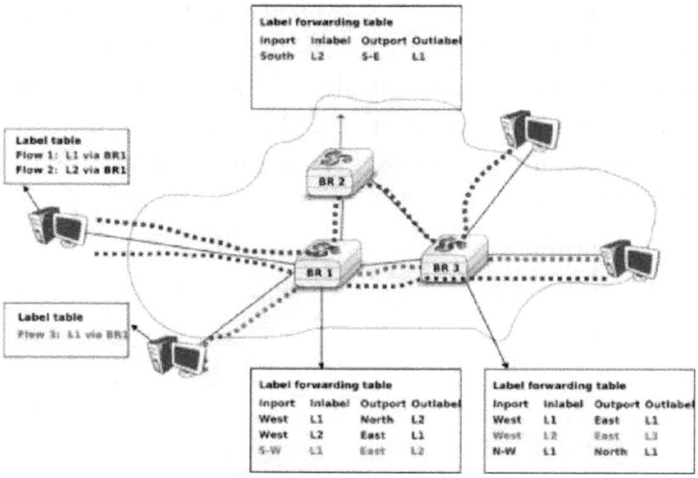

Figure 4.7: Label forwarding tables in a network using virtual circuits

The virtual circuit organisation has been mainly used in public networks, starting from X.25 and then Frame Relay and Asynchronous Transfer Mode (ATM) network.

Both the datagram and virtual circuit organisations have advantages and drawbacks. The main advantage of the datagram organisation is that hosts can easily send packets to any number of destinations while the virtual circuit organisation requires the establishment of a virtual circuit before the transmission of a data packet. This solution can be costly for hosts that exchange small amounts of data. On the other hand, the main advantage of the virtual circuit organisation is that the forwarding algorithm used by routers is simpler than when using the datagram organisation. Furthermore, the utilisation of virtual circuits may allow the load to be better spread through the network thanks to the utilisation of multiple virtual circuits. The MultiProtocol Label Switching (MPLS) technique that we will discuss in another revision of this book can be considered as a good compromise between datagram and virtual circuits. MPLS uses virtual circuits between routers, but does not extend them to the endhosts. Additional information about MPLS may be found in [ML2011].

4.1.2 The control plane

One of the objectives of the *control plane* in the network layer is to maintain the routing tables that are used on all routers. As indicated earlier, a routing table is a data structure that contains, for each destination address (or block of addresses) known by the router, the outgoing interface over which the router must forward a packet destined to this address. The routing table may also contain additional information such as the address of the next router on the path towards the destination or an estimation of the cost of this path.

In this section, we discuss the three main techniques that can be used to maintain the routing tables in a network.

Static routing

The simplest solution is to pre-compute all the routing tables of all routers and to install them on each router. Several algorithms can be used to compute these tables.

A simple solution is to use shortest path routing and to minimise the number of intermediate routers to reach each destination. More complex algorithms can take into account the expected load on the links to ensure that congestion does not occur for a given traffic demand. These algorithms must all ensure that:

- all routers are configured with a route to reach each destination
- none of the paths composed with the entries found in the routing tables contain a cycle. Such a cycle would lead to a forwarding loop.

The figure below shows sample routing tables in a five routers network.

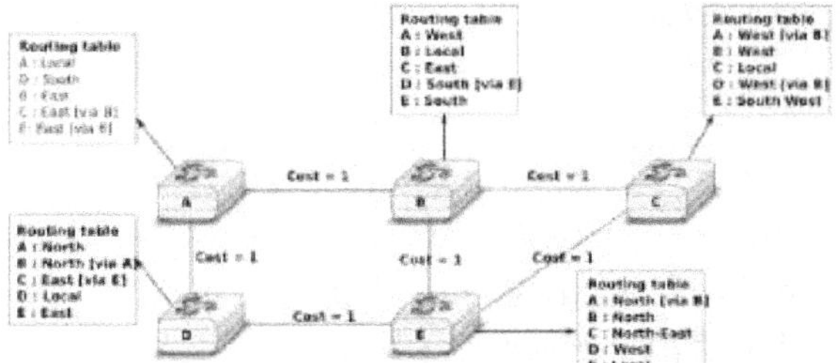

Figure 4.8: Routing tables in a simple network

The main drawback of static routing is that it does not adapt to the evolution of the network. When a new router or link is added, all routing tables must be recomputed. Furthermore, when a link or router fails, the routing tables must be updated as well.

Distance vector routing

Distance vector routing is a simple distributed routing protocol. Distance vector routing allows routers to automatically discover the destinations reachable inside the network as well as the shortest path to reach each of these destinations. The shortest path is computed based on *metrics* or *costs* that are associated to each link. We use *l.cost* to represent the metric that has been configured for link *l* on a router.

Each router maintains a routing table. The routing table *R* can be modelled as a data structure that stores, for each known destination address *d*, the following attributes:

- *R[d].link* is the outgoing link that the router uses to forward packets towards destination d
- *R[d].cost* is the sum of the metrics of the links that compose the shortest path to reach destination *d*
- *R[d].time* is the timestamp of the last distance vector containing destination *d*

A router that uses distance vector routing regularly sends its distance vector over all its interfaces. The distance vector is a summary of the router's routing table that indicates the distance towards each known destination. This distance vector can be computed from the routing table by using the pseudo-code below.

```
Every N seconds:
v=Vector()
for d in R[]:
# add destination d to vector
v.add(Pair(d,R[d].cost))
for i in interfaces
# send vector v on this interface
send(v,interface)
```

When a router boots, it does not know any destination in the network and its routing table only contains itself. It thus sends to all its neighbours a distance vector that contains only its address at a distance of *0*. When a router receives a distance vector on link l, it processes it as follows.

```
# V : received Vector
# l : link over which vector is received
def received(V,l):
# received vector from link l
for d in V[]
if not (d in R[]) :
# new route
R[d].cost=V[d].cost+l.cost
R[d].link=l
R[d].time=now
else :
# existing route, is the new better ?
```

```
if ( ((V[d].cost+l.cost) < R[d].cost) or ( R[d].link == l) )   :
# Better route or change to current route
R[d].cost=V[d].cost+l.cost
R[d].link=l
R[d].time=now
```

The router iterates over all addresses included in the distance vector. If the distance vector contains an address that the router does not know, it inserts the destination inside its routing table via link *l* and at a distance which is the sum between the distance indicated in the distance vector and the cost associated to link l. If the destination was already known by the router, it only updates the corresponding entry in its routing table if either :

- the cost of the new route is smaller than the cost of the already known route *((V[d].cost+l.cost) < R[d].cost)*
- the new route was learned over the same link as the current best route towards this destination *(R[d].link = =l)*

The first condition ensures that the router discovers the shortest path towards each destination. The second condition is used to take into account the changes of routes that may occur after a link failure or a change of the metric associated to a link.

To understand the operation of a distance vector protocol, let us consider the network of five routers shown below.

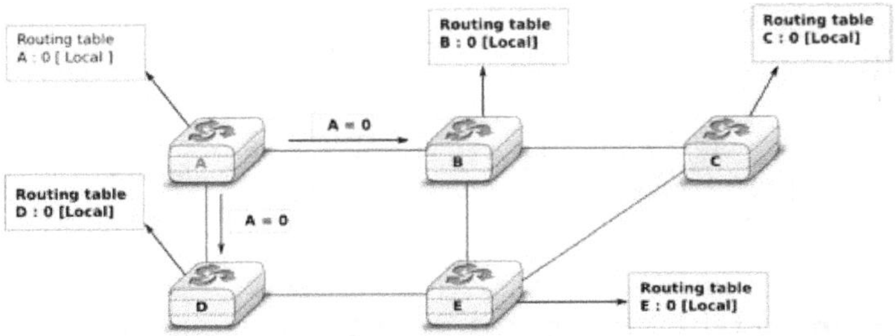

Figure 4.9: Operation of distance vector routing in a simple network

Assume that *A* is the first to send its distance vector *[A=0]*.

- *B* and *D* process the received distance vector and update their routing table with a route towards A.
- *D* sends its distance vector *[D=0,A=1]* to *A* and E. *E* can now reach *A* and D.
- *C* sends its distance vector *[C=0]* to B and *E*
- *E* sends its distance vector *[E=0,D=1,A=2,C=2]* to D, *B* and C. *B* can now reach A, C, *D* and *E*

- *B* sends its distance vector *[B=0,A=1,C=1,D=2,E=1]* to A, *C* and E. A, B, *C* and *E* can now reach all destinations.
- *A* sends its distance vector *[A=0,B=1,C=2,D=1,E=2]* to *B* and D.

At this point, all routers can reach all other routers in the network thanks to the routing tables shown in the figure below.

To deal with link and router failures, routers use the timestamp stored in their routing table. As all routers send their distance vector every *N* seconds, the timestamp of each route should be regularly refreshed. Thus no route should have a timestamp older than *N* seconds, unless the route is not reachable anymore. In practice, to cope with the possible loss of a distance vector due to transmission errors, routers check the timestamp of the routes stored in their routing table every *N* seconds and remove the routes that are older than 3 x *N* seconds. When a router notices that a route towards a destination has expired, it must first associate an to cost to this route and send its distance vector to its neighbours to inform them. The route can then be removed from the routing table after some time (e.g. 3 x *N* seconds), to ensure that the neighbouring routers have received the bad news, even if some distance vectors do not reach them due to transmission errors.

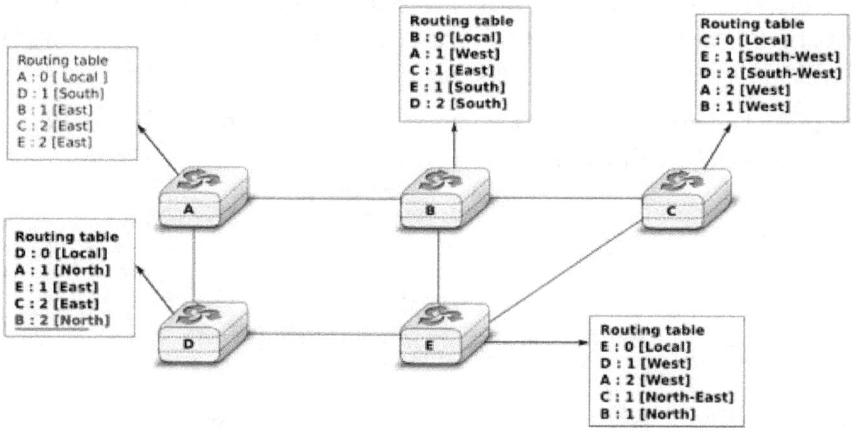

Figure 4.10: Routing tables computed by distance vector in a simple network

Consider the example above and assume that the link between routers *A* and *B* fails. Before the failure, *A* used *B* to reach destinations B, C and *E* while B only used the A-B link to reach A. The affected entries timeout on routers A and B and they both send their distance vector.

- A sends its distance vector [A = 0, *D* = rc, C = rc, D = 1, *E* = rc]. *D* knows that it cannot reach B anymore via A
- D sends its distance vector [D = 0,*B* = rc, A = 1, C = 2, E =1] to A and E. A recovers routes towards C and E via D.

- B sends its distance vector [B = 0, A = rc, C = 1, D = 2, E =1] to E and C. D learns that there is no route anymore to reach A via B.
- E sends its distance vector [E = 0,A = 2, C = 1, D = 1, B = 1] to D, B and C. D learns a route towards B. C and B learn a route towards A.

At this point, all routers have a routing table allowing them to reach all another routers, except router A, which cannot yet reach router B. A recovers the route towards B once router D sends its updated distance vector [A = 1, B = 2, C = 2, D = 1, E =1]. This last step is illustrated in figure *Routing tables computed by distance vector after a failure,* which shows the routing tables on all routers.

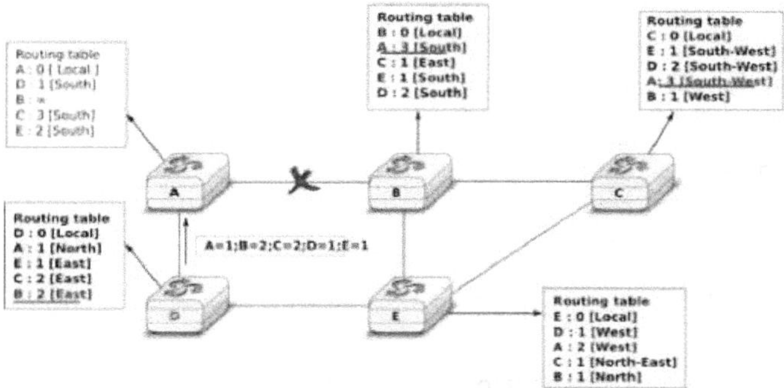

Figure 4.11: Routing tables computed by distance vector after a failure

Consider now that the link between *D* and *E* fails. The network is now partitioned into two disjoint parts : *(A , D)* and *(B, E, C)*. The routes towards *B, C* and *E* expire first on router *D*. At this time, router *D* updates its routing table.

If *D* sends [D = 0,A = 1,B = rc, C = rc, E = rc], *A* learns that B, *C* and *E* are unreachable and updates its routing table.

Unfortunately, if the distance vector sent to *A* is lost or if *A* sends its own distance vector ([A = 0, D = 1,B = 3, C = 3, E = 2]) at the same time as *D* sends its distance vector, *D* updates its routing table to use the shorter routes advertised by *A* towards *B, C* and *E.* After some time *D* sends a new distance vector : [*D* = 0, A = 1,*E* = 3, *C* = 4, *B* = 4]. A updates its routing table and after some time sends its own distance vector [A = 0, D = 1, B = 5, C = 5, E = 4], etc. This problem is known as the *count to infinity problem* in networking literature. Routers *A* and *D* exchange distance vectors with increasing costs until these costs reach to. This problem may occur in other scenarios than the one depicted in the above figure. In fact, distance vector routing may suffer from count to infinity problems as soon as there is a cycle in the network. Cycles are necessary to have enough redundancy to deal with link and router failures. To mitigate the impact of counting to infinity, some distance vector protocols consider that 16 = to. Unfortunately, this limits the metrics that network operators can use and the diameter of the networks using distance vectors.

This count to infinity problem occurs because router *A* advertises to router *D* a route that it has learned via router *D*. A possible solution to avoid this problem could be to change how a router creates its distance vector. Instead of computing one distance vector and sending it to all its neighbors, a router could create a distance vector that is specific to each neighbour and only contains the routes that have not been learned via this neighbour. This could be implemented by the following pseudocode.

```
Every N seconds:
# one vector for each interface
for l in interfaces:
v=Vector()
for d in R[]:
if (R[d].link != i) :
v=v+Pair(d,R[d.cost])
send(v)
end for d in R[]
#end for l in interfaces
```

This technique is called *split-horizon*. With this technique, the count to infinity problem would not have happened in the above scenario, as router *A* would have advertised [A = 0], since it learned all its other routes via router D. Another variant called *split-horizon with poison reverse* is also possible. Routers using this variant advertise a cost of to for the destinations that they reach via the router to which they send the distance vector. This can be implemented by using the pseudo-code below.

```
Every N seconds:
for l in interfaces:
one vector for each interface
v=Vector()
for d in R[]:
if (R[d].link != i) :
v=v+Pair(d,R[d.cost])
else:
v=v+Pair(d,infinity);
send(v)
end for d in R[]
#end for l in interfaces
```

Unfortunately, split-horizon, is not sufficient to avoid all count to infinity problems with distance vector routing. Consider the failure of link *A-B* in the network of four routers below.

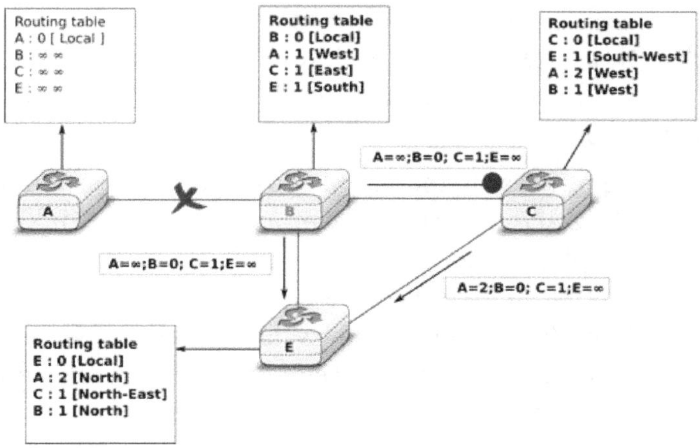

Figure 4.12: Count to infinity problem

After having detected the failure, router *A* sends its distance vectors:

- [A = ∞, B = 0,*C* = ∞, *E* =1] to router C
- [A = ∞, B = 0, C = 1, E = ∞] to router *E*

If, unfortunately, the distance vector sent to router C is lost due to a transmission error or because router C is overloaded, a new count to infinity problem can occur. If router C sends its distance vector [A = 2, B = 1, C = 0, E = ∞] to router E, this router installs a route of distance *3* to reach A via C. Router E sends its distance vectors [A = 3, B = ∞, C = 1, E =1] to router *B* and [A = to, B = 1, C = ∞, E = 0] to router C. This distance vector allows B to recover a route of distance *4* to reach A.

Link state routing

Link state routing is the second family of routing protocols. While distance vector routers use a distributed algorithm to compute their routing tables, link-state routers exchange messages to allow each router to learn the entire network topology. Based on this learned topology, each router is then able to compute its routing table by using a shortest path computation [Dijkstra1959].

For link-state routing, a network is modelled as a *directed weighted graph.* Each router is a node, and the links between routers are the edges in the graph. A positive weight is associated to each directed edge and routers use the shortest path to reach each destination. In practice, different types of weight can be associated to each directed edge :

- unit weight. If all links have a unit weight, shortest path routing prefers the paths with the least number of intermediate routers.

- weight proportional to the propagation delay on the link. If all link weights are configured this way, shortest path routing uses the paths with the smallest propagation delay.
- $weight = \frac{C}{bandwidth}$ where C is a constant larger than the highest link bandwidth in the network. If all link weights are configured this way, shortest path routing prefers higher bandwidth paths over lower bandwidth paths

Usually, the same weight is associated to the two directed edges that correspond to a physical link (i.e. R1 R2 and R2 R1). However, nothing in the link state protocols requires this. For example, if the weight is set in function of the link bandwidth, then an asymmetric ADSL link could have a different weight for the upstream and downstream directions. Other variants are possible. Some networks use optimisation algorithms to find the best set of weights to minimize congestion inside the network for a given traffic demand [FRT2002].

When a link-state router boots, it first needs to discover to which routers it is directly connected. For this, each router sends a HELLO message every *N* seconds on all of its interfaces. This message contains the router's address. Each router has a unique address. As its neighbouring routers also send HELLO messages, the router automatically discovers to which neighbours it is connected. These HELLO messages are only sent to neighbours who are directly connected to a router, and a router never forwards the HELLO messages that they receive. HELLO messages are also used to detect link and router failures. A link is considered to have failed if no HELLO message has been received from the neighbouring router for a period of *k* x *N* seconds.

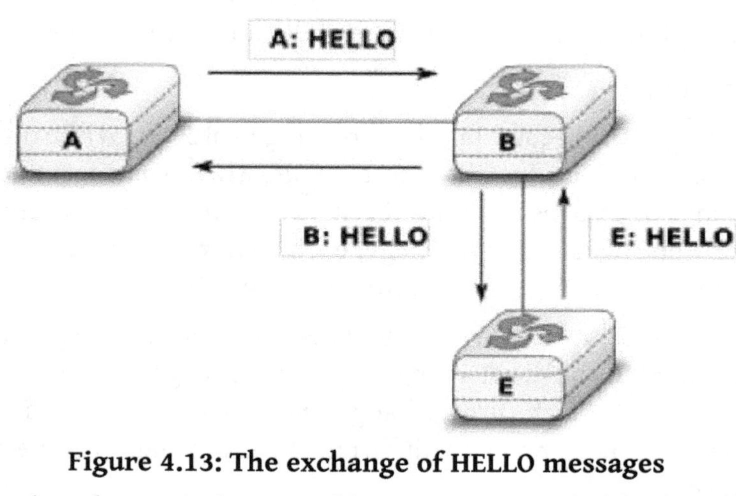

Figure 4.13: The exchange of HELLO messages

Once a router has discovered its neighbours, it must reliably distribute its local links to all routers in the network to allow them to compute their local view of the network topology. For this, each router builds a *link-state packet* (LSP) containing the following information :

- LSP.Router : identification (address) of the sender of the LSP
- LSP.age : age or remaining lifetime of the LSP
- LSP.seq : sequence number of the LSP
- LSP.Links[] : links advertised in the LSP. Each directed link is represented with the following information : - LSP.Links[i].Id : identification of the neighbour - LSP.Links[i].cost: cost of the link

These LSPs must be reliably distributed inside the network without using the router's routing table since these tables can only be computed once the LSPs have been received. The *Flooding* algorithm is used to efficiently distribute the LSPs of all routers. Each router that implements *flooding* maintains a *link state database* (LSDB) containing the most recent LSP sent by each router. When a router receives an LSP, it first verifies whether this LSP is already stored inside its LSDB. If so, the router has already distributed the LSP earlier and it does not need to forward it. Otherwise, the router forwards the LSP on all links except the link over which the LSP was received. Reliable flooding can be implemented by using the following pseudo-code.

```
# links is the set of all links on the router
# Router R's LSP arrival on link l
if newer(LSP, LSDB(LSP.Router)) :
LSDB.add(LSP)
for i in links :
if i!=l :
send(LSP,i)
else:
# LSP has already been flooded
```

In this pseudo-code, *LSDB(r)* returns the most recent *LSP* originating from router *r* that is stored in the *LSDB. newer(lsp1,lsp2)* returns true if *lsp1* is more recent than *lsp2.* See the note below for a discussion on how *newer* can be implemented.

Note: Which is the most recent LSP ?

A router that implements flooding must be able to detect whether a received LSP is newer than the stored LSP. This requires a comparison between the sequence number of the received LSP and the sequence number of the LSP stored in the link state database. The ARPANET routing protocol [MRR1979] used a 6 bits sequence number and implemented the comparison as follows **RFC 789**

```
def newer( lsp1, lsp2 ):
return ( ( ( lsp1.seq > lsp2.seq) and ( (lsp1.seq-lsp2.seq)<=32) ) or
( ( lsp1.seq < lsp2.seq) and ( (lsp2.seq-lsp1.seq)> 32) ) )
```

This comparison takes into account the modulo 2^6 arithmetic used to increment the sequence numbers. Intuitively, the comparison divides the circle of all sequence numbers into two halves. Usually, the sequence number of the received LSP is equal to the sequence number of the stored LSP incremented by one, but sometimes the sequence numbers of two successive LSPs may differ, e.g. if one router has been disconnected from the network for some time. The comparison above worked well until October 27, 1980. On this day, the ARPANET crashed completely. The crash was complex and involved several routers. At one point, LSP *40* and LSP *44* from one of the routers were stored in the LSDB of some routers in the ARPANET. As LSP *44* was the newest, it should have replaced by LSP *40* on all routers. Unfortunately, one of the ARPANET routers suffered from a memory problem and sequence number *40 (101000* in binary) was replaced by *8 (001000* in binary) in the buggy router and flooded. Three LSPs were present in the network and *44* was newer than *40* which is newer than 8, but unfortunately *8* was considered to be newer than 44... All routers started to exchange these three link state packets for ever and the only solution to recover from this problem was to shutdown the entire network **RFC 789**.

Current link state routing protocols usually use 32 bits sequence numbers and include a special mechanism in the unlikely case that a sequence number reaches the maximum value (using a 32 bits sequence number space takes 136 years if a link state packet is generated every second).

To deal with the memory corruption problem, link state packets contain a checksum. This checksum is computed by the router that generates the LSP. Each router must verify the checksum when it receives or floods an LSP. Furthermore, each router must periodically verify the checksums of the LSPs stored in its LSDB.

Flooding is illustrated in the figure below. By exchanging HELLO messages, each router learns its direct neighbours. For example, router *E* learns that it is directly connected to routers *D, B* and C. Its first LSP has sequence number *0* and contains the directed links *E->D, E->B* and *E->C.* Router E sends its LSP on all its links and routers *D, B* and *C* insert the LSP in their LSDB and forward it over their other links.

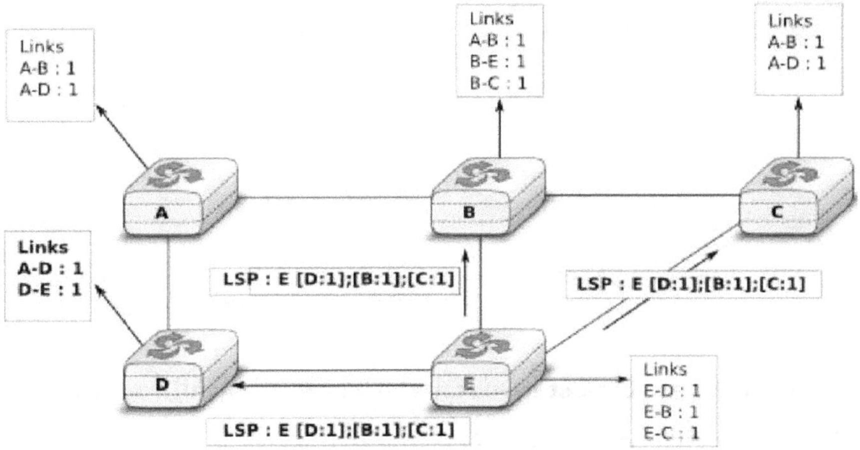

Figure 4.14: Flooding : example

Flooding allows LSPs to be distributed to all routers inside the network without relying on routing tables. In the example above, the LSP sent by router *E* is likely to be sent twice on some links in the network. For example, routers B and C receive E's LSP at almost the same time and forward it over the B-C link. To avoid sending the same LSP twice on each link, a possible solution is to slightly change the pseudo-code above so that a router waits for some random time before forwarding a LSP on each link. The drawback of this solution is that the delay to flood an LSP to all routers in the network increases. In practice, routers immediately flood the LSPs that contain new information (e.g. addition or removal of a link) and delay the flooding of refresh LSPs (i.e. LSPs that contain exactly the same information as the previous LSP originating from this router) [FFEB2005].

To ensure that all routers receive all LSPs, even when there are transmissions errors, link state routing protocols use *reliable flooding.* With *reliable flooding,* routers use acknowledgements and if necessary retransmissions to ensure that all link state packets are successfully transferred to all neighbouring routers. Thanks to reliable flooding, all routers store in their LSDB the most recent LSP sent by each router in the network. By combining the received LSPs with its own LSP, each router can compute the entire network topology.

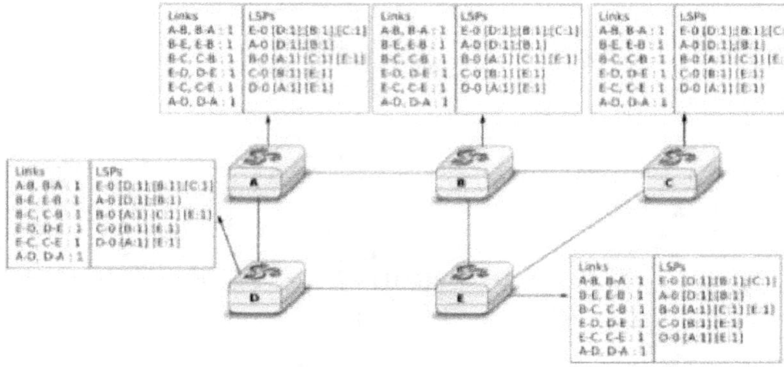

Figure 4.15: Link state databases received by all routers

Note: Static or dynamic link metrics ?

As link state packets are flooded regularly, routers are able to measure the quality (e.g. delay or load) of their links and adjust the metric of each link according to its current quality. Such dynamic adjustments were included in the ARPANET routing protocol [MRR1979]. However, experience showed that it was difficult to tune the dynamic adjustments and ensure that no forwarding loops occur in the network [KZ1989]. Today's link state routing protocols use metrics that are manually configured on the routers and are only changed by the network operators or network management tools [FRT2002].

When a link fails, the two routers attached to the link detect the failure by the lack of HELLO messages received in the last *k* x *N* seconds. Once a router has detected a local link failure, it generates and floods a new LSP that no longer contains the failed link and the new LSP replaces the previous LSP in the network. As the two routers attached to a link do not detect this failure exactly at the same time, some links may be announced in only one direction. This is illustrated in the figure below. Router *E* has detected the failures of link *E-B* and flooded a new LSP, but router B has not yet detected the failure.

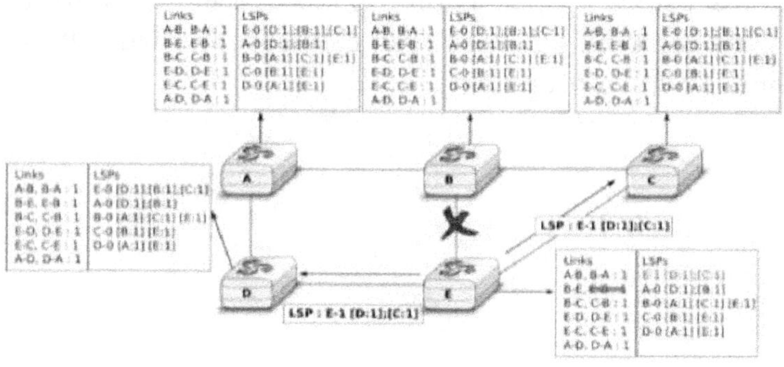

Figure 4.16: The two-way connectivity check

When a link is reported in the LSP of only one of the attached routers, routers consider the link as having failed and they remove it from the directed graph that they compute from their LSDB. This is called the *two-way connectivity check.* This check allows link failures to be flooded quickly as a single LSP is sufficient to announce such bad news. However, when a link comes up, it can only be used once the two attached routers have sent their LSPs. The *two-way connectivity check* also allows for dealing with router failures. When a router fails, all its links fail by definition. Unfortunately, it does not, of course, send a new LSP to announce its failure. The *two-way connectivity check* ensures that the failed router is removed from the graph.

When a router has failed, its LSP must be removed from the LSDB of all routers. This can be done by using the *age* field that is included in each LSP. The *age* field is used to bound the maximum lifetime of a link state packet in the network. When a router generates a LSP, it sets its lifetime (usually measured in seconds) in the *age* field. All routers regularly decrement the *age* of the LSPs in their LSDB and a LSP is discarded once its *age* reaches *0*. Thanks to the *age* field, the LSP from a failed router does not remain in the LSDBs forever.

To compute its routing table, each router computes the spanning tree rooted at itself by using Dijkstra's shortest path algorithm [Dijkstra1959]. The routing table can be derived automatically from the spanning as shown in the figure below.

4.2 INTERNET PROTOCOL

The Internet Protocol (IP) is the network layer protocol of the TCP/IP protocol suite. IP allows the applications running above the transport layer (UDP/TCP) to use a wide range of heterogeneous datalink layers. IP was designed when most point-to-point links were telephone lines with modems. Since then, IP has been able to use Local Area Networks (Ethernet, Token Ring, FDDI,...), new wide area data link layer technologies (X.25, ATM, Frame Relay, ...) and more recently wireless networks (802.11, 802.15, UMTS, GPRS, ...). The flexibility of IP and its ability to use various types of underlying data link layer technologies is one of its key advantages.

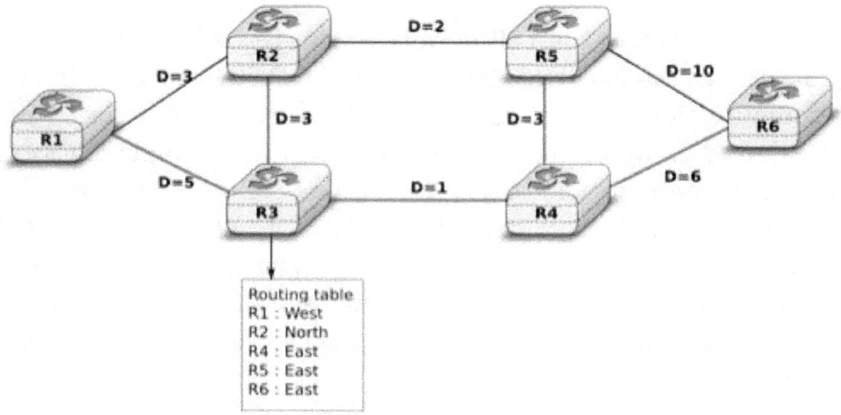

Figure 4.17: Computation of the routing table

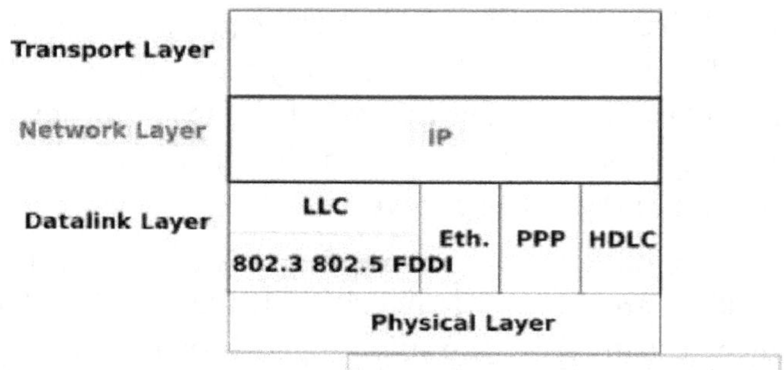

Figure 4.18: IP and the reference model

The current version of IP is version 4 specified in **RFC 791**. We first describe this version and later explain IP version 6, which is expected to replace IP version 4 in the not so distant future.

4.2.1 IP version 4

IP version 4 is the data plane protocol of the network layer in the TCP/IP protocol suite. The design of IP version 4 was based on the following assumptions :

- IP should provide an unreliable connectionless service (TCP provides reliability when required by the application)
- IP operates with the datagram transmission mode
- IP addresses have a fixed size of 32 bits
- IP must be usable above different types of datalink layers
- IP hosts exchange variable length packets

The addresses are an important part of any network layer protocol. In the late 1970s, the developers of IPv4 designed IPv4 for a research network that would interconnect some research labs and universities. For this utilisation, 32 bits wide addresses were much larger than the expected number of hosts on the network. Furthermore, 32 bits was a nice address size for software-based routers. None of the developers of IPv4 were expecting that IPv4 would become as widely used as it is today.

IPv4 addresses are encoded as a 32 bits field. IPv4 addresses are often represented in *dotted-decimal* format as a sequence of four integers separated by a dot. The first integer is the decimal representation of the most significant byte of the 32 bits IPv4 address,... For example,

- 1.2.3.4 corresponds to 00000001000000100000001100000100
- 127.0.0.1 corresponds to 01111111000000000000000000000001
- 255.255.255.255 corresponds to 11111111111111111111111111111111

An IPv4 address is used to identify an interface on a router or a host. A router has thus as many IPv4 addresses as the number of interfaces that it has in the datalink layer. Most hosts have a single datalink layer interface and thus have a single IPv4 address. However, with the growth of wireless, more and more hosts have several datalink layer interfaces (e.g. an Ethernet interface and a WiFi interface). These hosts are said to be *multihomed.* A multihomed host with two interfaces has thus two IPv4 addresses.

An important point to be defined in a network layer protocol is the allocation of the network layer addresses. A naive allocation scheme would be to provide an IPv4 address to each host when the host is attached to the Internet on a first come first served basis. With this solution, a host in Belgium could have address 2.3.4.5 while another host located in Africa would use address 2.3.4.6. Unfortunately, this would force all routers to maintain a specific route towards each host. The figure below shows a simple enterprise network with two routers and three hosts and the associated routing tables if such isolated addresses were used.

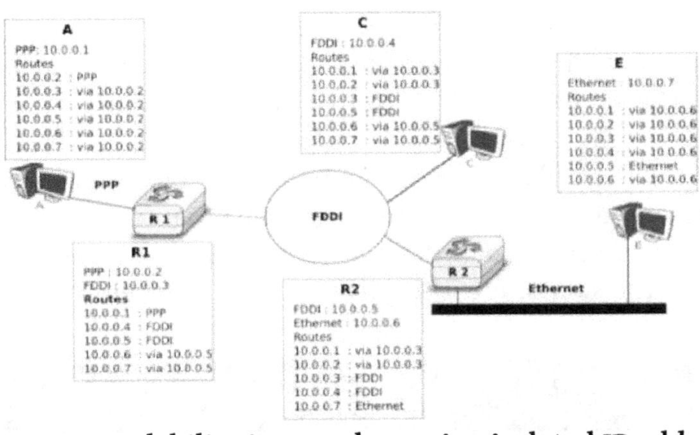

Figure 4.19: Scalability issues when using isolated IP addresses

To preserve the scalability of the routing system, it is important to minimize the number of routes that are stored on each router. A router cannot store and maintain one route for each of the almost 1 billion hosts that are connected to today's Internet. Routers should only maintain routes towards blocks of addresses and not towards individual hosts. For this, hosts are grouped in *subnets* based on their location in the network. A typical subnet groups all the hosts that are part of the same enterprise. An enterprise network is usually composed of several LANs interconnected by routers. A small block of addresses from the Enterprise's block is usually assigned to each LAN. An IPv4 address is composed of two parts : a *subnetwork identifier* and a *host identifier*. The *subnetwork identifier* is composed of the high order bits of the address and the host identifier is encoded in the low order bits of the address. This is illustrated in the figure below.

10001010 00110000 0001101 *0 00000001*

subnetwork id *host id*

Figure 4.20: The subnetwork and host identifiers inside an IPv4 address

When a router needs to forward a packet, it must know the *subnet* of the destination address to be able to consult its forwarding table to forward the packet. **RFC 791** proposed to use the high-order bits of the address to encode the length of the subnet identifier. This led to the definition of three *classes* of unicast addresses

Class	High-order bits	Length of subnet id	Number of networks	Addresses per network
Class A	*0*	8 bits	128	16,777,216 (2^{24})
Class B	*10*	16 bits	16,384	65,536 (2^{16})
Class C	*110*	24 bits	2,097,152	256 (2^{8})

However, these three classes of addresses were not flexible enough. A class *A* subnet was too large for most organisations and a class C subnet was too small. Flexibility was added by the introduction of *variable-length subnets* in **RFC 1519.** With *variable-length* subnets, the subnet identifier can be any size, from *1* to *31* bits. *Variable-length* subnets allow the network operators to use a subnet that better matches the number of hosts that are placed inside the subnet. A subnet identifier or IPv4 prefix is usually represented as *A.B.C.D/p* where *A.B.C.D* is the network address obtained by concatenating the subnet identifier with a host identifier containing only *0* and *p* is the length of the subnet identifier in bits. The table below provides examples of IP subnets.

Subnet	Number of addresses	Smallest address	Highest address

10.0.0.0/8	16,777,216	10.0.0.0	10.255.255.255
192.168.0.0/16	65,536	192.168.0.0	192.168.255.255
198.18.0.0/15	131,072	198.18.0.0	198.19.255.255
192.0.2.0/24	256	192.0.2.0	192.0.2.255
10.0.0.0/30	4	10.0.0.0	10.0.0.3
10.0.0.0/31	2	10.0.0.0	10.0.0.1

The figure below provides a simple example of the utilisation of IPv4 subnets in an enterprise network. The length of the subnet identifier assigned to a LAN usually depends on the expected number of hosts attached to the LAN. For point-to-point links, many deployments have used */30* prefixes, but recent routers are now using */31* subnets on point-to-point links **RFC 3021** or do not even use IPv4 addresses on such links .

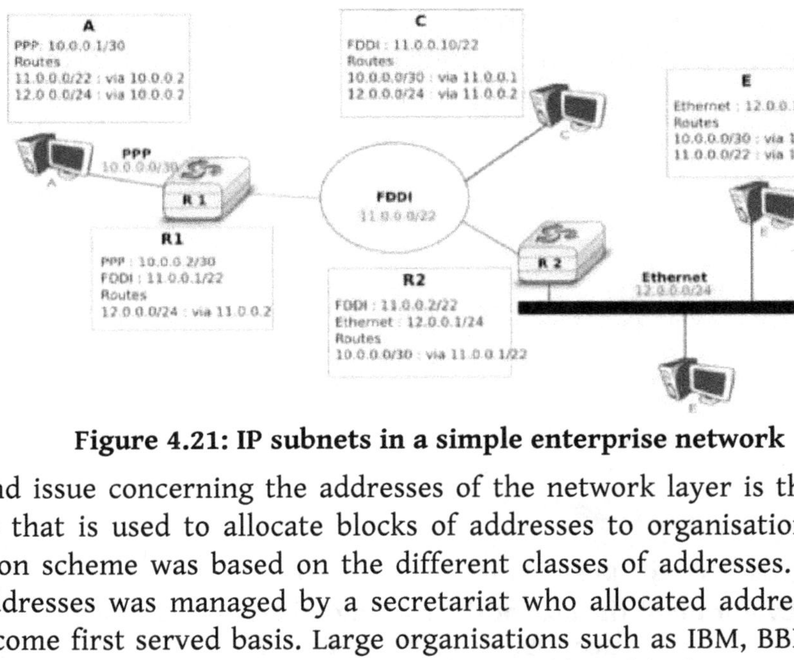

Figure 4.21: IP subnets in a simple enterprise network

A second issue concerning the addresses of the network layer is the allocation scheme that is used to allocate blocks of addresses to organisations. The first allocation scheme was based on the different classes of addresses. The pool of IPv4 addresses was managed by a secretariat who allocated address blocks on a first-come first served basis. Large organisations such as IBM, BBN, as well as Stanford or the MIT were able to obtain a class *A* address block. Most organisations requested a class *B* address block containing 65536 addresses, which was suitable for most enterprises and universities. The table below provides examples of some IPv4 address blocks in the class *B* space.

Subnet	Organisation
130.100.0.0/16	Ericsson, Sweden
130.101.0.0/16	University of Akron, USA
130.102.0.0/16	The University of Queensland, Australia
130.103.0.0/16	Lotus Development, USA
130.104.0.0/16	Universite catholique de Louvain, Belgium
130.105.0.0/16	Open Software Foundation, USA

However, the Internet was a victim of its own success and in the late 1980s, many organisations were requesting blocks of IPv4 addresses and started connecting to the Internet. Most of these organisations requested class *B* address blocks, as class *A* address blocks were too large and in limited supply while class C address blocks were considered to be too small. Unfortunately, there were only 16,384 different class B address blocks and this address space was being consumed quickly. As a consequence, the routing tables maintained by the routers were growing quickly and some routers had difficulties maintaining all these routes in their limited memory.

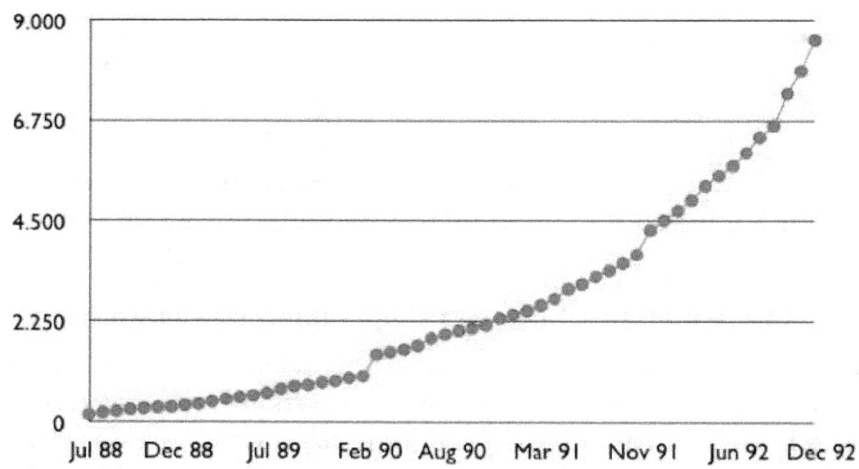

Figure 4.22: Evolution of the size of the routing tables on the Internet (Jul 1988-Dec 1992 - source : RFC 1518)

Faced with these two problems, the Internet Engineering Task Force decided to develop the Classless Interdomain Routing (CIDR) architecture **RFC 1518.** This architecture aims at allowing IP routing to scale better than the class-based architecture. CIDR contains three important modifications compared to **RFC 791.**

1. IP address classes are deprecated. All IP equipment must use and support variable-length subnets.
2. IP address blocks are no longer allocated on a first-come-first-served basis. Instead, CIDR introduces a hierarchical address allocation scheme.

3. IP routers must use longest-prefix match when they lookup a destination address in their forwarding table

The last two modifications were introduced to improve the scalability of the IP routing system. The main drawback of the first-come-first-served address block allocation scheme was that neighbouring address blocks were allocated to very different organisations and conversely, very different address blocks were allocated to similar organisations. With CIDR, address blocks are allocated by Regional IP Registries (RIR) in an aggregatable manner. A RIR is responsible for a large block of addresses and a region. For example, RIPE is the RIR that is responsible for Europe. A RIR allocates smaller address blocks from its large block to Internet Service Providers **RFC 2050**. Internet Service Providers then allocate smaller address blocks to their customers. When an organisation requests an address block, it must prove that it already has or expects to have in the near future, a number of hosts or customers that is equivalent to the size of the requested address block.

The main advantage of this hierarchical address block allocation scheme is that it allows the routers to maintain fewer routes. For example, consider the address blocks that were allocated to some of the Belgian universities as shown in the table below.

Address block	Organisation
130.104.0.0/16	Universite catholique de Louvain
134.58.0.0/16	Katholiek Universiteit Leuven
138.48.0.0/16	Facultes universitaires Notre-Dame de la Paix
139.165.0.0/16	Universite de Liege
164.15.0.0/16	Universite Libre de Bruxelles

These universities are all connected to the Internet exclusively via Belnet. As each university has been allocated a different address block, the routers of Belnet must announce one route for each university and all routers on the Internet must maintain a route towards each university. In contrast, consider all the high schools and the government institutions that are connected to the Internet via Belnet. An address block was assigned to these institutions after the introduction of CIDR in the *193.190.0.0/15* address block owned by Belnet. With CIDR, Belnet can announce a single route towards *193.190.0.0/15* that covers all of these high schools.

However, there is one difficulty with the aggregatable variable length subnets used by CIDR. Consider for example FEDICT, a government institution that uses the *193.191.244.0/23* address block. Assume that in addition to being connected to the Internet via Belnet , FEDICT also wants to be connected to another Internet Service Provider. The FEDICT network is then said to be multihomed. This is shown in the figure below.

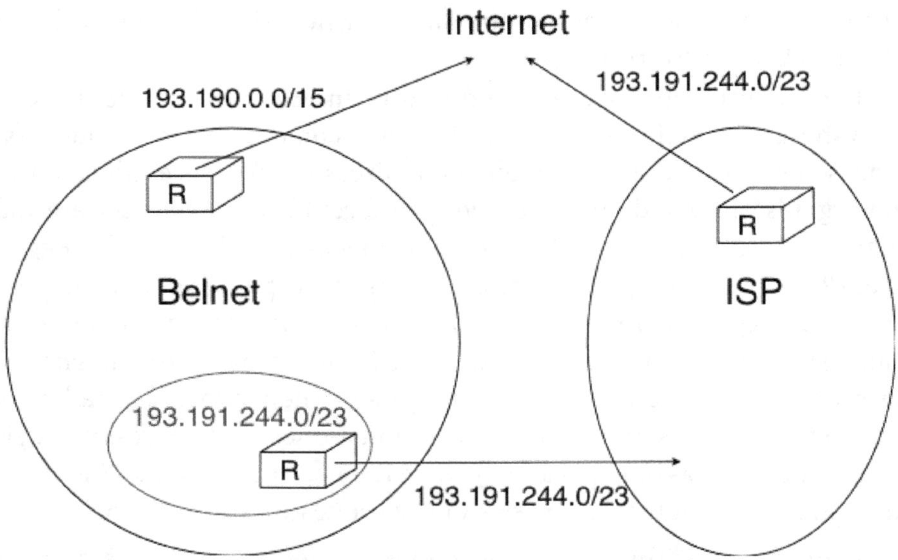

Figure 4.23: Multihoming and CIDR

With such a multihomed network, routers *R1* and *R2* would have two routes towards IPv4 address *193.191.245.88* : one route via Belnet *(193.190.0.0/15)* and one direct route *(193.191.244.0/23)*. Both routes match IPv4 address *193.192.145.88*. Since **RFC 1519** when a router knows several routes towards the same destination address, it must forward packets along the route having the longest prefix length. In the case of *193.191.245.88*, this is the route *193.191.244.0/23* that is used to forward the packet. This forwarding rule is called the *longest prefix match* or the *more specific match*. All IPv4 routers implement this forwarding rule.

To understand the *longest prefix match* forwarding, consider the figure below. With this rule, the route *0.0.0.0/0* plays a particular role. As this route has a prefix length of *0* bits, it matches all destination addresses. This route is often called the *default* route.

- a packet with destination *192.168.1.1* received by router *R* is destined to the router itself. It is delivered to the appropriate transport protocol.
- a packet with destination *11.2.3.4* matches two routes : *11.0.0.0/8* and *0.0.0.0/0*. The packet is forwarded on the *West* interface.
- a packet with destination *130.4.3.4* matches one route : *0.0.0.0/0*. The packet is forwarded on the *North* interface.
- a packet with destination *4.4.5.6* matches two routes : *4.0.0.0/8* and *0.0.0.0/0*. The packet is forwarded on the *West* interface.
- a packet with destination *4.10.11.254* matches three routes : *4.0.0.0/8*, *4.10.11.0/24 and '0.0.0.0/0*. The packet is forwarded on the *South* interface.

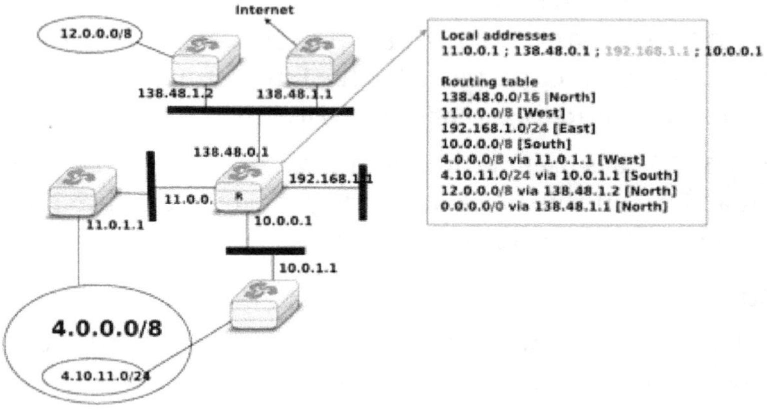

Figure 4.24: Longest prefix match example

The longest prefix match can be implemented by using different data structures. One possibility is to use a trie. The figure below shows a trie that encodes six routes having different outgoing interfaces.

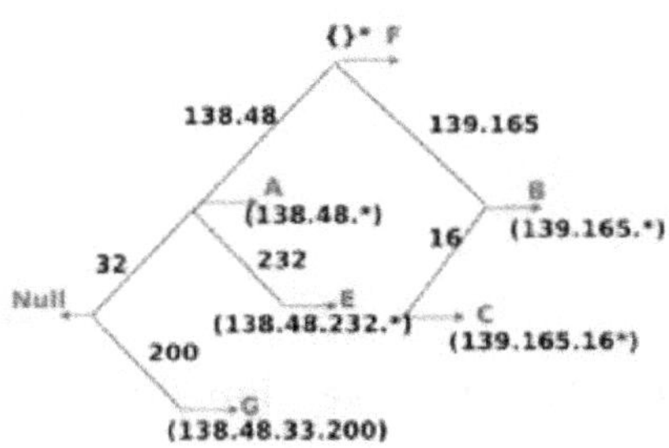

Figure 4.25: A trie representing a routing table

Note: Special IPv4 addresses

Most unicast IPv4 addresses can appear as source and destination addresses in packets on the global Internet. However, it is worth noting that some blocks of IPv4 addresses have a special usage, as described in **RFC 5735**. These include :

- *0.0.0.0/8,* which is reserved for self-identification. A common address in this block is *0.0.0.0,* which is sometimes used when a host boots and does not yet know its IPv4 address.
- *127.0.0.0/8,* which is reserved for loopback addresses. Each host implementing IPv4 must have a loopback interface (that is not attached to a datalink layer). By convention, IPv4 address *127.0.0.1* is assigned to this interface. This allows processes running on a host to use TCP/IP

to contact other processes running on the same host. This can be very useful for testing purposes.

- *10.0.0.0/8,172.16.0.0/12* and *192.168.0.0/16* are reserved for private networks that are not directly attached to the Internet. These addresses are often called private addresses or **RFC 1918** addresses.
- *169.254.0.0/16* is used for link-local addresses **RFC 3927**. Some hosts use an address in this block when they are connected to a network that does not allocate addresses as expected.

IPv4 packets

Now that we have clarified the allocation of IPv4 addresses and the utilisation of the longest prefix match to forward IPv4 packets, we can have a more detailed look at IPv4 by starting with the format of the IPv4 packets. The IPv4 packet format was defined in **RFC 791**. Apart from a few clarifications and some backward compatible changes, the IPv4 packet format did not change significantly since the publication of **RFC 791**. All IPv4 packets use the 20 bytes header shown below. Some IPv4 packets contain an optional header extension that is described later.

```
 0                   1                   2                   3
 0 1 2 3 4 5 6 7 8 9 0 1 2 3 4 5 6 7 8 9 0 1 2 3 4 5 6 7 8 9 0 1
+-+-+-+-+-+-+-+-+-+-+-+-+-+-+-+-+-+-+-+-+-+-+-+-+-+-+-+-+-+-+-+-+
|Version|  IHL  |   DS Field    |          Total Length         |
+-+-+-+-+-+-+-+-+-+-+-+-+-+-+-+-+-+-+-+-+-+-+-+-+-+-+-+-+-+-+-+-+
|         Identification        |Flags|      Fragment Offset    |
+-+-+-+-+-+-+-+-+-+-+-+-+-+-+-+-+-+-+-+-+-+-+-+-+-+-+-+-+-+-+-+-+
|  Time to Live |    Protocol   |         Header Checksum       |
+-+-+-+-+-+-+-+-+-+-+-+-+-+-+-+-+-+-+-+-+-+-+-+-+-+-+-+-+-+-+-+-+
|                       Source Address                          |
+-+-+-+-+-+-+-+-+-+-+-+-+-+-+-+-+-+-+-+-+-+-+-+-+-+-+-+-+-+-+-+-+
|                    Destination Address                        |
+-+-+-+-+-+-+-+-+-+-+-+-+-+-+-+-+-+-+-+-+-+-+-+-+-+-+-+-+-+-+-+-+
```

Figure 4.26: The IP version 4 header

The main fields of the IPv4 header are :

- a 4 bits *version* that indicates the version of IP used to build the header. Using a version field in the header allows the network layer protocol to evolve.
- a 4 bits *IP Header Length (IHL)* that indicates the length of the IP header in 32 bits words. This field allows IPv4 to use options if required, but as it is encoded as a 4 bits field, the IPv4 header cannot be longer than 64 bytes.
- an 8 bits *DS* field that is used for Quality of Service and whose usage is described later.
- an 8 bits *Protocol* field that indicates the transport layer protocol that must process the packet's payload at the destination. Common values for this field are *6* for TCP and *17* for UDP

- a 16 bits *length* field that indicates the total length of the entire IPv4 packet (header and payload) in bytes. This implies that an IPv4 packet cannot be longer than 65535 bytes.
- a 32 bits *source address* field that contains the IPv4 address of the source host
- a 32 bits *destination address* field that contains the IPv4 address of the destination host
- a 16 bits *checksum* that protects only the IPv4 header against transmission errors

The other fields of the IPv4 header are used for specific purposes. The first is the 8 bits *Time To Live (TTL)* field. This field is used by IPv4 to avoid the risk of having an IPv4 packet caught in an infinite loop due to a transient or permanent error in routing tables. Consider for example the situation depicted in the figure below where destination *D* uses address *11.0.0.56.* If *S* sends a packet towards this destination, the packet is forwarded to router *B* which forwards it to router C that forwards it back to router *A*, etc.

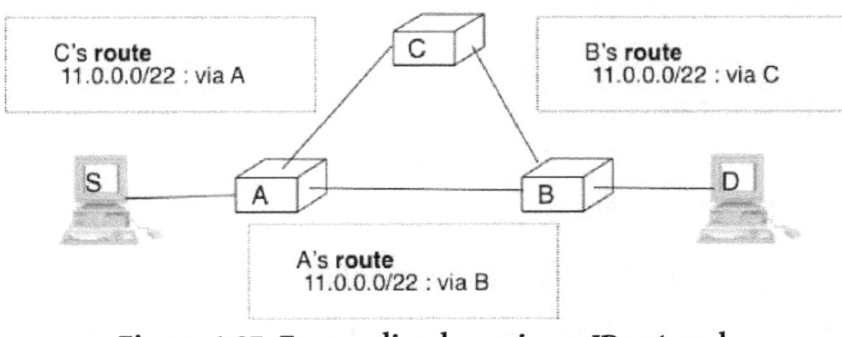

Figure 4.27: Forwarding loops in an IP network

Unfortunately, such loops can occur for two reasons in IP networks. First, if the network uses static routing, the loop can be caused by a simple configuration error. Second, if the network uses dynamic routing, such a loop can occur transiently, for example during the convergence of the routing protocol after a link or router failure. The *TTL* field of the IPv4 header ensures that even if there are forwarding loops in the network, packets will not loop forever. Hosts send their IPv4 packets with a positive TTL (usually *64* or more). When a router receives an IPv4 packet, it first decrements the *TTL* by one. If the *TTL* becomes *0*, the packet is discarded and a message is sent back to the packet's source (see section ICMP). Otherwise, the router performs a lookup in its forwarding table to forward the packet.

A second problem for IPv4 is the heterogeneity of the datalink layer. IPv4 is used above many very different datalink layers. Each datalink layer has its own characteristics and as indicated earlier, each datalink layer is characterised by a maximum frame size. From IP's point of view, a datalink layer interface is characterised by its *Maximum Transmission Unit (MTU).* The MTU of an interface is the largest IPv4 packet (including header) that it can send. The table below provides some common MTU sizes.

Datalink layer	MTU
Ethernet	1500 bytes
WiFi	2272 bytes
ATM (AAL5)	9180 bytes
802.15.4	102 or 81 bytes
Token Ring	4464 bytes
FDDI	4352 bytes

Although IPv4 can send 64 KBytes long packets, few datalink layer technologies that are used today are able to send a 64 KBytes IPv4 packet inside a frame. Furthermore, as illustrated in the figure below, another problem is that a host may send a packet that would be too large for one of the datalink layers used by the intermediate routers.

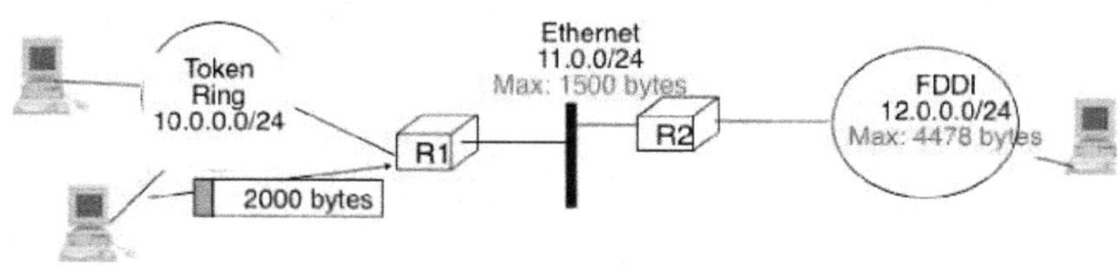

Figure 4.28: The need for fragmentation and reassembly

To solve these problems, IPv4 includes a packet fragmentation and reassembly mechanism. Both hosts and intermediate routers may fragment an IPv4 packet if the packet is too long to be sent via the datalink layer. In IPv4, fragmentation is completely performed in the IP layer and a large IPv4 is fragmented into two or more IPv4 packets (called fragments). The IPv4 fragments of a large packet are normal IPv4 packets that are forwarded towards the destination of the large packet by intermediate routers.

The IPv4 fragmentation mechanism relies on four fields of the IPv4 header : *Length, Identification,* the *flags* and the *Fragment Offset.* The IPv4 header contains two flags: *More fragments* and *Don't Fragment (DF).* When the *DF* flag is set, this indicates that the packet cannot be fragmented.

The basic operation of the IPv4 fragmentation is as follows. A large packet is fragmented into two or more fragments. The size of all fragments, except the last one, is equal to the Maximum Transmission Unit of the link used to forward the packet. Each IPv4 packet contains a 16 bits *Identification* field. When a packet is fragmented, the *Identification* of the large packet is copied in all fragments to allow the destination to reassemble the received fragments together. In each fragment, the *Fragment Offset* indicates, in units of 8 bytes, the position of the payload of the fragment in the payload of the original packet. The *Length* field in each fragment indicates the length of the payload of the fragment as in a normal IPv4 packet. Finally, the *More fragments* flag is set only in the last fragment of a large packet.

The following pseudo-code details the IPv4 fragmentation, assuming that the packet does not contain options.

```
#mtu : maximum size of the packet (including header) of outgoing link if p.len < mtu :
send(p)
# packet is too large
maxpayload=8*int((mtu-20)/8) # must be n times 8 bytes
if p.flags=='DF' :
discard(p)
# packet must be fragmented
payload=p[IP].payload
pos=0
while len(payload) > 0 :
if len(payload) > maxpayload :
toSend=IP(dest=p.dest,src=p.src,
ttl=p.ttl, id=p.id,
frag=p.frag+(pos/8),
len=mtu, proto=p.proto)/payload[0:maxpayload]
pos=pos+maxpayload
payload=payload[maxpayload+1:]
else
toSend=IP(dest=p.dest,src=p.src,
ttl=p.ttl, id=p.id,
frag=p.frag+(pos/8),
flags=p.flags,
len=len(payload), proto=p.proto)/payload
forward(toSend)
```

The fragments of an IPv4 packet may arrive at the destination in any order, as each fragment is forwarded independently in the network and may follow different paths. Furthermore, some fragments may be lost and never reach the destination.

The reassembly algorithm used by the destination host is roughly as follows. First, the destination can verify whether a received IPv4 packet is a fragment or not by checking the value of the *More fragments* flag and the *Fragment Offset.* If the *Fragment Offset* is set to *0* and the *More fragments* flag is reset, the received packet has not been fragmented. Otherwise, the packet has been fragmented and must be reassembled. The reassembly algorithm relies on the *Identification* field of the received fragments to associate a fragment with the corresponding packet being reassembled. Furthermore, the *Fragment Offset* field indicates the position of the fragment payload in the original unfragmented packet. Finally, the packet with the *More fragments* flag reset allows the destination to determine the total length of the original unfragmented packet.

Note that the reassembly algorithm must deal with the unreliability of the IP network. This implies that a fragment may be duplicated or a fragment may never reach the destination. The destination can easily detect fragment duplication thanks to the *Fragment Offset.* To deal with fragment losses, the reassembly algorithm must bound the time during which the fragments of a packet are stored in its buffer while the packet is being reassembled. This can be implemented by starting a timer when the first fragment of a packet is received. If the packet has not been reassembled upon expiration of the timer, all fragments are discarded and the packet is considered to be lost.

The original IP specification, in **RFC 791**, defined several types of options that can be added to the IP header. Each option is encoded using a *type length value* format. They are not widely used today and are thus only briefly described. Additional details may be found in **RFC 791**.

The most interesting options in IPv4 are the three options that are related to routing. The *Record route* option was defined to allow network managers to determine the path followed by a packet. When the *Record route* option was present, routers on the packet's path had to insert their IP address in the option. This option was implemented, but as the optional part of the IPv4 header can only contain 44 bytes, it is impossible to discover an entire path on the global Internet. *traceroute(8)*, despite its limitations, is a better solution to record the path towards a destination.

The other routing options are the *Strict source route* and the *Loose source route* option. The main idea behind these options is that a host may want, for any reason, to specify the path to be followed by the packets that it sends. The *Strict source route* option allows a host to indicate inside each packet the exact path to be followed. The *Strict source route* option contains a list of IPv4 address and a pointer to indicate the next address in the list. When a router receives a packet containing this option, it does not lookup the destination address in its routing table but forwards the packet directly to the next router in the list and advances the pointer. This is illustrated in the figure below where *S* forces its packets to follow the *RA-RB-RD* path.

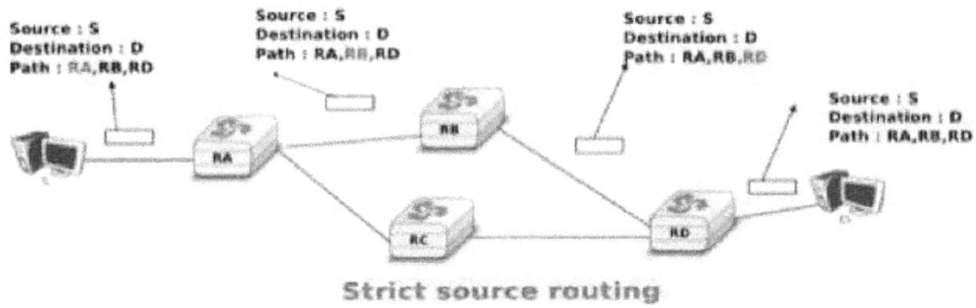

Figure 4.29: Usage of the Strict source route option

The maximum length of the optional part of the IPv4 header is a severe limitation for the *Strict source route* option as for the *Record Route* option. The *Loose source route* option does not suffer from this limitation. This option allows the sending host to indicate inside its packet *some* of the routers that must be traversed to reach the destination. This is shown in the figure below. *S* sends a packet containing a list of addresses and a pointer to the next router in the list. Initially, this pointer points to *RB*. When *RA* receives the packet sent by *S*, it looks up in its forwarding table the address pointed in the *Loose source route* option and not the destination address. The packet is then forwarded to router *RB* that recognises its address in the option and advances the pointer. As there is no address listed in the *Loose source route* option anymore, *RB* and other downstream routers forward the packet by performing a lookup for the destination address.

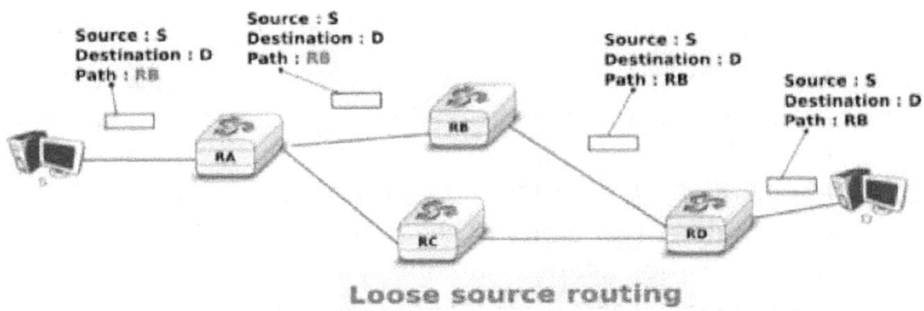

Figure 4.30: Usage of the Loose source route option

These two options are usually ignored by routers because they cause security problems **RFC 6274**.

4.2.2 ICMP version 4

It is sometimes necessary for intermediate routers or the destination host to inform the sender of the packet of a problem that occurred while processing a packet. In the TCP/IP protocol suite, this reporting is done by the Internet Control Message Protocol (ICMP). ICMP is defined in **RFC 792.** ICMP messages are carried as the payload of IP packets (the protocol value reserved for ICMP is 1). An ICMP message is composed of an 8 byte header and a variable length payload that usually contains the first bytes of the packet that triggered the transmission of the ICMP message.

```
 0                   1                   2                   3
 0 1 2 3 4 5 6 7 8 9 0 1 2 3 4 5 6 7 8 9 0 1 2 3 4 5 6 7 8 9 0 1
+-+-+-+-+-+-+-+-+-+-+-+-+-+-+-+-+-+-+-+-+-+-+-+-+-+-+-+-+-+-+-+-+
|Version|  IHL  |   DS Field    |          Total Length         |
+-+-+-+-+-+-+-+-+-+-+-+-+-+-+-+-+-+-+-+-+-+-+-+-+-+-+-+-+-+-+-+-+
|         Identification        |Flags|     Fragment Offset     |
+-+-+-+-+-+-+-+-+-+-+-+-+-+-+-+-+-+-+-+-+-+-+-+-+-+-+-+-+-+-+-+-+
|  Time to Live |    Protocol   |         Header Checksum       |
+-+-+-+-+-+-+-+-+-+-+-+-+-+-+-+-+-+-+-+-+-+-+-+-+-+-+-+-+-+-+-+-+
|                       Source Address                          |
+-+-+-+-+-+-+-+-+-+-+-+-+-+-+-+-+-+-+-+-+-+-+-+-+-+-+-+-+-+-+-+-+
|                    Destination Address                        |
+-+-+-+-+-+-+-+-+-+-+-+-+-+-+-+-+-+-+-+-+-+-+-+-+-+-+-+-+-+-+-+-+
|     Type      |     Code      |          Checksum             |
+-+-+-+-+-+-+-+-+-+-+-+-+-+-+-+-+-+-+-+-+-+-+-+-+-+-+-+-+-+-+-+-+
|                             Data                              |
~                                                               ~
+-+-+-+-+-+-+-+-+-+-+-+-+-+-+-+-+-+-+-+-+-+-+-+-+-+-+-+-+-+-+-+-+
|      IPv4 header of errored packet + 64 bits of payload       |
+-+-+-+-+-+-+-+-+-+-+-+-+-+-+-+-+-+-+-+-+-+-+-+-+-+-+-+-+-+-+-+-+
```

Figure 4.31: ICMP version 4 (RFC 792)

In the ICMP header, the *Type* and *Code* fields indicate the type of problem that was detected by the sender of the ICMP message. The *Checksum* protects the entire ICMP message against transmission errors and the *Data* field contains additional information for some ICMP messages.

The main types of ICMP messages are :

- *Destination unreachable* : a *Destination unreachable* ICMP message is sent when a packet cannot be delivered to its destination due to routing problems. Different types of unreachability are distinguished :
    - *Network unreachable* : this ICMP message is sent by a router that does not have a route for the subnet containing the destination address of the packet
    - *Host unreachable* : this ICMP message is sent by a router that is attached to the subnet that contains the destination address of the packet, but this destination address cannot be reached at this time
    - *Protocol unreachable* : this ICMP message is sent by a destination host that has received a packet, but does not support the transport protocol indicated in the packet's *Protocol* field
    - *Port unreachable* : this ICMP message is sent by a destination host that has received a packet destined to a port number, but no server process is bound to this port
- *Fragmentation needed* : this ICMP message is sent by a router that receives a packet with the *Don't Fragment* flag set that is larger than the MTU of the outgoing interface
- *Redirect*: this ICMP message can be sent when there are two routers on the same LAN. Consider a LAN with one host and two routers : *R1* and R2. Assume that *R1* is also connected to subnet *130.104.0.0/16* while *R2* is

connected to subnet *138.48.0.0/16.* If a host on the LAN sends a packet towards *130.104.1.1* to R2, *R2* needs to forward the packet again on the LAN to reach R1. This is not optimal as the packet is sent twice on the same LAN. In this case, *R2* could send an ICMP *Redirect* message to the host to inform it that it should have sent the packet directly to R1. This allows the host to send the other packets to *130.104.1.1* directly via R1.

- *Parameter problem* : this ICMP message is sent when a router or a host receives an IP packet containing an error (e.g. an invalid option)

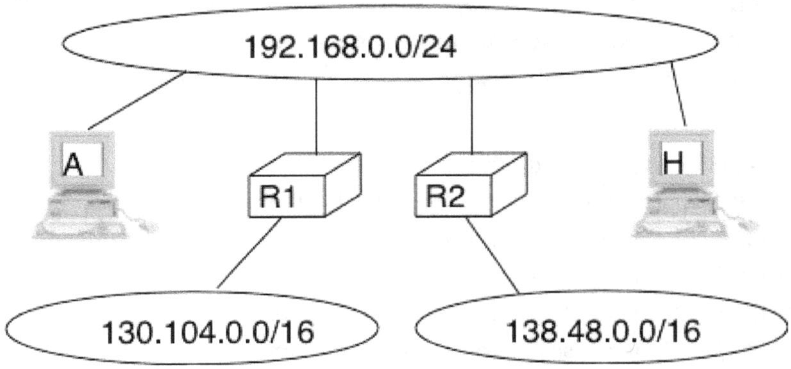

Figure 4.32: ICMP redirect

- *Source quench* : a router was supposed to send this message when it had to discard packets due to congestion. However, sending ICMP messages in case of congestion was not the best way to reduce congestion and since the inclusion of a congestion control scheme in TCP, this ICMP message has been deprecated.
- *Time Exceeded* : there are two types of *Time Exceeded* ICMP messages
  - *TTL exceeded*: a *TTL exceeded* message is sent by a router when it discards an IPv4 packet because its *TTL* reached *0.*
  - *Reassembly time exceeded* : this ICMP message is sent when a destination has been unable to reassemble all the fragments of a packet before the expiration of its reassembly timer.
- *Echo request* and *Echo reply* : these ICMP messages are used by the *ping(8)* network debugging software.

Note: Redirection attacks

ICMP redirect messages are useful when several routers are attached to the same LAN as hosts. However, they should be used with care as they also create an important security risk. One of the most annoying attacks in an IP network is called the *man in the middle attack.* Such an attack occurs if an attacker is able to receive, process, possibly modify and forward all the packets exchanged between a source and a destination. As the attacker receives all the packets it can easily collect passwords or credit card numbers or even inject fake information in an established TCP connection. ICMP redirects unfortunately enable an attacker to easily perform such an attack. In the figure above, consider host *H* that is attached to the same LAN as *A* and R1. If *H* sends to *A* an ICMP redirect for prefix *138.48.0.0/16*, *A* forwards to *H* all the packets that it wants to send to this prefix. *H* can then forward them to R2. To avoid these attacks, hosts should ignore the ICMP redirect messages that they receive.

ping(8) is often used by network operators to verify that a given IP address is reachable. Each host is supposed to reply with an ICMP *Echo reply* message when its receives an ICMP *Echo request* message. A sample usage of *ping(8)* is shown below.

```
ping 130.104.1.1
PING 130.104.1.1 (130.104.1.1): 56 data bytes
64 bytes from 130.104.1.1: icmp_seq=0 ttl=243 time=19.961 ms
64 bytes from 130.104.1.1: icmp_seq=1 ttl=243 time=22.072 ms
64 bytes from 130.104.1.1: icmp_seq=2 ttl=243 time=23.064 ms
64 bytes from 130.104.1.1: icmp_seq=3 ttl=243 time=20.026 ms
64 bytes from 130.104.1.1: icmp_seq=4 ttl=243 time=25.099 ms
--- 130.104.1.1 ping statistics ---
5 packets transmitted, 5 packets received, 0% packet loss
round-trip min/avg/max/stddev = 19.961/22.044/25.099/1.938 ms
```

Another very useful debugging tool is *traceroute(8)*. The traceroute man page describes this tool as *"print the route packets take to network host"*. traceroute uses the *TTL exceeded* ICMP messages to discover the intermediate routers on the path towards a destination. The principle behind traceroute is very simple. When a router receives an IP packet whose *TTL* is set to *1* it decrements the *TTL* and is forced to return to the sending host a *TTL exceeded* ICMP message containing the header and the first bytes of the discarded IP packet. To discover all routers on a network path, a simple solution is to first send a packet whose *TTL* is set to 1, then a packet whose *TTL* is set to 2, etc. A sample traceroute output is shown below.

```
traceroute www.ietf.org
traceroute to www.ietf.org (64.170.98.32), 64 hops max, 40 byte packets
1 CsHalles3.sri.ucl.ac.be (192.168.251.230) 5.376 ms 1.217 ms 1.137 ms
2 CtHalles.sri.ucl.ac.be (192.168.251.229) 1.444 ms 1.669 ms 1.301 ms
3 CtPythagore.sri.ucl.ac.be (130.104.254.230) 1.950 ms 4.688 ms 1.319 ms
4 fe.m20.access.lln.belnet.net (193.191.11.9) 1.578 ms 1.272 ms 1.259 ms
5 10ge.cr2.brueve.belnet.net (193.191.16.22) 5.461 ms 4.241 ms 4.162 ms
6 212.3.237.13 (212.3.237.13) 5.347 ms 4.544 ms 4.285 ms
```

```
7 ae-11-11.car1.Brussels1.Level3.net (4.69.136.249) 5.195 ms 4.304 ms 4.329 ms
8 ae-6-6.ebr1.London1.Level3.net (4.69.136.246) 8.892 ms 8.980 ms 8.830 ms
9 ae-100-100.ebr2.London1.Level3.net (4.69.141.166) 8.925 ms 8.950 ms 9.006 ms
10 ae-41-41.ebr1.NewYork1.Level3.net (4.69.137.66) 79.590 ms
ae-43-43.ebr1.NewYork1.Level3.net (4.69.137.74) 78.140 ms
ae-42-42.ebr1.NewYork1.Level3.net (4.69.137.70) 77.663 ms
11 ae-2-2.ebr1.Newark1.Level3.net (4.69.132.98) 78.290 ms 83.765 ms 90.006 ms
12 ae-14-51.car4.Newark1.Level3.net (4.68.99.8) 78.309 ms 78.257 ms 79.709 ms
13 ex1-tg2-0.eqnwnj.sbcglobal.net (151.164.89.249) 78.460 ms 78.452 ms 78.292 ms
14 151.164.95.190 (151.164.95.190) 157.198 ms 160.767 ms 159.898 ms
15 ded-p10-0.pltn13.sbcglobal.net (151.164.191.243) 161.872 ms 156.996 ms 159.425 ms
16 AMS-1152322.cust-rtr.swbell.net (75.61.192.10) 158.735 ms 158.485 ms 158.588 ms
17 mail.ietf.org (64.170.98.32) 158.427 ms 158.502 ms 158.567 ms
```

The above *traceroute(8)* output shows a 17 hops path between a host at UCLouvain and one of the main IETF servers. For each hop, traceroute provides the IPv4 address of the router that sent the ICMP message and the measured round-trip-time between the source and this router. traceroute sends three probes with each *TTL* value. In some cases, such as at the 10th hop above, the ICMP messages may be received from different addresses. This is usually because different packets from the same source have followed different paths [11] in the network.

Another important utilisation of ICMP messages is to discover the maximum MTU that can be used to reach a destination without fragmentation. As explained earlier, when an IPv4 router receives a packet that is larger than the MTU of the outgoing link, it must fragment the packet. Unfortunately, fragmentation is a complex operation and routers cannot perform it at line rate [KM1995]. Furthermore, when a TCP segment is transported in an IP packet that is fragmented in the network, the loss of a single fragment forces TCP to retransmit the entire segment (and thus all the fragments). If TCP was able to send only packets that do not require fragmentation in the network, it could retransmit only the information that was lost in the network. In addition, IP reassembly causes several challenges at high speed as discussed in **RFC 4963**. Using IP fragmentation to allow UDP applications to exchange large messages raises several security issues [KPS2003].

ICMP, combined with the *Don't fragment (DF)* IPv4 flag, is used by TCP implementations to discover the largest MTU size that is allowed to reach a destination host without causing network fragmentation. This is the *Path MTU discovery* mechanism defined in **RFC 1191**. A TCP implementation that includes *Path MTU discovery* (most do) requests the IPv4 layer to send all segments inside IPv4 packets having the *DF* flag set. This prohibits intermediate routers from fragmenting these packets. If a router needs to forward an unfragmentable packet over a link with a smaller MTU, it returns a *Fragmentation needed* ICMP message to the source, indicating the MTU of its outgoing link. This ICMP message contains in the MTU of the router's outgoing link in its *Data* field. Upon reception of this ICMP message, the source TCP implementation adjusts its Maximum Segment Size (MSS) so that the packets containing the segments that it sends can be forwarded by this router without requiring fragmentation.

Interactions between IPv4 and the datalink layer

As mentioned in the first section of this chapter, there are three main types of datalink layers: *point-to-point* links, LANs supporting broadcast and multicast and *NBMA* networks. There are two important issues to be addressed when using IPv4 in these types of networks. The first issue is how an IPv4 device obtains its IPv4 address. The second issue is how IPv4 packets are exchanged over the datalink layer service.

On a *point-to-point* link, the IPv4 addresses of the communicating devices can be configured manually or by using a simple protocol. IPv4 addresses are often configured manually on *point-to-point* links between routers. When *point-to-point* links are used to attach hosts to the network, automatic configuration is often preferred in order to avoid problems with incorrect IPv4 addresses. For example, the PPP, specified in **RFC 1661**, includes an IP network control protocol that can be used by the router in the figure below to send the IPv4 address that the attached host must configure for its interface. The transmission of IPv4 packets on a point-to-point link will be discussed in chapter *chap:lan.*

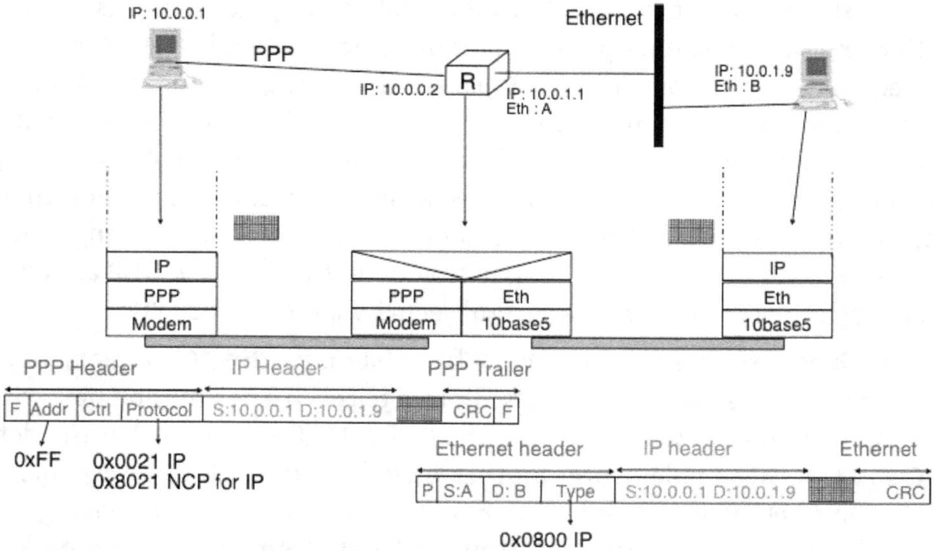

Figure 4.33: IPv4 on point-to-point links

Using IPv4 in a LAN introduces an additional problem. On a LAN, each device is identified by its unique datalink layer address. The datalink layer service can be used by any host attached to the LAN to send a frame to any other host attached to the same LAN. For this, the sending host must know the datalink layer address of the destination host. For example, the figure below shows four hosts attached to the same LAN configured with IPv4 addresses in the *10.0.1.0/24* subnet and datalink layer addresses represented as a single character. In this network, if host *10.0.1.22/24* wants to send an IPv4 packet to the host having address *10.0.1.8,* it must know that the datalink layer address of this host is *C*.

Figure 4.34: A simple LAN

In a simple network such as the one shown above, it could be possible to manually configure the mapping between the IPv4 addresses of the hosts and the corresponding datalink layer addresses. However, in a larger LAN this is impossible. To ease the utilisation of LANs, IPv4 hosts must be able to automatically obtain the datalink layer address corresponding to any IPv4 address on the same LAN. This is the objective of the *Address Resolution Protocol (ARP)* defined in **RFC 826.** ARP is a datalink layer protocol that is used by IPv4. It relies on the ability of the datalink layer service to easily deliver a broadcast frame to all devices attached to the same LAN.

The easiest way to understand the operation of ARP is to consider the simple network shown above and assume that host *10.0.1.22/24* needs to send an IPv4 packet to host *10.0.1.8.* As this IP address belongs to the same subnet, the packet must be sent directly to its destination via the datalink layer service. To use this service, the sending host must find the datalink layer address that is attached to host *10.0.1.8.* Each IPv4 host maintains an *ARP cache* containing the list of all mappings between IPv4 addresses and datalink layer addresses that it knows. When an IPv4 hosts boots, its ARP cache is empty. *10.0.1.22* thus first consults its ARP cache. As the cache does not contain the requested mapping, host *10.0.1.22* sends a broadcast ARP query frame on the LAN. The frame contains the datalink layer address of the sending host (A) and the requested IPv4 address *(10.0.1.8).* This broadcast frame is received by all devices on the LAN and only the host that owns the requested IPv4 address replies by returning a unicast ARP reply frame with the requested mapping. Upon reception of this reply, the sending host updates its ARP cache and sends the IPv4 packet by using the datalink layer service. To deal with devices that move or whose addresses are reconfigured, most ARP implementations remove the cache entries that have not been used for a few minutes. Some implementations re-validate ARP cache entries from time to time by sending ARP queries.

Note: Security issues with the Address Resolution Protocol

ARP is an old and widely used protocol that was unfortunately designed when security issues were not a concern. *ARP* is almost insecure by design. Hosts using *ARP* can be subject to several types of attack. First, a malicious host could create a denial of service attack on a LAN by sending random replies to the received ARP queries. This would pollute the ARP cache of the other hosts on the same LAN. On a fixed network, such attacks can be detected by the system administrator who can physically remove the malicious hosts from the LAN. On a wireless network, removing a malicious host is much more difficult.

A second type of attack are the *man-in-the-middle* attacks. This name is used for network attacks where the attacker is able to read and possibly modify all the messages sent by the attacked devices. Such an attack is possible in a LAN. Assume, in the figure above, that host *10.0.1.9* is malicious and would like to receive and modify all the packets sent by host *10.0.1.22* to host *10.0.1.8*. This can be achieved easily if host *10.0.1.9* manages, by sending fake ARP replies, to convince host *10.0.1.22* (resp. *10.0.1.8)* that its own datalink layer address must be used to reach *10.0.1.8* (resp. *10.0.1.22)*.

ARP is used by all devices that are connected to a LAN and implement IPv4. Both routers and endhosts implement ARP. When a host needs to send an IPv4 packet to a destination outside of its local subnet, it must first send the packet to one of the routers that reside on this subnet. Consider for example the network shown in the figure below. Each host is configured with an IPv4 address in the *10.0.1.0/24* subnet and uses *10.0.1.1* as its default router. To send a packet to address *1.2.3.4*, host *10.0.1.8* will first need to know the datalink layer of the default router. It will thus send an ARP request for *10.0.1.1*. Upon reception of the ARP reply, host *10.0.1.8* updates its ARP table and sends its packet in a frame to its default router. The router will then forward the packet towards its final destination.

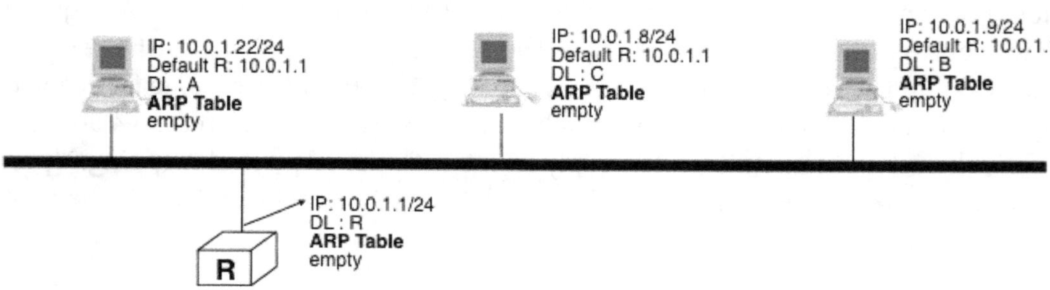

Figure 4.35: A simple LAN with a router

In the early days of the Internet, IP addresses were manually configured on both hosts and routers and almost never changed. However, this manual configuration can be complex and often causes errors that are sometimes difficult to debug. Recent TCP/IP implementations are able to detect some of these misconfigurations. For example, if two hosts are attached to the same subnet with the same IPv4 address they will be unable to communicate. To detect this problem hosts send an ARP request for their configured address each time their addressed is changed **RFC 5227**. If they receive an answer to this ARP request, they trigger an alarm or inform the system administrator.

To ease the attachment of hosts to subnets, most networks now support the Dynamic Host Configuration Protocol (DHCP) **RFC 2131**. DHCP allows a host to automatically retrieve its assigned IPv4 address. A DHCP server is associated to each subnet. Each DHCP server manages a pool of IPv4 addresses assigned to the subnet. When a host is first attached to the subnet, it sends a DHCP request message in a UDP segment (the DHCP server listens on port 67). As the host knows neither its IPv4 address nor the IPv4 address of the DHCP server, this UDP segment is sent inside an IPv4 packet whose source and destination addresses are respectively *0.0.0.0* and 255.255.255.255. The DHCP request may contain various options such as the name of the host, its datalink layer address, etc. The server captures the DHCP request and selects an unassigned address in its address pool. It then sends the assigned IPv4 address in a DHCP reply message which contains the datalink layer address of the host and additional information such as the subnet mask of the IPv4 address, the address of the default router or the address of the DNS resolver. This DHCP reply message is sent in an IPv4 packet whose source and destination addresses are respectively the IPv4 address of the DHCP server and the 255.255.255.255 broadcast address. The DHCP reply also specifies the lifetime of the address allocation. This forces the host to renew its address allocation once it expires. Thanks to the limited lease time, IP addresses are automatically returned to the pool of addresses hosts are powered off. This reduces the waste of IPv4 addresses.

In an NBMA network, the interactions between IPv4 and the datalink layer are more complex as the ARP protocol cannot be used as in a LAN. Such NBMA networks use special servers that store the mappings between IP addresses and the corresponding datalink layer address. Asynchronous Transfer Mode (ATM) networks for example can use either the ATMARP protocol defined in **RFC 2225** or the NextHop Resolution Protocol (NHRP) defined in **RFC 2332**. ATM networks are less frequently used today and we will not describe the detailed operation of these servers.

Operation of IPv4 devices

At this point of the description of IPv4, it is useful to have a detailed look at how an IPv4 implementation sends, receives and forwards IPv4 packets. The simplest case is when a host needs to send a segment in an IPv4 packet. The host performs two operations. First, it must decide on which interface the packet will be sent. Second it must create the corresponding IP packet(s).

To simplify the discussion in this section, we ignore the utilisation of IPv4 options. This is not a severe limitation as today IPv4 packets rarely contain options. Details about the processing of the IPv4 options may be found in the relevant RFCs, such as **RFC 791**. Furthermore, we also assume that only point-to-point links are used. We defer the explanation of the operation of IPv4 over Local Area Networks until the next chapter.

An IPv4 host having *n* datalink layer interfaces manages *n* +1 IPv4 addresses:

- the *127.0.0.1/32* IPv4 address assigned by convention to its loopback address
- one *A.B.C.D/p* IPv4 address assigned to each of its n datalink layer interfaces

Such a host maintains a routing table containing one entry for its loopback address and one entry for each subnet identifier assigned to its interfaces. Furthermore, the host usually uses one of its interfaces as the *default* interface when sending packets that are not addressed to a directly connected destination. This is represented by the *default* route : *0.0.0.0/0* that is associated to one interface.

When a transport protocol running on the host requests the transmission of a segment, it usually provides the IPv4 destination address to the IPv4 layer in addition to the segment. The IPv4 implementation first performs a longest prefix match with the destination address in its routing table. The lookup returns the identification of the interface that must be used to send the packet. The host can then create the IPv4 packet containing the segment. The source IPv4 address of the packet is the IPv4 address of the host on the interface returned by the longest prefix match. The *Protocol* field of the packet is set to the identification of the local transport protocol which created the segment. The *TTL* field of the packet is set to the default *TTL* used by the host. The host must now choose the packet's *Identification.* This *Identification* is important if the packet becomes fragmented in the network, as it ensures that the destination is able to reassemble the received fragments. Ideally, a sending host should never send a packet twice with the same *Identification* to the same destination host, in order to ensure that all fragments are correctly reassembled by the destination. Unfortunately, with a 16 bits *Identification* field and an expected MSL of 2 minutes, this implies that the maximum bandwidth to a given destination is limited to roughly 286 Mbps. With a more realistic 1500 bytes MTU, that bandwidth drops to 6.4 Mbps **RFC 4963** if fragmentation must be possible. This is very low and is another reason why hosts are highly encouraged to avoid fragmentation. If; despite all of this, the MTU of the outgoing interface is smaller than the packet's length, the packet is fragmented. Finally, the packet's checksum is computed before transmission.

When a host receives an IPv4 packet destined to itself, there are several operations that it must perform. First, it must check the packet's checksum. If the checksum is incorrect, the packet is discarded. Then, it must check whether the packet has been fragmented. If yes, the packet is passed to the reassembly algorithm described earlier. Otherwise, the packet must be passed to the upper layer. This is done by looking at the *Protocol* field (*6* for TCP, *17* for UDP). If the host does not implement the transport layer protocol corresponding to the received *Protocol* field, it sends a *Protocol unreachable* ICMP message to the sending host. If the received packet contains an ICMP message (*Protocol* field set to 1), the processing is more complex. An *Echo-request* ICMP message triggers the transmission of an *ICMP Echo-reply* message. The other types of ICMP messages indicate an error that was caused by a previously transmitted packet. These ICMP messages are usually forwarded to the transport protocol that sent the erroneous packet. This can be done by inspecting the contents of the ICMP message that includes the header and the first 64 bits of the erroneous packet. If the IP packet did not contain options, which is the case for most IPv4 packets, the transport protocol can find in the first 32 bits of the transport header the source and destination ports to determine the affected transport flow. This is important for Path MTU discovery for example.

When a router receives an IPv4 packet, it must first check the packet's checksum. If the checksum is invalid, it is discarded. Otherwise, the router must check whether the destination address is one of the IPv4 addresses assigned to the router. If so, the router must behave as a host and process the packet as described above. Although routers mainly forward IPv4 packets, they sometimes need to be accessed as hosts by network operators or network management software.

If the packet is not addressed to the router, it must be forwarded on an outgoing interface according to the router's routing table. The router first decrements the packet's *TTL*. If the *TTL* reaches 0, a *TTL Exceeded* ICMP message is sent back to the source. As the packet header has been modified, the checksum must be recomputed. Fortunately, as IPv4 uses an arithmetic checksum, a router can incrementally update the packet's checksum as described in **RFC 1624**. Then, the router performs a longest prefix match for the packet's destination address in its forwarding table. If no match is found, the router must return a *Destination unreachable* ICMP message to the source. Otherwise, the lookup returns the interface over which the packet must be forwarded. Before forwarding the packet over this interface, the router must first compare the length of the packet with the MTU of the outgoing interface. If the packet is smaller than the MTU, it is forwarded. Otherwise, a *Fragmentation needed* ICMP message is sent if the *DF* flag was sent or the packet is fragmented if the *DF* was not set.

Note: Longest prefix match in IP routers

Performing the longest prefix match at line rate on routers requires highly tuned data structures and algorithms. Consider for example an implementation of the longest match based on a Radix tree on a router with a 10 Gbps link. On such a link, a router can receive 31,250,000 40 bytes IPv4 packets every second. To forward the packets at line rate, the router must process one IPv4 packet every 32 nanoseconds. This cannot be achieved by a software implementation. For a hardware implementation, the main difficulty lies in the number of memory accesses that are necessary to perform the longest prefix match. 32 nanoseconds is very small compared to the memory accesses that are required by a naive longest prefix match implement. Additional information about faster longest prefix match algorithms may be found in [Varghese2005].

4.2.3 IP version 6

In the late 1980s and early 1990s the growth of the Internet was causing several operational problems on routers. Many of these routers had a single CPU and up to 1 MByte of RAM to store their operating system, packet buffers and routing tables. Given the rate of allocation of IPv4 prefixes to companies and universities willing to join the Internet, the routing tables where growing very quickly and some feared that all IPv4 prefixes would quickly be allocated. In 1987, a study cited in **RFC 1752**, estimated that there would be 100,000 networks in the near future. In August 1990, estimates indicated that the class B space would be exhausted by March 1994. Two types of solution were developed to solve this problem. The first short term solution was the introduction of Classless Inter Domain Routing *(CIDR)*. A second short term solution was the Network Address Translation *(NAT)* mechanism, defined in **RFC 1631**. NAT allowed multiple hosts to share a single public IP address, it is explained in section *Middleboxes*.

However, in parallel with these short-term solutions, which have allowed the IPv4 Internet to continue to be usable until now, the Internet Engineering Task Force started to work on developing a replacement for IPv4. This work started with an open call for proposals, outlined in **RFC 1550**. Several groups responded to this call with proposals for a next generation Internet Protocol (IPng) :

- TUBA proposed in **RFC 1347** and **RFC 1561**
- PIP proposed in **RFC 1621**

- SIPP proposed in **RFC 1710**

The IETF decided to pursue the development of IPng based on the SIPP proposal. As IP version 5 was already used by the experimental ST-2 protocol defined in **RFC 1819**, the successor of IP version 4 is IP version 6. The initial IP version 6 defined in **RFC 1752** was designed based on the following assumptions :

- IPv6 addresses are encoded as a 128 bits field
- The IPv6 header has a simple format that can easily be parsed by hardware devices
- A host should be able to configure its IPv6 address automatically
- Security must be part of IPv6

Note: The IPng address size

When the work on IPng started, it was clear that 32 bits was too small to encode an IPng address and all proposals used longer addresses. However, there were many discussions about the most suitable address length. A first approach, proposed by SIP in **RFC 1710**, was to use 64 bit addresses. A 64 bits address space was 4 billion times larger than the IPv4 address space and, furthermore, from an implementation perspective, 64 bit CPUs were being considered and 64 bit addresses would naturally fit inside their registers. Another approach was to use an existing address format. This was the TUBA proposal (**RFC 1347**) that reuses the ISO CLNP 20 bytes addresses. The 20 bytes addresses provided room for growth, but using ISO CLNP was not favored by the IETF partially due to political reasons, despite the fact that mature CLNP implementations were already available. 128 bits appeared to be a reasonable compromise at that time.

IPv6 addressing architecture

The experience of IPv4 revealed that the scalability of a network layer protocol heavily depends on its addressing architecture. The designers of IPv6 spent a lot of effort defining its addressing architecture RFC 3513. All IPv6 addresses are 128 bits wide. This implies that there are 340; 282; 366; 920; 938; 463; 463; 374; 607; 431; 768; 211; 456(3:4 X 10^{38}) different IPv6 addresses. As the surface of the Earth is about 510,072,000 km^2, this implies that there are about 6:67 X 10^{23} IPv6 addresses per square meter on Earth. Compared to IPv4, which offers only 8 addresses per square kilometer, this is a significant improvement on paper.

IPv6 supports unicast, multicast and anycast addresses. As with IPv4, an IPv6 unicast address is used to identify one datalink-layer interface on a host. If a host has several datalink layer interfaces (e.g. an Ethernet interface and a WiFi interface), then it needs several IPv6 addresses. In general, an IPv6 unicast address is structured as shown in the figure below.

An IPv6 unicast address is composed of three parts :

1. A global routing prefix that is assigned to the Internet Service Provider that owns this block of addresses
2. A subnet identifier that identifies a customer of the ISP
3. An interface identifier that identifies a particular interface on an endsystem

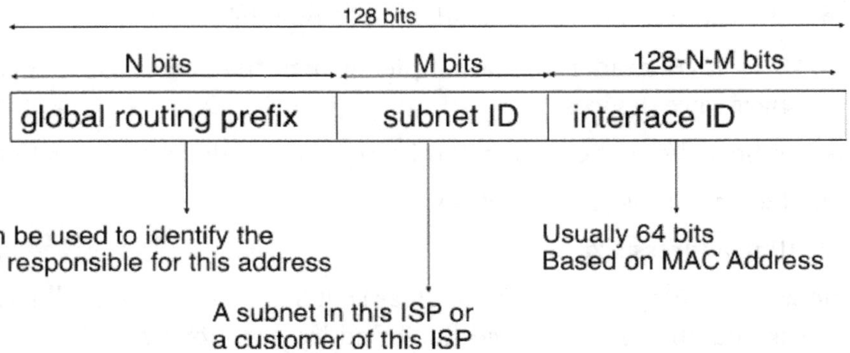

Figure 4.36: Structure of IPv6 unicast addresses

In today's deployments, interface identifiers are always 64 bits wide. This implies that while there are 2^{128} different IPv6 addresses, they must be grouped in 2 subnets. This could appear as a waste of resources, however using 64 bits for the host identifier allows IPv6 addresses to be auto-configured and also provides some benefits from a security point of view, as explained in section ICMPv6

Note: Textual representation of IPv6 addresses

It is sometimes necessary to write IPv6 addresses in text format, e.g. when manually configuring addresses or for documentation purposes. The preferred format for writing IPv6 addresses is *x:x:x:x:x:x:x:x,* where the *x* 's are hexadecimal digits representing the eight 16-bit parts of the address. Here are a few examples of IPv6 addresses:

- ABCD:EF01:2345:6789:ABCD:EF01:2345:6789
- 2001:DB8:0:0:8:800:200C:417A
- FE80:0:0:0:219:E3FF:FED7:1204

IPv6 addresses often contain a long sequence of bits set to *0.* In this case, a compact notation has been defined. With this notation, :: is used to indicate one or more groups of 16 bits blocks containing only bits set to 0. For example,

- 2001:DB8:0:0:8:800:200C:417A is represented as *2001:DB8::8:800:200C:417A*
- FF01:0:0:0:0:0:0:101 is represented as *FF01::101*
- 0:0:0:0:0:0:0:1 is represented as *::1*
- 0:0:0:0:0:0:0:0 is represented as*::*

An IPv6 prefix can be represented as *address/length,* where *length* is the length of the prefix in bits. For example, the three notations below correspond to the same IPv6 prefix :

- 2001:0DB8:0000:CD30:0000:0000:0000:0000/60
- 2001:0DB8::CD30:0:0:0:0/60
- 2001:0DB8:0:CD30::/60

The drawback of PA addresses is that when a company using a PA address block changes its provider, it needs to change all the addresses that it uses. This can be a nightmare from an operational perspective and many companies are lobbying to obtain *PI* address blocks even if they are small and connected to a single provider. The typical size of the IPv6 address blocks are :

- /32 for an Internet Service Provider
- /48 for a single company
- /64 for a single user (e.g. a home user connected via ADSL)
- /128 in the rare case when it is known that no more than one endhost will be attached

For the companies that want to use IPv6 without being connected to the IPv6 Internet, **RFC 4193** defines the *Unique Local Unicast (ULA)* addresses *(FC00::/7).* These ULA addresses play a similar role as the private IPv4 addresses defined in **RFC 1918.** However, the size of the *FC00::/7* address block allows ULA to be much more flexible than private IPv4 addresses.

Furthermore, the IETF has reserved some IPv6 addresses for a special usage. The two most important ones are :

- *0:0:0:0:0:0:0:1* (*::1* in compact form) is the IPv6 loopback address. This is the address of a logical interface that is always up and running on IPv6 enabled hosts. This is the equivalent of *127.0.0.1* in IPv4.
- *0:0:0:0:0:0:0:0* (:: in compact form) is the unspecified IPv6 address. This is the IPv6 address that a host can use as source address when trying to acquire an official address.

The last type of unicast IPv6 addresses are the *Link Local Unicast* addresses. These addresses are part of the *FE80::/10* address block and are defined in **RFC 4291.** Each host can compute its own link local address by concatenating the *FE80::/64* prefix with the 64 bits identifier of its interface. Link local addresses can be used when hosts that are attached to the same link (or local area network) need to exchange packets. They are used notably for address discovery and auto-configuration purposes. Their usage is restricted to each link and a router cannot forward a packet whose source or destination address is a link local address. Link local addresses have also been defined for IPv4 **RFC 3927**. However, the IPv4 link local addresses are only used when a host cannot obtain a regular IPv4 address, e.g. on an isolated LAN.

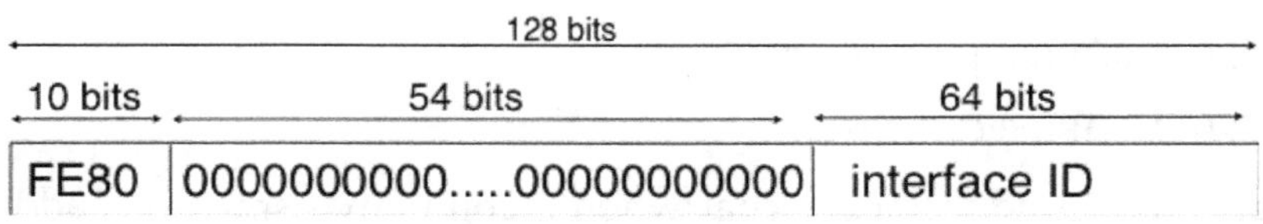

Figure 4.37: IPv6 link local address structure

An important consequence of the IPv6 unicast addressing architecture and the utilisation of link-local addresses is that an IPv6 host has several IPv6 addresses. This implies that an IPv6 stack must be able to handle multiple IPv6 addresses. This was not always the case with IPv4.

RFC 4291 defines a special type of IPv6 anycast address. On a subnetwork having prefix *p/n*, the IPv6 address whose *128-n* low-order bits are set to *0* is the anycast address that corresponds to all routers inside this subnetwork. This anycast address can be used by hosts to quickly send a packet to any of the routers inside their own subnetwork.

Finally, **RFC 4291** defines the structure of the IPv6 multicast addresses. This structure is depicted in the figure below

The low order 112 bits of an IPv6 multicast address are the group's identifier. The high order bits are used as a marker to distinguish multicast addresses from unicast addresses. Notably, the 4 bits flag field indicates whether the address is temporary or permanent. Finally, the scope field indicates the boundaries of the forwarding of packets destined to a particular address. A link-local scope indicates that a router should not forward a packet destined to such a multicast address. An organisation local-scope indicates that a packet sent to such a multicast destination address should not leave the organisation. Finally the global scope is intended for multicast groups spanning the global Internet.

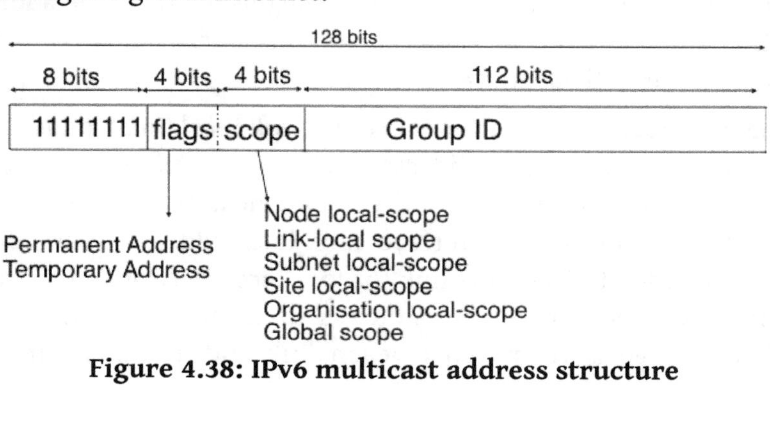

Figure 4.38: IPv6 multicast address structure

Among these addresses, some are well known. For example, all endsystem automatically belong to the *FF02::1* multicast group while all routers automatically belong to the *FF02::2* multicast group. We discuss IPv6 multicast later.

IPv6 packet format

The IPv6 packet format was heavily inspired by the packet format proposed for the SIPP protocol in **RFC 1710**. The standard IPv6 header defined in **RFC 2460** occupies 40 bytes and contains 8 different fields, as shown in the figure below.

```
 0                   1                   2                   3
 0 1 2 3 4 5 6 7 8 9 0 1 2 3 4 5 6 7 8 9 0 1 2 3 4 5 6 7 8 9 0 1
+-+-+-+-+-+-+-+-+-+-+-+-+-+-+-+-+-+-+-+-+-+-+-+-+-+-+-+-+-+-+-+-+
|Version|    DS Field   |               Flow Label              |
+-+-+-+-+-+-+-+-+-+-+-+-+-+-+-+-+-+-+-+-+-+-+-+-+-+-+-+-+-+-+-+-+
|         Payload Length        |  Next Header  |   Hop Limit   |
+-+-+-+-+-+-+-+-+-+-+-+-+-+-+-+-+-+-+-+-+-+-+-+-+-+-+-+-+-+-+-+-+
|                                                               |
+                                                               +
|                                                               |
+                         Source Address                        +
|                                                               |
+                                                               +
|                                                               |
+-+-+-+-+-+-+-+-+-+-+-+-+-+-+-+-+-+-+-+-+-+-+-+-+-+-+-+-+-+-+-+-+
|                                                               |
+                                                               +
|                                                               |
+                      Destination Address                      +
|                                                               |
+                                                               +
|                                                               |
+-+-+-+-+-+-+-+-+-+-+-+-+-+-+-+-+-+-+-+-+-+-+-+-+-+-+-+-+-+-+-+-+
```

Figure 4.39: The IP version 6 header (RFC 2460)

Apart from the source and destination addresses, the IPv6 header contains the following fields :

- *version* : a 4 bits field set to *6* and intended to allow IP to evolve in the future if needed
- *Traffic class* : this 8 bits field plays a similar role as the *DS* byte in the IPv4 header
- *Flow label*: this field was initially intended to be used to tag packets belonging to the same *flow*. However, as of this writing, there is no clear guideline on how this field should be used by hosts and routers
- *Payload length* : this is the size of the packet payload in bytes. As the length is encoded as a 16 bits field, an IPv6 packet can contain up to 65535 bytes of payload.
- *Next Header* : this 8 bits field indicates the type of header that follows the IPv6 header. It can be a transport layer header (e.g. *6* for TCP or *17* for UDP) or an IPv6 option. Handling options as a next header allows simplifying the processing of IPv6 packets compared to IPv4.

- *Hop Limit*: this 8 bits field indicates the number of routers that can forward the packet. It is decremented by one by each router and has the same purpose as the TTL field of the IPv4 header.

In comparison with IPv4, the IPv6 packets are much simpler and easier to process by routers. A first important difference is that there is no checksum inside the IPv6 header. This is mainly because all datalink layers and transport protocols include a checksum or a CRC to protect their frames/segments against transmission errors. Adding a checksum in the IPv6 header would have forced each router to recompute the checksum of all packets, with limited benefit in detecting errors. In practice, an IP checksum allows for catching errors that occur inside routers (e.g. due to memory corruption) before the packet reaches its destination. However, this benefit was found to be too small given the reliability of current memories and the cost of computing the checksum on each router.

A second difference with IPv4 is that the IPv6 header does not support fragmentation and reassembly. Experience with IPv4 has shown that fragmenting packets in routers was costly [KM1995] and the developers of IPv6 have decided that routers would not fragment packets anymore. If a router receives a packet that is too long to be forwarded, the packet is dropped and the router returns an ICMPv6 messages to inform the sender of the problem. The sender can then either fragment the packet or perform Path MTU discovery. In IPv6, packet fragmentation is performed only by the source by using IPv6 options.

The third difference are the IPv6 options, which are simpler and easier to process than the IPv4 options.

Note: Header compression on low bandwidth links

Given the size of the IPv6 header, it can cause huge overhead on low bandwidth links, especially when small packets are exchanged such as for Voice over IP applications. In such environments, several techniques can be used to reduce the overhead. A first solution is to use data compression in the datalink layer to compress all the information exchanged [Thomborson1992]. These techniques are similar to the data compression algorithms used in tools such as *compress(l)* or *gzip(l)* **RFC 1951**. They compress streams of bits without taking advantage of the fact that these streams contain IP packets with a known structure. A second solution is to compress the IP and TCP header. These header compression techniques, such as the one defined in **RFC 2507** take advantage of the redundancy found in successive packets from the same flow to significantly reduce the size of the protocol headers. Another solution is to define a compressed encoding of the IPv6 header that matches the capabilities of the underlying datalink layer **RFC 4944**.

IPv6 options

In IPv6, each option is considered as one header containing a multiple of 8 bytes to ensure that IPv6 options in a packet are aligned on 64 bit boundaries. IPv6 defines several type of options :

- the hop-by-hop options are options that must be processed by the routers on the packet's path
- the type 0 routing header, which is similar to the IPv4 loose source routing option
- the fragmentation option, which is used when fragmenting an IPv6 packet • the destination options
- the security options that allow IPv6 hosts to exchange packets with cryptographic authentication (AH header) or encryption and authentication (ESP header)

RFC 2460 provides lots of detail on the encodings of the different types of options. In this section, we only discus some of them. The reader may consult RFC 2460 for more information about the other options. The first point to note is that each option contains a Next Header field, which indicates the type of header that follows the option. A second point to note is that in order to allow routers to efficiently parse IPv6 packets, the options that must be processed by routers (hop-by-hop options and type 0 routing header) must appear first in the packet. This allows the router to process a packet without being forced to analyse all the packet's options. A third point to note is that hop-by-hop and destination options are encoded using a type length value format. Furthermore, the type field contains bits that indicate whether a router that does not understand this option should ignore the option or discard the packet. This allows the introduction of new options into the network without forcing all devices to be upgraded to support them at the same time.

Two hop-by-hop options have been defined. RFC 2675 specifies the jumbogram that enables IPv6 to support packets containing a payload larger than 65535 bytes. These jumbo packets have their payload length set to 0 and the jumbogram option contains the packet length as a 32 bits field. Such packets can only be sent from a source to a destination if all the routers on the path support this option. However, as of this writing it does not seem that the jumbogram option has been implemented. The router alert option defined in **RFC 2711** is the second example of a *hop-by-hop* option. The packets that contain this option should be processed in a special way by intermediate routers. This option is used for IP packets that carry Resource Reservation Protocol (RSVP) messages. Its usage is explained later.

The type 0 routing header defined in **RFC 2460** is an example of an IPv6 option that must be processed by some routers. This option is encoded as shown below.

```
 0                   1                   2                   3
 0 1 2 3 4 5 6 7 8 9 0 1 2 3 4 5 6 7 8 9 0 1 2 3 4 5 6 7 8 9 0 1
+-+-+-+-+-+-+-+-+-+-+-+-+-+-+-+-+-+-+-+-+-+-+-+-+-+-+-+-+-+-+-+-+
|  Next Header  |  Hdr Ext Len  | Routing Type=0| Segments Left |
+-+-+-+-+-+-+-+-+-+-+-+-+-+-+-+-+-+-+-+-+-+-+-+-+-+-+-+-+-+-+-+-+
|                            Reserved                           |
+-+-+-+-+-+-+-+-+-+-+-+-+-+-+-+-+-+-+-+-+-+-+-+-+-+-+-+-+-+-+-+-+
|                                                               |
+                                                               +
|                                                               |
+                           Address[1]                          +
|                                                               |
+                                                               +
|                                                               |
+-+-+-+-+-+-+-+-+-+-+-+-+-+-+-+-+-+-+-+-+-+-+-+-+-+-+-+-+-+-+-+-+
|                                                               |
+                                                               +
|                                                               |
+                           Address[2]                          +
|                                                               |
+                                                               +
|                                                               |
+-+-+-+-+-+-+-+-+-+-+-+-+-+-+-+-+-+-+-+-+-+-+-+-+-+-+-+-+-+-+-+-+
.                               .                               .
.                               .                               .
.                               .                               .
+-+-+-+-+-+-+-+-+-+-+-+-+-+-+-+-+-+-+-+-+-+-+-+-+-+-+-+-+-+-+-+-+
|                                                               |
+                                                               +
|                                                               |
+                           Address[n]                          +
|                                                               |
+                                                               +
|                                                               |
+-+-+-+-+-+-+-+-+-+-+-+-+-+-+-+-+-+-+-+-+-+-+-+-+-+-+-+-+-+-+-+-+
```

Figure 4.40: The Type 0 routing header (RFC 2460)

The type 0 routing option was intended to allow a host to indicate a loose source route that should be followed by a packet by specifying the addresses of some of the routers that must forward this packet. Unfortunately, further work with this routing header, including an entertaining demonstration with scapy [BE2007] , revealed some severe security problems with this routing header. For this reason, loose source routing with the type 0 routing header has been removed from the IPv6 specification **RFC 5095.**

In IPv6, fragmentation is performed exclusively by the source host and relies on the fragmentation header. This 64 bits header is composed of six fields :

- a *Next Header* field that indicates the type of the header that follows the fragmentation header
- a *reserved* field set to *0.*
- the *Fragment Offset* is a 13-bit unsigned integer that contains the offset, in 8 bytes units, of the data following this header, relative to the start of the original packet.
- the *More* flag, which is set to *0* in the last fragment of a packet and to *1* in all other fragments.
- the 32 bits *Identification* field indicates to which original packet a fragment belongs. When a host sends fragmented packets, it should ensure that it does not reuse the same *identification* field for packets sent

to the same destination during a period of *MSL* seconds. This is easier with the 32 bits *identification* used in the IPv6 fragmentation header, than with the 16 bits *identification* field of the IPv4 header.

Some IPv6 implementations send the fragments of a packet in increasing fragment offset order, starting from the first fragment. Others send the fragments in reverse order, starting from the last fragment. The latter solution can be advantageous for the host that needs to reassemble the fragments, as it can easily allocate the buffer required to reassemble all fragments of the packet upon reception of the last fragment. When a host receives the first fragment of an IPv6 packet, it cannot know a priori the length of the entire IPv6 packet.

The figure below provides an example of a fragmented IPv6 packet containing a UDP segment. The *Next Header* type reserved for the IPv6 fragmentation option is 44.

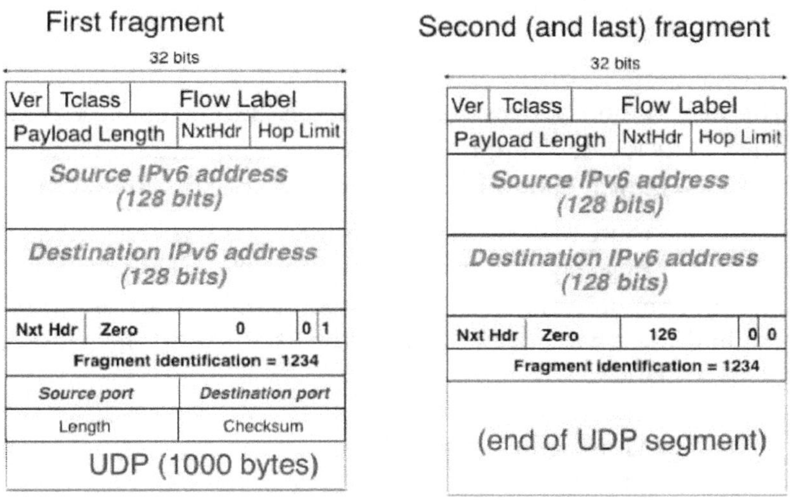

Figure 4.41: IPv6 fragmentation example

Finally, the last type of IPv6 options is the Encaspulating Security Payload (ESP) defined in **RFC 4303** and the Authentication Header (AH) defined in **RFC 4302**. These two headers are used by IPSec **RFC 4301**. They are discussed in another chapter.

4.2.4 ICMP version 6

ICMPv6 defined in **RFC 4443** is the companion protocol for IPv6 as ICMPv4 is the companion protocol for IPv4. ICMPv6 is used by routers and hosts to report problems when processing IPv6 packets. However, as we will see in chapter *The datalink layer and the Local Area Networks*, ICMPv6 is also used when auto-configuring addresses.

The traditional utilisation of ICMPv6 is similar to ICMPv4. ICMPv6 messages are carried inside IPv6 packets (the *Next Header* field for ICMPv6 is 58). Each ICMP message contains an 8 bits header with a *type* field, a *code* field and a 16 bits checksum computed over the entire ICMPv6 message. The message body contains a copy of the IPv6 packet in error.

```
 0                   1                   2                   3
 0 1 2 3 4 5 6 7 8 9 0 1 2 3 4 5 6 7 8 9 0 1 2 3 4 5 6 7 8 9 0 1
+-+-+-+-+-+-+-+-+-+-+-+-+-+-+-+-+-+-+-+-+-+-+-+-+-+-+-+-+-+-+-+-+
|     Type      |     Code      |          Checksum             |
+-+-+-+-+-+-+-+-+-+-+-+-+-+-+-+-+-+-+-+-+-+-+-+-+-+-+-+-+-+-+-+-+
|                                                               |
+                         Message Body                          +
|                                                               |
```

Figure 4.42: ICMP version 6 packet format

ICMPv6 specifies two classes of messages : error messages that indicate a problem in handling a packet and informational messages. Four types of error messages are defined in **RFC 4443** :

- **1** [Destination Unreachable. Such an ICMPv6 message is sent when the destination address of a packet is unreachable. The *code* field of the ICMP header contains additional information about the type of unreachability. The following codes are specified in **RFC 4443**]
  - 0 : No route to destination. This indicates that the router that sent the ICMPv6 message did not have a route towards the packet's destination
  - 1: Communication with destination administratively prohibited. This indicates that a firewall has refused to forward the packet towards its destination.
  - 2 : Beyond scope of source address. This message can be sent if the source is using link-local addresses to reach a global unicast address outside its subnet.
  - 3 : Address unreachable. This message indicates that the packet reached the subnet of the destination, but the host that owns this destination address cannot be reached.
  - 4 : Port unreachable. This message indicates that the IPv6 packet was received by the destination, but there was no application listening to the specified port.
- 2 : Packet Too Big. The router that was to send the ICMPv6 message received an IPv6 packet that is larger than the MTU of the outgoing link. The ICMPv6 message contains the MTU of this link in bytes. This allows the sending host to implement Path MTU discovery **RFC 1981**
- 3 : Time Exceeded. This error message can be sent either by a router or by a host. A router would set *code* to *0* to report the reception of a packet whose *Hop Limit* reached *0*. A host would set code to *1* to report that it was unable to reassemble received IPv6 fragments.

- 4 : Parameter Problem. This ICMPv6 message is used to report either the reception of an IPv6 packet with an erroneous header field (type 0) or an unknown *Next Header* or IP option (types 1 and 2). In this case, the message body contains the erroneous IPv6 packet and the first 32 bits of the message body contain a pointer to the error.

Two types of informational ICMPv6 messages are defined in **RFC 4443** : *echo request* and *echo reply,* which are used to test the reachability of a destination by using *ping6(8).*

ICMPv6 also allows the discovery of the path between a source and a destination by using *traceroute6(8).* The output below shows a traceroute between a host at UCLouvain and one of the main IETF servers. Note that this IPv6 path is different than the IPv4 path that was described earlier although the two traceroutes were performed at the same time.

traceroute6 www.ietf.org
traceroute6 to www.ietf.org (2001:1890:1112:1::20) from 2001:6a8:3080:2:217:f2ff:fed6:65c0, 30 hops 1 2001:6a8:3080:2::1 13.821 ms 0.301 ms 0.324 ms
2 2001:6a8:3000:8000::1 0.651 ms 0.51 ms 0.495 ms
3 10ge.cr2.bruvil.belnet.net 3.402 ms 3.34 ms 3.33 ms
4 10ge.cr2.brueve.belnet.net 3.668 ms 10ge.cr2.brueve.belnet.net 3.988 ms 10ge.cr2.brueve.belnet.5 belnet.rt1.ams.nl.geant2.net 10.598 ms 7.214 ms 10.082 ms
6 so-7-0-0.rt2.cop.dk.geant2.net 20.19 ms 20.002 ms 20.064 ms
7 kbn-ipv6-b1.ipv6.telia.net 21.078 ms 20.868 ms 20.864 ms
8 s-ipv6-b1-link.ipv6.telia.net 31.312 ms 31.113 ms 31.411 ms
9 s-ipv6-b1-link.ipv6.telia.net 61.986 ms 61.988 ms 61.994 ms
10 2001:1890:61:8909::1 121.716 ms 121.779 ms 121.177 ms
11 2001:1890:61:9117::2 203.709 ms 203.305 ms 203.07 ms
12 mail.ietf.org 204.172 ms 203.755 ms 203.748 ms

Note: Rate limitation of ICMP messages

High-end hardware based routers use special purpose chips on their interfaces to forward IPv6 packets at line rate. These chips are optimised to process *correct* IP packets. They are not able to create ICMP messages at line rate. When such a chip receives an IP packet that triggers an ICMP message, it interrupts the main CPU of the router and the software running on this CPU processes the packet. This CPU is much slower than the hardware acceleration found on the interfaces [Gill2004]. It would be overloaded if it had to process IP packets at line rate and generate one ICMP message for each received packet. To protect this CPU, high-end routers limit the rate at which the hardware can interrupt the main CPU and thus the rate at which ICMP messages can be generated. This implies that not all erroneous

IP packets cause the transmission of an ICMP message. The risk of overloading the main CPU of the router is also the reason why using hop-by-hop IPv6 options, including the router alter option is discouraged.

Interactions between IPv6 and the datalink layer

There are several differences between IPv6 and IPv4 when considering their interactions with the datalink layer. In IPv6, the interactions between the network and the datalink layer is performed using ICMPv6.

First ICMPv6 is used to resolve the datalink layer address that corresponds to a given IPv6 address. This part of ICMPv6 is the Neighbour Discovery Protocol (NDP) defined in **RFC 4861.** NDP is similar to ARP, but there are two important differences. First, NDP messages are exchanged in ICMPv6 messages while ARP messages are sent as datalink layer frames. Second, an ARP request is sent as a broadcast frame while an NDP solicitation message is sent as a multicast ICMPv6 packet that is transported inside a multicast frame. The operation of the NDP protocol is similar to ARP. To obtain an address mapping, a host sends a Neighbour Solicitation message. This message is sent inside an ICMPv6 message that is placed in an IPv6 packet whose source address is the IPv6 address of the requesting host and the destination address is the all-hosts IPv6 multicast address *(FF02::1)* to which all IPv6 hosts listen. The Neighbour Solicitation contains the requested IPv6 address. The owner of the requested address replies by sending a unicast Neighbour Advertisement message to the requesting host. NDP suffers from similar security issues as the ARP protocol. However, it is possible to secure NDP by using the *Cryptographically Generated IPv6 Addresses* (CGA) defined in **RFC 3972.** The Secure Neighbour Discovery Protocol is defined in **RFC 3971**, but a detailed description of this protocol is outside the scope of this chapter.

IPv6 networks also support the Dynamic Host Configuration Protocol. The IPv6 extensions to DHCP are defined in **RFC 3315.** The operation of DHCPv6 is similar to DHCP that was described earlier. In addition to DHCPv6, IPv6 networks support another mechanism to assign IPv6 addresses to hosts. This is the Stateless Address Configuration (SLAC) defined in **RFC 4862.** When a host boots, it derives its identifier from its datalink layer address and concatenates this 64 bits identifier to the *FE80::/64* prefix to obtain its link-local IPv6 address. It then sends a Neighbour Solicitation with its link-local address as a target to verify whether another host is using the same link-local address on this subnet. If it receives a Neighbour Advertisement indicating that the link-local address is used by another host, it generates another 64 bits identifier and sends again a Neighbour Solicitation. If there is no answer, the host considers its link-local address to be valid. This address will be used as the source address for all NDP messages sent on the subnet. To automatically configure its global IPv6 address, the host must know the globally routable IPv6 prefix that is used on the local subnet. IPv6 routers regularly send ICMPv6 Router Advertisement messages that indicate the IPv6 prefix assigned to each subnet. Upon reception of this message, the host can derive its global IPv6 address by concatenating its 64 bits identifier with the received prefix. It concludes the SLAC by sending a Neighbour Solicitation message targeted at its global IPv6 address to ensure that another host is not using the same IPv6 address.

4.2.5 Middleboxes

When the TCP/IP architecture and the IP protocol were defined, two type of devices were considered in the network layer : endhosts and routers. Endhosts are the sources and destinations of IP packets while routers forward packets. When a router forwards an IP packet, it consults its forwarding table, updates the packet's TTL, recomputes its checksum and forwards it to the next hop. A router does not need to read or change the contents of the packet's payload.

However, in today's Internet, there exist devices that are not strictly routers but which process, sometimes modify, and forward IP packets. These devices are often called *middleboxes* **RFC 3234**. Some middleboxes only operate in the network layer, but most middleboxes are able to analyse the payload of the received packets and extract the transport header, and in some cases the application layer protocols.

In this section, we briefly describe two type of middleboxes : firewalls and network address translation (NAT) devices. A discussion of the different types of middleboxes with references may be found in **RFC 3234**.

Firewalls

When the Internet was only a research network interconnecting research labs, security was not a concern, and most hosts agreed to exchange packets over TCP connections with most other hosts. However, as more and more users and companies became connected to the Internet, allowing unlimited access to hosts that they managed started to concern companies. Furthermore, at the end of the 1980s, several security issues affected the Internet, such as the first Internet worm [RE1989] and some widely publicised security breaches [Stoll1988] [CB2003] [Cheswick1990] .

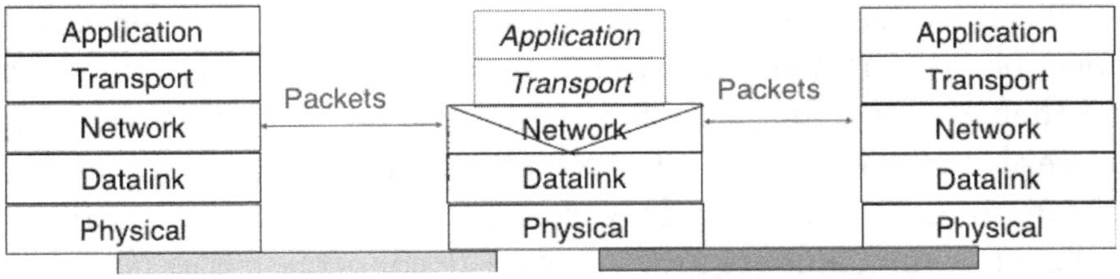

Figure 4.43: IP middleboxes and the reference model

These security problems convinced the industry that IP networks are a key part of a company's infrastructure, that should be protected by special devices like security guards and fences are used to protect buildings. These special devices were quickly called *firewalls.* A typical firewall has two interfaces:

- an external interface connected to the global Internet
- an internal interface connected to a trusted network

The first firewalls included configurable packet filters. A packet filter is a set of rules defining the security policy of a network. In practice, these rules are based on the values of fields in the IP or transport layer headers. Any field of the IP or transport header can be used in a firewall rule, but the most common ones are:

- filter on the source address. For example, a company may decide to discard all packets received from one of its competitors. In this case, all packets whose source address belong to the competitor's address block would be rejected
- filter on destination address. For example, the hosts of the research lab of a company may receive packets from the global Internet, but not the hosts of the financial department
- filter on the *Protocol* number found in the IP header. For example, a company may only allow its hosts to use TCP or UDP, but not other, more experimental, transport protocols
- filter on the TCP or UDP port numbers. For example, only the DNS server of a company should received UDP segments whose destination port is set to *53* or only the official SMTP servers of the company can send TCP segments whose source ports are set to 25
- filter on the TCP flags. For example, a simple solution to prohibit external hosts from opening TCP connections with hosts inside the company is to discard all TCP segments received from the external interface with only the *SYN* flag set.

Such firewalls are often called *stateless* firewalls because they do not maintain any state about the TCP connections that pass through them.

Another type of firewalls are *stateful* firewalls. A stateful firewall tracks the state of each TCP connection passing through it and maintains a TCB for each of these TCP connection. This TCB allows it to reassemble the received segments in order to extract their payload and perform verifications in the application layer. Some firewalls are able to inspect the URLs accessed using HTTP and log all URLs visited or block TCP connections where a dangerous URL is exchanged. Some firewalls can verify that SMTP commands are used when a TCP connection is established on port *25* or that a TCP connection on port *80* carries HTTP commands and responses.

Note: Beyond firewalls

Apart from firewalls, different types of "security" devices have been installed at the periphery of corporate networks. Intrusion Detection Systems (IDS), such as the popular snort , are stateful devices that are capable of matching reassembled segments against regular expressions corresponding to signatures of viruses, worms or other types of attacks. Deep Packet Inspection (DPI) is another type of middlebox that analyses the packet's payload and is able to reassemble TCP segments in order to detect inappropriate usages. While IDS are mainly used in corporate networks, DPI is mainly used in Internet Service Providers. Some ISPs use DPI to detect and limit the bandwidth consumed by peer-to-peer applications. Some countries such as China or Iran use DPI to detect inappropriate Internet usage.

NAT

Network Address Translation (NAT) was proposed in [TE1993] and **RFC 3022** as a short term solution to deal with the expected shortage of IPv4 addresses in the late 1980s - early 1990s. Combined with CIDR, NAT helped to significantly slow down the consumption of IPv4 addresses. A NAT is a middlebox that interconnects two networks that are using IPv4 addresses from different addressing spaces. Usually, one of these addressing spaces is the public Internet while the other is using the private IPv4 addresses defined in **RFC 1918.**

A very common deployment of NAT is in broadband access routers as shown in the figure below. The broadband access router interconnects a home network, either WiFi or Ethernet based, and the global Internet via one ISP over ADSL or CATV. A single IPv4 address is allocated to the broadband access router and network address translation allows all of the hosts attached to the home network to share a single public IPv4 address.

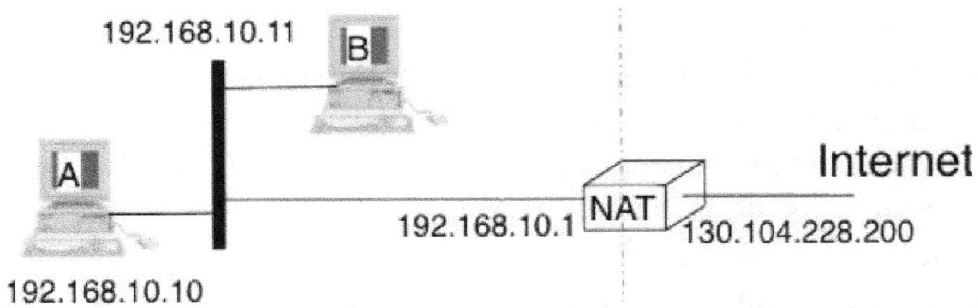

Figure 4.44: A simple NAT with one public IPv4 address

A second type of deployment is in enterprise networks as shown in the figure below. In this case, the NAT functionality is installed on a border router of the enterprise. A private IPv4 address is assigned to each enterprise host while the border router manages a pool containing several public IPv4 addresses.

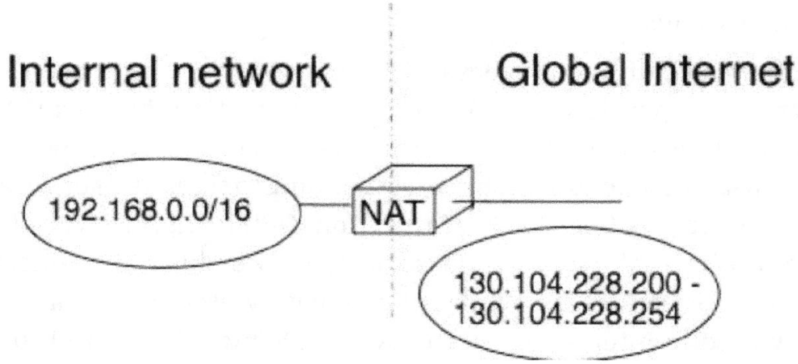

Figure 4.45: An enterprise NAT with several public IPv4 addresses

As the name implies, a NAT is a device that "translates" IP addresses. A NAT maintains a mapping table between the private IP addresses used in the internal network and the public IPv4 addresses. NAT allows a large number of hosts to share a pool of IP addresses, as these hosts do not all access the global Internet at the same time.

The simplest NAT is a middlebox that uses a one-to-one mapping between a private IP address and a public IP address. To understand its operation, let us assume that a NAT, such as the one shown above, has just booted. When the NAT receives the first packet from source *S* in the internal network which is destined to the public Internet, it creates a mapping between internal address S and the first address of its pool of public addresses *(P1)*. Then, it translates the received packet so that it can be sent to the public Internet. This translation is performed as followed :

- the source address of the packet *(S)* is replaced by the mapped public address (P1)
- the checksum of the IP header is incrementally updated as its content has changed
- if the packet carried a TCP or UDP segment, the transport layer checksum found in the included segment must also be updated as it is computed over the segment and a pseudo-header that includes the source and destination addresses

When a packet destined to *P1* is received from the public Internet, the NAT consults its mapping table to find S. The received packet is translated and forwarded in the internal network.

This works as long as the pool of public IP addresses of the NAT does not become empty. In this case, a mapping must be removed from the mapping table to allow a packet from a new host to be translated. This garbage collection can be implemented by adding to each entry in the mapping table a timestamp that contains the last utilisation time of a mapping entry. This timestamp is updated each time the corresponding entry is used. Then, the garbage collection algorithm can remove the oldest mapping entry in the table.

A drawback of such a simple enterprise NAT is the size of the pool of public IPv4 addresses which is often too small to allow a large number of hosts share such a NAT. In this case, a better solution is to allow the NAT to translate both IP addresses and port numbers.

Such a NAT maintains a mapping table that maps an internal IP address and TCP port number with an external IP address and TCP port number. When such a NAT receives a packet from the internal network, it performs a lookup in the mapping table with the packet's source IP address and source TCP port number. If a mapping is found, the source IP address and the source TCP port number of the packet are translated with the values found in the mapping table, the checksums are updated and the packet is sent to the global Internet. If no mapping is found, a new mapping is created with the first available couple *(IP address, TCP port number)* and the packet is translated. The entries of the mapping table are either removed at the end of the corresponding TCP connection as the NAT tracks TCP connection state like a stateful firewall or after some idle time.

When such a NAT receives a packet from the global Internet, it looks up its mapping table for the packet's destination IP address and destination TCP port number. If a mapping is found, the packet is translated and forwarded into the internal network. Otherwise, the packet is discarded as the NAT cannot determine to which particular internal host the packet should be forwarded. For this reason,

With 2^{16} different port numbers, a NAT may support a large number of hosts with a single public IPv4 address. However, it should be noted that some applications open a large number of TCP connections [Miyakawa2008]. Each of these TCP connections consumes one mapping entry in the NAT's mapping table.

NAT allows many hosts to share one or a few public IPv4 addresses. However, using NAT has two important drawbacks. First, it is difficult for external hosts to open TCP connections with hosts that are behind a NAT. Some consider this to be a benefit from a security perspective. However, a NAT should not be confused with a firewall as there are some techniques to traverse NATs. Second, NAT breaks the end-to-end transparency of the network and transport layers. The main problem is when an application layer protocol uses IP addresses in some of the ADUs that it sends. A popular example is ftp defined in **RFC 959**. In this case, there is a mismatch between the packet header translated by the NAT and the packet payload. The only solution to solve this problem is to place an Application Level Gateway (ALG) on the NAT that understands the application layer protocol and can thus translate the IP addresses and port numbers found in the ADUs. However, defining an ALG for each application is costly and application developers should avoid using IP addresses in the messages exchanged in the application layer **RFC 3235**.

Note: IPv6 and NAT

NAT has been very successful with IPv4. Given the size of the IPv6 addressing space, the IPv6 designers expected that NAT would never be useful with IPv6. The end-to-end transparency of IPv6 has been one of its key selling points compared to IPv4. However, the expected shortage of IPv4 addresses lead enterprise network administrators to consider IPv6 more seriously. One of the results of this analysis is that the IETF defined NAT devices [WB2008] that are IPv6 specific. Another usage of NAT with IPv6 is to allow IPv6 hosts to access IPv4 destinations and conversely. The early IPv6 specifications included the Network Address Translation - Protocol Translation (NAT- PT) mechanism defined in **RFC 2766**. This mechanism was later deprecated in **RFC 4966** but has been recently restarted under the name NAT64 [BMvB2009]. A NAT64 is a middlebox that performs the IPv6<->IPv4 packet translation to allow IPv6 hosts to contact IPv4 servers **RFC 6144**.

4.3 ROUTING IN IP NETWORKS

In a large IP network such as the global Internet, routers need to exchange routing information. The Internet is an interconnection of networks, often called domains, that are under different responsibilities. As of this writing, the Internet is composed on more than 30,000 different domains and this number is still growing. A domain can be a small enterprise that manages a few routers in a single building, a larger enterprise with a hundred routers at multiple locations, or a large Internet Service Provider managing thousands of routers. Two classes of routing protocols are used to allow these domains to efficiently exchange routing information.

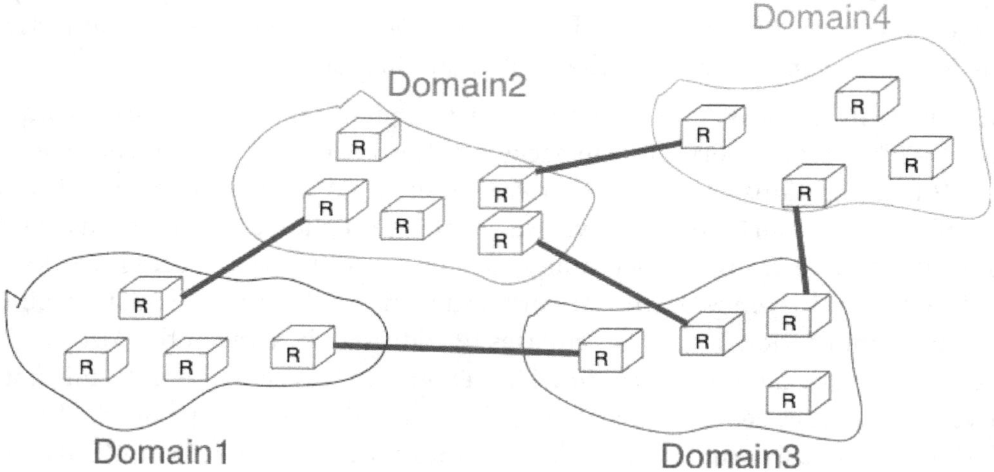

Figure 4.46: Organisation of a small Internet

The first class of routing protocols are the *intradomain routing protocols* (sometimes also called the interior gateway protocols or *IGP).* An intradomain routing protocol is used by all routers inside a domain to exchange routing information about the destinations that are reachable inside the domain. There are several intradomain routing protocols. Some domains use *RIP,* which is a distance vector protocol. Other domains use link-state routing protocols such as *OSPF* or *IS-IS.* Finally, some domains use static routing or proprietary protocols such as *IGRP* or *EIGRP.*

These intradomain routing protocols usually have two objectives. First, they distribute routing information that corresponds to the shortest path between two routers in the domain. Second, they should allow the routers to quickly recover from link and router failures.

The second class of routing protocols are the *interdomain routing protocols* (sometimes also called the exterior gateway protocols or *EGP*). The objective of an interdomain routing protocol is to distribute routing information between domains. For scalability reasons, an interdomain routing protocol must distribute aggregated routing information and considers each domain as a black box.

A very important difference between intradomain and interdomain routing are the *routing policies* that are used by each domain. Inside a single domain, all routers are considered equal, and when several routes are available to reach a given destination prefix, the best route is selected based on technical criteria such as the route with the shortest delay, the route with the minimum number of hops or the route with the highest bandwidth.

When we consider the interconnection of domains that are managed by different organisations, this is no longer true. Each domain implements its own routing policy. A routing policy is composed of three elements : an *import filter* that specifies which routes can be accepted by a domain, an *export filter* that specifies which routes can be advertised by a domain and a ranking algorithm that selects the best route when a domain knows several routes towards the same destination prefix. As we will see later, another important difference is that the objective of the interdomain routing protocol is to find the *cheapest* route towards each destination. There is only one interdomain routing protocol : *BGP*.

4.3.1 Intradomain routing

In this section, we briefly describe the key features of the two main intradomain unicast routing protocols : RIP and OSPF.

RIP

The Routing Information Protocol (RIP) is the simplest routing protocol that was standardised for the TCP/IP protocol suite. RIP is defined in **RFC 2453**. Additional information about RIP may be found in [Malkin1999]

RIP routers periodically exchange RIP messages. The format of these messages is shown below. A RIP message is sent inside a UDP segment whose destination port is set to *521*. A RIP message contains several fields. The *Cmd* field indicates whether the RIP message is a request or a response. Routers send one of more RIP response messages every 30 seconds. These messages contain the distance vectors that summarize the router's routing table. The RIP request messages can be used by routers or hosts to query other routers about the content of their routing table. A typical usage is when a router boots and quickly wants to receive the RIP responses from its neighbours to compute its own routing table. The current version of RIP is version 2 defined in **RFC 2453** for IPv4 and **RFC**

```
 0                   1                   2                   3
 0 1 2 3 4 5 6 7 8 9 0 1 2 3 4 5 6 7 8 9 0 1 2 3 4 5 6 7 8 9 0 1
+-+-+-+-+-+-+-+-+-+-+-+-+-+-+-+-+-+-+-+-+-+-+-+-+-+-+-+-+-+-+-+-+
| Command (1)   | Version (1)   |            unused             |
+---------------+---------------+-------------------------------+
|             0xFFFF            |    Authentication Type (2)    |
+-------------------------------+-------------------------------+
~                       Authentication (16)                     ~
+---------------------------------------------------------------+
~                     Up to 20 Route Entries                    ~
+---------------------------------------------------------------+
```

Figure 4.47: RIP message format

The RIP header contains an authentication field. This authentication can be used by network administrators to ensure that only the RIP messages sent by the routers that they manage are used to build the routing tables. **RFC 2453** only supports a basic authentication scheme where all routers are configured with the same password and include this password in all RIP messages. This is not very secure since an attacker can know the password by capturing a single RIP message. However, this password can protect against configuration errors. Stronger authentication schemes are described in **RFC 2082** and **RFC 4822,** but the details of these mechanisms are outside the scope of this section.

Each RIP message contains a set of route entries. Each route entry is encoded as a 20 bytes field whose format is shown below. RIP was initially designed to be suitable for different network layer protocols. Some implementations of RIP were used in XNS or IPX networks. The first field of the RIP route entry is the *Address Family Identifier (AFI).* This identifier indicates the type of address found in the route entry [22]. IPv4 uses *AFI=1.* The other important fields of the route entry are the IPv4 prefix, the netmask that indicates the length of the subnet identifier and is encoded as a 32 bits netmask and the metric. Although the metric is encoded as a 32 bits field, the maximum RIP metric is *15* (for RIP, 16 = to)

```
 0                   1                   2                   3 3
 0 1 2 3 4 5 6 7 8 9 0 1 2 3 4 5 6 7 8 9 0 1 2 3 4 5 6 7 8 9 0 1
+-+-+-+-+-+-+-+-+-+-+-+-+-+-+-+-+-+-+-+-+-+-+-+-+-+-+-+-+-+-+-+-+
| Address Family Identifier (2) |        Route Tag (2)          |
+-------------------------------+-------------------------------+
|                         IP Address (4)                        |
+---------------------------------------------------------------+
|                         Subnet Mask (4)                       |
+---------------------------------------------------------------+
|                         Next Hop (4)                          |
+---------------------------------------------------------------+
|                         Metric (4)                            |
+---------------------------------------------------------------+
```

Figure 4.48: Format of the RIP IPv4 route entries (RFC 2453)

With a 20 bytes route entry, it was difficult to use the same format as above to support IPv6. Instead of defining a variable length route entry format, the designers of **RFC 2080** defined a new format that does not include an *AFI* field. The format of the route entries used by **RFC 2080** is shown below. *Plen* is the length of the subnet identifier in bits and the metric is encoded as one byte. The maximum metric is still *15*.

```
 0                   1                   2                   3
 0 1 2 3 4 5 6 7 8 9 0 1 2 3 4 5 6 7 8 9 0 1 2 3 4 5 6 7 8 9 0 1
+-+-+-+-+-+-+-+-+-+-+-+-+-+-+-+-+-+-+-+-+-+-+-+-+-+-+-+-+-+-+-+-+
|                                                               |
~                        IPv6 prefix (16)                       ~
|                                                               |
+---------------------------------------------------------------+
|         route tag (2)         | prefix len (1)|  metric (1)   |
+-+-+-+-+-+-+-+-+-+-+-+-+-+-+-+-+-+-+-+-+-+-+-+-+-+-+-+-+-+-+-+-+
```

Figure 4.49: Format of the RIP IPv6 route entries

Note: A note on timers

The first RIP implementations sent their distance vector exactly every 30 seconds. This worked well in most networks, but some researchers noticed that routers were sometimes overloaded because they were processing too many distance vectors at the same time [FJ1994]. They collected packet traces in these networks and found that after some time the routers' timers became synchronised, i.e. almost all routers were sending their distance vectors at almost the same time. This synchronisation of the transmission times of the distance vectors caused an overload on the routers' CPU but also increased the convergence time of the protocol in some cases. This was mainly due to the fact that all routers set their timers to the same expiration time after having processed the received distance vectors. Sally Floyd and Van Jacobson proposed in [FJ1994] a simple solution to solve this synchronisation problem. Instead of advertising their distance vector exactly after 30 seconds, a router should send its next distance vector after a delay chosen randomly in the [15,45] interval **RFC 2080.** This randomisation of the delays prevents the synchronisation that occurs with a fixed delay and is now a recommended practice for protocol designers.

OSPF

Link-state routing protocols are used in IP networks. Open Shortest Path First (OSPF), defined in **RFC 2328,** is the link state routing protocol that has been standardised by the IETF. The last version of OSPF, which supports IPv6, is defined in **RFC 5340.** OSPF is frequently used in enterprise networks and in some ISP networks. However, ISP networks often use the IS-IS link-state routing protocol [ISO10589], which was developed for the ISO CLNP protocol but was adapted to be used in IP **RFC 1195** networks before the finalisation of the standardisation of OSPF. A detailed analysis of ISIS and OSPF may be found in [BMO2006] and [Perlman2000]. Additional information about OSPF may be found in [Moy1998].

Compared to the basics of link-state routing protocols that we discussed in section *Link state routing,* there are some particularities of OSPF that are worth discussing. First, in a large network, flooding the information about all routers and links to thousands of routers or more may be costly as each router needs to store all the information about the entire network. A better approach would be to introduce hierarchical routing. Hierarchical routing divides the network into regions. All the routers inside a region have detailed information about the topology of the region but only learn aggregated information about the topology of the other regions and their interconnections. OSPF supports a restricted variant of hierarchical routing. In OSPF's terminology, a region is called an area.

OSPF imposes restrictions on how a network can be divided into areas. An area is a set of routers and links that are grouped together. Usually, the topology of an area is chosen so that a packet sent by one router inside the area can reach any other router in the area without leaving the area. An OSPF area contains two types of routers **RFC 2328:**

- Internal router : A router whose directly connected networks belong to the area
- Area border routers: A router that is attached to several areas.

For example, the network shown in the figure below has been divided into three areas: *area 1,* containing routers *R1, R3, R4, R5* and *RA, area 2* containing *R7, R8, R9, R10, RB* and *RC.* OSPF areas are identified by a 32 bit integer, which is sometimes represented as an IP address. Among the OSPF areas, *area 0,* also called the *backbone area* has a special role. The backbone area groups all the area border routers (routers

RA, *RB* and *RC* in the figure below) and the routers that are directly connected to the backbone routers but do not belong to another area (router *RD* in the figure below). An important restriction imposed by OSPF is that the path between two routers that belong to two different areas (e.g. *R1* and *R8* in the figure below) must pass through the backbone area.

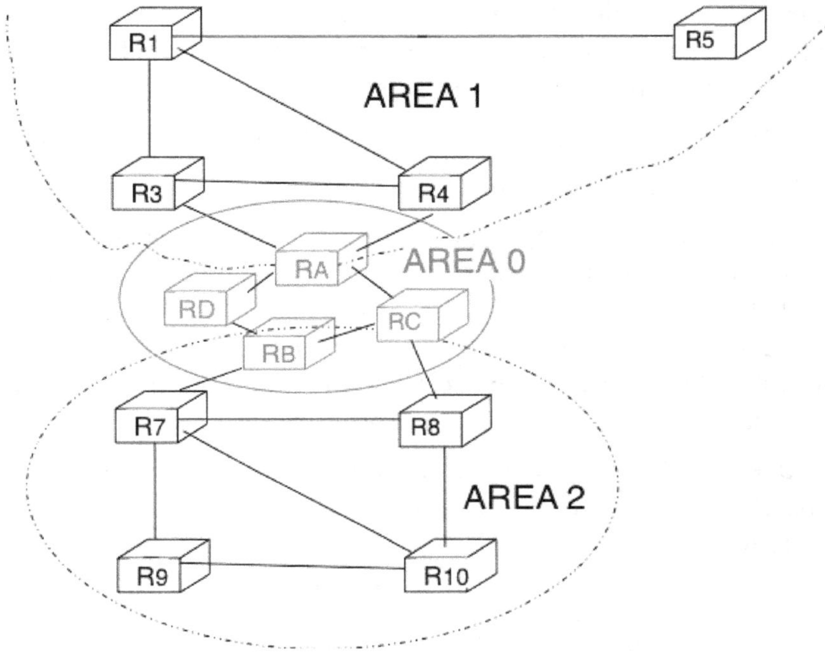

Figure 4.50: OSPF areas

Inside each non-backbone area, routers distribute the topology of the area by exchanging link state packets with the other routers in the area. The internal routers do not know the topology of other areas, but each router knows how to reach the backbone area. Inside an area, the routers only exchange link-state packets for all destinations that are reachable inside the area. In OSPF, the inter-area routing is done by exchanging distance vectors. This is illustrated by the network topology shown below.

Let us first consider OSPF routing inside *area 2*. All routers in the area learn a route towards *192.168.1.0/24* and *192.168.10.0/24*. The two area border routers, *RB* and RC, create network summary advertisements. Assuming that all links have a unit link metric, these would be:

- *RB* advertises *192.168.1.0/24* at a distance of *2* and *192.168.10.0/24* at a distance of *3*
- *RC* advertises *192.168.1.0/24* at a distance of *3* and *192.168.10.0/24* at a distance of *2*

These summary advertisements are flooded through the backbone area attached to routers *RB* and RC. In its routing table, router *RA* selects the summary advertised by *RB* to reach *192.168.1.0/24* and the summary advertised by *RC* to reach *192.168.10.0/24.* Inside *area 1,* router *RA* advertises a summary indicating that *192.168.1.0/24* and *192.168.10.0/24* are both at a distance of *3* from itself.

On the other hand, consider the prefixes *10.0.0.0/24* and *10.0.1.0/24* that are inside *area 1.* Router *RA* is the only area border router that is attached to this area. This router can create two different network summary advertisements :

- *10.0.0.0/24* at a distance of *1* and *10.0.1.0/24* at a distance of *2* from *RA*
- *10.0.0.0/23* at a distance of *2* from *RA*

The first summary advertisement provides precise information about the distance used to reach each prefix. However, all routers in the network have to maintain a route towards *10.0.0.0/24* and a route towards *10.0.1.0/24* that are both via router *RA.* The second advertisement would improve the scalability of OSPF by reducing the number of routes that are advertised across area boundaries. However, in practice this requires manual configuration on the border routers.

The second OSPF particularity that is worth discussing is the support of Local Area Networks (LAN). As shown in the example below, several routers may be attached to the same LAN.

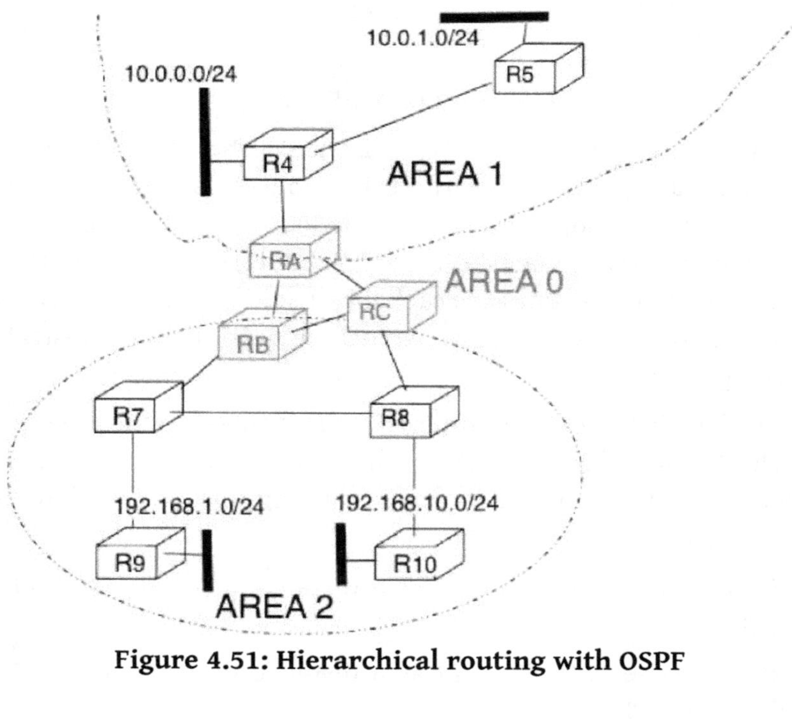

Figure 4.51: Hierarchical routing with OSPF

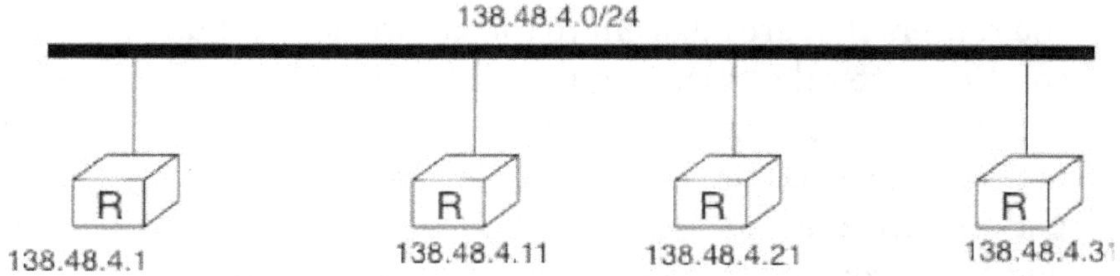

Figure 4.52: An OSPF LAN containing several routers

A first solution to support such a LAN with a link-state routing protocol would be to consider that a LAN is equivalent to a full-mesh of point-to-point links as if each router can directly reach any other router on the LAN. However, this approach has two important drawbacks:

Each router must exchange HELLOs and link state packets with all the other routers on the LAN. This increases the number of OSPF packets that are sent and processed by each router.

Remote routers, when looking at the topology distributed by OSPF, consider that there is a full-mesh of links between all the LAN routers. Such a full-mesh implies a lot of redundancy in case of failure, while in practice the entire LAN may completely fail. In case of a failure of the entire LAN, all routers need to detect the failures and flood link state packets before the LAN is completely removed from the OSPF topology by remote routers.

To better represent LANs and reduce the number of OSPF packets that are exchanged, OSPF handles LAN differently. When OSPF routers boot on a LAN, they elect one of them as the *Designated Router (DR)* **RFC 2328**. The DR router *represents* the local area network, and advertises the LAN's subnet *(138.48.4.0/24* in the example above). Furthermore, LAN routers only exchange HELLO packets with the DR. Thanks to the utilisation of a DR, the topology of the LAN appears as a set of point-to-point links connected to the *DR* as shown in the figure below.

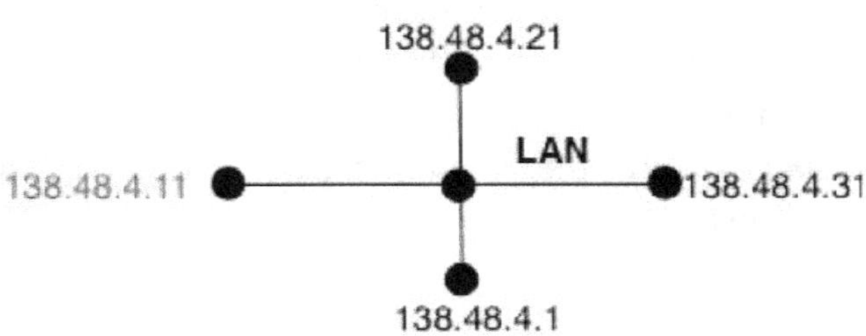

Figure 4.53: OSPF representation of a LAN

Note: How to quickly detect a link failure ?

Network operators expect an OSPF network to be able to quickly recover from link or router failures [VPD2004]. In an OSPF network, the recovery after a failure is performed in three steps [FFEB2005] :

- the routers that are adjacent to the failure detect it quickly. The default solution is to rely on the regular exchange of HELLO packets. However, the interval between successive HELLOs is often set to 10 seconds... Setting the HELLO timer down to a few milliseconds is difficult as HELLO packets are created and processed by the main CPU of the routers and these routers cannot easily generate and process a HELLO packet every millisecond on each of their interfaces. A better solution is to use a dedicated failure detection protocol such as the Bidirectional Forwarding Detection (BFD) protocol defined in [KW2009] that can be implemented directly on the router interfaces. Another solution to be able to detect the failure is to instrument the physical and the datalink layer so that they can interrupt the router when a link fails. Unfortunately, such a solution cannot be used on all types of physical and datalink layers.
- the routers that have detected the failure flood their updated link state packets in the network
- all routers update their routing table

4.3.2 Interdomain routing

As explained earlier, the Internet is composed of more than 30,000 different networks called *domains*. Each domain is composed of a group of routers and hosts that are managed by the same organisation. Example domains include belnet, sprint, level3, geant, abilene, cisco or google .

Each domain contains a set of routers. From a routing point of view, these domains can be divided into two classes: the *transit* and the *stub* domains. A *stub* domain sends and receives packets whose source or destination are one of its own hosts. A *transit* domain is a domain that provides a transit service for other domains, i.e. the routers in this domain forward packets whose source and destination do not belong to the transit domain. As of this writing, about 85% of the domains in the Internet are stub domains. A *stub* domain that is connected to a single transit domain is called a *single-homed stub*. A *multihomed stub* is a *stub* domain connected to two or more transit providers.

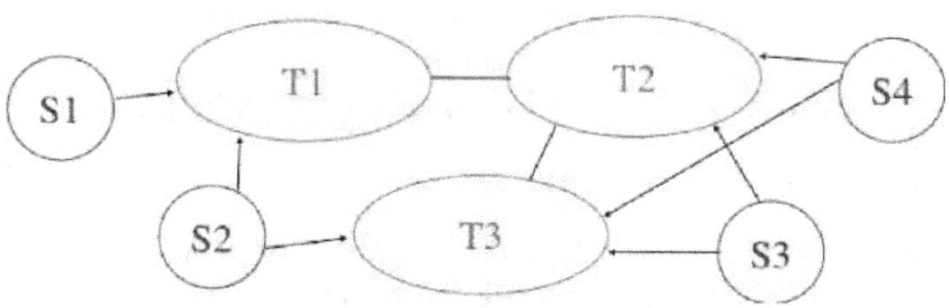

Figure 4.54: Transit and stub domains

The stub domains can be further classified by considering whether they mainly send or receive packets. An *accessrich* stub domain is a domain that contains hosts that mainly receive packets. Typical examples include small ADSL- or cable modem-based Internet Service Providers or enterprise networks. On the other hand, a *contentrich* stub domain is a domain that mainly produces packets. Examples of *content-rich* stub domains include google, yahoo, microsoft, facebook or content distribution networks such as akamai or limelight For the last few years, we have seen a rapid growth of these *content-rich* stub domains. Recent measurements [ATLAS2009] indicate that a growing fraction of all the packets exchanged on the Internet are produced in the data centers managed by these content providers.

Domains need to be interconnected to allow a host inside a domain to exchange IP packets with hosts located in other domains. From a physical perspective, domains can be interconnected in two different ways. The first solution is to directly connect a router belonging to the first domain with a router inside the second domain. Such links between domains are called private interdomain links or *private peering links.* In practice, for redundancy or performance reasons, distinct physical links are usually established between different routers in the two domains that are interconnected.

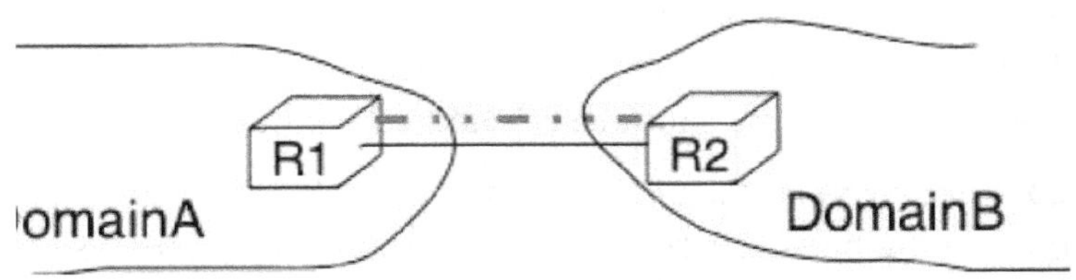

Figure 4.55: Interconnection of two domains via a private peering link

Such *private peering links* are useful when, for example, an enterprise or university network needs to be connected to its Internet Service Provider. However, some domains are connected to hundreds of other domain. For some of these domains, using only private peering links would be too costly. A better solution to allow many domains to interconnect cheaply are the *Internet exchange Points (IXP).* An *IXP* is usually some space in a data center that hosts routers belonging to different domains. A domain willing to exchange packets with other domains present at the *IXP* installs one of its routers on the *IXP* and connects it to other routers inside its own network. The IXP contains a Local Area Network to which all the participating routers are connected. When two domains that are present at the IXP wish to exchange packets, they simply use the Local Area Network. IXPs are very popular in Europe and many Internet Service Providers and Content providers are present in these IXPs.

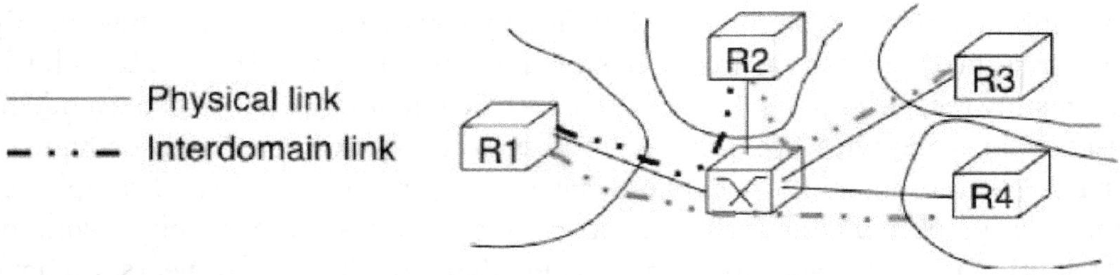

Figure 4.56: Interconnection of two domains at an Internet eXchange Point

In the early days of the Internet, domains would simply exchange all the routes they know to allow a host inside one domain to reach any host in the global Internet. However, in today's highly commercial Internet, this is no longer true as interdomain routing mainly needs to take into account the economical relationships between the domains. Furthermore, while intradomain routing usually prefers some routes over others based on their technical merits (e.g. prefer route with the minimum number of hops, prefer route with the minimum delay, prefer high bandwidth routes over low bandwidth ones, etc) interdomain routing mainly deals with economical issues. For interdomain routing, the cost of using a route is often more important than the quality of the route measured by its delay or bandwidth.

There are different types of economical relationships that can exist between domains. Interdomain routing converts these relationships into peering relationships between domains that are connected via peering links.

The first category of peering relationship is the *customer->provider* relationship. Such a relationship is used when a customer domain pays an Internet Service Provider to be able to exchange packets with the global Internet over an interdomain link. A similar relationship is used when a small Internet Service Provider pays a larger Internet Service Provider to exchange packets with the global Internet.

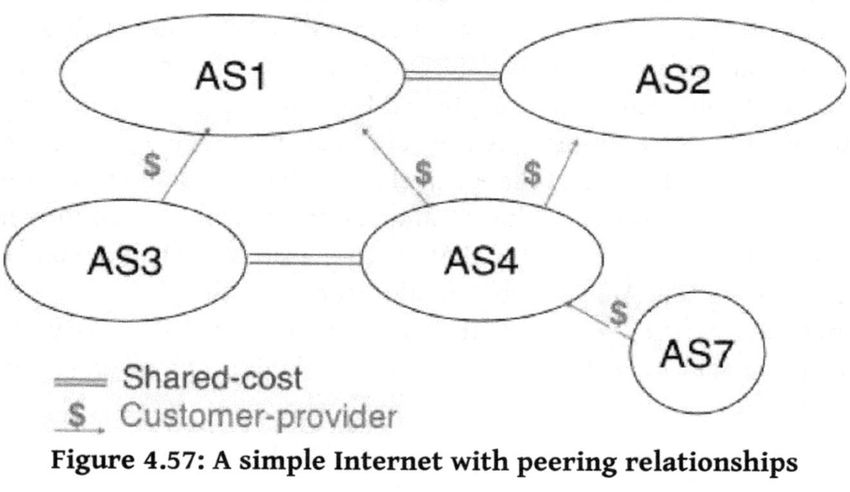

Figure 4.57: A simple Internet with peering relationships

To understand the *customer->provider* relationship, let us consider the simple internetwork shown in the figure above. In this internetwork, *AS7* is a stub domain that is connected to one provider : *AS4.* The contract between *AS4* and *AS7* allows a host inside *AS7* to exchange packets with any host in the internetwork. To enable this exchange of packets, *AS7* must know a route towards any domain and all the domains of the internetwork must know a route via *AS4* that allows them to reach hosts inside AS7. From a routing perspective, the commercial contract between *AS7* and *AS4* leads to the following routes being exchanged :

- over a *customer->provider* relationship, the *customer* domain advertises to its *provider* all its routes and all the routes that it has learned from its own customers.
- over a*provider->customer* relationship, the *provider* advertises all the routes that it knows to its *customer.*

The second rule ensures that the customer domain receives a route towards all destinations that are reachable via its provider. The first rule allows the routes of the customer domain to be distributed throughout the Internet.

Coming back to the figure above, *AS4* advertises to its two providers *AS1* and *AS2* its own routes and the routes learned from its customer, AS7. On the other hand, AS4 advertises to AS7 all the routes that it knows.

The second type of peering relationship is the *shared-cost* peering relationship. Such a relationship usually does not involve a payment from one domain to the other in contrast with the *customer->provider* relationship. A *shared-cost* peering relationship is usually established between domains having a similar size and geographic coverage. For example, consider the figure above. If *AS3* and *AS4* exchange many packets via AS1, they both need to pay AS1. A cheaper alternative for *AS3* and *AS4* would be to establish a *shared-cost* peering. Such a peering can be established at IXPs where both *AS3* and *AS4* are present or by using private peering links. This *shared-cost* peering should be used to exchange packets between hosts inside *AS3* and hosts inside AS4. However, *AS3* does not want to receive on the *AS3-AS4 shared-cost* peering links packets whose destination belongs to *AS1* as *AS3* would have to pay to send these packets to *AS1.*

From a routing perspective, over a *shared-cost* peering relationship a domain only advertises its internal routes and the routes that it has learned from its customers. This restriction ensures that only packets destined to the local domain or one of its customers is received over the *shared-cost* peering relationship. This implies that the routes that have been learned from a provider or from another *shared-cost* peer is not advertised over a *shared-cost* peering relationship. This is motivated by economical reasons. If a domain were to advertise the routes that it learned from a provider over a *shared-cost* peering relationship that does not bring revenue, it would have allowed its *shared-cost* peer to use the link with its provider without any payment. If a domain were to advertise the routes it learned over a *shared cost* peering over another *shared-cost* peering relationship, it would have allowed these *shared-cost* peers to use its own network (which may span one or more continents) freely to exchange packets.

Finally, the last type of peering relationship is the *sibling.* Such a relationship is used when two domains exchange all their routes in both directions. In practice, such a relationship is only used between domains that belong to the same company.

These different types of relationships are implemented in the *interdomain routing policies* defined by each domain. The *interdomain routing policy* of a domain is composed of three main parts:

- the *import filter* that specifies, for each peering relationship, the routes that can be accepted from the neighbouring domain (the non-acceptable routes are ignored and the domain never uses them to forward packets)
- the *export filter* that specifies, for each peering relationship, the routes that can be advertised to the neighbouring domain
- the *ranking* algorithm that is used to select the best route among all the routes that the domain has received towards the same destination prefix

A domain's import and export filters can be defined by using the Route Policy Specification Language (RPSL) specified in **RFC 2622** [GAVE1999]. Some Internet Service Providers, notably in Europe, use RPSL to document [29] their import and export policies. Several tools help to easily convert a RPSL policy into router commands.

The figure below provides a simple example of import and export filters for two domains in a simple internetwork. In RPSL, the keyword *ANY* is used to replace any route from any domain. It is typically used by a provider to indicate that it announces all its routes to a customer over a *provider->customer* relationship. This is the case for *AS4*'s export policy. The example below clearly shows the difference between a *provider->customer* and a *shared-cost* peering relationship. *AS4*'s export filter indicates that it announces only its internal routes (AS4) and the routes learned from its clients (*AS7*) over its *shared-cost* peering with *AS3*, while it advertises all the routes that it uses (including the routes learned from *AS3*) to *AS7*.

The Border Gateway Protocol

The Internet uses a single interdomain routing protocol : the Border Gateway Protocol (BGP). The current version of BGP is defined in **RFC 4271**. BGP differs from the intradomain routing protocols that we have already discussed in several ways. First, BGP is a *path-vector* protocol. When a BGP router advertises a route towards a prefix, it announces the IP prefix and the interdomain path used to reach this prefix. From BGP's point of view, each domain is identified by a unique *Autonomous System* (AS) number and the interdomain path contains the AS numbers of the transit domains that are used to reach the associated prefix. This interdomain path is called the *AS Path.* Thanks to these AS-Paths, BGP does not suffer from the count-to-infinity problems that affect distance vector routing protocols. Furthermore, the AS-Path can be used to implement some routing policies. Another difference between BGP and the intradomain routing protocols is that a BGP router does not send the entire contents of its routing table to its neighbours regularly. Given the size of the global Internet, routers would be overloaded by the number of BGP messages that they would need to process. BGP uses incremental updates, i.e. it only announces the routes that have changed to its neighbours.

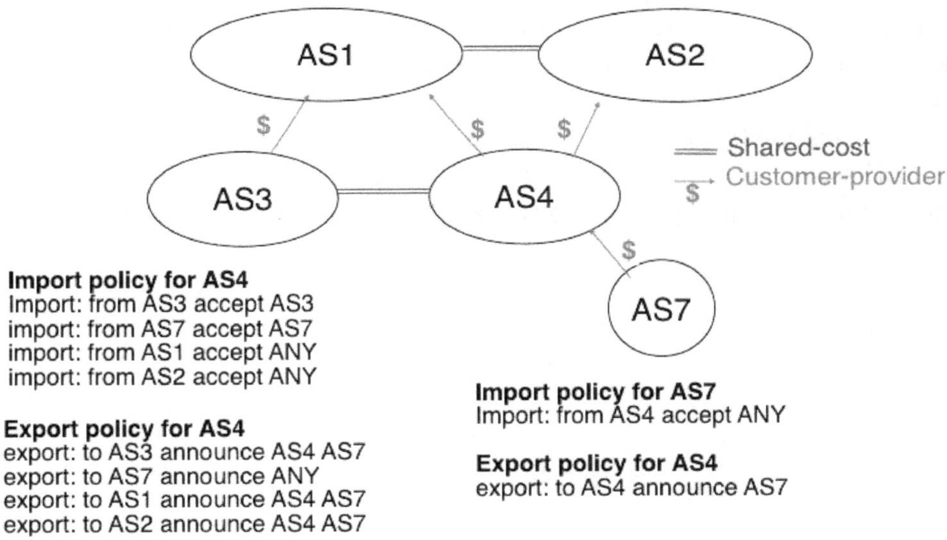

Figure 4.58: Import and export policies

The figure below shows a simple example of the BGP routes that are exchanged between domains. In this example, prefix *1.0.0.0/8* is announced by *AS1. AS1* advertises a BGP route towards this prefix to AS2. The AS-Path of this route indicates that AS1 is the originator of the prefix. When *AS4* receives the BGP route from AS1, it re-announces it to AS2 and adds its AS number to the AS-Path. AS2 has learned two routes towards prefix *1.0.0.0/8.* It compares the two routes and prefers the route learned from AS4 based on its own ranking algorithm. AS2 advertises to AS5 a route towards *1.0.0.0/8* with its AS-Path set to *AS2:AS4:AS1.* Thanks to the AS-Path, *AS5* knows that if it sends a packet towards *1.0.0.0/8* the packet first passes through AS2, then through *AS4* before reaching its destination inside *AS1.*

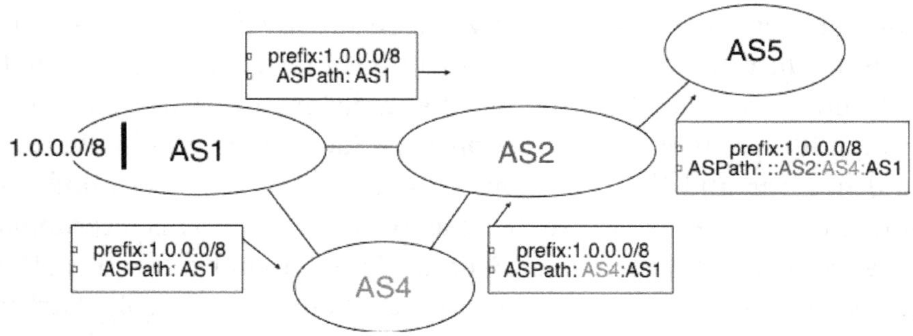

Figure 4.59: Simple exchange of BGP routes

BGP routers exchange routes over BGP sessions. A BGP session is established between two routers belonging to two different domains that are directly connected. As explained earlier, the physical connection between the two routers can be implemented as a private peering link or over an Internet eXchange Point. A BGP session between two adjacent routers runs above a TCP connection (the default BGP port is 179). In contrast with intradomain routing protocols that exchange IP packets or UDP segments, BGP runs above TCP because TCP ensures a reliable delivery of the BGP messages sent by each router without forcing the routers to implement acknowledgements, checksums, etc. Furthermore, the two routers consider the peering link to be up as long as the BGP session and the underlying TCP connection remain up. The two endpoints of a BGP session are called *BGP peers.*

Figure 4.60: A BGP peering session between two directly connected routers

In practice, to establish a BGP session between routers *R1* and *R2* in the figure above, the network administrator of *AS3* must first configure on R1 the IP address of R2 on the *R1-R2* link and the AS number of R2. Router R1 then regularly tries to establish the BGP session with *R2*. *R2* only agrees to establish the BGP session with *R1* once it has been configured with the IP address of R1 and its AS number.

For security reasons, a router never establishes a BGP session that has not been manually configured on the router.

The BGP protocol **RFC 4271** defines several types of messages that can be exchanged over a BGP session :

- *OPEN* : this message is sent as soon as the TCP connection between the two routers has been established. It initialises the BGP session and allows the negotiation of some options. Details about this message may be found in **RFC 4271**
- *NOTIFICATION* : this message is used to terminate a BGP session, usually because an error has been detected by the BGP peer. A router that sends or receives a *NOTIFICATION* message immediately shutdowns the corresponding BGP session.
- *UPDATE:* this message is used to advertise new or modified routes or to withdraw previously advertised routes.
- *KEEPALIVE* : this message is used to ensure a regular exchange of messages on the BGP session, even when no route changes. When a BGP router has not sent an *UPDATE* message during the last 30 seconds, it shall send a *KEEPALIVE* message to confirm to the other peer that it is still up. If a peer does not receive any BGP message during a period of 90 seconds, the BGP session is considered to be down and all the routes learned over this session are withdrawn.

As explained earlier, BGP relies on incremental updates. This implies that when a BGP session starts, each router first sends BGP *UPDATE* messages to advertise to the other peer all the exportable routes that it knows. Once all these routes have been advertised, the BGP router only sends BGP *UPDATE* messages about a prefix if the route is new, one of its attributes has changed or the route became unreachable and must be withdrawn. The BGP *UPDATE* message allows BGP routers to efficiently exchange such information while minimising the number of bytes exchanged. Each *UPDATE* message contains :

- a list of IP prefixes that are withdrawn
- a list of IP prefixes that are (re-)advertised
- the set of attributes (e.g. AS-Path) associated to the advertised prefixes

In the remainder of this chapter, and although all routing information is exchanged using BGP *UPDATE* messages, we assume for simplicity that a BGP message contains only information about one prefix and we use the words :

- *Withdraw message* to indicate a BGP *UPDATE* message containing one route that is withdrawn

- *Update message* to indicate a BGP *UPDATE* containing a new or updated route towards one destination prefix with its attributes

From a conceptual point of view, a BGP router connected to *N* BGP peers, can be described as being composed of four parts as shown in the figure below.

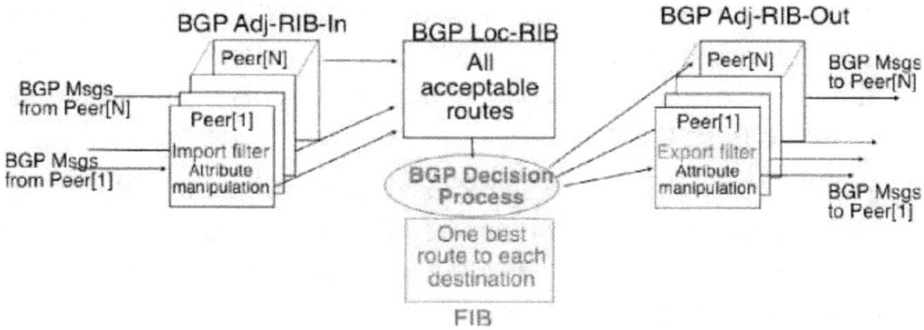

Figure 4.61: Organisation of a BGP router

In this figure, the router receives BGP messages on the left part of the figure, processes these messages and possibly sends BGP messages on the right part of the figure. A BGP router contains three important data structures :

- the *Adj-RIB-In* contains the BGP routes that have been received from each BGP peer. The routes in the *Adj-RIB-In* are filtered by the *import filter* before being placed in the *BGP-Loc-RIB.* There is one *import filter* per BGP peer.
- the *Local Routing Information Base (Loc-RIB)* contains all the routes that are considered as acceptable by the router. The *Loc-RIB* may contain several routes, learned from different BGP peers, towards the same destination prefix.
- the *Forwarding Information Base (FIB)* is used by the dataplane to forward packets towards their destination. The *FIB* contains, for each destination, the best route that has been selected by the *BGP decision process.* This decision process is an algorithm that selects, for each destination prefix, the best route according to the router's ranking algorithm that is part of its policy.
- the *Adj-RIB-Out* contains the BGP routes that have been advertised to each BGP peer. The *Adj-RIB-Out* for a given peer is built by applying the peer's *export filter* on the routes that have been installed in the FIB. There is one *export filter* per BGP peer. For this reason, the Adj-RIB-Out of a peer may contain different routes than the Adj-RIB-Out of another peer.

When a BGP session starts, the routers first exchange *OPEN* messages to negotiate the options that apply throughout the entire session. Then, each router extracts from its FIB the routes to be advertised to the peer. It is important to note that, for each known destination prefix, a BGP router can only advertise to a peer the route that it has itself installed inside its FIB. The routes that are advertised to a peer must pass the peer's *export filter*. The *export filter* is a set of rules that define which routes can be advertised over the corresponding session, possibly after having modified some of its attributes. One *export filter* is associated to each BGP session. For example, on a *shared-cost peering*, the *export filter* only selects the internal routes and the routes that have been learned from a *customer*. The pseudo-code below shows the initialisation of a BGP session.

```
def initiliaze_BGP_session( RemoteAS, RemotelP):
# Initialize and start BGP session
# Send BGP OPEN Message to RemoteIP on port 179
# Follow BGP state machine
# advertise local routes and routes learned from peers*/
for d in BGPLocRIB :
B=build_BGP_Update(d)
S=Apply_Export_Filter(RemoteAS,B)
if (S != None) :
send_Update(S,RemoteAS,RemoteIP)
# entire RIB has been sent
# new Updates will be sent to reflect local or distant
# changes in routers
```

In the above pseudo-code, the *build_BGP_UPDATE(d)* procedure extracts from the *BGP Loc-RIB* the best path towards destination *d* (i.e. the route installed in the FIB) and prepares the corresponding BGP *UPDATE* message.

This message is then passed to the *export filter* that returns NULL if the route cannot be advertised to the peer or the (possibly modified) BGP *UPDATE* message to be advertised. BGP routers allow network administrators to specify very complex *export filters*, see e.g. [WMS2004]. A simple *export filter* that implements the equivalent of *split horizon* is shown below.

```
def apply_export_filter(RemoteAS, BGPMsg) :
# check if RemoteAS already received route
if RemoteAS is BGPMsg.ASPath :
BGPMsg=None
Many additional export policies can be configured :
Accept or refuse the BGPMsg
Modify selected attributes inside BGPMsg
return BGPMsg
```

At this point, the remote router has received all the exportable BGP routes. After this initial exchange, the router only sends *BGP UPDATE* messages when there is a change (addition of a route, removal of a route or change in the attributes of a route) in one of these exportable routes. Such a change can happen when the router receives a BGP message. The pseudo-code below summarizes the processing of these BGP messages.

```
def Recvd_BGPMsg(Msg, RemoteAS) :
B=apply_import_filer(Msg,RemoteAS)
if (B== None): # Msg not acceptable
return
if IsUPDATE(Msg):
Old_Route=BestRoute(Msg.prefix)
Insert_in_RIB(Msg)
Run_Decision_Process(RIB)
if (BestRoute(Msg.prefix) != Old_Route) :
# best route changed
B=build_BGP_Message(Msg.prefix);
S=apply_export_filter(RemoteAS,B);
if (S!=None) : # announce best route
send_UPDATE(S,RemoteAS,RemoteIP);
else if (Old_Route != None) :
send_WITHDRAW(Msg.prefix,RemoteAS, RemoteIP)
else : # Msg is WITHDRAW
Old_Route=BestRoute(Msg.prefix)
Remove_from_RIB(Msg)
Run_Decision_Process(RIB)
if (Best_Route(Msg.prefix) !=Old_Route):
# best route changed
B=build_BGP_Message(Msg.prefix)
S=apply_export_filter(RemoteAS,B)
if (S != None) : # still one best route towards Msg.prefix
send_UPDATE(S,RemoteAS, RemoteIP);
else if(Old_Route != None) : # No best route anymore
send_WITHDRAW(Msg.prefix,RemoteAS,RemoteIP);
```

When a BGP message is received, the router first applies the peer's *import filter* to verify whether the message is acceptable or not. If the message is not acceptable, the processing stops. The pseudo-code below shows a simple *import filter*. This *import filter* accepts all routes, except those that already contain the local AS in their AS-Path. If such a route was used, it would cause a routing loop. Another example of an *import filter* would be a filter used by an Internet Service Provider on a session with a customer to only accept routes towards the IP prefixes assigned to the customer by the provider. On real routers, *import filters* can be much more complex and some *import filters* modify the attributes of the received BGP *UPDATE* [WMS2004] .

```
def apply_import_filter(RemoteAS, BGPMsg):
if MysAS in BGPMsg.ASPath :
BGPMsg=None
# Many additional import policies can be configured :
# Accept or refuse the BGPMsg
# Modify selected attributes inside BGPMsg
return BGPMsg
```

Note: The bogon filters

Another example of frequently used *import filters* are the filters that Internet Service Providers use to ignore bogon routes. In the ISP community, a bogon route is a route that should not be advertised on the global Internet. Typical examples include the private IPv4 prefixes defined in **RFC 1918**, the loopback prefixes *(127.0.0.1/8* and *::1/128)* or the IP prefixes that have not yet been allocated by IANA. A well managed BGP router should ensure that it never advertises bogons on the global Internet. Detailed information about these bogons may be found at http://www.team-cymru.org/Services/Bogons/

If the import filter accepts the BGP message, the pseudo-code distinguishes two cases. If this is an *Update message* for prefix p, this can be a new route for this prefix or a modification of the route's attributes. The router first retrieves from its *RIB* the best route towards prefix *p*. Then, the new route is inserted in the *RIB* and the *BGP decision process* is run to find whether the best route towards destination *p* changes. A BGP message only needs to be sent to the router's peers if the best route has changed. For each peer, the router applies the *export filter* to verify whether the route can be advertised. If yes, the filtered BGP message is sent. Otherwise, a *Withdraw message* is sent. When the router receives a *Withdraw message*, it also verifies whether the removal of the route from its *RIB* caused its best route towards this prefix to change. It should be noted that, depending on the content of the *RIB* and the *export filters*, a BGP router may need to send a *Withdraw message* to a peer after having received an *Update message* from another peer and conversely.

Let us now discuss in more detail the operation of BGP in an IPv4 network. For this, let us consider the simple network composed of three routers located in three different ASes and shown in the figure below.

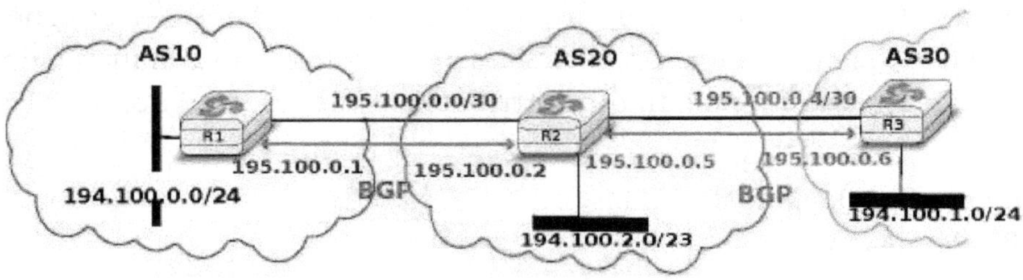

Figure 4.62: Utilisation of the BGP nexthop attribute

This network contains three routers: R1, *R2* and R3. Each router is attached to a local IPv4 subnet that it advertises using BGP. There are two BGP sessions, one between *R1* and *R2* and the second between *R2* and *R3*. A */30* subnet is used on each interdomain link *(195.100.0.0/30* on *R1-R2* and *195.100.0.4/30* on *R2-R3).* The BGP sessions run above TCP connections established between the neighbouring routers (e.g. *195.100.0.1 -195.100.0.2* for the *R1-R2* session).

Let us assume that the *R1-R2* BGP session is the first to be established. A *BGP Update* message sent on such a session contains three fields :

- the advertised prefix
- the *BGP nexthop*
- the attributes including the AS-Path

We use the notation *U(prefix, nexthop, attributes)* to represent such a *BGP Update* message in this section. Similarly, *W(prefix)* represents a *BGP withdraw* for the specified prefix. Once the *R1-R2* session has been established, *R1* sends *U(194.100.0.0 /24,195.100.0.1,AS10)* to *R2* and *R2* sends *U(194.100.2.0/23,195.100.0.2,AS20).* At this point, *R1* can reach *194.100.2.0/23* via *195.100.0.2* and *R2* can reach *194.100.0.0/24* via *195.100.0.1.*

Once the *R2-R3* has been established, *R3* sends *U(194.100.1.0/24,195.100.0.6,AS30). R2* announces on the *R2- R3* session all the routes inside its RIB. It thus sends to *R3* : *U(194.100.0.0/24,195.100.0.5,AS20:AS10)* and *U(194.100.2.0/23,195.100.0.5,AS20).* Note that when *R2* advertises the route that it learned fromR1, it updates the BGP nexthop and adds its AS number to the AS-Path. *R2* also sends *U(194.100.1.0/24,195.100.0.2,AS20 :AS30)* to *R1* on the *R1-R3* session. At this point, all BGP routes have been exchanged and all routers can reach *194.100.0.0/24,194.100.2.0/23* and *194.100.1.0/24.*

If the link between *R2* and *R3* fails, *R3* detects the failure as it did not receive *KEEPALIVE* messages recently from *R2.* At this time, *R3* removes from its RIB all the routes learned over the *R2-R3* BGP session. R2 also removes from its RIB the routes learned from R3. R2 also sends *W(194.100.1.0/24)* to *R1* over the *R1-R3* BGP session since it does not have a route anymore towards this prefix.

Note: Origin of the routes advertised by a BGP router

A frequent practical question about the operation of BGP is how a BGP router decides to originate or advertise a route for the first time. In practice, this occurs in two situations :

- the router has been manually configured by the network operator to always advertise one or several routes on a BGP session. For example, on the BGP session between UCLouvain and its provider, belnet , UCLouvain's router always advertises the *130.104.0.0/16* IPv4 prefix assigned to the campus network
- the router has been configured by the network operator to advertise over its BGP session some of the routes that it learns with its intradomain routing protocol. For example, an enterprise router may advertise over a BGP session with its provider the routes to remote sites when these routes are reachable and advertised by the intradomain routing protocol

The first solution is the most frequent. Advertising routes learned from an intradomain routing protocol is not recommended, this is because if the route flaps, this would cause a large number of BGP messages being exchanged in the global Internet.

Most networks that use BGP contain more than one router. For example, consider the network shown in the figure below where *AS20* contains two routers attached to interdomain links : *R2* and R4. In this network, two routing protocols are used by *R2* and *R4*. They use an intradomain routing protocol such as OSPF to distribute the routes towards the internal prefixes: *195.100.0.8/30,195.100.0.0/30,...* *R2* and *R4* also use BGP. *R2* receives the routes advertised by *AS10* while *R4* receives the routes advertised by *AS30.* These two routers need to exchange the routes that they have respectively received over their BGP sessions.

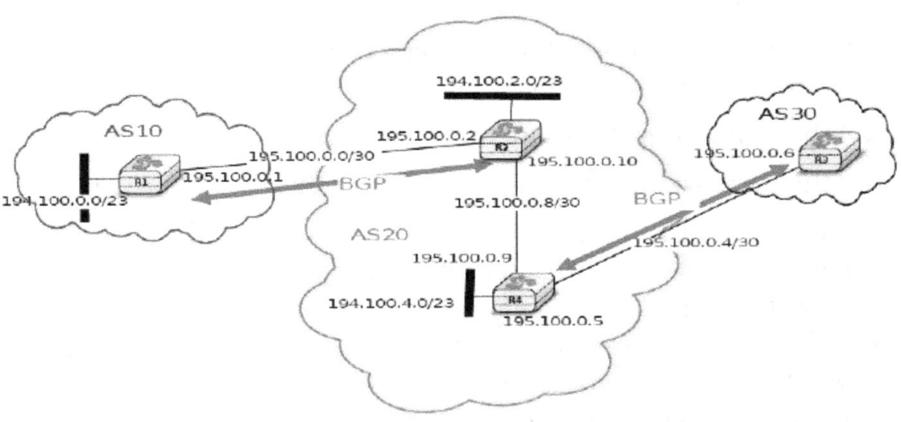

Figure 4.63: A larger network using BGP

A first solution to allow *R2* and *R3* to exchange the interdomain routes that they have learned over their respective BGP sessions would be to configure the intradomain routing protocol to distribute inside *AS20* the routes learned over the BGP sessions. Although current routers support this feature, this is a bad solution for two reasons :

1. Intradomain routing protocols cannot distribute the attributes that are attached to a BGP route. If *R4* received via the intradomain routing protocol a route towards *194.100.0.0/23* that *R2* learned via BGP, it would not know that the route was originated by *AS10* and the only advertisement that it could send to *R3* would contain an incorrect AS-Path
2. Intradomain routing protocols have not been designed to support the hundreds of thousands of routes that a BGP router can receive on today's global Internet.

The best solution to allow BGP routers to distribute, inside an AS, all the routes learned over BGP sessions is to establish BGP sessions among all the BGP routers inside the AS. In practice, there are two types of BGP sessions

- *eBGP* session or *external BGP session.* Such a BGP session is established between two routers that are directly connected and belong to two different domains.
- *iBGP* session or *internal BGP session.* Such a BGP session is established between two routers belonging to the same domain. These two routers do not need to be directly connected.

In practice, each BGP router inside a domain maintains an *iBGP session* with every other BGP router in the domain. This creates a full-mesh of *iBGP sessions* among all BGP routers of the domain. *iBGP sessions,* like *eBGP sessions* run over TCP connections. Note that in contrast with *eBGP sessions* that are established between directly connected routers, *iBGP sessions* are often established between routers that are not directly connected.

An important point to note about *iBGP sessions* is that a BGP router only advertises a route over an *iBGP session* provided that :

- the router uses this route to forward packets, and
- the route was learned over one of the router's *eBGP sessions*

A BGP router does not advertise a route that it has learned over an *iBGP session* over another *iBGP session.* Note that a router can, of course, advertise over an *eBGP session* a route that it has learned over an *iBGP session.* This difference between the behaviour of a BGP router over *iBGP* and *eBGP* session is due to the utilisation of a full-mesh of *iBGP sessions.* Consider a network containing three BGP routers : *A, B* and *C* interconnected via a full-mesh of iBGP sessions. If router *A* learns a route towards prefix *p* from router B, router *A* does not need to advertise the received route to router *C* since router *C* also learns the same route over the *C-B iBGP session.*

To understand the utilisation of an *iBGP session,* let us consider what happens when router *R1* sends *U(194.100.0.0/23,195.100.0.1,AS10)* in the network shown below. This BGP message is processed by *R2* which advertises it over its *iBGP session* with R4. The *BGP Update* sent by *R2* contains the same nexthop and the same AS-Path as in the *BGP Update* received by R2. *R4* then sends *U(194.100.0.0/23,195.100.0.5,AS20:AS10)* to *R3.* Note that the BGP nexthop and the AS-Path are only updated when a BGP route is advertised over an *eBGP session.*

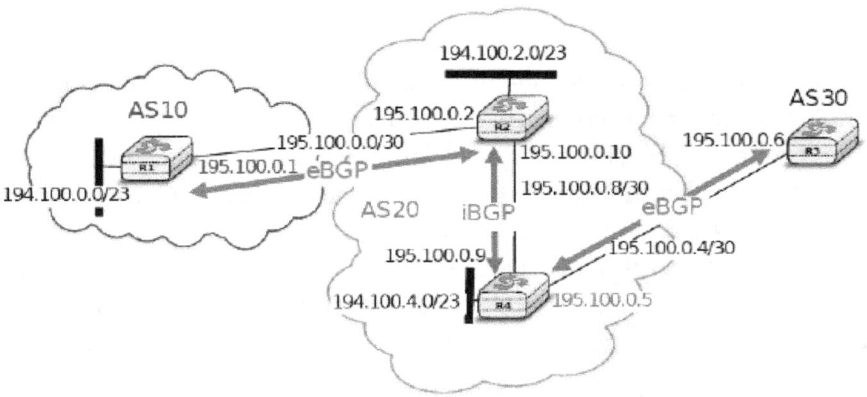

Figure 4.64: iBGP and eBGP sessions

Note: Loopback interfaces and iBGP sessions

In addition to their physical interfaces, routers can also be configured with a special loopback interface. A loopback interface is a software interface that is always up. When a loopback interface is configured on a router, the address associated to this interface is advertised by the intradomain routing protocol. Consider for example a router with two point-to-point interfaces and one loopback interface. When a point-to-point interface fails, it becomes unreachable and the router cannot receive anymore packets via this IP address. This is not the case for the loopback interface. It remains reachable as long as at least one of the router's interfaces remains up. *iBGP sessions* are usually established using the router's loopback addresses as endpoints. This allows the *iBGP session* and its underlying TCP connection to remain up even if physical interfaces fail on the routers.

Now that routers can learn interdomain routes over iBGP and eBGP sessions, let us examine what happens when router *R3* sends a packet destined to *194.100.1.234. R3* forwards this packet to *R4. R4* uses an intradomain routing protocol and BGP. Its BGP routing table contains the following longest prefix match :

- *194.100.0.0/23* via *195.100.0.1*

This routes indicates that to forward a packet towards *194.100.0.0/23, R4* needs to forward the packet along the route towards *195.100.0.1.* However, *R4* is not directly connected to *195.100.0.1. R4* learned a route that matches this address thanks to its intradomain routing protocol that distributed the following routes :

- *195.100.0.0/30* via *195.100.0.10*
- *195.100.0.4/30* East
- *195.100.0.8/30* North
- *194.100.2.0/23* via *195.100.0.10*
- *194.100.0.4/23* West

To build its forwarding table, *R4* must combine the routes learned from the intradomain routing protocol with the routes learned from BGP. Thanks to its intradomain routing table, for each interdomain route *R4* replaces the BGP nexthop with its shortest path computed by the intradomain routing protocol. In the figure above, *R4* forwards packets to *194.100.0.0/23* via *195.100.0.10* to which it is directly connected via its North interface. *R4* 's resulting forwarding table, which associates an outgoing interface for a directly connected prefix or a directly connected nexthop and an outgoing interface for prefixes learned via BGP, is shown below :

- *194.100.0.0/23* via *195.100.0.10* (North)
- *195.100.0.0/30* via *195.100.0.10* (North)
- *195.100.0.4/30* East
- *195.100.0.8/30* North
- *194.100.2.0/23* via *195.100.0.10* (North)
- *194.100.4.0/23* West

There is thus a coupling between the interdomain and the intradomain routing tables. If the intradomain routes change, e.g. due to link failures or changes in link metrics, then the forwarding table must be updated on each router as the shortest path towards a BGP nexthop may have changed.

The last point to be discussed before looking at the BGP decision process is that a network may contain routers that do not maintain any eBGP session. These routers can be stub routers attached to a single router in the network or core routers that reside on the path between two border routers that are using BGP as illustrated in the figure below.

In the scenario above, router *R2* needs to be able to forward a packet towards any destination in the *12.0.0.0/8* prefix inside *AS30.* Such a packet would need to be forwarded by router *R5* since this router resides on the path between *R2* and its BGP nexthop attached to *R4*. Two solutions can be used to ensure that *R2* is able to forward such interdomain packets :

- enable BGP on router *R5* and include this router in the *iBGP* full-mesh. Two iBGP sessions would be added in the figure above : *R2-R5* and *R4-R5*. This solution works and is used by many ASes. However, it forces all routers to have enough resources (CPU and memory) to run BGP and maintain a large forwarding table
- encapsulate the interdomain packets sent through the AS so that router *R5* never needs to forward a packet whose destination is outside the local AS. Different encapsulation mechanisms exist. MultiProtocol Label Switching (MPLS) **RFC 3031** and the Layer 2 Tunneling Protocol (L2TP) **RFC 3931** are frequently used in large domains, but a detailed explanation of these techniques is outside the scope of this section. The simplest encapsulation scheme to understand is in IP in IP defined in RFC 2003. This encapsulation scheme places an IP packet (called the inner packet), including its payload, as the payload of a larger IP packet (called the outer packet). It can be used by border routers to forward packets via routers that do not maintain a BGP routing table. For example, in the figure above, if router R2 needs to forward a packet towards destination 12.0.0.1, it can add at the front of this packet an IPv4 header whose source address is set to one of its IPv4 addresses and whose destination address is one of the IPv4 addresses of R4. The Protocol field of the IP header is set to 4 to indicate that it contains an IPv4 packet. The packet is forwarded by R5 to R4 based on the forwarding table that it built thanks to its intradomain routing table. Upon reception of the packet, R4 removes the outer header and consults its (BGP) forwarding table to forward the packet towards R3.

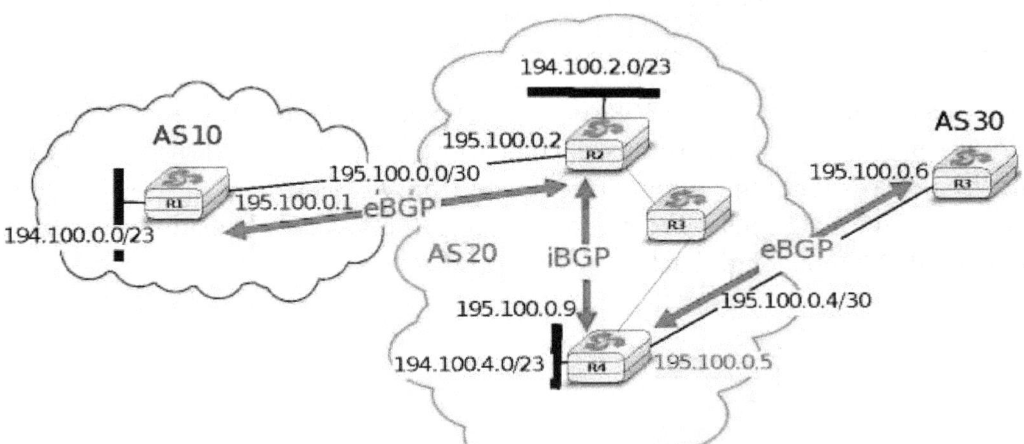

Figure 4.65: How to deal with non-BGP routers ?

The BGP decision process

Besides the import and export filters, a key difference between BGP and the intradomain routing protocols is that each domain can define is own ranking algorithm to determine which route is chosen to forward packets when several routes have been learned towards the same prefix. This ranking depends on several BGP attributes that can be attached to a BGP route.

The first BGP attribute that is used to rank BGP routes is the *local-preference* (local-pref) attribute. This attribute is an unsigned integer that is attached to each BGP route received over an eBGP session by the associated import filter.

When comparing routes towards the same destination prefix, a BGP router always prefers the routes with the highest *local-pref.* If the BGP router knows several routes with the same *local-pref,* it prefers among the routes having this *local-pref* the ones with the shortest AS-Path.

The *local-pref* attribute is often used to prefer some routes over others. This attribute is always present inside *BGP Updates* exchanged over *iBGP sessions,* but never present in the messages exchanged over *eBGP sessions.*

A common utilisation of *local-pref* is to support backup links. Consider the situation depicted in the figure below. *AS1* would always like to use the high bandwidth link to send and receive packets via *AS2* and only use the backup link upon failure of the primary one.

As BGP routers always prefer the routes with the highest *local-pref* attribute, this policy can be implemented using the following import filter on *R1*

```
import: from AS2 RA at R1 set localpref=100;
from AS2 RB at R1 set localpref=200;
accept ANY
```

With this import filter, all the BGP routes learned from *RB* over the high bandwidth links are preferred over the routes learned over the backup link. If the primary link fails, the corresponding routes are removed from *R1* ‘s RIB and *R1* uses the route learned from *RA*. *R1* reuses the routes via *RB* as soon as they are advertised by *RB* once the *R1-RB* link comes back.

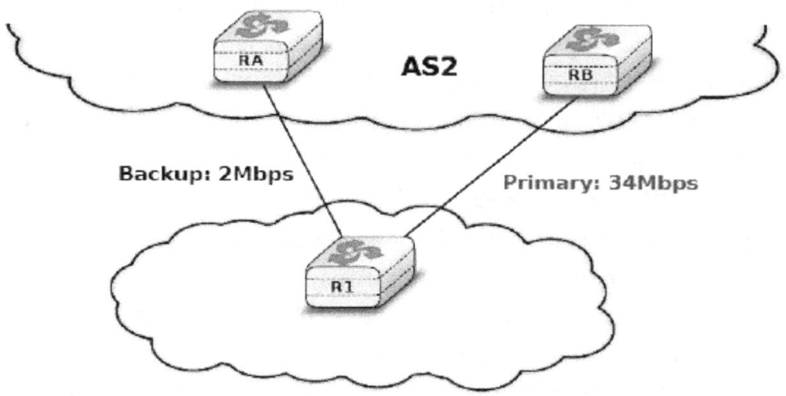

Figure 4.66: How to create a backup link with BGP ?

The import filter above modifies the selection of the BGP routes inside *AS1*. Thus, it influences the route followed by the packets forwarded by AS1. In addition to using the primary link to send packets, AS1 would like to receive its packets via the high bandwidth link. For this, AS2 also needs to set the *local-pref* attribute in its import filter.

import: from AS1 R1 at RA set localpref=100;
from AS1 R1 at RB set localpref=200;
accept AS1

Sometimes, the *local-pref* attribute is used to prefer a *cheap* link compared to a more expensive one. For example, in the network below, AS1 could wish to send and receive packets mainly via its interdomain link with *AS4*.

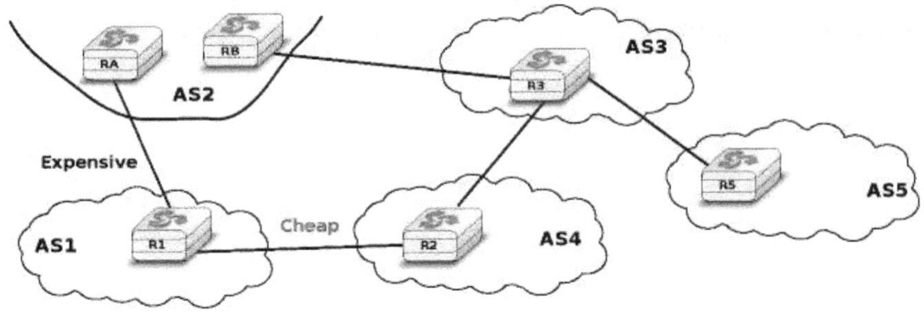

Figure 4.67: How to prefer a cheap link over an more expensive one ?

AS1 can install the following import filter on *R1* to ensure that it always sends packets via *R2* when it has learned a route via *AS2* and another via *AS4*.

import: from AS2 RA at R1 set localpref=100;
from AS4 R2 at R1 set localpref=200;
accept ANY

However, this import filter does not influence how *AS3* , for example, prefers some routes over others. If the link between *AS3* and *AS2* is less expensive than the link between *AS3* and AS4, *AS3* could send all its packets via *AS2* and *AS1* would receive packets over its expensive link. An important point to remember about *local-pref* is that it can be used to prefer some routes over others to send packets, but it has no influence on the routes followed by received packets.

Another important utilisation of the *local-pref* attribute is to support the *customer->provider* and *shared-cost* peering relationships. From an economic point of view, there is an important difference between these three types of peering relationships. A domain usually earns money when it sends packets over a *provider->customer* relationship. On the other hand, it must pay its provider when it sends packets over a *customer->provider* relationship.

Using a *shared-cost* peering to send packets is usually neutral from an economic perspective. To take into account these economic issues, domains usually configure the import filters on their routers as follows:

- insert a high *local-pref* attribute in the routes learned from a customer
- insert a medium *local-pref* attribute in the routes learned over a shared-cost peering
- insert a low *local-pref* attribute in the routes learned from a provider

With such an import filter, the routers of a domain always prefer to reach destinations via their customers whenever such a route exists. Otherwise, they prefer to use *shared-cost* peering relationships and they only send packets via their providers when they do not know any alternate route. A consequence of setting the *local-pref* attribute like this is that Internet paths are often asymmetrical. Consider for example the internetwork shown in the figure below.

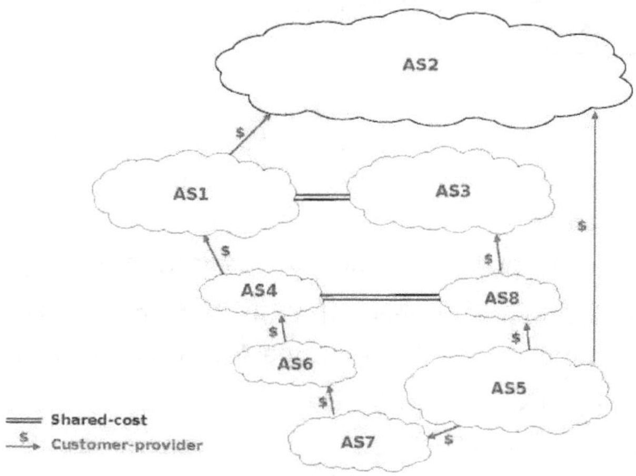

Figure 4.68: Asymmetry of Internet paths

Consider in this internetwork the routes available inside *AS1* to reach AS5. *AS1* learns the *AS4:AS6:AS7:AS5* path from AS4, the *AS3:AS8:AS5* path from *AS3* and the *AS2:AS5* path from AS2. The first path is chosen since it was from learned from a customer. *AS5* on the other hand receives three paths towards *AS1* via its providers. It may select any of these paths to reach *AS1* , depending on how it prefers one provider over the others.

Coming back to the organisation of a BGP router shown in figure *Organisation of a BGP router*, the last part to be discussed is the BGP decision process. The *BGP Decision Process* is the algorithm used by routers to select the route to be installed in the FIB when there are multiple routes towards the same prefix. The BGP decision process receives a set of candidate routes towards the same prefix and uses seven steps. At each step, some routes are removed from the candidate set and the process stops when the set only contains one route :

1. Ignore routes having an unreachable BGP nexthop
2. Prefer routes having the highest local-pref
3. Prefer routes having the shortest AS-Path
4. Prefer routes having the smallest MED
5. Prefer routes learned via eBGP sessions over routes learned via iBGP sessions
6. Prefer routes having the closest next-hop
7. Tie breaking rules: prefer routes learned from the router with lowest router id

The first step of the BGP decision process ensures that a BGP router does not install in its FIB a route whose nexthop is considered to be unreachable by the intradomain routing protocol. This could happen, for example, when a router has crashed. The intradomain routing protocol usually advertises the failure of this router before the failure of the BGP sessions that it terminates. This rule implies that the BGP decision process must be re-run each time the intradomain routing protocol reports a change in the reachability of a prefix containing one of more BGP nexthops.

The second rule allows each domain to define its routing preferences. The *local-pref* attribute is set by the import filter of the router that learned a route over an eBGP session.

In contrast with intradomain routing protocols, BGP does not contain an explicit metric. This is because in the global Internet it is impossible for all domains to agree on a common metric that meets the requirements of all domains. Despite this, BGP routers prefer routes having a short AS-Path attribute over routes with a long AS- Path. This step of the BGP decision process is motivated by the fact that operators expect that a route with a long AS-Path is lower quality than a route with a shorter AS-Path. However, studies have shown that there was not always a strong correlation between the quality of a route and the length of its AS-Path [HFPMC2002].

Before explaining the fourth step of the BGP decision process, let us first describe the fifth and the sixth steps of the BGP decision process. These two steps are used to implement *hot potato* routing. Intuitively, when a domain implements hot *potato routing,* it tries to forward packets that are destined to addresses outside of its domain, to other domains as quickly as possible.

To understand *hot potato routing,* let us consider the two domains shown in the figure below. *AS2* advertises prefix *1.0.0.0/8* over the *R2-R6* and *R3-R7* peering links. The routers inside *AS1* learn two routes towards *1.0.0.0/8:* one via *R6-R2* and the second via *R7-R3.*

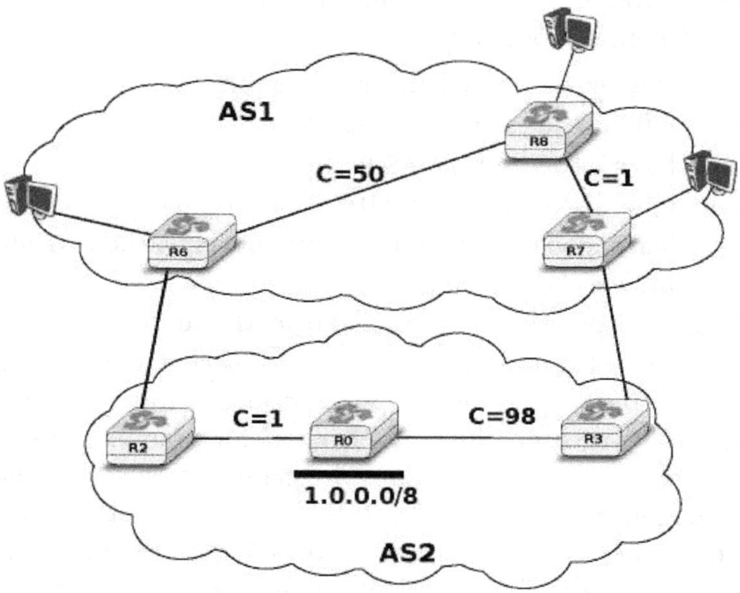

Figure 4.69: Hot and cold potato routing

With the fifth step of the BGP decision process, a router always prefers to use a route learned over an *eBGP session* compared to a route learned over an *iBGP session.* Thus, router *R6* (resp. *R7*) prefers to use the route via router *R2* (resp. *R3)* to reach prefix *1.0.0.0/8.*

The sixth step of the BGP decision process takes into account the distance, measured as the length of the shortest intradomain path, between a BGP router and the BGP nexthop for routes learned over *iBGP sessions.* This rule is used on router *R8* in the example above. This router has received two routes towards *1.0.0.0/8:*

- *1.0.0.0/8* via *R7* that is at a distance of *1* from *R8*
- *1.0.0.0/8* via *R6* that is at a distance of *50* from *R8*

The first route, via *R7* is the one that router *R8* prefers, as this is the route that minimises the cost of forwarding packets inside *AS1* before sending them to *AS2.*

Hot potato routing allows *AS1* to minimise the cost of forwarding packets towards *AS2.* However, there are situations where this is not desirable. For example, assume that *AS1* and *AS2* are domains with routers on both the East and the West coast of the US. In these two domains, the high metric associated to links *R6-R8* and *R0-R2* correspond to the cost of forwarding a packet across the USA. If *AS2* is a customer that pays AS1, it would prefer to receive the packets destined to *1.0.0.0/8* via the *R2-R6* link instead of the *R7-R3* link. This is the objective of *cold potato routing.*

Cold potato routing is implemented using the *Multi-Exit Discriminator (MED)* attribute. This attribute is an optional BGP attribute that may be set by border routers when advertising a BGP route over an *eBGP session.* The MED attribute is usually used to indicate over an *eBGP session* the cost to reach the BGP nexthop for the advertised route. The *MED* attribute is set by the router that advertises a route over an *eBGP session.* In the example above, router *R2* sends *U(1.0.0.0/8,R2,AS2,MED=1)* while *R3* sends *U(1.0.0.0/8,R3,AS2,MED=98).*

Assume that the BGP session *R7-3* is the first to be established. *R7* sends *U(1.0.0.0/8,R3,AS2,MED=98)* to both *R8* and R6. At this point, all routers inside *AS1* send the packets towards *1.0.0.0/8* via *R7-R3.* Then, the *R6- R2* BGP session is established and router *R6* receives *U(1.0.0.0/8,R2,AS2,MED=1).* Router *R6* runs its decision process for destination *1.0.0.0/8* and selects the route via *R2* as its chosen route to reach this prefix since this is the only route that it knows. *R6* sends *U(1.0.0.0/8,R2,AS2,MED=1)* to routers *R8* and R7. They both run their decision process and prefer the route advertised by R6, as it contains the smallest *MED.* Now, all routers inside *AS1* forward the packets to *1.0.0.0/8* via link *R6-R2* as expected by AS2. As router *R7* no longer uses the BGP route learned via R3, it must stop advertising it over *iBGP sessions* and sends *W(1.0.0.0/8)* over its *iBGP sessions* with *R6* and *R8*. However, router *R7* still keeps the route learned from *R3* inside its Adj-RIB-In. If the *R6-R2* link fails, *R6* sends *W(1.0.0.0/8)* over its iBGP sessions and router *R7* responds by sending *U(1.0.0.0/8,R3,AS2,MED=98)* over its iBGP sessions.

In practice, the fifth step of the BGP decision process is slightly more complex, as the routes towards a given prefix can be learned from different ASes. For example, assume that in figure *Hot and cold potato routing, 1.0.0.0/8* is also advertised by *AS3* (not shown in the figure) that has peering links with routers *R6* and *R8*. If *AS3* advertises a route whose MED attribute is set to *2* and another with a MED set to 3, how should *AS1* 's router compare the four BGP routes towards *1.0.0.0/8* ? Is a MED value of *1* from *AS2* better than a MED value of *2* from *AS3* ? The fifth step of the BGP decision process solves this problem by only comparing the MED attribute of the routes learned from the same neighbour AS. Additional details about the MED attribute may be found in **RFC 4451**. It should be noted that using the MED attribute may cause some problems in BGP networks as explained in [GW2002]. In practice, the *MED* attribute is not used on *eBGP sessions* unless the two domains agree to enable it.

The last step of the BGP decision allows the selection of a single route when a BGP router has received several routes that are considered as equal by the first six steps of the decision process. This can happen for example in a dual-homed stub attached to two different providers. As shown in the figure below, router *R1* receives two equally good BGP routes towards *1.0.0.0/8*. To break the ties, each router is identified by a unique *router-id* which in practice is one of the IP addresses assigned to the router. On some routers, the lowest router id step in the BGP decision process is replaced by the selection of the oldest route **RFC 5004**. Preferring the oldest route when breaking ties is used to prefer stable paths over unstable paths. However, a drawback of this approach is that the selection of the BGP routes depends on the arrival times of the corresponding messages. This makes the BGP selection process non-deterministic and can lead to problems that are difficult to debug.

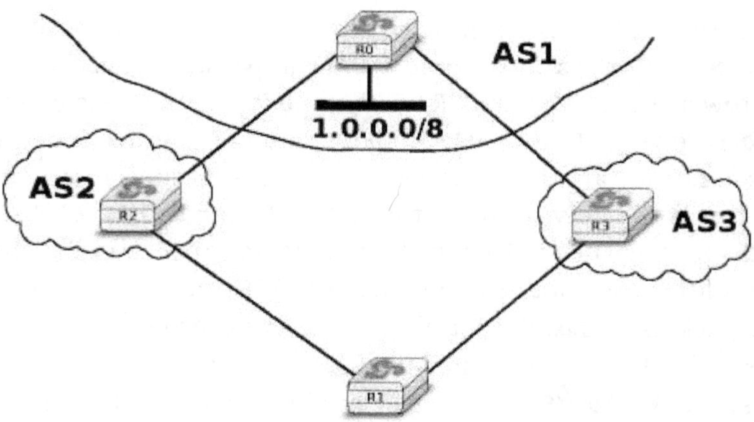

Figure 4.70: A stub connected to two providers

BGP convergence

In the previous sections, we have explained the operation of BGP routers. Compared to intradomain routing protocols, a key feature of BGP is its ability to support interdomain routing policies that are defined by each domain as its import and export filters and ranking process. A domain can define its own routing policies and router vendors have implemented many configuration tweaks to support complex routing policies. However, the routing policy chosen by a domain may interfere with the routing policy chosen by another domain. To understand this issue, let us first consider the simple internetwork shown below.

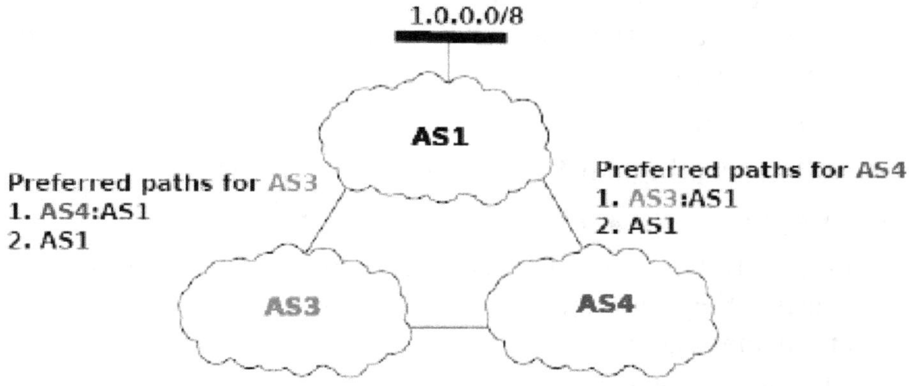

Figure 4.71: The disagree internetwork

In this internetwork, we focus on the route towards *1.0.0.0/8* which is advertised by *AS1.* Let us also assume that *AS3* (resp. *AS4)* prefers, e.g. for economic reasons, a route learned from *AS4 (AS3)* over a route learned from AS1. When AS1 sends *U(1.0.0.0/8,AS1)* to *AS3* and AS4, three sequences of exchanges of BGP messages are possible :

1. *AS3* sends first *U(1.0.0.0/8,AS3:AS1)* to AS4. *AS4* has learned two routes towards *1.0.0.0/8.* It runs its BGP decision process and selects the route via *AS3* and does not advertise a route to *AS3*
2. *AS4* first sends *U(1.0.0.0/8,AS3:AS1)* to AS3. *AS3* has learned two routes towards *1.0.0.0/8.* It runs its BGP decision process and selects the route via *AS4* and does not advertise a route to *AS4*
3. *AS3* sends *U(1.0.0.0/8,AS3:AS1)* to *AS4* and, at the same time, *AS4* sends *U(1.0.0.0/8,AS4:AS1). AS3* prefers the route via *AS4* and thus sends *W(1.0.0.0/8)* to AS4. In the mean time, *AS4* prefers the route via *AS3* and thus sends *W(1.0.0.0/8)* to AS3. Upon reception of the *BGP Withdraws, AS3* and *AS4* only know the direct route towards *1.0.0.0/8. AS3* (resp. AS4) sends *U(1.0.0.0/8,AS3:AS1)* (resp. *U(1.0.0.0/8,AS4:AS1))* to *AS4* (resp. *AS3*). *AS3* and *AS4* could in theory continue to exchange BGP messages for ever. In practice, one of them sends one message faster than the other and BGP converges.

The example above has shown that the routes selected by BGP routers may sometimes depend on the ordering of the BGP messages that are exchanged. Other similar scenarios may be found in **RFC 4264.**

From an operational perspective, the above configuration is annoying since the network operators cannot easily predict which paths are chosen. Unfortunately, there are even more annoying BGP configurations. For example, let us consider the configuration below which is often named *Bad Gadget* [GW1999]

In this internetwork, there are four ASes. *AS0* advertises one route towards one prefix and we only analyse the routes towards this prefix. The routing preferences of AS1, *AS3* and *AS4* are the following :

- *AS1* prefers the path *AS3:AS0* over all other paths
- *AS3* prefers the path *AS4:AS0* over all other paths
- *AS4* prefers the path *AS1:AS0* over all other paths

AS0 sends *U(p,AS0)* to AS1, *AS3* and AS4. As this is the only route known by AS1, *AS3* and *AS4* towards p, they all select the direct path. Let us now consider one possible exchange of BGP messages :

1. *AS1* sends *U(p, AS1:AS0)* to *AS3* and AS4. *AS4* selects the path via *AS1* since this is its preferred path. *AS3* still uses the direct path.
2. *AS4* advertises *U(p,AS4:AS1:AS0)* to AS3.

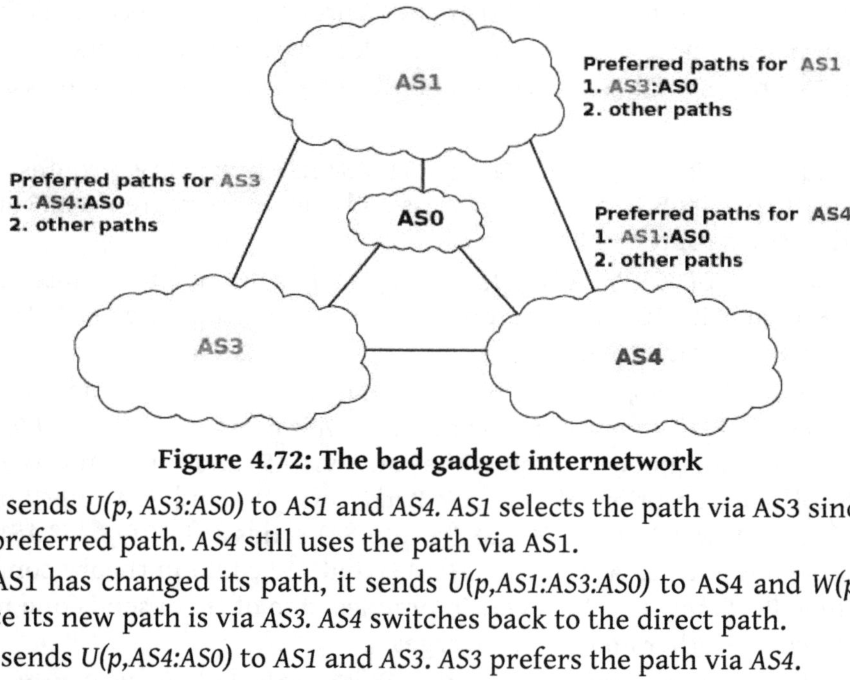

Figure 4.72: The bad gadget internetwork

3. AS3 sends *U(p, AS3:AS0)* to *AS1* and *AS4. AS1* selects the path via AS3 since this is its preferred path. *AS4* still uses the path via AS1.
4. As AS1 has changed its path, it sends *U(p,AS1:AS3:AS0)* to AS4 and *W(p)* to *AS3* since its new path is via *AS3. AS4* switches back to the direct path.
5. *AS4* sends *U(p,AS4:AS0)* to *AS1* and *AS3*. *AS3* prefers the path via *AS4*.
6. *AS3* sends *U(p,AS3:AS4:AS0)* to *AS1* and *W(p)* to AS4. *AS1* switches back to the direct path and we are back at the first step.

This example shows that the convergence of BGP is unfortunately not always guaranteed as some interdomain routing policies may interfere with each other in complex ways. [GW1999] have shown that checking for global convergence is either NP-complete or NP-hard. See [GSW2002] for a more detailed discussion.

Fortunately, there are some operational guidelines [GR2001] [GGR2001] that can guarantee BGP convergence in the global Internet. To ensure that BGP will converge, these guidelines consider that there are two types of peering relationships : *customer->provider* and *shared-cost*. In this case, BGP convergence is guaranteed provided that the following conditions are fulfilled :

1. The topology composed of all the directed *customer->provider* peering links is an acyclic graph
2. An AS always prefers a route received from a *customer* over a route received from a *shared-cost* peer or a *provider*.

The first guideline implies that the provider of the provider of *ASx* cannot be a customer of ASx. Such a relationship would not make sense from an economic perspective as it would imply circular payments. Furthermore, providers are usually larger than customers.

The second guideline also corresponds to economic preferences. Since a provider earns money when sending packets to one of its customers, it makes sense to prefer such customer learned routes over routes learned from providers. [GR2001] also shows that BGP convergence is guaranteed even if an AS associates the same preference to routes learned from a *shared-cost* peer and routes learned from a customer.

From a theoretical perspective, these guidelines should be verified automatically to ensure that BGP will always converge in the global Internet. However, such a verification cannot be performed in practice because this would force all domains to disclose their routing policies (and few are willing to do so) and furthermore the problem is known to be NP-hard [GW1999].

In practice, researchers and operators expect that these guidelines are verified in most domains. Thanks to the large amount of BGP data that has been collected by operators and researchers , several studies have analysed the AS-level topology of the Internet. [SARK2002] is one of the first analysis. More recent studies include [COZ2008] and [DKF+2007]

Based on these studies and [ATLAS2009], the AS-level Internet topology can be summarised as shown in the figure below.

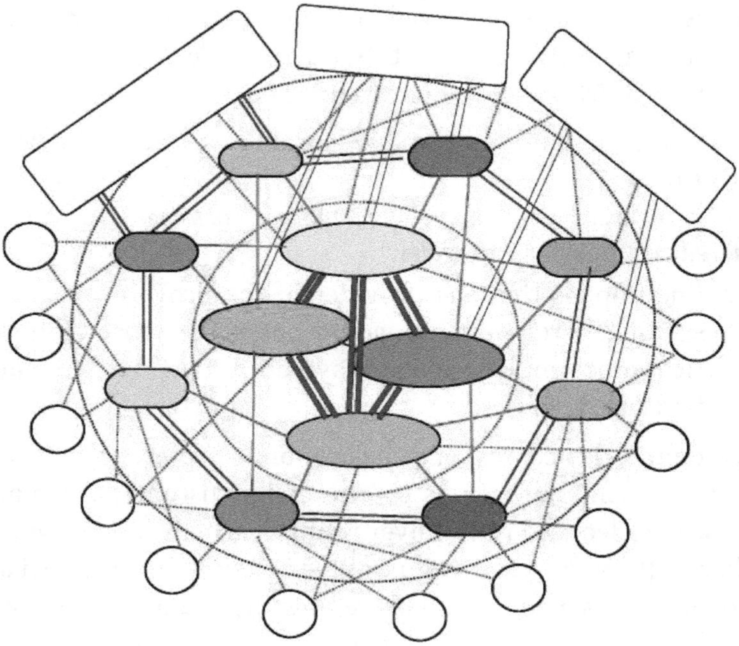

Figure 4.73: The layered structure of the global Internet

The domains on the Internet can be divided in about four categories according to their role and their position in the AS-level topology.

- the core of the Internet is composed of a dozen-twenty *Tier-1* ISPs. A *Tier-1* is a domain that has no *provider.* Such an ISP has *shared-cost* peering relationships with all other *Tier-1* ISPs and *provider->customer* relationships with smaller ISPs. Examples of *Tier-1* ISPs include sprint, level3 or opentransit
- the *Tier-2* ISPs are national or continental ISPs that are customers of *Tier-1* ISPs. These *Tier-2* ISPs have smaller customers and *shared-cost* peering relationships with other *Tier-2* ISPs. Example of *Tier-2* ISPs include France Telecom, Belgacom, British Telecom, ...
- the *Tier-3* networks are either stub domains such as enterprise or campus networks networks and smaller ISPs. They are customers of Tier-1 and Tier-2 ISPs and have sometimes *shared-cost* peering relationships
- the large content providers that are managing large datacenters. These content providers are producing a growing fraction of the packets exchanged on the global Internet [ATLAS2009]. Some of these content providers are customers of Tier-1 or Tier-2 ISPs, but they often try to establish *shared-cost* peering relationships, e.g. at IXPs, with many Tier-1 and Tier-2 ISPs.

Due to this organisation of the Internet and due to the BGP decision process, most AS-level paths on the Internet have a length of 3-5 AS hops.

4.4 EXERCISES

4.4.1 Principles

1. Routing protocols used in data networks only use positive link weights. What would happen with a distance vector routing protocol in the network below that contains a negative link weight ?

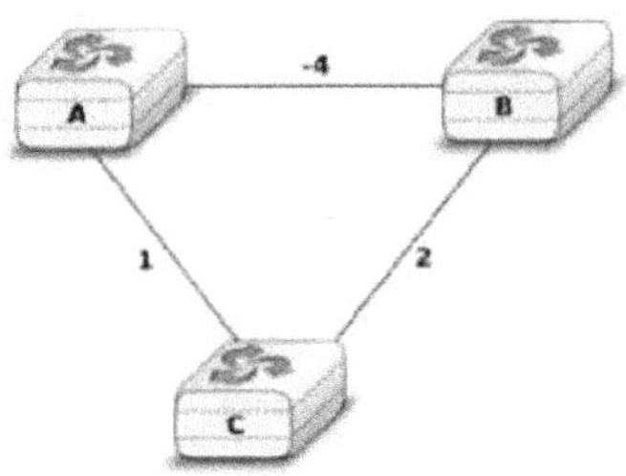

Figure 4.74: Simple network

2. When a network specialist designs a network, one of the problems that he needs to solve is to set the metrics the links in his network. In the USA, the Abilene network interconnects most of the research labs and universities. The figure below shows the topology of this network in 2009.

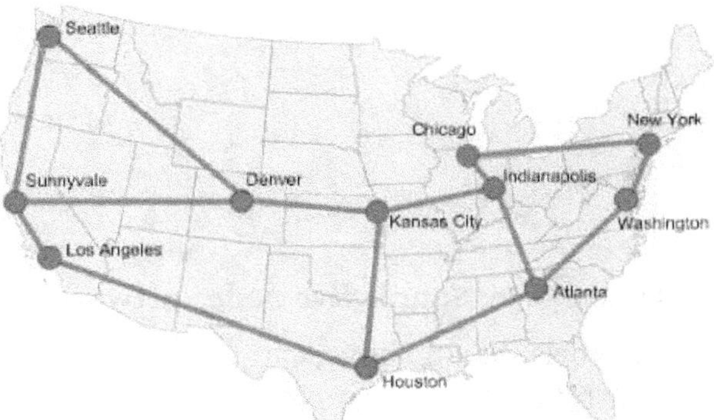

Figure 4.75: The Abilene network

In this network, assume that all the link weights are set to 1. What is the paths followed by a packet sent by the router located in *Los Angeles* to reach :

- the router located in *New York*
- the router located in *Washington* ?

Is it possible to configure the link metrics so that the packets sent by the router located in *Los Angeles* to the routers located in respectively *New York* and *Washington* do not follow the same path ?

Is it possible to configure the link weights so that the packets sent by the router located in *Los Angeles* to router located in *New York* follow one path while the packets sent by the router located in *New York* to the router located in *Los Angeles* follow a completely different path ?

Assume that the routers located in *Denver* and *Kansas City* need to exchange lots of packets. Can you configure the link metrics such that the link between these two routers does not carry any packet sent by another router in the network ?

3. In the five nodes network shown below, can you configure the link metrics so that the packets sent by router *E* to router *A* use link *B->A* while the packets sent by router *B* use links *B->D* and *D->A?*

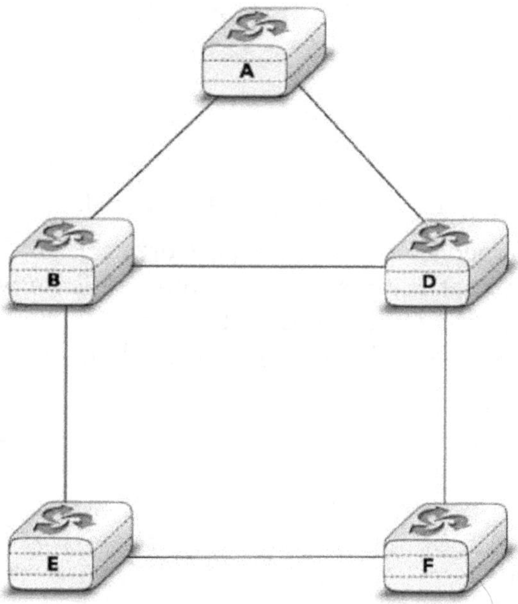

Figure 4.76: Simple five nodes network

4. In the five nodes network shown above, can you configure the link weights so that the packets sent by router *E* (resp. *F)* follow the *E->B->A* path (resp. *F->D->B->A)* ?
5. In the above questions, you have worked on the stable state of the routing tables computed by routing protocols. Let us now consider the transient problems that main happen when the network topology changes. For this, consider the network topology shown in the figure below and assume that all routers use a distance vector protocol that uses split horizon.

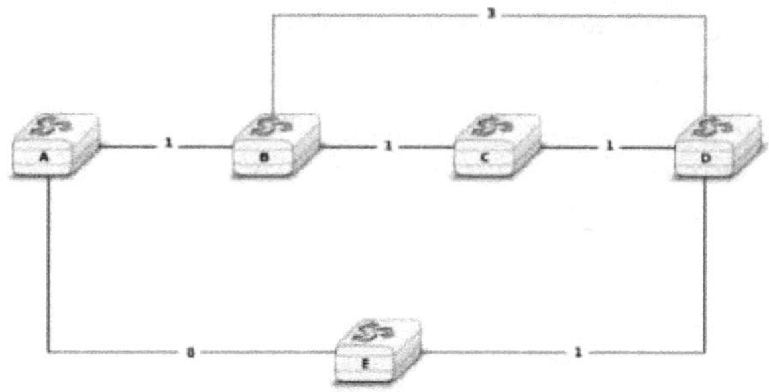

Figure 4.77: Simple network with redundant links

If you compute the routing tables of all routers in this network, you would obtain a table such as the table below :

Destination	Routes on A	Routes on B	Routes on C	Routes on D	Routes on E
A	0	1 via A	2 viaB	3 via C	4 viaD
B	1 viaB	0	1 viaB	2 viaC	3 viaD
C	2 viaB	1 via C	0	1 viaC	2 viaD
D	3 viaB	2 via C	1 viaD	0	1 viaD
E	4 viaB	3 via C	2 viaD	1 viaE	0

Distance vector protocols can operate in two different modes: *periodic updates* and *triggered updates. Periodic updates* is the default mode for a distance vector protocol. For example, each router could advertise its distance vector every thirty seconds. With the *triggered updates* a router sends its distance vector when its routing table changes (and periodically when there are no changes).

- Consider a distance vector protocol using split horizon and *periodic updates.* Assume that the link *B-C* fails. *B* and *C* update their local routing table but they will only advertise it at the end of their period. Select one ordering for the *periodic updates* and every time a router sends its distance vector, indicate the vector sent to each neighbor and update the table above. How many periods are required to allow the network to converge to a stable state ?
- Consider the same distance vector protocol, but now with *triggered updates.* When link *B-C* fails, assume that *B* updates its routing table immediately and sends its distance vector to *A* and *D.* Assume that both *A* and *D* process the received distance vector and that *A* sends its own distance vector, ... Indicate all the distance vectors that are exchanged and update the table above each time a distance vector is sent by a router (and received by other routers) until all routers have learned a new route to each destination. How many distance vector messages must be exchanged until the network converges to a stable state ?

6. Consider the network shown below. In this network, the metric of each link is set to *1* except link *A-B* whose metric is set to *4* in both directions. In this network, there are two paths with the same cost between *D* and *C*. Old routers would randomly select one of these equal cost paths and install it in their forwarding table. Recent routers are able to use up to *N* equal cost paths towards the same destination.

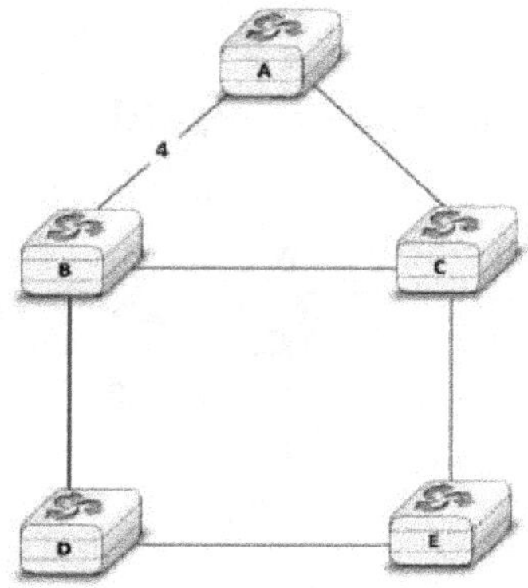

Figure 4.78: A simple network running OSPF

On recent routers, a lookup in the forwarding table for a destination address returns a set of outgoing interfaces. How would you design an algorithm that selects the outgoing interface used for each packet, knowing that to avoid reordering, all segments of a given TCP connection should follow the same path?

7. Consider again the network shown above. After some time, OSPF converges and all routers compute the following routing tables :

Destination	Routes on A	Routes on B	Routes on C	Routes on D	Routes on E
A	0	2 viaC	1 via A	3 via B,E	2 viaC
B	2 viaC	0	1 viaB	1 viaB	2 via D,C
C	1 viaC	1 viaC	0	2 via B,E	1 viaC
D	3 via C	1 viaD	2 via B,E	0	1 viaD
E	2 viaC	2 via C,D	1 viaE	1 viaE	0

An important difference between OSPF and RIP is that OSPF routers flood link state packets that allow the other routers to recompute their own routing tables while RIP routers exchange distance vectors. Consider that link *B-C* fails and that router *B* is the first to detect the failure. At this point, *B* cannot reach anymore *A*, *C* and 50% of its paths towards *E* have failed. C cannot reach B anymore and half of its paths towards *D* have failed.

Router *B* will flood its updated link state packet through the entire network and all routers will recompute their forwarding table. Upon reception of a link state packet, routers usually first flood the received link-state packet and then recompute their forwarding table. Assume that *B* is the first to recompute its forwarding table, followed by *D*, *A* , *C* and finally *E*

8. After each update of a forwarding table, verify which pairs of routers are able to exchange packets. Provide your answer using a table similar to the one shown above.
9. Can you find an ordering of the updates of the forwarding tables that avoids all transient problems ?
10. Consider the network shown in the figure below and explain the path that will be followed by the packets to reach *194.100.10.0/23*

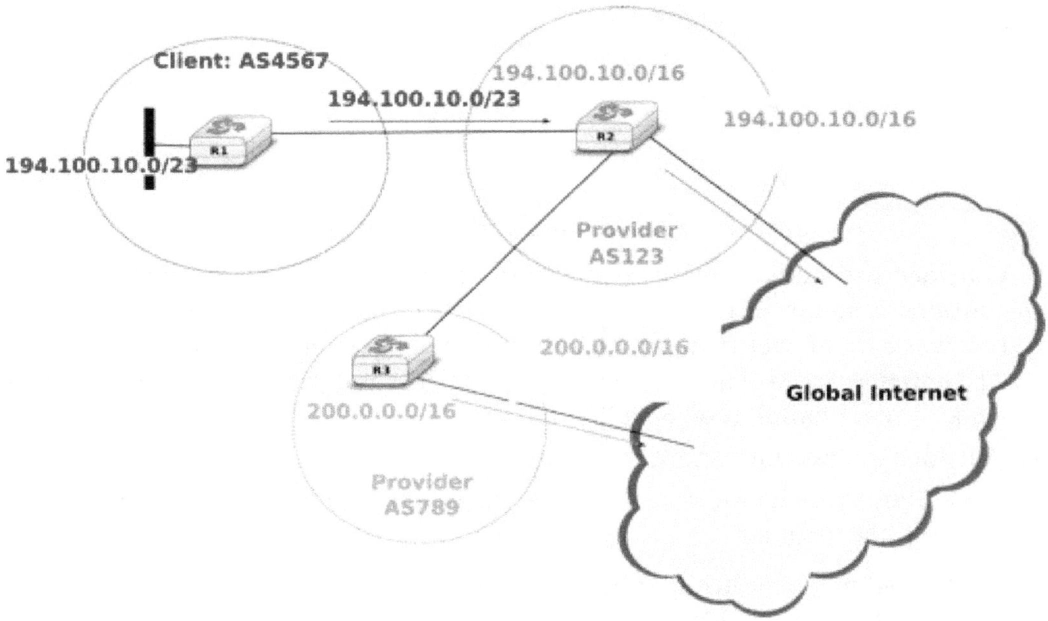

Figure 4.79: A stub connected to one provider

11. Consider, now, as shown in the figure below that the stub AS is now also connected to provider *AS789*. Via which provider will the packets destined to *194.100.10.0/23* will be received by *AS4567* ? Should *AS123* change its configuration?
12. Consider that stub shown in the figure below decides to advertise two */24* prefixes instead of its allocated */23* prefix.
    1. Via which provider does *AS4567* receive the packets destined to *194.100.11.99* and *194.100.10.1*
    2. How is the reachability of these addresses affected when link *R1-R3* fails ?
    3. Propose a configuration on *R1* that achieves the same objective as the one shown in the figure but also preserves the reachability of all IP addresses inside *AS4567* if one of *AS4567*'s interdomain links fails?

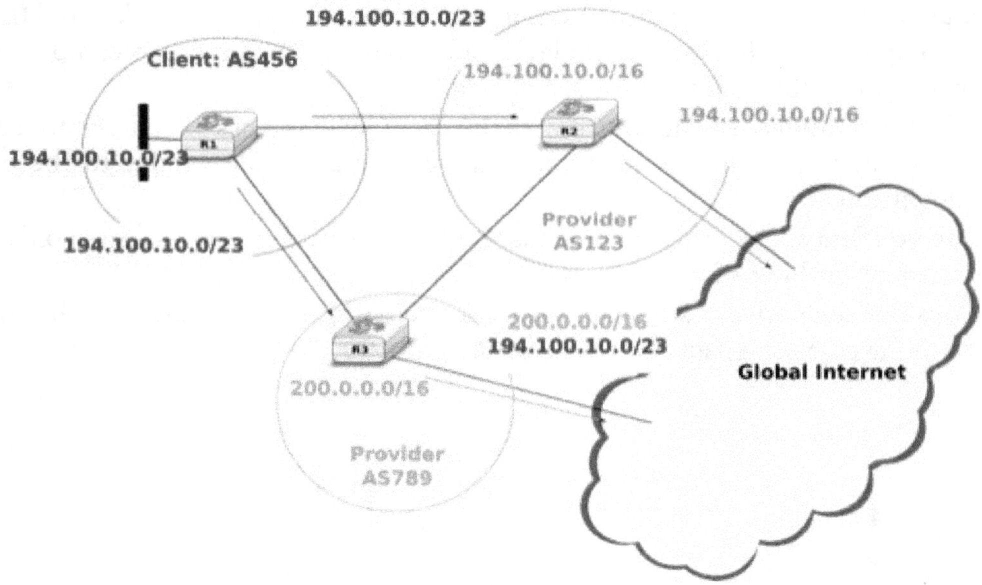

Figure 4.80: A stub connected to two providers

13. Consider the network shown in the figure below. In this network, each AS contains a single BGP router. Assume that *R1* advertises a single prefix. *R1* receives a lot of packets from *R9*. Without any help from *R2*, *R9* or *R4*, how could R1 configure its BGP advertisement such that it receives the packets from R9 via *R3* ? What happens when a link fails ?
14. Consider the network show in the figure below.
    1. Show which BGP messages are exchanged when router R1 advertises prefix *10.0.0.0/8*.
    2. How many and which routes are known by router R5 ? Which route does it advertise to R6?
    3. Assume now that the link between R1 and R2 fails. Show the messages exchanged due to this event. Which BGP messages are sent to *R6* ?
15. Consider the network shown in the figure below where R1 advertises a single prefix. In this network, the link between *R1* and *R2* is considered as a backup link. It should only be used only when the primary link *(R1-R4)* fails. This can be implemented on R2 by setting a low *local-pref* to the routes received on link R2-R1
    1. In this network, what are the paths used by all routers to reach *R1* ?
    2. Assume now that the link *R1-R4* fails. Which BGP messages are exchanged and what are now the paths used to reach *R1* ?
    3. Link *R1-R4* comes back. Which BGP messages are exchanged and what do the paths used to reach *R1* become ?

16. On February 22, 2008, the Pakistan Telecom Authority issued an order to Pakistan ISPs to block access to three IP addresses belonging to youtube: *208.65.153.238, 208.65.153.253, 208.65.153.251.* One operator noted that these addresses were belonging to the same */24* prefix. Read http://www.ripe.net/news/study- youtube-hijacking.html to understand what happened really.
    1. What should have done youtube to avoid this problem ?

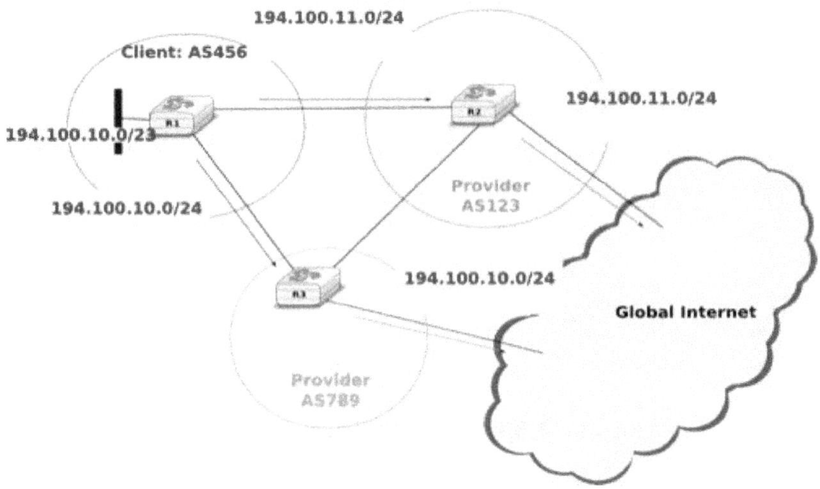

Figure 5.81: A stub connected to two providers

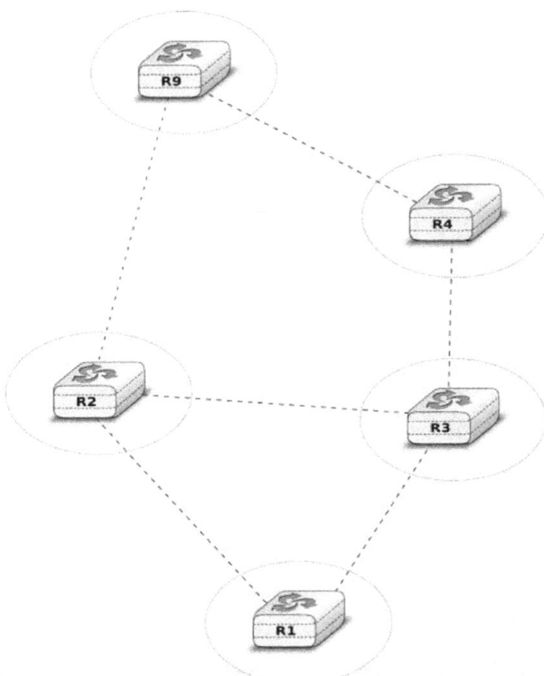

Figure 4.82: A simple internetwork

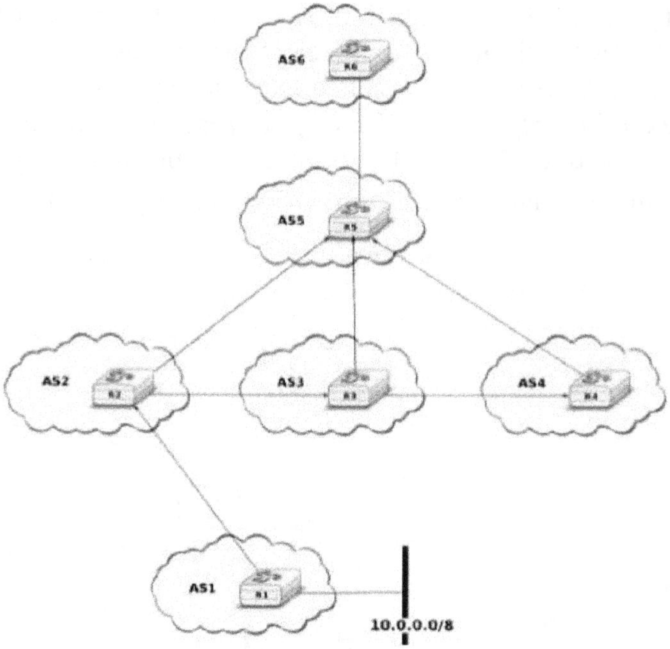

Figure 4.83: A simple internetwork

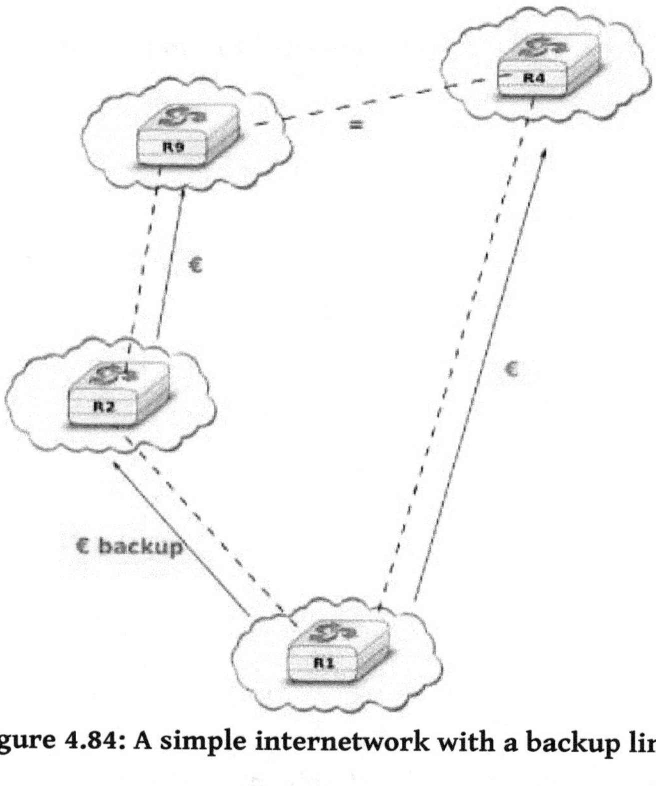

Figure 4.84: A simple internetwork with a backup link

2. What kind of solutions would you propose to improve the security of interdomain routing ?

17. There are currently 13 IPv4 addresses that are associated to the root servers of the Domain Name System. However, http://www.root-servers.org/ indicates that there are more than 100 different physical servers that support. This is a large anycast service. How would you configure BGP routers to provide such anycast service ?
18. Consider the network shown in the figure below. In this network, *R0* advertises prefix *p* and all link metrics are set to *1*
    - Draw the iBGP and eBGP sessions
    - Assume that session *R0-R8* is down when R0 advertises p over *R0-R7.* What are the BGP messages exchanged and the routes chosen by each router in the network ?
    - Session *R0-R8* is established and R0 advertises prefix p over this session as well
    - Do the routes selected by each router change if the *MED* attribute is used on the *R7-R6* and *R3-R10* sessions, but not on the *R4-R9* and *R6-R8* sessions ?
    - Is it possible to configure the routers in the *R1 - R6* network such that *R4* reaches prefix *p* via *R6-R8* while *R2‘uses the ‘R3-R10* link ?

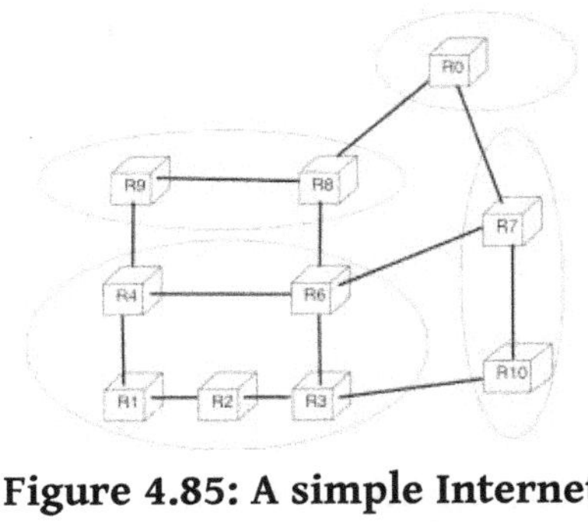

Figure 4.85: A simple Internet

19. The BGP *MED* attribute is often set at the IGP cost to reach the BGP nexthop of the advertised prefix. However, routers can also be configured to always use the same *MED* values for all routes advertised over a given session. How would you use it in the figure above so that link *R10-R3* is the primary link while *R7-R6* is a backup link ? Is there an advantage or drawback of using the *MED* attribute for this application compared to *local-pref* ?
20. In the figure above, assume that the managers of *R8* and *R9* would like to use the *R8-R6* link as a backup link, but the managers of *R4* and *R6* do no agree to use the BGP *MED* attribute nor to use a different *local-pref* for the routes learned from

4.5.2 Practice

1. For the following IPv4 subnets, indicate the smallest and the largest IPv4 address inside the subnet :
    - *8.0.0.0/8*
    - *172.12.0.0/16*
    - *200.123.42.128/25*
    - *12.1.2.0/13*
2. For the following IPv6 subnets, indicate the smallest and the largest IPv6 address inside the subnet:
    - *FE80::/64*
    - *2001:db8::/48*
    - *2001:6a8:3080::/48*
3. Researchers and network operators collect and expose lots of BGP data. For this, they establish eBGP sessions between *data collection* routers and production routers located in operational networks. Several *data collection* routers are available, the most popular ones are :
    - http://www.routeviews.org
    - http://www.ripe.net/ris
4. For this exercise, you will use one of the *routeviews* BGP routers. You can access one of these routers by using telnet. Once logged on the router, you can use the router's command line interface to analyse its BGP routing table.

```
telnet route-views.routeviews.org
Trying 128.223.51.103...
Connected to route-views.routeviews.org.
Escape character is '^]'.
C
**********************************************************************
Oregon Exchange BGP Route Viewer route-views.oregon-ix.net / route-views.
routeviews.org
route views data is archived on http://archive.routeviews.org
This hardware is part of a grant from Cisco Systems.
Please contact help@routeviews.org if you have questions or
comments about this service, its use, or if you might be able to contribute your view.
This router has views of the full routing tables from several ASes. The list of ASes is
documented under "Current Participants" on http://www.routeviews.org/.
**************
```

route-views.routeviews.org is now using AAA for logins. Login with username "rviews". See http://routeviews.org/aaa.html

****

User Access Verification

Username: rviews

route-views.oregon-ix.net>

This router has eBGP sessions with routers from several ISPs. See http://www.routeviews.org/peers/route-views.oregon-ix.net.txt for an up-to-date list of all eBGP sessions maintained by this router.

Among all the commands supported by this router, the *show ip bgp* command is very useful. This command takes an IPv4 prefix as parameter and allows you to retrieve all the routes that this routers has received in its Adj-RIB-In for the specified prefix.

1. Use *show ip bgp 130.104.0.0/16* to find the best path used by this router to reach UCLouvain
2. Knowing that *130.104.0.0/16* is announced by belnet (AS2611), what are, according to this BGP routing tables, the ASes that peer with belnet
3. Do the same analysis for one of the IPv4 prefixes assigned to Skynet (AS5432): *62.4.128.0/17.* The output of the *show ip bgp 62.4.128.0/17* reveals something strange as it seems that one of the paths towards this prefix passes twice via *AS5432.* Can you explain this ?

2905 702 1239 5432 5432

196.7.106.245 from 196.7.106.245 (196.7.106.245)

Origin IGP, metric 0, localpref 100, valid, external

4. netkit allows to easily perform experiments by using an emulated environment is is composed of virtual machines running User Model Linux. netkit allows to setup a small network in a lab and configure it as if you had access to several PCs interconnected by using cables and network equipments.

A netkit lab is defined as a few configuration files and scripts:

lab.conf is a textfile that defines the virtual machines and the network topology. A simple *lab.conf*

file is shown below.

LAB_DESCRIPTION="a string describing the lab"

LAB_VERSION=1.0

LAB_AUTHOR="the author of the lab"

LAB_EMAIL="email address of the author"

h1[0]="lan"

h2[0]="lan"

This configuration file requests the creation of two virtual machines, named hl **and** h2. **Each of these hosts has one ne** A *host.startup* file for each host *(hl.startup* and *h2.startup* in the example above). This file is a shell script that is executed at the end of the boot of the virtual host. This is typically in this script that the network interfaces are configured and the daemons are launched. A directory for each host (hl and *h2* in the example above). This directory is used to store configuration files that must be copied on the virtual machine's filesystems when they are first created.

netkit contains several scripts that can be used to run a lab. *Istart* allows to launch a lab and *lhalt* allows to halt the machines at the end of a lab. If you need to exchange files between the virtual machines and the Linux host on which netkit runs, note that the virtual hosts mount the directory that contains the running lab in */hostlab* and your home directory in */hosthome.*

For this exercise, you will use a netkit lab containing 4 hosts and two routers. The configuration files are available exercises/labs/lab-2routers.tar.gz. The network topology of this lab is shown in the figure below.

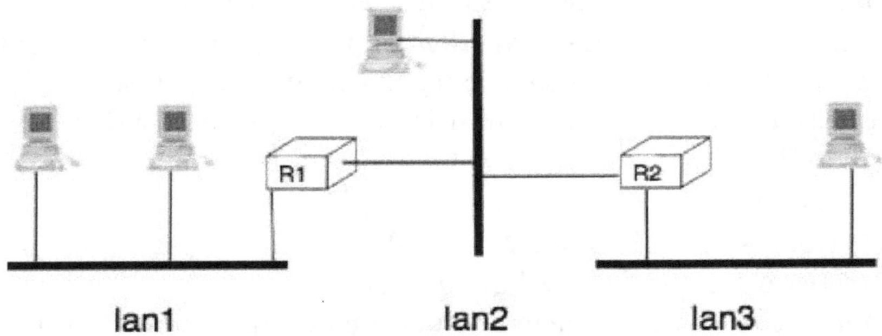

Figure 4.86: The two routers lab

The *lab.conf* file for this lab is shown below.

h1[0]="lan1"
h2[0]="lan1"
h3[0]="lan2"
router1[0]="lan1"
router1[1]="lan2"
router2[0]="lan2"
router2[1]="lan3"
h4[0]="lan3"

In this network, we will use subnet *172.12.1.0/24* for *lanl, 172.12.2.0/24* for *lan2* and *172.12.3.0/24* for *lan3.*

On Linux, the IP addresses assigned on an interface can be configured by using *ifconfig(8)*. When *ifconfig(8)* is used without parameters, it lists all the existing interfaces of the host with their configuration. A sample *ifconfig(8)* output is shown below.

```
host:~# ifconfig
eth0 Link encap:Ethernet HWaddr FE:3A:59:CD:59:AD
Inet addr:192.168.1.1    Bcast:192.168.1.255    Mask:255.255.255.0
inet6 addr: fe80::fc3a:59ff:fecd:59ad/64 Scope:Link UP BROADCAST RUNNING
MULTICAST MTU:1500 Metric:1
errors:0 dropped:0 errors:0 dropped:0 txqueuelen:1000 overruns:0 frame:0 overruns:0
carrier:0
RX bytes:216 (216.0 b) TX bytes:258 (258.0 b) Interrupt:5

lo Link encap:Local Loopback
inet addr:127.0.0.1     Mask:255.0.0.0
inet6 addr: ::1/128 Scope:Host
UP LOOPBACK RUNNING MTU:16436 Metric:1
RX packets:0 errors:0 dropped:0 overruns:0 frame:0
TX packets:0 errors:0 dropped:0 overruns:0 carrier:0 collisions:0 txqueuelen:0
RX bytes:0 (0.0 b) TX bytes:0 (0.0 b)
```

This host has two interfaces : the loopback interface (*lo* with IPv4 address *127.0.0.1* and IPv6 address ::1) and the *eth0* interface. The *192.168.1.1/24* address and a link local IPv6 address *(fe80::fc3a:59ff:fecd:59ad/64)* have been assigned to interface *eth0.* The broadcast address is used in some particular cases, this is outside the scope of this exercise. *ifconfig(8)* also provides statistics such as the number of packets sent and received over this interface. Another important information that is provided by *ifconfig(8)* is the hardware address (HWaddr) used by the datalink layer of the interface. On the example above, the *eth0* interface uses the 48 bits *FE:3A:59:CD:59:AD* hardware address.

You can configure the IPv4 address assigned to an interface by specifying the address and the netmask. ifconfig eth0 192.168.1.2 netmask 255.255.255.128 up

You can also specify the prefix length

.. code-block:: text

ifconfig eth0 192.168.1.2/25 up

In both cases, *ifconfig eth0* allows you to verify that the interface has been correctly configured.

```
eth0    Link encap:Ethernet HWaddr FE:3A:59:CD:59:AD
        inet addr:192.168.1.2  Bcast:192.168.1.127   Mask:255.255.255.128
        inet6 addr: fe80::fc3a:59ff:fecd:59ad/64 Scope:Link
        UP BROADCAST RUNNING MULTICAST MTU:1500 Metric:1
        RX packets:3 errors:0 dropped:0 overruns:0 frame:0
        TX packets:3 errors:0 dropped:0 overruns:0 carrier:0 collisions:0
        txqueuelen:1000
        RX bytes:216 (216.0 b) TX bytes:258 (258.0 b)
        Interrupt:5
```

Another important command on Linux is *route(8)* that allows to look at the contents of the routing table stored in the Linux kernel and change it. For example, *route -n* returns the contents of the IPv4 routing table. See *route(8)* for a detailed description on how you can configure routes by using this tool.

1. Use *ifconfig(8)* to configure the following IPv4 addresses:
    - *172.16.1.11/24* on interface *eth0* on *h1*
    - *172.16.1.12/24* on interface *eth0* on *h2*
2. Use *route -n* to look at the contents of the routing table on the two hosts.
3. Verify by using *ping(8)* that *h1* can reach *172.16.1.12*
4. Use *ifconfig(8)* to configure IPv4 address *172.16.1.1/24* on the *eth0* interface of *router1* and *172.16.2.1/24* on the *eth1* interface on this router.
5. Since hosts *hl* and *h2* are attached to a local area network that contains a single router, this router can act as a default router. Add a default route on hl and h2 so that they can use *routerl* as their default router to reach any remote IPv4 address. Verify by using *ping(8)* that hl can reach address *172.16.2.1.*
6. What do you need to configure on *router2, h3* and *h4* so that all hosts and routers can reach all hosts and routers in the emulated network ? Add the *ifconfig* and *route* commands in the *.startup* files of all the hosts so that the network is correctly configured when it is started by using *Istart.*

Use the network configured above to test how IP packets are fragmented. The *ifconfig* command allows you to specify the Maximum Transmission Unit (MTU), i.e. the largest size of the frames that are allowed on a given interface. The default MTU on the *eth?* interfaces is 1500 bytes.

1. Force an MTU of 500 bytes on the three interfaces attached to *lan2.*
2. Use *ping -s 1000* to send a 1000 bytes ping packet from *h3* to one of the routers attached to *lan2* and capture the packets on the other router by using *tcpdump(8)*. In which order does the emulated host sends the IP fragments ?
3. Use *ping -s 2000* to send a 2000 bytes ping packet from *h1* to *h4* and capture the packets on *lan2* and *lan3* by using *tcpdump(8)*. In which order does the emulated host sends the IP fragments ?

4. From your measurements, how does an emulated host generate the identifiers of the IP packets that it sends
5. Reset the MTU on the *eth1* interface of router *r1* at 1500 bytes, but leave the MTU on the *eth0* interface of router *r2* at 500 bytes. Check whether host *h1* can ping host *h4*. Use *tcpdump(8)* to analyse what is happening.
6. The Routing Information Protocol (RIP) is a distance vector protocol that is often used in small IP networks. There are various implementations of RIP. For this exercise, you will use quagga, an open-source implementation of several IP routing protocols that runs on Linux and other Unix compatible operating systems. *quagga(8)* is in fact a set of daemons that interact together and with the Linux kernel. For this exercise, you will use two of these daemons : *zebra(8)* and *ripd(8)*. *zebra(8)* is the master daemon that handles the interactions between the Linux kernel routing table and the routing protocols. *ripd(8)* is the implementation of the RIP protocol. It interacts with the Linux routing tables through the *zebra(8)* daemon.

To use a Linux real or virtual machine as a router, you need to first configure the IP addresses of the interfaces of the machine. Once this configuration has been verified, you can configure the *zebra(8)* and *ripd(8)* daemons. The configuration files for these daemons reside in */etc/zebra*. The first configuration file is */etc/zebra/daemons*. It lists the daemons that are launched when zebra is started by */etc/init.d/zebra*. To enable *ripd(8)* and *zebra(8)*, this file will be configured as follows.

```
# This file tells the zebra package
# which daemons to start.
# Entries are in the format: <daemon>=(yes|no|priority)
# where 'yes' is equivalent to infinitely low priority, and
# lower numbers mean higher priority. Read
#/usr/doc/zebra/README.Debian for details.
# Daemons are: bgpd zebra ospfd ospf6d ripd ripngd
zebra=yes
bgpd=no
ospfd=yes
ospf6d=no
ripd=no
ripngd=no
```

The second configuration file is the */etc/zebra/zebra.conf* file. It defines the global configuration rules that apply to *zebra(8)*. For this exercise, we use the default configuration file shown below.

```
! -*- zebra -*-
! zebra configuration file
```

```
hostname zebra
password zebra
enable password zebra
! Static default route sample.
!ip route 0.0.0.0/0 203.181.89.241
log file /var/log/zebra/zebra.log
```

In the zebra configuration file, lines beginning with ! are comments. This configuration defines the hostname as *zebra* and two passwords. The default password *(password zebra)* is the one that must be given when connecting to the *zebra(8)* management console over a TCP connection. This management console can be use like a shell on a Unix host to specify commands to the *zebra(8)* daemons. The second one *(enable password zebra)* specifies the password to be provided before giving commands that change the configuration of the daemon. It is also possible to specify static routes in this configuration file, but we do not use this facility in this exercise. The last parameter that is specified is the log file where *zebra(8)* writes debugging information. Additional information about quagga are available from http://www.quagga.net/docs/docs-info.php

The most interesting configuration file for this exercise is the*/etc/zebra/ripd.conf* file. It contains all the parameters that are specific to the operation of the RIP protocol. A sample *ripd(8)* configuration file is shown below.

```
!
hostname ripd
password zebra
enable password zebra
!
router rip
network 100.1.0.0/16
redistribute connected
!
log file /var/log/zebra/ripd.log
```

This configuration files shown the two different ways to configure *ripd(8)*. The statement *router rip* indicates the beginning of the configuration for the RIP routing protocol. The indented lines that follow are part of the configuration of this protocol. The first line, *network 100.1.0.0/16* is used to enable RIP on the interface whose IP subnet matches *100.1.0.0/16.* The second line, *redistribute connected* indicates that all the subnetworks that are directly connected on the router should be advertised. When this configuration line is used, *ripd(8)* interacts with the Linux kernel routing table and advertises all the subnetworks that are directly connected on the router.

If a new interface is enabled and configured on the router, its subnetwork prefix will be automatically advertised. Similarly, the subnetwork prefix will be automatically removed if the subnetwork interface is shutdown.

To experiment with RIP, you will use the emulated routers shown in the figure below. You can download the entire lab from exercises/labs/lab-5routers-rip.tar.gz

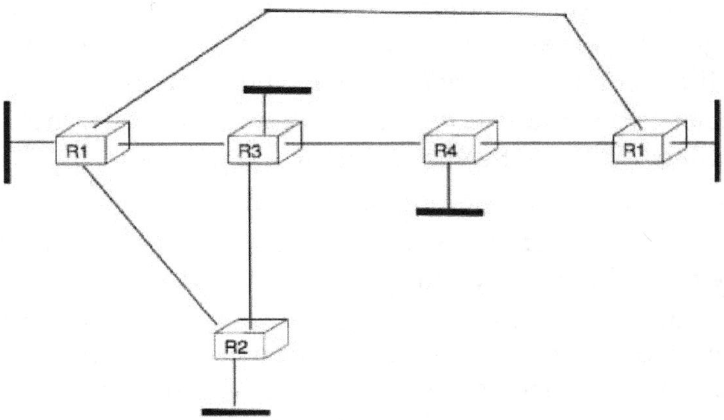

Figure 4.87: The five routers lab

The *lab.conf* describing the topology and the interfaces used on all hosts is shown below/

r1[0]="A"
r1[1]="B"
r1[2]="F"
r1[3]="V"
r2[0]="A"
r2[1]="C"
r2[2]="W"
r3[0]="B"
r3[1]="C"
r3[2]="D"
r3[3]="X"
r4[0]="D"
r4[1]="E"
r4[2]="Y"
r5[0]="E"
r5[1]="F"
r5[2]="Z"

There are two types of subnetworks in this topology. The subnetworks from the *172.16.0.0/16* prefix are used on the links between routers while the subnetworks from the *192.168.0.0/16* prefix are used on the local area networks that are attached to a single router.

A router can be configured in two different ways: by specifying configuration files and by typing the commands directly on the router by using *telnet(1)*. The first four routers have been configured in the provided configuration files. Look at *r1.startup* and the configurations files in *r1/tmp/zebra* in the lab's directory for router *r1*. The *r?.startup* files contain the *ifconfig(8)* commands that are used to configure the interfaces of each virtual router. The configuration files located in *r?/tmp/zebra* are also copied automatically on the virtual router when it boots.

1. Launch the lab by using *lstart* and verify that router *r1* can reach *192.168.1.1*, *192.168.2.2*, *192.168.3.3* and *192.168.4.4*. You can also *traceroute(8)* to determine what is the route followed by your packets.
2. The *ripd(8)* daemon can also be configured by typing commands over a TCP connection. *ripd(8)* listens on port 2602. On router *r1*, use *telnet 127.0.0.1 2602* to connect to the *ripd(8)* daemon. The default password is *zebra*. Once logged on the *ripd(8)* daemon, you reach the > prompt where you can query the status of the router. By typing *?* at the prompt, you will find the list of supported commands. The *show* command is particularly useful, type *show ?* to obtain the list of its sub options. For example, *show ip rip* will return the routing table that is maintained by the *ripd(8)* daemon.
3. Disable interface *eth3* on router *r1* by typing *ifconfig eth3 down* on this router. Verify the impact of this command on the routing tables of the other routers in the network. Re-enable this interface by typing *ifconfig eth3 up*.
4. Do the same with the *eth1* interface on router *r3*.
5. Edit the */etc/zebra/ripd.conf* configuration file on router *r5* so that this router becomes part of the network. Verify that *192.168.5.5* is reachable by all routers inside the network.

The Open Shortest Path First (OSPF) protocol is a link-state protocol that is often used in enterprise IP networks. OSPF is implemented in the *ospfd(8)* daemon that is part of quagga. We use the same topology as in the previous exercise. The netkit lab may be downloaded from exercises/labs/lab-5routers-ospf.tar.gz.

The *ospfd(8)* daemon supports a more complex configuration that the *ripd(8)* daemon. A sample configuration is shown below.

```
!
hostname ospfd
password zebra
enable password zebra
```

```
!
interface eth0
ip ospf cost 1
interface eth1
ip ospf cost 1
interface eth2
ip ospf cost 1
interface eth3
ip ospf cost 1
!
router ospf
router-id 192.168.1.1
network 172.16.1.0/24 area 0.0.0.0
network 172.16.2.0/24 area 0.0.0.0
network 172.16.3.0/24 area 0.0.0.0
network 192.168.1.0/24 area 0.0.0.0
passive-interface eth3
!
log file /var/log/zebra/ospfd.log
```

In this configuration file, the *ip ospf cost 1* specify a metric of *1* for each interface. The *ospfd(8)* configuration is composed of three parts. First, each router must have one identifier that is unique inside the network. Usually, this identifier is one of the IP addresses assigned to the router. Second, each subnetwork on the router is associated with an area. In this example, we only use the backbone area (i.e. *0.0.0.0).* The last command specifies that the OSPF Hello messages should not be sent over interface *eth3* although its subnetwork will be advertised by the router. Such a command is often used on interfaces that are attached to endhosts to ensure that no problem will occur if a student configures a software OSPF router on his laptop attached to this interface.

The netkit lab contains already the configuration for routers *r1* - *r4.*

The *ospfd(8)* daemon listens on TCP port *2604.* You can follow the evolution of the OSPF protocol by using the *show ip ospf ?* commands.

1. Launch the lab by using *lstart* and verify that the *192.168.1.1, 192.168.2.2, 192.168.3.3* and *192.168.4.4* addresses are reachable from any router inside the network.
2. Configure router *r5* by changing the */etc/zebra/ospfd.conf* file and restart the daemon. Verify that the *192.168.5.5* address is reachable from any router inside the network.

3. How can you update the network configuration so that the packets sent by router *r1* to router *r5* use the direct link between the two routers while the packets sent by *r5* are forwarded via *r4* ?
4. Disable interface *eth3* on router *r1* and see how quickly the network converges ? You can follow the evolution of the routing table on a router by typing *netstat -rnc*. Re-enable interface *eth3* on router *r1*.
5. Change the MTU of *eth0* on router *r1* but leave it unchanged on interface *eth0* of router *r2*. What is the impact of this change ? Can you explain why ?
6. Disable interface *eth1* on router *r3* and see how quickly the network converges ? Re-enable this interface.
7. Halt router *r2* by using *vcrash r2*. How quickly does the network react to this failure?

CHAPTER

The Datalink Layer and The Local Area Networks

5

The datalink layer is the lowest layer of the reference model that we discuss in detail. As mentioned previously, there are two types of datalink layers. The first datalink layers that appeared are the ones that are used on point- to-point links between devices that are directly connected by a physical link. We will briefly discuss one of these datalink layers in this chapter. The second type of datalink layers are the ones used in Local Area Networks (LANs). The main difference between the point-to-point and the LAN datalink layers is that the latter need to regulate the access to the Local Area Network which is usually a shared medium.

This chapter is organised as follows. We first discuss the principles of the datalink layer as well as the services that it uses from the physical layer. We then describe in more detail several Medium Access Control algorithms that are used in Local Area Networks to regulate the access to the shared medium. Finally we discuss in detail important datalink layer technologies with an emphasis on Ethernet and WiFi networks.

5.1 PRINCIPLES

The datalink layer uses the service provided by the physical layer. Although there are many different implementations of the physical layer from a technological perspective, they all provide a service that enables the datalink layer to send and receive bits between directly connected devices. The datalink layer receives packets from the network layer. Two datalink layer entities exchange *frames*. As explained in the previous chapter, most datalink layer technologies impose limitations on the size of the frames. Some technologies only impose a maximum frame size, others enforce both minimum and maximum frames sizes and finally some technologies only support a single frame size. In the latter case, the datalink layer will usually include an adaptation sublayer to allow the network layer to send and receive variable-length packets. This adaptation layer may include fragmentation and reassembly mechanisms.

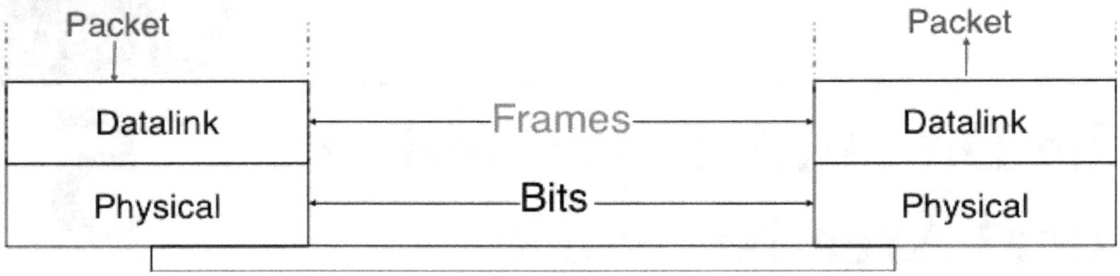

Figure 5.1: The datalink layer and the reference model

The physical layer service facilitates the sending and receiving of bits. Furthermore, it is usually far from perfect as explained in the introduction :

- the Physical layer may change, e.g. due to electromagnetic interferences, the value of a bit being transmitted
- the Physical layer may deliver *more* bits to the receiver than the bits sent by the sender
- the Physical layer may deliver *fewer* bits to the receiver than the bits sent by the sender

The datalink layer must allow endsystems to exchange frames containing packets despite all of these limitations. On point-to-point links and Local Area Networks, the first problem to be solved is how to encode a frame as a sequence of bits, so that the receiver can easily recover the received frame despite the limitations of the physical layer.

If the physical layer were perfect, the problem would be very simple. The datalink layer would simply need to define how to encode each frame as a sequence of consecutive bits. The receiver would then easily be able to extract the frames from the received bits. Unfortunately, the imperfections of the physical layer make this framing problem slightly more complex. Several solutions have been proposed and are used in practice in different datalink layer technologies.

5.1.1 Framing

This is the *framing* problem. It can be defined as : *"How does a sender encode frames so that the receiver can efficiently extract them from the stream of bits that it receives from the physical layer"*.

A first solution to solve the framing problem is to require the physical layer to remain idle for some time after the transmission of each frame. These idle periods can be detected by the receiver and serve as a marker to delineate frame boundaries. Unfortunately, this solution is not sufficient for two reasons. First, some physical layers cannot remain idle and always need to transmit bits. Second, inserting an idle period between frames decreases the maximum bandwidth that can be achieved by the datalink layer.

Some physical layers provide an alternative to this idle period. All physical layers are able to send and receive physical symbols that represent values *0* and 1. However, for various reasons that are outside the scope of this chapter, several physical layers are able to exchange other physical symbols as well. For example, the Manchester encoding used in several physical layers can send four different symbols. The Manchester encoding is a differential encoding scheme in which time is divided into fixed-length periods. Each period is divided in two halves and two different voltage levels can be applied. To send a symbol, the sender must set one of these two voltage levels during each half period. To send a *1* (resp. *0*), the sender must set a high (resp. low) voltage during the first half of the period and a low (resp. high) voltage during the second half. This encoding ensures that there will be a transition at the middle of each period and allows the receiver to synchronise its clock to the sender's clock. Apart from the encodings for *0* and 1, the Manchester encoding also supports two additional symbols : *InvH* and *InvB* where the same voltage level is used for the two half periods. By definition, these two symbols cannot appear inside a frame which is only composed of *0* and *1*. Some technologies use these special symbols as markers for the beginning or end of frames.

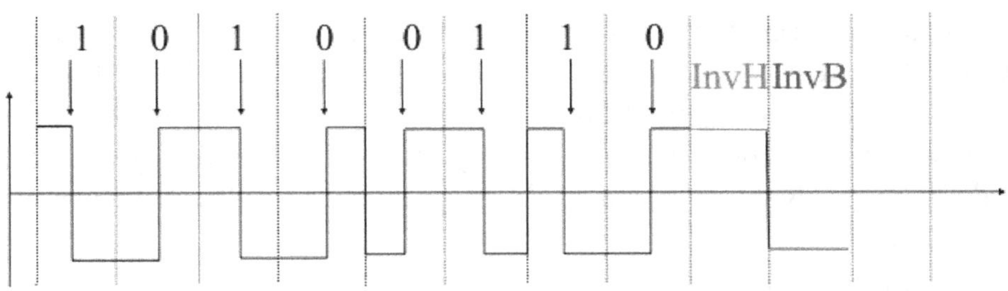

Figure 5.2: Manchester encoding

Unfortunately, multi-symbol encodings cannot be used by all physical layers and a generic solution which can be used with any physical layer that is able to transmit and receive only *0* and *1* is required. This generic solution is called *stuffing* and two variants exist: *bit stuffing* and *character stuffing*. To enable a receiver to easily delineate the frame boundaries, these two techniques reserve special bit strings as frame boundary markers and encode the frames so that these special bit strings do not appear inside the frames.

Bit stuffing reserves the *01111110* bit string as the frame boundary marker and ensures that there will never be six consecutive *1* symbols transmitted by the physical layer inside a frame. With bit stuffing, a frame is sent as follows. First, the sender transmits the marker, i.e. *01111110*. Then, it sends all the bits of the frame and inserts an additional bit set to *0* after each sequence of five consecutive *1* bits.

This ensures that the sent frame never contains a sequence of six consecutive bits set to 1. As a consequence, the marker pattern cannot appear inside the frame sent. The marker is also sent to mark the end of the frame. The receiver performs the opposite to decode a received frame. It first detects the beginning of the frame thanks to the *01111110* marker. Then, it processes the received bits and counts the number of consecutive bits set to 1. If a 0 follows five consecutive bits set to 1, this bit is removed since it was inserted by the sender. If a 1 follows five consecutive bits sets to 1, it indicates a marker if it is followed by a bit set to 0. The table below illustrates the application of bit stuffing to some frames.

Original frame	Transmitted frame
0001001001001001001000011	01111110000100100100100100100001101111110
0110111111111111111110010	01111110011011111011111011111011001001111110
01111110	0111111001111101001111110

For example, consider the transmission of *0110111111111111111110010.* The sender will first send the *01111110* marker followed by *011011111.* After these five consecutive bits set to 1, it inserts a bit set to *0* followed by 11111. A new *0* is inserted, followed by 11111. A new *0* is inserted followed by the end of the frame *110010* and the *01111110* marker.

Bit stuffing increases the number of bits required to transmit each frame. The worst case for bit stuffing is of course a long sequence of bits set to *1* inside the frame. If transmission errors occur, stuffed bits or markers can be in error. In these cases, the frame affected by the error and possibly the next frame will not be correctly decoded by the receiver, but it will be able to resynchronise itself at the next valid marker.

Bit stuffing can be easily implemented in hardware. However, implementing it in software is difficult given the higher overhead of bit manipulations in software. Software implementations prefer to process characters than bits, software-based datalink layers usually use *character stuffing.* This technique operates on frames that contain an integer number of 8-bit characters. Some characters are used as markers to delineate the frame boundaries. Many *character stuffing* techniques use the *DLE, STX* and *ETX* characters of the ASCII character set. *DLE STX* (resp. *DLE ETX)* is used to mark the beginning (end) of a frame. When transmitting a frame, the sender adds a *DLE* character after each transmitted *DLE* character. This ensures that none of the markers can appear inside the transmitted frame. The receiver detects the frame boundaries and removes the second *DLE* when it receives two consecutive *DLE* characters. For example, to transmit frame *12 3 DLE STX 4,* a sender will first send *DLE STX* as a marker, followed by *12 3 DLE.* Then, the sender transmits an additional *DLE* character followed by *STX 4* and the *DLE ETX* marker.

Original frame	Transmitted frame
12 34	*DLE STX 12 34 DLE ETX*
1 2 3 DLESTX4	*DLE STX 12 3 DLE DLE STX 4 DLE ETX*
DLE STX DLE ETX	*DLE STX DLE DLE STX DLE DLE ETX DLE ETX*

Character stuffing, like bit stuffing, increases the length of the transmitted frames. For *character stuffing*, the worst frame is a frame containing many *DLE* characters. When transmission errors occur, the receiver may incorrectly decode one or two frames (e.g. if the errors occur in the markers). However, it will be able to resynchronise itself with the next correctly received markers.

5.1.2 Error detection

Besides framing, datalink layers also include mechanisms to detect and sometimes even recover from transmission error. To allow a receiver to detect transmission errors, a sender must add some redundant information as an *error detection* code to the frame sent. This *error detection* code is computed by the sender on the frame that it transmits. When the receiver receives a frame with an error detection code, it recomputes it and verifies whether the received *error detection code* matches the computer *error detection code*. If they match, the frame is considered to be valid. Many error detection schemes exist and entire books have been written on the subject. A detailed discussion of these techniques is outside the scope of this book, and we will only discuss some examples to illustrate the key principles.

To understand *error detection codes*, let us consider two devices that exchange bit strings containing *N* bits. To allow the receiver to detect a transmission error, the sender converts each string of *N* bits into a string of *N+r* bits. Usually, the *r* redundant bits are added at the beginning or the end of the transmitted bit string, but some techniques interleave redundant bits with the original bits. An *error detection code* can be defined as a function that computes the *r* redundant bits corresponding to each string of *N* bits. The simplest error detection code is the parity bit. There are two types of parity schemes: even and odd parity. With the *even* (resp. *odd)* parity scheme, the redundant bit is chosen so that an even (resp. odd) number of bits are set to *1* in the transmitted bit string of N+r bits. The receiver can easily recompute the parity of each received bit string and discard the strings with an invalid parity. The parity scheme is often used when 7-bit characters are exchanged. In this case, the eighth bit is often a parity bit. The table below shows the parity bits that are computed for bit strings containing three bits.

3 bits string	Odd parity	Even parity
000	1	0
001	0	1

3 bits string	Odd parity	Even parity
010	0	1
100	0	1
111	0	1
110	1	0
101	1	0
011	1	0

The parity bit allows a receiver to detect transmission errors that have affected a single bit among the transmitted N+r bits. If there are two or more bits in error, the receiver may not necessarily be able to detect the transmission error. More powerful error detection schemes have been defined. The Cyclical Redundancy Checks (CRC) are widely used in datalink layer protocols. An N-bits CRC can detect all transmission errors affecting a burst of less than N bits in the transmitted frame and all transmission errors that affect an odd number of bits. Additional details about CRCs may be found in [Williams1993].

It is also possible to design a code that allows the receiver to correct transmission errors. The simplest *error correction code* is the triple modular redundancy (TMR). To transmit a bit set to 1 (resp. 0), the sender transmits 111 (resp. *000).* When there are no transmission errors, the receiver can decode 111 as 1. If transmission errors have affected a single bit, the receiver performs majority voting as shown in the table below. This scheme allows the receiver to correct all transmission errors that affect a single bit.

Received bits	Decoded bit
000	0
001	0
010	0
100	0
111	1
110	1
101	1
011	1

Other more powerful error correction codes have been proposed and are used in some applications. The Hamming Code is a clever combination of parity bits that provides error detection and correction capabilities.

In practice, datalink layer protocols combine bit stuffing or character stuffing with a length indication in the frame header and a checksum or CRC. The checksum/CRC is computed by the sender and placed in the frame before applying bit/character stuffing.

5.2 MEDIUM ACCESS CONTROL

Point-to-point datalink layers need to select one of the framing techniques described above and optionally add retransmission algorithms such as those explained for the transport layer to provide a reliable service. Datalink layers for Local Area Networks face two additional problems. A LAN is composed of several hosts that are attached to the same shared physical medium. From a physical layer perspective, a LAN can be organised in four different ways :

- a bus-shaped network where all hosts are attached to the same physical cable
- a ring-shaped where all hosts are attached to an upstream and a downstream node so that the entire network forms a ring
- a star-shaped network where all hosts are attached to the same device
- a wireless network where all hosts can send and receive frames using radio signals

These four basic physical organisations of Local Area Networks are shown graphically in the figure below. We will first focus on one physical organisation at a time.

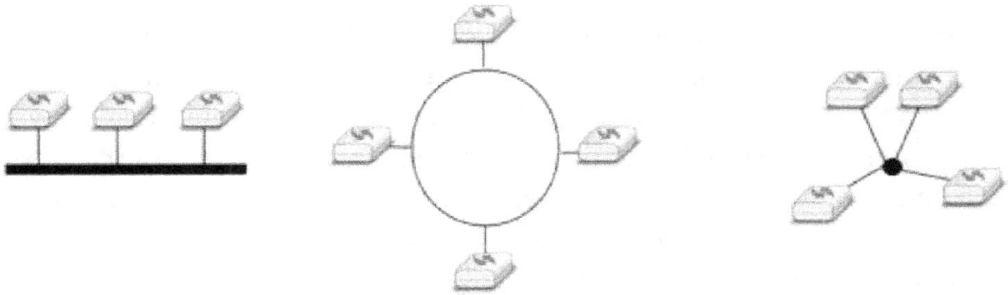

Figure 5.3: Bus, ring and star-shaped Local Area Network

The common problem among all of these network organisations is how to efficiently share the access to the Local Area Network. If two devices send a frame at the same time, the two electrical, optical or radio signals that correspond to these frames will appear at the same time on the transmission medium and a receiver will not be able to decode either frame. Such simultaneous transmissions are called *collisions.* A *collision* may involve frames transmitted by two or more devices attached to the Local Area Network. Collisions are the main cause of errors in wired Local Area Networks.

All Local Area Network technologies rely on a *Medium Access Control* algorithm to regulate the transmissions to either minimise or avoid collisions. There are two broad families of *Medium Access Control* algorithms:

1. *Deterministic* or *pessimistic* MAC algorithms. These algorithms assume that collisions are a very severe problem and that they must be completely avoided. These algorithms ensure that at any time, at most one device is allowed to send a frame on the LAN. This is usually achieved by using a distributed protocol which elects one device that is allowed to transmit at each time. A deterministic MAC algorithm ensures that no collision will happen, but there is some overhead in regulating the transmission of all the devices attached to the LAN.
2. *Stochastic* or *optimistic* MAC algorithms. These algorithms assume that collisions are part of the normal operation of a Local Area Network. They aim to minimise the number of collisions, but they do not try to avoid all collisions. Stochastic algorithms are usually easier to implement than deterministic ones.

We first discuss a simple deterministic MAC algorithm and then we describe several important optimistic algorithms, before coming back to a distributed and deterministic MAC algorithm.

5.2.1 Static allocation methods

A first solution to share the available resources among all the devices attached to one Local Area Network is to define, *a priori*, the distribution of the transmission resources among the different devices. If N devices need to share the transmission capacities of a LAN operating at b Mbps, each device could be allocated a bandwidth of N Mbps.

Limited resources need to be shared in other environments than Local Area Networks. Since the first radio transmissions by Marconi more than one century ago, many applications that exchange information through radio signals have been developed. Each radio signal is an electromagnetic wave whose power is centered around a given frequency. The radio spectrum corresponds to frequencies ranging between roughly 3 KHz and 300 GHz. Frequency allocation plans negotiated among governments reserve most frequency ranges for specific applications such as broadcast radio, broadcast television, mobile communications, aeronautical radio navigation, amateur radio, satellite, etc. Each frequency range is then subdivided into channels and each channel can be reserved for a given application, e.g. a radio broadcaster in a given region.

Frequency Division Multiplexing (FDM) is a static allocation scheme in which a frequency is allocated to each device attached to the shared medium. As each device uses a different transmission frequency, collisions cannot occur. In optical networks, a variant of FDM called *Wavelength Division Multiplexing* (WDM) can be used. An optical fiber can transport light at different wavelengths without interference. With WDM, a different wavelength is allocated to each of the devices that share the same optical fiber.

Time Division Multiplexing (TDM) is a static bandwidth allocation method that was initially defined for the telephone network. In the fixed telephone network, a voice conversation is usually transmitted as a 64 Kbps signal. Thus, a telephone conservation generates 8 KBytes per second or one byte every 125 microsecond. Telephone conversations often need to be multiplexed together on a single line. For example, in Europe, thirty 64 Kbps voice signals are multiplexed over a single 2 Mbps (E1) line. This is done by using *Time Division Multiplexing* (TDM). TDM divides the transmission opportunities into slots. In the telephone network, a slot corresponds to 125 microseconds. A position inside each slot is reserved for each voice signal. The figure below illustrates TDM on a link that is used to carry four voice conversations. The vertical lines represent the slot boundaries and the letters the different voice conversations. One byte from each voice conversation is sent during each 125 microsecond slot. The byte corresponding to a given conversation is always sent at the same position in each slot.

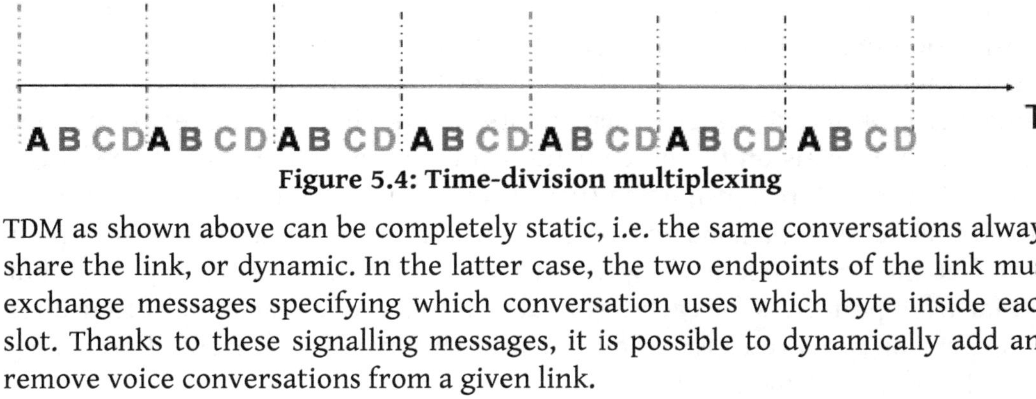

Figure 5.4: Time-division multiplexing

TDM as shown above can be completely static, i.e. the same conversations always share the link, or dynamic. In the latter case, the two endpoints of the link must exchange messages specifying which conversation uses which byte inside each slot. Thanks to these signalling messages, it is possible to dynamically add and remove voice conversations from a given link.

TDM and FDM are widely used in telephone networks to support fixed bandwidth conversations. Using them in Local Area Networks that support computers would probably be inefficient. Computers usually do not send information at a fixed rate. Instead, they often have an on-off behaviour. During the on period, the computer tries to send at the highest possible rate, e.g. to transfer a file. During the off period, which is often much longer than the on period, the computer does not transmit any packet. Using a static allocation scheme for computers attached to a LAN would lead to huge inefficiencies, as they would only be able to transmit at N of the total bandwidth during their on period, despite the fact that the other computers are in their off period and thus do not need to transmit any information. The dynamic MAC algorithms discussed in the remainder of this chapter aim solve this problem.

5.2.2 ALOHA

In the 1960s, computers were mainly mainframes with a few dozen terminals attached to them. These terminals were usually in the same building as the mainframe and were directly connected to it. In some cases, the terminals were installed in remote locations and connected through a *modem* attached to a *dial-up line*. The university of Hawaii chose a different organisation. Instead of using telephone lines to connect the distant terminals, they developed the first *packet radio* technology [Abramson1970]. Until then, computer networks were built on top of either the telephone network or physical cables. ALOHANet showed that it was possible to use radio signals to interconnect computers.

The first version of ALOHANet, described in [Abramson1970], operated as follows: First, the terminals and the mainframe exchanged fixed-length frames composed of 704 bits. Each frame contained 80 8-bit characters, some control bits and parity information to detect transmission errors. Two channels in the 400 MHz range were reserved for the operation of ALOHANet. The first channel was used by the mainframe to send frames to all terminals. The second channel was shared among all terminals to send frames to the mainframe. As all terminals share the same transmission channel, there is a risk of collision. To deal with this problem as well as transmission errors, the mainframe verified the parity bits of the received frame and sent an acknowledgement on its channel for each correctly received frame. The terminals on the other hand had to retransmit the unacknowledged frames. As for TCP, retransmitting these frames immediately upon expiration of a fixed timeout is not a good approach as several terminals may retransmit their frames at the same time leading to a network collapse. A better approach, but still far from perfect, is for each terminal to wait a random amount of time after the expiration of its retransmission timeout. This avoids synchronisation among multiple retransmitting terminals.

The pseudo-code below shows the operation of an ALOHANet terminal. We use this python syntax for all Medium Access Control algorithms described in this chapter. The algorithm is applied to each new frame that needs to be transmitted. It attempts to transmit a frame at most *max* times *(while loop)*. Each transmission attempt is performed as follows: First, the frame is sent. Each frame is protected by a timeout. Then, the terminal waits for either a valid acknowledgement frame or the expiration of its timeout. If the terminal receives an acknowledgement, the frame has been delivered correctly and the algorithm terminates. Otherwise, the terminal waits for a random time and attempts to retransmit the frame.

```
# ALOHA
N=1
while N<= max :
```

```
send(frame)
wait(ack_on_return_channel or timeout)
if (ack_on_return_channel):
break # transmission was successful
else:
# timeout
wait(random_time)
N=N+1
else:
# Too many transmission attempts
```

[Abramson1970] analysed the performance of ALOHANet under particular assumptions and found that ALO- HANet worked well when the channel was lightly loaded. In this case, the frames are rarely retransmitted and the *channel traffic,* i.e. the total number of (correct and retransmitted) frames transmitted per unit of time is close to the *channel utilization,* i.e. the number of correctly transmitted frames per unit of time. Unfortunately, the analysis also reveals that the *channel utilization* reaches its maximum at *jle* = 0-186 times the channel bandwidth. At higher utilization, ALOHANet becomes unstable and the network collapses due to collided retransmissions.

Note: Amateur packet radio

Packet radio technologies have evolved in various directions since the first experiments performed at the University of Hawaii. The Amateur packet radio service developed by amateur radio operators is one of the descendants ALOHANet. Many amateur radio operators are very interested in new technologies and they often spend countless hours developing new antennas or transceivers. When the first personal computers appeared, several amateur radio operators designed radio modems and their own datalink layer protocols [KPD1985] [BNT1997]. This network grew and it was possible to connect to servers in several European countries by only using packet radio relays. Some amateur radio operators also developed TCP/ IP protocol stacks that were used over the packet radio service. Some parts of the amateur packet radio network are connected to the global Internet and use the *44.0.0.0/8* prefix.

Many improvements to ALOHANet have been proposed since the publication of [Abramson1970], and this technique, or some of its variants, are still found in wireless networks today. The slotted technique proposed in [Roberts1975] is important because it shows that a simple modification can significantly improve channel utilization. Instead of allowing all terminals to transmit at any time, [Roberts1975] proposed to divide time into slots and allow terminals to transmit only at the beginning of each slot. Each slot corresponds to the time required to transmit one fixed size frame. In practice, these slots can be imposed by a single clock that is received by all terminals. In ALOHANet, it could have been located on the central mainframe. The analysis in [Roberts1975] reveals that this simple modification improves the channel utilization by a factor of two.

5.2.3 Carrier Sense Multiple Access

ALOHA and slotted ALOHA can easily be implemented, but unfortunately, they can only be used in networks that are very lightly loaded. Designing a network for a very low utilisation is possible, but it clearly increases the cost of the network. To overcome the problems of ALOHA, many Medium Access Control mechanisms have been proposed which improve channel utilization. Carrier Sense Multiple Access (CSMA) is a significant improvement compared to ALOHA. CSMA requires all nodes to listen to the transmission channel to verify that it is free before transmitting a frame [KT1975]. When a node senses the channel to be busy, it defers its transmission until the channel becomes free again. The pseudo-code below provides a more detailed description of the operation of CSMA.

```
# persistent CSMA
N=1
while N<= max :
wait(channel_becomes_free)
send(frame)
wait(ack or timeout)
if ack :
break # transmission was successful
else :
# timeout
N=N+1
end of while loop
# Too many transmission attempts
```

The above pseudo-code is often called *persistent CSMA* [KT1975] as the terminal will continuously listen to the channel and transmit its frame as soon as the channel becomes free. Another important variant of CSMA is the *non-persistent CSMA* [KT1975]. The main difference between persistent and non-persistent CSMA described in the pseudo-code below is that a non-persistent CSMA node does not continuously listen to the channel to determine when it becomes free. When a non-persistent CSMA terminal senses the transmission channel to be busy, it waits for a random time before sensing the channel again. This improves channel utilization compared to persistent CSMA. With persistent CSMA, when two terminals sense the channel to be busy, they will both transmit (and thus cause a collision) as soon as the channel becomes free. With non-persistent CSMA, this synchronisation does not occur, as the terminals wait a random time after having sensed the transmission channel. However, the higher channel utilization achieved by non-persistent CSMA comes at the expense of a slightly higher waiting time in the terminals when the network is lightly loaded.

```
# Non persistent CSMA
N=1
while N<= max :
listen(channel)
if free(channel):
send(frame)
wait(ack or timeout)
if received(ack) :
break # transmission was successful
else :
# timeout
N=N+1
else:
wait(random_time)
# end of while loop
# Too many transmission attempts
```

[KT1975] analyzes in detail the performance of several CSMA variants. Under some assumptions about the transmission channel and the traffic, the analysis compares ALOHA, slotted ALOHA, persistent and non-persistent CSMA. Under these assumptions, ALOHA achieves a channel utilization of only 18.4% of the channel capacity. Slotted ALOHA is able to use 36.6% of this capacity. Persistent CSMA improves the utilization by reaching 52.9% of the capacity while non-persistent CSMA achieves 81.5% of the channel capacity.

5.2.4 Carrier Sense Multiple Access with Collision Detection

CSMA improves channel utilization compared to ALOHA. However, the performance can still be improved, especially in wired networks. Consider the situation of two terminals that are connected to the same cable. This cable could, for example, be a coaxial cable as in the early days of Ethernet [Metcalfe1976]. It could also be built with twisted pairs. Before extending CSMA, it is useful to understand more intuitively, how frames are transmitted in such a network and how collisions can occur. The figure below illustrates the physical transmission of a frame on such a cable. To transmit its frame, host A must send an electrical signal on the shared medium. The first step is thus to begin the transmission of the electrical signal. This is point *(1)* in the figure below. This electrical signal will travel along the cable. Although electrical signals travel fast, we know that information cannot travel faster than the speed of light (i.e. 300.000 kilometers/second). On a coaxial cable, an electrical signal is slightly slower than the speed of light and 200.000 kilometers per second is a reasonable estimation. This implies that if the cable has a length of one kilometer, the electrical signal will need 5 microseconds to travel from one end of the cable to the other. The ends of coaxial cables are equipped with termination points that ensure that the electrical signal is not reflected back to its source. This is illustrated at point *(3)* in the figure, where the electrical signal has reached the left endpoint and host B. At this point, B starts to receive the frame being transmitted by A. Notice that there is a delay between the transmission of a bit on host A and its reception by host B. If there were other hosts attached to the cable, they would receive the first bit of the frame at slightly different times. As we will see later, this timing difference is a key problem for MAC algorithms. At point *(4)*, the electrical signal has reached both ends of the cable and occupies it completely. Host A continues to transmit the electrical signal until the end of the frame. As shown at point (5), when the sending host stops its transmission, the electrical signal corresponding to the end of the frame leaves the coaxial cable. The channel becomes empty again once the entire electrical signal has been removed from the cable.

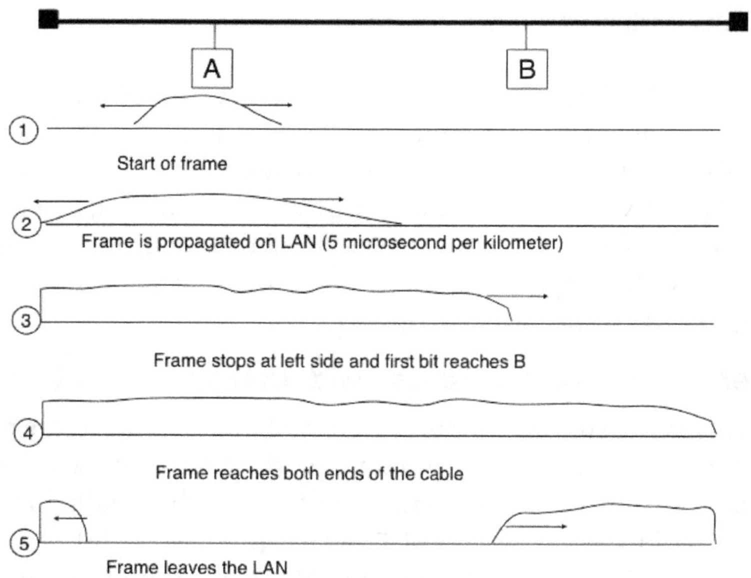

Figure 5.5: Frame transmission on a shared bus

Now that we have looked at how a frame is actually transmitted as an electrical signal on a shared bus, it is interesting to look in more detail at what happens when two hosts transmit a frame at almost the same time. This is illustrated in the figure below, where hosts A and B start their transmission at the same time (point (1)). At this time, if host C senses the channel, it will consider it to be free. This will not last a long time and at point (2) the electrical signals from both host A and host B reach host C. The combined electrical signal (shown graphically as the superposition of the two curves in the figure) cannot be decoded by host C. Host C detects a collision, as it receives a signal that it cannot decode. Since host C cannot decode the frames, it cannot determine which hosts are sending the colliding frames. Note that host A (and host B) will detect the collision after host C (point (3) in the figure below).

As shown above, hosts detect collisions when they receive an electrical signal that they cannot decode. In a wired network, a host is able to detect such a collision both while it is listening (e.g. like host C in the figure above) and also while it is sending its own frame. When a host transmits a frame, it can compare the electrical signal that it transmits with the electrical signal that it senses on the wire. At points *(1)* and (2) in the figure above, host A senses only its own signal. At point (3), it senses an electrical signal that differs from its own signal and can thus detects the collision. At this point, its frame is corrupted and it can stop its transmission. The ability to detect collisions while transmitting is the starting point for the *Carrier Sense Multiple Access with Collision Detection (CSMA/CD)* Medium Access Control algorithm, which is used in Ethernet networks [Metcalfe1976] [802.3]. When an Ethernet host detects a collision while it is transmitting, it immediately stops its transmission. Compared with pure CSMA, CSMA/CD is an important improvement since when collisions occur, they only last until colliding hosts have detected it and stopped their transmission. In practice, when a host detects a collision, it sends a special jamming signal on the cable to ensure that all hosts have detected the collision.

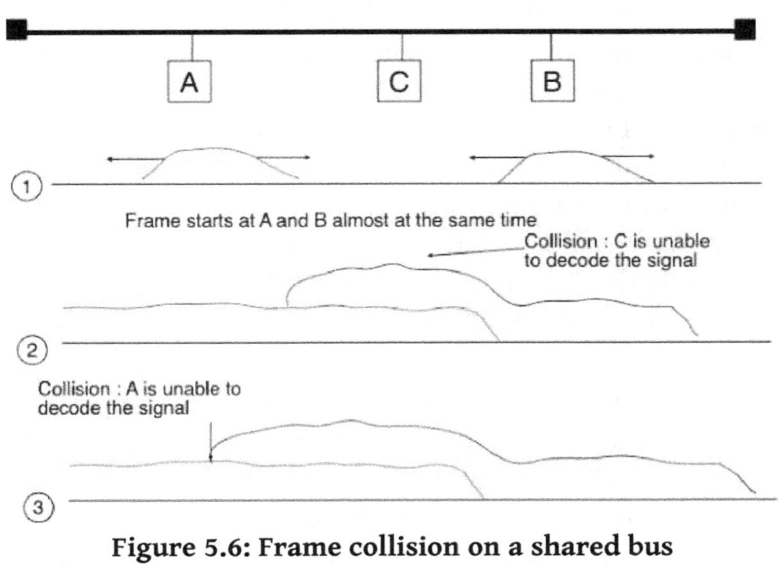

Figure 5.6: Frame collision on a shared bus

To better understand these collisions, it is useful to analyse what would be the worst collision on a shared bus network. Let us consider a wire with two hosts attached at both ends, as shown in the figure below. Host A starts to transmit its frame and its electrical signal is propagated on the cable. Its propagation time depends on the physical length of the cable and the speed of the electrical signal. Let us use τ to represent this propagation delay in seconds. Slightly less than τ seconds after the beginning of the transmission of A's frame, B decides to start transmitting its own frame. After ϵ seconds, B senses A's frame, detects the collision and stops transmitting. The beginning of B's frame travels on the cable until it reaches host A. Host A can thus detect the collision at time $\tau - \epsilon + \tau \approx 2 \times \tau$. An important point to note is that a collision can only occur during the first $2 \times \tau$ seconds of its transmission. If a collision did not occur during this period, it cannot occur afterwards since the transmission channel is busy after t seconds and CSMA/CD hosts sense the transmission channel before transmitting their frame.

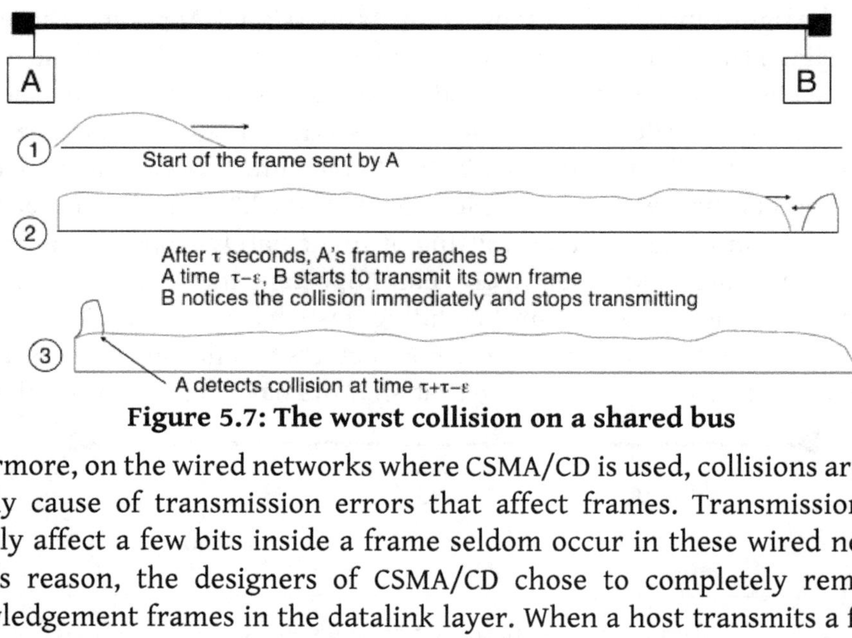

Figure 5.7: The worst collision on a shared bus

Furthermore, on the wired networks where CSMA/CD is used, collisions are almost the only cause of transmission errors that affect frames. Transmission errors that only affect a few bits inside a frame seldom occur in these wired networks. For this reason, the designers of CSMA/CD chose to completely remove the acknowledgement frames in the datalink layer. When a host transmits a frame, it verifies whether its transmission has been affected by a collision. If not, given the negligible Bit Error Ratio of the underlying network, it assumes that the frame was received correctly by its destination. Otherwise the frame is retransmitted after some delay.

Removing acknowledgements is an interesting optimisation as it reduces the number of frames that are exchanged on the network and the number of frames that need to be processed by the hosts. However, to use this optimisation, we must ensure that all hosts will be able to detect all the collisions that affect their frames. The problem is important for short frames. Let us consider two hosts, A and B, that are sending a small frame to host C as illustrated in the figure below. If the frames sent by A and B are very short, the situation illustrated below may occur. Hosts A and B send their frame and stop transmitting (point *(1)*). When the two short frames arrive at the location of host C, they collide and host C cannot decode them (point (2)). The two frames are absorbed by the ends of the wire. Neither host A nor host B have detected the collision. They both consider their frame to have been received correctly by its destination.

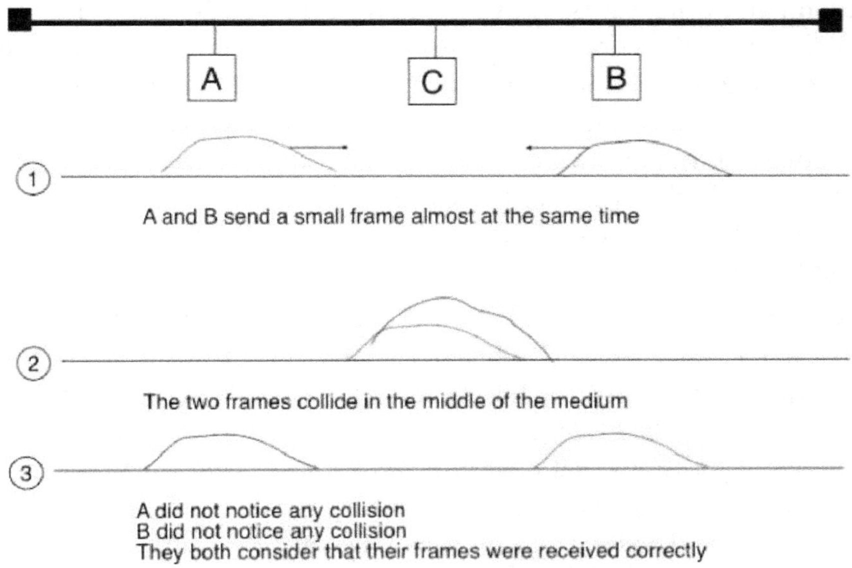

Figure 5.8: The short-frame collision problem

To solve this problem, networks using CSMA/CD require hosts to transmit for at least 2 x *t* seconds. Since the network transmission speed is fixed for a given network technology, this implies that a technology that uses CSMA/CD enforces a minimum frame size. In the most popular CSMA/CD technology, Ethernet, 2 x t is called the *slot time* .

The last innovation introduced by CSMA/CD is the computation of the retransmission timeout. As for ALOHA, this timeout cannot be fixed, otherwise hosts could become synchronised and always retransmit at the same time. Setting such a timeout is always a compromise between the network access delay and the amount of collisions. A short timeout would lead to a low network access delay but with a higher risk of collisions. On the other hand, a long timeout would cause a long network access delay but a lower risk of collisions. The *binary exponential back-off* algorithm was introduced in CSMA/CD networks to solve this problem.

To understand *binary exponential back-off*, let us consider a collision caused by exactly two hosts. Once it has detected the collision, a host can either retransmit its frame immediately or defer its transmission for some time. If each colliding host flips a coin to decide whether to retransmit immediately or to defer its retransmission, four cases are possible :

1. Both hosts retransmit immediately and a new collision occurs
2. The first host retransmits immediately and the second defers its retransmission
3. The second host retransmits immediately and the first defers its retransmission
4. Both hosts defer their retransmission and a new collision occurs

In the second and third cases, both hosts have flipped different coins. The delay chosen by the host that defers its retransmission should be long enough to ensure that its retransmission will not collide with the immediate retransmission of the other host. However the delay should not be longer than the time necessary to avoid the collision, because if both hosts decide to defer their transmission, the network will be idle during this delay. The *slot time* is the optimal delay since it is the shortest delay that ensures that the first host will be able to retransmit its frame completely without any collision.

If two hosts are competing, the algorithm above will avoid a second collision 50% of the time. However, if the network is heavily loaded, several hosts may be competing at the same time. In this case, the hosts should be able to automatically adapt their retransmission delay. The *binary exponential back-off* performs this adaptation based on the number of collisions that have affected a frame. After the first collision, the host flips a coin and waits 0 or 1 *slot time.* After the second collision, it generates a random number and waits 0, 1, 2 or 3 *slot times,* etc. The duration of the waiting time is doubled after each collision. The complete pseudo-code for the CSMA/CD algorithm is shown in the figure below.

```
# CSMA/CD pseudo-code
N=1
while N<= max :
wait(channel_becomes_free)
send(frame)
wait_until (end_of_frame) or (collision)
if collision detected:
stop transmitting
send(jamming)
k = min (10, N)
r = random(0, 2k - 1)     * slotTime
wait(r*slotTime)
N=N+1
else :
wait(inter-frame_delay)
break
```

end of while loop
Too many transmission attempts

The inter-frame delay used in this pseudo-code is a short delay corresponding to the time required by a network adapter to switch from transmit to receive mode. It is also used to prevent a host from sending a continuous stream of frames without leaving any transmission opportunities for other hosts on the network. This contributes to the fairness of CSMA/CD. Despite this delay, there are still conditions where CSMA/CD is not completely fair [RY1994]. Consider for example a network with two hosts : a server sending long frames and a client sending acknowledgments. Measurements reported in [RY1994] have shown that there are situations where the client could suffer from repeated collisions that lead it to wait for long periods of time due to the exponential back-off algorithm.

5.2.5 Carrier Sense Multiple Access with Collision Avoidance

The *Carrier Sense Multiple Access with Collision Avoidance* (CSMA/CA) Medium Access Control algorithm was designed for the popular WiFi wireless network technology [802.11]. CSMA/CA also senses the transmission channel before transmitting a frame. Furthermore, CSMA/CA tries to avoid collisions by carefully tuning the timers used by CSMA/CA devices.

CSMA/CA uses acknowledgements like CSMA. Each frame contains a sequence number and a CRC. The CRC is used to detect transmission errors while the sequence number is used to avoid frame duplication. When a device receives a correct frame, it returns a special acknowledgement frame to the sender. CSMA/CA introduces a small delay, named *Short Inter Frame Spacing* (SIFS), between the reception of a frame and the transmission of the acknowledgement frame. This delay corresponds to the time that is required to switch the radio of a device between the reception and transmission modes.

Compared to CSMA, CSMA/CA defines more precisely when a device is allowed to send a frame. First, CSMA/CA defines two delays : *DIFS* and *EIFS*. To send a frame, a device must first wait until the channel has been idle for at least the *Distributed Coordination Function Inter Frame Space* (DIFS) if the previous frame was received correctly. However, if the previously received frame was corrupted, this indicates that there are collisions and the device must sense the channel idle for at least the *Extended Inter Frame Space* (EIFS), with *SIFS < DIFS < EIFS*. The exact values for SIFS, DIFS and EIFS depend on the underlying physical layer [802.11].

The figure below shows the basic operation of CSMA/CA devices. Before transmitting, host *A* verifies that the channel is empty for a long enough period. Then, its sends its data frame. After checking the validity of the received frame, the recipient sends an acknowledgement frame after a short SIFS delay. Host C, which does not participate in the frame exchange, senses the channel to be busy at the beginning of the data frame. Host C can use this information to determine how long the channel will be busy for. Note that as *SIFS < DIFS < EIFS,* even a device that would start to sense the channel immediately after the last bit of the data frame could not decide to transmit its own frame during the transmission of the acknowledgement frame.

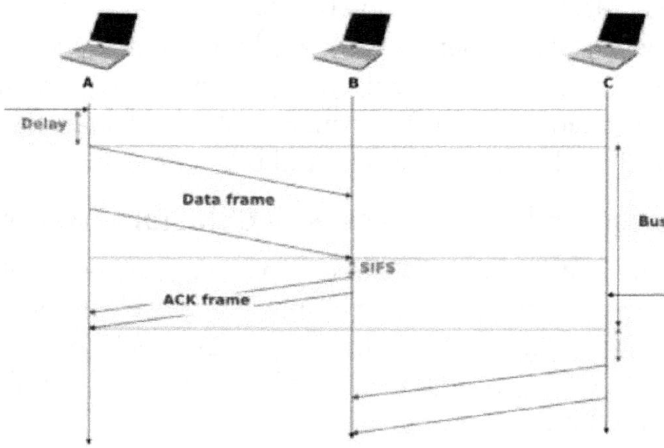

Figure 5.9: Operation of a CSMA/CA device

The main difficulty with CSMA/CA is when two or more devices transmit at the same time and cause collisions. This is illustrated in the figure below, assuming a fixed timeout after the transmission of a data frame. With CSMA/CA, the timeout after the transmission of a data frame is very small, since it corresponds to the SIFS plus the time required to transmit the acknowledgement frame.

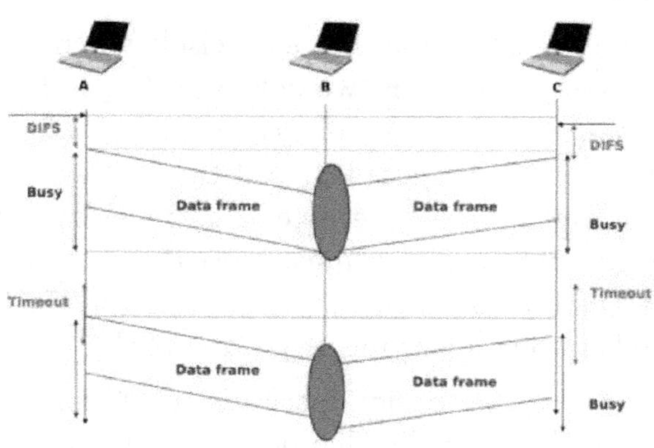

Figure 5.10: Collisions with CSMA/CA

To deal with this problem, CSMA/CA relies on a backoff timer. This backoff timer is a random delay that is chosen by each device in a range that depends on the number of retransmissions for the current frame. The range grows exponentially with the retransmissions as in CSMA/CD. The minimum range for the backoff timer is [0,7 * *slotTime*] where the *slotTime* is a parameter that depends on the underlying physical layer. Compared to CSMA/CD's exponential backoff, there are two important differences to notice. First, the initial range for the backoff timer is seven times larger. This is because it is impossible in CSMA/CA to detect collisions as they happen. With CSMA/CA, a collision may affect the entire frame while with CSMA/CD it can only affect the beginning of the frame. Second, a CSMA/CA device must regularly sense the transmission channel during its back off timer. If the channel becomes busy (i.e. because another device is transmitting), then the back off timer must be frozen until the channel becomes free again. Once the channel becomes free, the back off timer is restarted. This is in contrast with CSMA/CD where the back off is recomputed after each collision. This is illustrated in the figure below. Host *A* chooses a smaller backoff than host C. When C senses the channel to be busy, it freezes its backoff timer and only restarts it once the channel is free again.

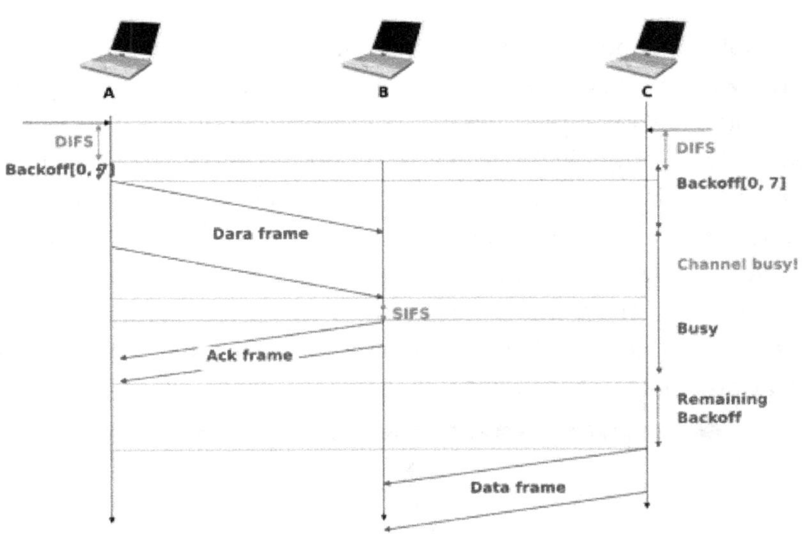

Figure 5.11: Detailed example with CSMA/CA

The pseudo-code below summarises the operation of a CSMA/CA device. The values of the SIFS, DIFS, EIFS and slotTime depend on the underlying physical layer technology [802.11]

```
# CSMA/CA simplified pseudo-code
N=1
while N<= max :
waitUntil(free(channel))
if correct(last_frame) :
wait(channel_free_during_t >=DIFS)
else:
wait(channel_free_during_t >=EIFS)
back-off_time = int(random[0,min(255,7*(2^(N-1)))])*slotTime
wait(channel free during backoff_time)
# backoff timer is frozen while channel is sensed to be busy
send(frame)
wait(ack or timeout)
if received(ack)
frame received correctly
break
else:
retransmission required
N=N+1
```

Another problem faced by wireless networks is often called the *hidden station problem.* In a wireless network, radio signals are not always propagated same way in all directions. For example, two devices separated by a wall may not be able to receive each other's signal while they could both be receiving the signal produced by a third host. This is illustrated in the figure below, but it can happen in other environments. For example, two devices that are on different sides of a hill may not be able to receive each other's signal while they are both able to receive the signal sent by a station at the top of the hill. Furthermore, the radio propagation conditions may change with time. For example, a truck may temporarily block the communication between two nearby devices.

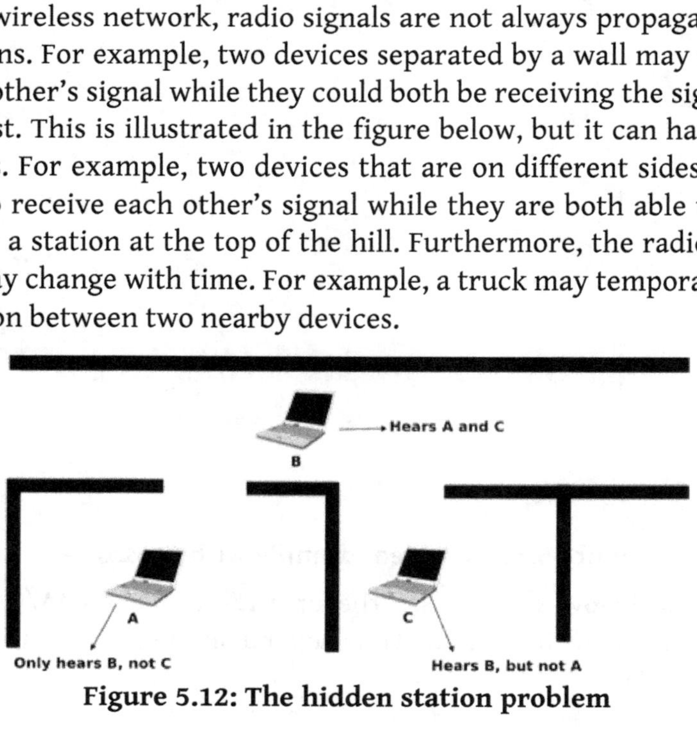

Figure 5.12: The hidden station problem

To avoid collisions in these situations, CSMA/CA allows devices to reserve the transmission channel for some time. This is done by using two control frames: *Request To Send* (RTS) and *Clear To Send* (CTS). Both are very short frames to minimize the risk of collisions. To reserve the transmission channel, a device sends a RTS frame to the intended recipient of the data frame. The RTS frame contains the duration of the requested reservation. The recipient replies, after a SIFS delay, with a CTS frame which also contains the duration of the reservation. As the duration of the reservation has been sent in both RTS and CTS, all hosts that could collide with either the sender or the reception of the data frame are informed of the reservation. They can compute the total duration of the transmission and defer their access to the transmission channel until then. This is illustrated in the figure below where host *A* reserves the transmission channel to send a data frame to host *B*. Host *C* notices the reservation and defers its transmission.

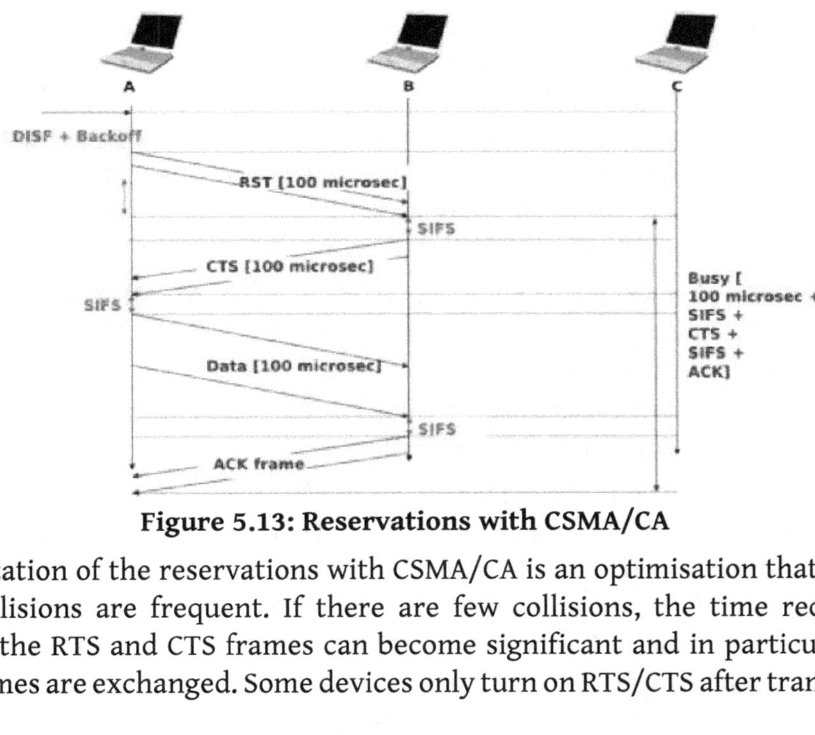

Figure 5.13: Reservations with CSMA/CA

The utilization of the reservations with CSMA/CA is an optimisation that is useful when collisions are frequent. If there are few collisions, the time required to transmit the RTS and CTS frames can become significant and in particular when short frames are exchanged. Some devices only turn on RTS/CTS after transmission errors.

5.2.6 Deterministic Medium Access Control algorithms

During the 1970s and 1980s, there were huge debates in the networking community about the best suited Medium Access Control algorithms for Local Area Networks. The optimistic algorithms that we have described until now were relatively easy to implement when they were designed. From a performance perspective, mathematical models and simulations showed the ability of these optimistic techniques to sustain load. However, none of the optimistic techniques are able to guarantee that a frame will be delivered within a given delay bound and some applications require predictable transmission delays. The deterministic MAC algorithms were considered by a fraction of the networking community as the best solution to fulfill the needs of Local Area Networks.

Both the proponents of the deterministic and the opportunistic techniques lobbied to develop standards for Local Area networks that would incorporate their solution. Instead of trying to find an impossible compromise between these diverging views, the IEEE 802 committee that was chartered to develop Local Area Network standards chose to work in parallel on three different LAN technologies and created three working groups. The IEEE 802.3 working group became responsible for CSMA/CD. The proponents of deterministic MAC algorithms agreed on the basic principle of exchanging special frames called tokens between devices to regulate the access to the transmission medium. However, they did not agree on the most suitable physical layout for the network. IBM argued in favor of Ring-shaped networks while the manufacturing industry, led by General Motors, argued in favor of a bus-shaped network. This led to the creation of the *IEEE 802.4 working group* to standardise Token Bus networks and the IEEE 802.5 working group to standardise Token Ring networks. Although these techniques are not widely used anymore today, the principles behind a token-based protocol are still important.

The IEEE 802.5 Token Ring technology is defined in [802.5]. We use Token Ring as an example to explain the principles of the token-based MAC algorithms in ring-shaped networks. Other ring-shaped networks include the almost defunct FDDI [Ross1989] or the more recent Resilient Pack Ring [DYGU2004]. A good survey of the token ring networks may be found in [Bux1989] .

A Token Ring network is composed of a set of stations that are attached to a unidirectional ring. The basic principle of the Token Ring MAC algorithm is that two types of frames travel on the ring : tokens and data frames. When the Token Ring starts, one of the stations sends the token. The token is a small frame that represents the authorization to transmit data frames on the ring. To transmit a data frame on the ring, a station must first capture the token by removing it from the ring. As only one station can capture the token at a time, the station that owns the token can safely transmit a data frame on the ring without risking collisions. After having transmitted its frame, the station must remove it from the ring and resend the token so that other stations can transmit their own frames.

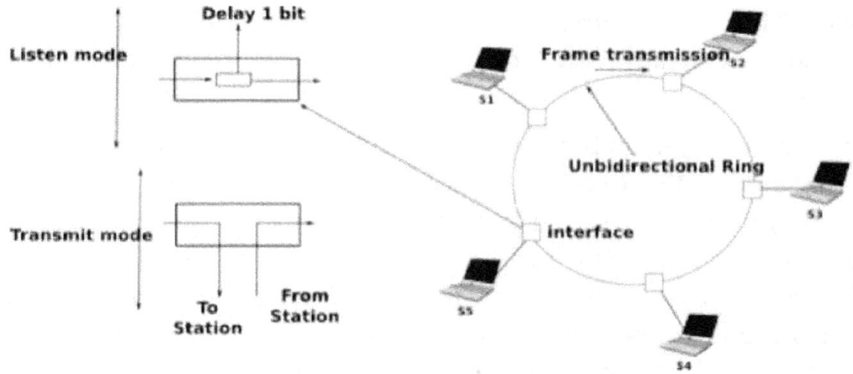

Figure 5.14: A Token Ring network

While the basic principles of the Token Ring are simple, there are several subtle implementation details that add complexity to Token Ring networks. To understand these details let us analyse the operation of a Token Ring interface on a station. A Token Ring interface serves three different purposes. Like other LAN interfaces, it must be able to send and receive frames. In addition, a Token Ring interface is part of the ring, and as such, it must be able to forward the electrical signal that passes on the ring even when its station is powered off.

When powered-on, Token Ring interfaces operate in two different modes : listen and transmit. When operating in listen mode, a Token Ring interface receives an electrical signal from its upstream neighbour on the ring, introduces a delay equal to the transmission time of one bit on the ring and regenerates the signal before sending it to its downstream neighbour on the ring.

The first problem faced by a Token Ring network is that as the token represents the authorization to transmit, it must continuously travel on the ring when no data frame is being transmitted. Let us assume that a token has been produced and sent on the ring by one station. In Token Ring networks, the token is a 24 bits frame whose structure is shown below.

```
0                   1                   2
0 1 2 3 4 5 6 7 8 9 0 1 2 3 4 5 6 7 8 9 0 1 2 3 4
+-+-+-+-+-+-+-+-+-+-+-+-+-+-+-+-+-+-+-+-+-+-+-+-+
| Start Delim.  |Access Control | Ending Delim. |
+-+-+-+-+-+-+-+-+-+-+-+-+-+-+-+-+-+-+-+-+-+-+-+-+
```

Figure 5.15: 802.5 token format

The token is composed of three fields. First, the *Starting Delimiter* is the marker that indicates the beginning of a frame. The first Token Ring networks used Manchester coding and the *Starting Delimiter* contained both symbols representing *0* and symbols that do not represent bits. The last field is the *Ending Delimiter* which marks the end of the token. The *Access Control* field is present in all frames, and contains several flags. The most important is the *Token* bit that is set in token frames and reset in other frames.

Let us consider the five station network depicted in figure *A Token Ring network* above and assume that station *S1* sends a token. If we neglect the propagation delay on the inter-station links, as each station introduces a one bit delay, the first bit of the frame would return to *S1* while it sends the fifth bit of the token. If station *S1* is powered off at that time, only the first five bits of the token will travel on the ring. To avoid this problem, there is a special station called the *Monitor* on each Token Ring. To ensure that the token can travel forever on the ring, this *Monitor* inserts a delay that is equal to at least 24 bit transmission times. If station *S3* was the *Monitor* in figure *A Token Ring network*, *S1* would have been able to transmit the entire token before receiving the first bit of the token from its upstream neighbour.

Now that we have explained how the token can be forwarded on the ring, let us analyse how a station can capture a token to transmit a data frame. For this, we need some information about the format of the data frames. An 802.5 data frame begins with the *Starting Delimiter* followed by the *Access Control* field whose *Token* bit is reset, a *Frame Control* field that allows for the definition of several types of frames, destination and source address, a payload, a CRC, the *Ending Delimiter* and a *Frame Status* field. The format of the Token Ring data frames is illustrated below.

```
 0                   1                   2                   3
 0 1 2 3 4 5 6 7 8 9 0 1 2 3 4 5 6 7 8 9 0 1 2 3 4 5 6 7 8 9 0 1
                +-+-+-+-+-+-+-+-+-+-+-+-+-+-+-+-+-+-+-+-+-+-+-+-+
                | Start Delim.  |Access Control | Frame Control |
+-+-+-+-+-+-+-+-+-+-+-+-+-+-+-+-+-+-+-+-+-+-+-+-+-+-+-+-+-+-+-+-+
|                                                               |
+    48 bits                    +-+-+-+-+-+-+-+-+-+-+-+-+-+-+-+-+
|    Destination Address        |                               |
+-+-+-+-+-+-+-+-+-+-+-+-+-+-+-+-+        48 bits                +
|                                     Source Address            |
+-+-+-+-+-+-+-+-+-+-+-+-+-+-+-+-+-+-+-+-+-+-+-+-+-+-+-+-+-+-+-+-+
|                                                               |
-                    Payload                                    |
|                                                               |
+-+-+-+-+-+-+-+-+-+-+-+-+-+-+-+-+-+-+-+-+-+-+-+-+-+-+-+-+-+-+-+-+
|                    32 bits         CRC                        |
+-+-+-+-+-+-+-+-+-+-+-+-+-+-+-+-+-+-+-+-+-+-+-+-+-+-+-+-+-+-+-+-+
| End Delim.    | Frame Status  |
+-+-+-+-+-+-+-+-+-+-+-+-+-+-+-+-+
```

Figure 5.16: 802.5 data frame format

To capture a token, a station must operate in *Listen* mode. In this mode, the station receives bits from its upstream neighbour. If the bits correspond to a data frame, they must be forwarded to the downstream neighbour. If they correspond to a token, the station can capture it and transmit its data frame. Both the data frame and the token are encoded as a bit string beginning with the *Starting Delimiter* followed by the *Access Control* field. When the station receives the first bit of a *Starting Delimiter*, it cannot know whether this is a data frame or a token and must forward the entire delimiter to its downstream neighbour. It is only when it receives the fourth bit of the *Access Control* field (i.e. the *Token* bit) that the station knows whether the frame is a data frame or a token. If the *Token* bit is reset, it indicates a data frame and the remaining bits of the data frame must be forwarded to the downstream station. Otherwise (*Token* bit is set), this is a token and the station can capture it by resetting the bit that is currently in its buffer. Thanks to this modification, the beginning of the token is now the beginning of a data frame and the station can switch to *Transmit* mode and send its data frame starting at the fifth bit of the *Access Control* field. Thus, the one-bit delay introduced by each Token Ring station plays a key role in enabling the stations to efficiently capture the token.

After having transmitted its data frame, the station must remain in *Transmit* mode until it has received the last bit of its own data frame. This ensures that the bits sent by a station do not remain in the network forever. A data frame sent by a station in a Token Ring network passes in front of all stations attached to the network. Each station can detect the data frame and analyse the destination address to possibly capture the frame.

The *Frame Status* field that appears after the *Ending Delimiter* is used to provide acknowledgements without requiring special frames. The *Frame Status* contains two flags: *A* and C. Both flags are reset when a station sends a data frame. These flags can be modified by their recipients. When a station senses its address as the destination address of a frame, it can capture the frame, check its CRC and place it in its own buffers. The destination of a frame must set the *A* bit (resp. *C* bit) of the *Frame Status* field once it has seen (resp. copied) a data frame. By inspecting the *Frame Status* of the returning frame, the sender can verify whether its frame has been received correctly by its destination.

The text above describes the basic operation of a Token Ring network when all stations work correctly. Unfortunately, a real Token Ring network must be able to handle various types of anomalies and this increases the complexity of Token Ring stations. We briefly list the problems and outline their solutions below. A detailed description of the operation of Token Ring stations may be found in [802.5]. The first problem is when all the stations attached to the network start. One of them must bootstrap the network by sending the first token. For this, all stations implement a distributed election mechanism that is used to select the *Monitor.* Any station can become a *Monitor.* The *Monitor* manages the Token Ring network and ensures that it operates correctly. Its first role is to introduce a delay of 24 bit transmission times to ensure that the token can travel smoothly on the ring. Second, the *Monitor* sends the first token on the ring. It must also verify that the token passes regularly.

According to the Token Ring standard [802.5], a station cannot retain the token to transmit data frames for a duration longer than the *Token Holding Time* (THT) (slightly less than 10 milliseconds). On a network containing *N* stations, the *Monitor* must receive the token at least every *N* x *THT* seconds. If the *Monitor* does not receive a token during such a period, it cuts the ring for some time and then reinitialises the ring and sends a token.

Several other anomalies may occur in a Token Ring network. For example, a station could capture a token and be powered off before having resent the token. Another station could have captured the token, sent its data frame and be powered off before receiving all of its data frame. In this case, the bit string corresponding to the end of a frame would remain in the ring without being removed by its sender. Several techniques are defined in [802.5] to allow the *Monitor* to handle all these problems. If unfortunately, the *Monitor* fails, another station will be elected to become the new *Monitor*.

5.3 DATALINK LAYER TECHNOLOGIES

In this section, we review the key characteristics of several datalink layer technologies. We discuss in more detail the technologies that are widely used today. A detailed survey of all datalink layer technologies would be outside the scope of this book.

5.3.1 The Point-to-Point Protocol

Many point-to-point datalink layers[2] have been developed, starting in the 1960s [McFadyen1976]. In this section, we focus on the protocols that are often used to transport IP packets between hosts or routers that are directly connected by a point-to-point link. This link can be a dedicated physical cable, a leased line through the telephone network or a dial-up connection with modems on the two communicating hosts.

The first solution to transport IP packets over a serial line was proposed in **RFC 1055** and is known as *Serial Line IP* (SLIP). SLIP is a simple character stuffing technique applied to IP packets. SLIP defines two special characters : *END* (decimal 192) and *ESC* (decimal 219). *END* appears at the beginning and at the end of each transmitted IP packet and the sender adds *ESC* before each *END* character inside each transmitted IP packet. SLIP only supports the transmission of IP packets and it assumes that the two communicating hosts/routers have been manually configured with each other's IP address. SLIP was mainly used over links offering bandwidth of often less than 20 Kbps. On such a low bandwidth link, sending 20 bytes of IP header followed by 20 bytes of TCP header for each TCP segment takes a lot of time. This initiated the development of a family of compression techniques to efficiently compress the TCP/IP headers. The first header compression technique proposed in **RFC 1144** was designed to exploit the redundancy between several consecutive segments that belong to the same TCP connection. In all these segments, the IP addresses and port numbers are always the same. Furthermore, fields such as the sequence and acknowledgement numbers do not change in a random way. **RFC 1144** defined simple techniques to reduce the redundancy found in successive segments. The development of header compression techniques continued and there are still improvements being developed now **RFC 5795.**

While SLIP was implemented and used in some environments, it had several limitations discussed in **RFC 1055.** The *Point-to-Point Protocol* (PPP) was designed shortly after and is specified in **RFC 1548.** PPP aims to support IP and other network layer protocols over various types of serial lines. PPP is in fact a family of three protocols that are used together :

1. The *Point-to-Point Protocol* defines the framing technique to transport network layer packets.
2. The *Link Control Protocol* that is used to negotiate options and authenticate the session by using username and password or other types of credentials
3. The *Network Control Protocol* that is specific for each network layer protocol. It is used to negotiate options that are specific for each protocol. For example, IPv4's NCP **RFC 1548** can negotiate the IPv4 address to be used, the IPv4 address of the DNS resolver. IPv6's NCP is defined in **RFC 5072.**

The PPP framing **RFC 1662** was inspired by the datalink layer protocols standardised by ITU-T and ISO. A typical PPP frame is composed of the fields shown in the figure below. A PPP frame starts with a one byte flag containing *01111110.* PPP can use bit stuffing or character stuffing depending on the environment where the protocol is used. The address and control fields are present for backward compatibility reasons. The 16 bit Protocol field contains the identifier of the network layer protocol that is carried in the PPP frame. *0x002d* is used for an IPv4 packet compressed with **RFC 1144** while *0x002f* is used for an uncompressed IPv4 packet. *0xc021* is used by the Link Control Protocol, *0xc023* is used by the Password Authentication Protocol (PAP). *0x0057* is used for IPv6 packets. PPP supports variable length packets, but LCP can negotiate a maximum packet length. The PPP frame ends with a Frame Check Sequence. The default is a 16 bits CRC, but some implementations can negotiate a 32 bits CRC. The frame ends with the *01111110* flag.

Figure 5.17: PPP frame format

PPP played a key role in allowing Internet Service Providers to provide dial-up access over modems in the late 1990s and early 2000s. ISPs operated modem banks connected to the telephone network. For these ISPs, a key issue was to authenticate each user connected through the telephone network. This authentication was performed by using the *Extensible Authentication Protocol* (EAP) defined in **RFC 3748.** EAP is a simple, but extensible protocol that was initially used by access routers to authenticate the users connected through dialup lines. Several authentication methods, starting from the simple username/password pairs to more complex schemes have been defined and implemented. When ISPs started to upgrade their physical infrastructure to provide Internet access over *Asymmetric Digital Subscriber Lines* (ADSL), they tried to reuse their existing authentication (and billing) systems. To meet these requirements, the IETF developed specifications to allow PPP frames to be transported over other networks than the point-to-point links for which PPP was designed. Nowadays, most ADSL deployments use PPP over either ATM **RFC 2364** or Ethernet **RFC 2516.**

5.3.2 Ethernet

Ethernet was designed in the 1970s at the Palo Alto Research Center [Metcalfe1976]. The first prototype used a coaxial cable as the shared medium and 3 Mbps of bandwidth. Ethernet was improved during the late 1970s and in the 1980s, Digital Equipment, Intel and Xerox published the first official Ethernet specification [DIX]. This specification defines several important parameters for Ethernet networks. The first decision was to standardise the commercial Ethernet at 10 Mbps. The second decision was the duration of the *slot time.* In Ethernet, a long *slot time* enables networks to span a long distance but forces the host to use a larger minimum frame size. The compromise was a *slot time* of 51.2 microseconds, which corresponds to a minimum frame size of 64 bytes.

The third decision was the frame format. The experimental 3 Mbps Ethernet network built at Xerox used short frames containing 8 bit source and destination addresses fields, a 16 bit type indication, up to 554 bytes of payload and a 16 bit CRC. Using 8 bit addresses was suitable for an experimental network, but it was clearly too small for commercial deployments. Although the initial Ethernet specification [DIX] only allowed up to 1024 hosts on an Ethernet network, it also recommended three important changes compared to the networking technologies that were available at that time. The first change was to require each host attached to an Ethernet network to have a globally unique datalink layer address. Until then, datalink layer addresses were manually configured on each host. [DP1981] went against that state of the art and noted "*Suitable installation-specific administrative procedures are also needed for assigning numbers to hosts on a network. If a host is moved from one network to another it may be necessary to change its host number if its former number is in use on the new network. This is easier said than done, as each network must have an administrator who must record the continuously changing state of the system (often on a piece of paper tacked to the wall!). It is anticipated that in future office environments, hosts locations will change as often as telephones are changed in present-day offices.*" The second change introduced by Ethernet was to encode each address as a 48 bits field [DP1981]. 48 bit addresses were huge compared to the networking technologies available in the 1980s, but the huge address space had several advantages [DP1981] including the ability to allocate large blocks of addresses to manufacturers. Eventually, other LAN technologies opted for 48 bits addresses as well **[802]_**. The third change introduced by Ethernet was the definition of *broadcast* and *multicast* addresses. The need for *multicast* Ethernet was foreseen in [DP1981] and thanks to the size of the addressing space it was possible to reserve a large block of multicast addresses for each manufacturer.

The datalink layer addresses used in Ethernet networks are often called MAC addresses. They are structured as shown in the figure below. The first bit of the address indicates whether the address identifies a network adapter or a multicast group. The upper 24 bits are used to encode an Organisation Unique Identifier (OUI). This OUI identifies a block of addresses that has been allocated by the secretariat who is responsible for the uniqueness of Ethernet addresses to a manufacturer. Once a manufacturer has received an OUI, it can build and sell products with one of the 16 million addresses in this block.

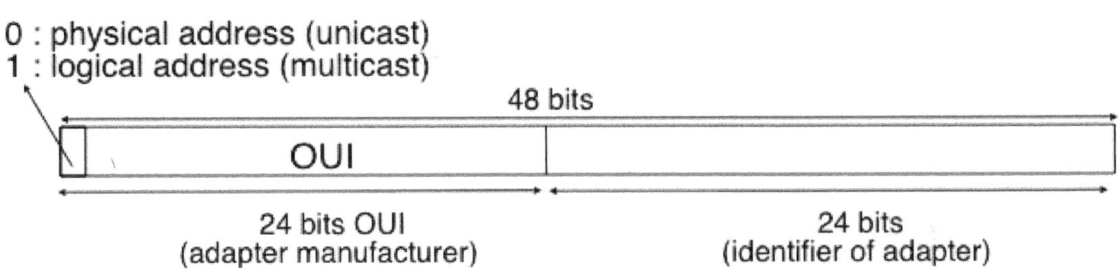

Figure 5.18: 48 bits Ethernet address format

The original 10 Mbps Ethernet specification [DIX] defined a simple frame format where each frame is composed of five fields. The Ethernet frame starts with a preamble (not shown in the figure below) that is used by the physical layer of the receiver to synchronise its clock with the sender's clock. The first field of the frame is the destination address. As this address is placed at the beginning of the frame, an Ethernet interface can quickly verify whether it is the frame recipient and if not, cancel the processing of the arriving frame. The second field is the source address. While the destination address can be either a unicast or a multicast/broadcast address, the source address must always be a unicast address. The third field is a 16 bits integer that indicates which type of network layer packet is carried inside the frame. This field is often called the *EtherType.* Frequently used *EtherType* values include *0x0800* for IPv4, *0x86DD* for IPv6 and *0x806* for the Address Resolution Protocol (ARP).

The fourth part of the Ethernet frame is the payload. The minimum length of the payload is 46 bytes to ensure a minimum frame size, including the header of 512 bits. The Ethernet payload cannot be longer than 1500 bytes. This size was found reasonable when the first Ethernet specification was written. At that time, Xerox had been using its experimental 3 Mbps Ethernet that offered 554 bytes of payload and **RFC 1122** required a minimum MTU of 572 bytes for IPv4. 1500 bytes was large enough to support these needs without forcing the network adapters to contain overly large memories. Furthermore, simulations and measurement studies performed in Ethernet networks revealed that CSMA/CD was able to achieve a very high utilization. This is illustrated in the figure below based on [SH1980], which shows the channel utilization achieved in Ethernet networks containing different numbers of hosts that are sending frames of different sizes.

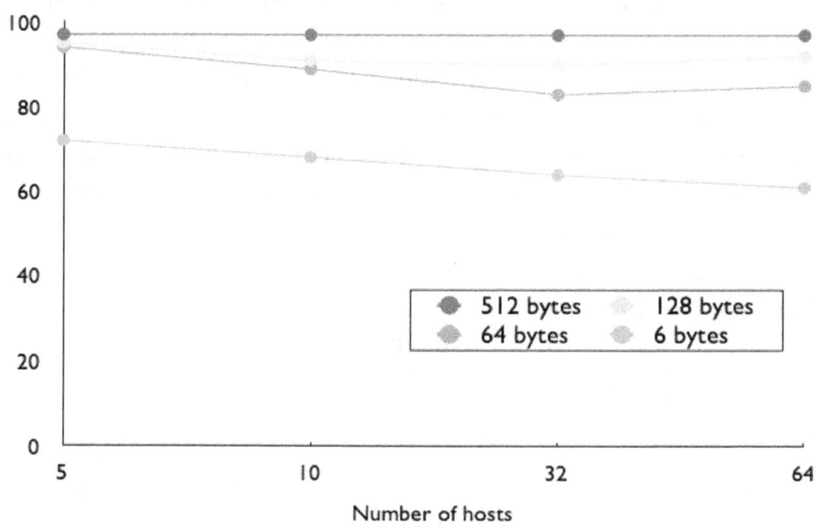

Figure 5.19: Impact of the frame length on the maximum channel utilisation [SH1980]

The last field of the Ethernet frame is a 32 bit Cyclical Redundancy Check (CRC). This CRC is able to catch a much larger number of transmission errors than the Internet checksum used by IP, UDP and TCP [SGP98]. The format of the Ethernet frame is shown below.

Note: Where should the CRC be located in a frame ?

The transport and datalink layers usually chose different strategies to place their CRCs or checksums. Transport layer protocols usually place their CRCs or checksums in the segment header. Datalink layer protocols sometimes place their CRC in the frame header, but often in a trailer at the end of the frame. This choice reflects implementation assumptions, but also influences performance **RFC 893.** When the CRC is placed in the trailer, as in Ethernet, the datalink layer can compute it while transmitting the frame and insert it at the end of the transmission. All Ethernet interfaces use this optimisation today. When the checksum is placed in the header, as in a TCP segment, it is impossible for the network interface to compute it while transmitting the segment. Some network interfaces provide hardware assistance to compute the TCP checksum, but this is more complex than if the TCP checksum were placed in the trailer .

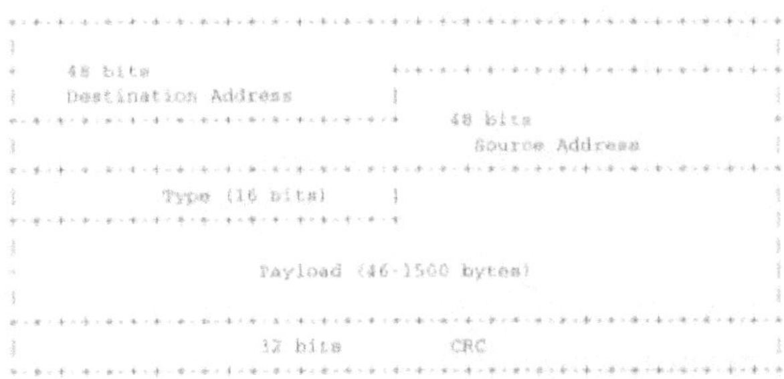

Figure 5.20: Ethernet DIX frame format

The Ethernet frame format shown above is specified in [DIX]. This is the format used to send both IPv4 **RFC 894** and IPv6 packets **RFC 2464.** After the publication of [DIX], the Institute of Electrical and Electronic Engineers (IEEE) began to standardise several Local Area Network technologies. IEEE worked on several LAN technologies, starting with Ethernet, Token Ring and Token Bus. These three technologies were completely different, but they all agreed to use the 48 bits MAC addresses specified initially for Ethernet **[802]**_. While developing its Ethernet standard [802.3], the IEEE 802.3 working group was confronted with a problem. Ethernet mandated a minimum payload size of 46 bytes, while some companies were looking for a LAN technology that could transparently transport short frames containing only a few bytes of payload. Such a frame can be sent by an Ethernet host by padding it to ensure that the payload is at least 46 bytes long. However since the Ethernet header [DIX] does not contain a length field, it is impossible for the receiver to determine how many useful bytes were placed inside the payload field. To solve this problem, the IEEE decided to replace the *Type* field of the Ethernet [DIX] header with a length field. This *Length* field contains the number of useful bytes in the frame payload. The payload must still contain at least 46 bytes, but padding bytes are added by the sender and removed by the receiver. In order to add the *Length* field without significantly changing the frame format, IEEE had to remove the *Type* field. Without this field, it is impossible for a receiving host to identify the type of network layer packet inside a received frame. To solve this new problem, IEEE developed a completely new sublayer called the Logical Link Control [802.2]. Several protocols were defined in this sublayer. One of them provided a slightly different version of the Type field of the original Ethernet frame format. Another contained acknowledgements and retransmissions to provide a reliable service... In practice, [802.2] is never used to support IP in Ethernet networks. The figure below shows the official [802.3] frame format.

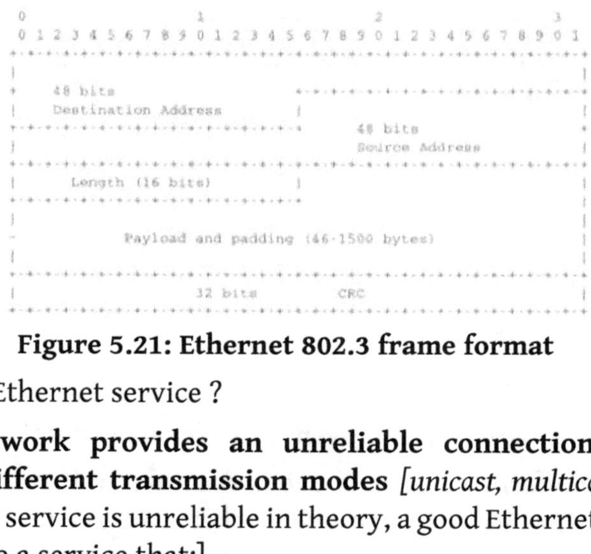

Figure 5.21: Ethernet 802.3 frame format

Note: What is the Ethernet service ?

An Ethernet network provides an unreliable connectionless service. It supports three different transmission modes *[unicast, multicast* and *broadcast.* While the Ethernet service is unreliable in theory, a good Ethernet network should, in practice, provide a service that:]

- delivers frames to their destination with a very high probability of successful delivery
- does not reorder the transmitted frames

The first property is a consequence of the utilisation of CSMA/CD. The second property is a consequence of the physical organisation of the Ethernet network as a shared bus. These two properties are important and all evolutions of the Ethernet technology have preserved them.

Several physical layers have been defined for Ethernet networks. The first physical layer, usually called 10Base5, provided 10 Mbps over a thick coaxial cable. The characteristics of the cable and the transceivers that were used then enabled the utilisation of 500 meter long segments. A 10Base5 network can also include repeaters between segments.

The second physical layer was 10Base2. This physical layer used a thin coaxial cable that was easier to install than the 10Base5 cable, but could not be longer than 185 meters. A 10BaseF physical layer was also defined to transport Ethernet over point-to-point optical links. The major change to the physical layer was the support of twisted pairs in the 10BaseT specification. Twisted pair cables are traditionally used to support the telephone service in office buildings. Most office buildings today are equipped with structured cabling. Several twisted pair cables are installed between any room and a central telecom closet per building or per floor in large buildings. These telecom closets act as concentration points for the telephone service but also for LANs.

The introduction of the twisted pairs led to two major changes to Ethernet. The first change concerns the physical topology of the network. 10Base2 and 10Base5 networks are shared buses, the coaxial cable typically passes through each room that contains a connected computer. A 10BaseT network is a star-shaped network. All the devices connected to the network are attached to a twisted pair cable that ends in the telecom closet. From a maintenance perspective, this is a major improvement. The cable is a weak point in 10Base2 and 10Base5 networks. Any physical damage on the cable broke the entire network and when such a failure occurred, the network administrator had to manually check the entire cable to detect where it was damaged. With 10BaseT, when one twisted pair is damaged, only the device connected to this twisted pair is affected and this does not affect the other devices. The second major change introduced by 10BaseT was that is was impossible to build a 10BaseT network by simply connecting all the twisted pairs together. All the twisted pairs must be connected to a relay that operates in the physical layer. This relay is called an *Ethernet hub*. A *hub* is thus a physical layer relay that receives an electrical signal on one of its interfaces, regenerates the signal and transmits it over all its other interfaces. Some *hubs* are also able to convert the electrical signal from one physical layer to another (e.g. 10BaseT to 10Base2 conversion).

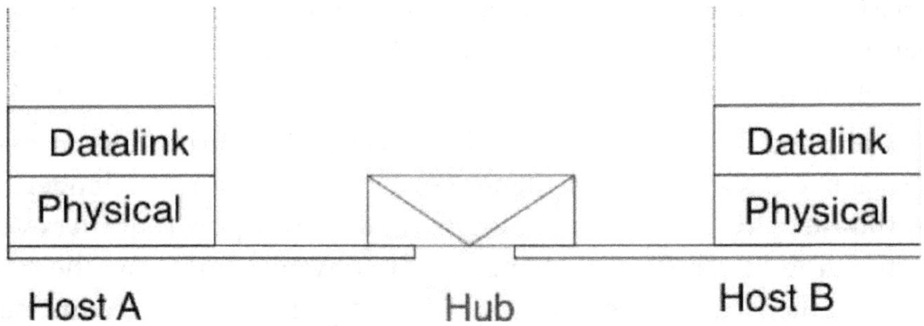

Figure 5.22: Ethernet hubs in the reference model

Computers can directly be attached to Ethernet hubs. Ethernet hubs themselves can be attached to other Ethernet hubs to build a larger network. However, some important guidelines must be followed when building a complex network with hubs. First, the network topology must be a tree. As hubs are relays in the physical layer, adding a link between *Hub2* and *Hub3* in the network below would create an electrical shortcut that would completely disrupt the network. This implies that there cannot be any redundancy in a hub-based network. A failure of a hub or of a link between two hubs would partition the network into two isolated networks. Second, as hubs are relays in the physical layer, collisions can happen and must be handled by CSMA/CD as in a 10Base5 network. This implies that the maximum delay between any pair of devices in the network cannot be longer than the 51.2 microseconds *slot time.* If the delay is longer, collisions between short frames may not be correctly detected. This constraint limits the geographical spread of 10BaseT networks containing hubs.

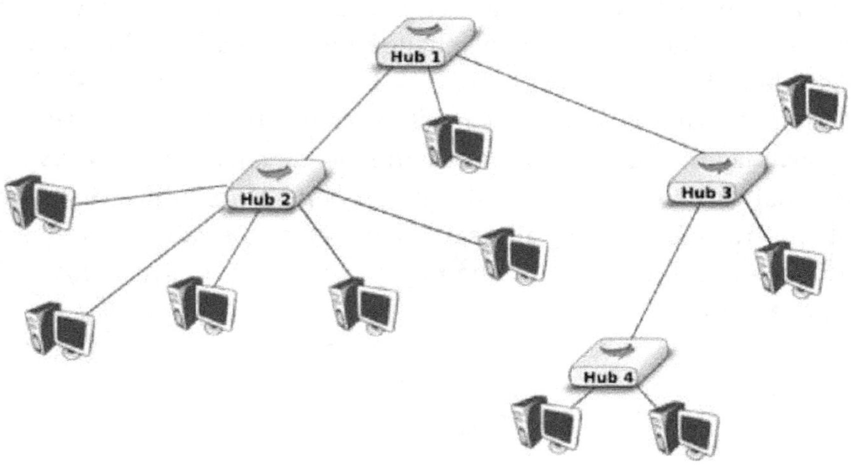

Figure 5.23: A hierarchical Ethernet network composed of hubs

In the late 1980s, 10 Mbps became too slow for some applications and network manufacturers developed several LAN technologies that offered higher bandwidth, such as the 100 Mbps FDDI LAN that used optical fibers. As the development of

10Base5, 10Base2 and 10BaseT had shown that Ethernet could be adapted to different physical layers, several manufacturers started to work on 100 Mbps Ethernet and convinced IEEE to standardise this new technology that was initially called *Fast Ethernet. Fast Ethernet* was designed under two constraints. First, *Fast Ethernet* had to support twisted pairs. Although it was easier from a physical layer perspective to support higher bandwidth on coaxial cables than on twisted pairs, coaxial cables were a nightmare from deployment and maintenance perspectives. Second, *Fast Ethernet* had to be perfectly compatible with the existing 10 Mbps Ethernets to allow *Fast Ethernet* technology to be used initially as a backbone technology to interconnect 10 Mbps Ethernet networks. This forced *Fast Ethernet* to use exactly the same frame format as 10 Mbps Ethernet. This implied that the minimum *Fast Ethernet* frame size remained at 512 bits. To preserve CSMA/CD with this minimum frame size and 100 Mbps instead of 10 Mbps, the duration of the *slot time* was decreased to 5.12 microseconds.

The evolution of Ethernet did not stop. In 1998, the IEEE published a first standard to provide Gigabit Ethernet over optical fibers. Several other types of physical layers were added afterwards. The 10 Gigabit Ethernet standard appeared in 2002. Work is ongoing to develop standards for 40 Gigabit and 100 Gigabit Ethernet and some are thinking about Terabit Ethernet. The table below lists the main Ethernet standards. A more detailed list may be found at http://en.wikipedia.org/wiki/Ethernet_physical_layer

Standard	Comments
10Base5	Thick coaxial cable, 500m
10Base2	Thin coaxial cable, 185m
10BaseT	Two pairs of category 3+ UTP
10Base-F	10 Mb/s over optical fiber
100Base-Tx	Category 5 UTP or STP, 100 m maximum
100Base-FX	Two multimode optical fiber, 2 km maximum
1000Base-CX	Two pairs shielded twisted pair, 25m maximum
1000Base-SX	Two multimode or single mode optical fibers with lasers
10 Gbps	Optical fiber but also Category 6 UTP
40-100 Gbps	Being developed, standard expected in 2010

Ethernet Switches

Increasing the physical layer bandwidth as in *Fast Ethernet* was only one of the solutions to improve the performance of Ethernet LANs. A second solution was to replace the hubs with more intelligent devices. As *Ethernet hubs* operate in the physical layer, they can only regenerate the electrical signal to extend the geographical reach of the network. From a performance perspective, it would be more interesting to have devices that operate in the datalink layer and can analyse the destination address of each frame and forward the frames selectively on the link that leads to the destination. Such devices are usually called *Ethernet switches* . An *Ethernet switch* is a relay that operates in the datalink layer as is illustrated in the figure below.

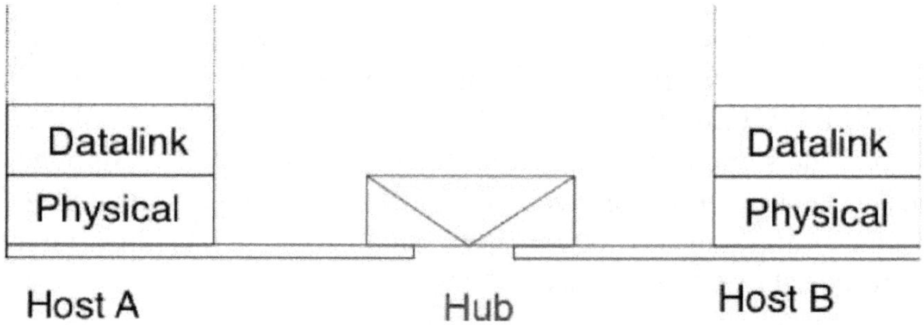

Figure 5.24: Ethernet switches and the reference model

An *Ethernet switch* understands the format of the Ethernet frames and can selectively forward frames over each interface. For this, each *Ethernet switch* maintains a *MAC address table.* This table contains, for each MAC address known by the switch, the identifier of the switch's port over which a frame sent towards this address must be forwarded to reach its destination. This is illustrated below with the *MAC address table* of the bottom switch. When the switch receives a frame destined to address *B,* it forwards the frame on its South port. If it receives a frame destined to address *D,* it forwards it only on its North port.

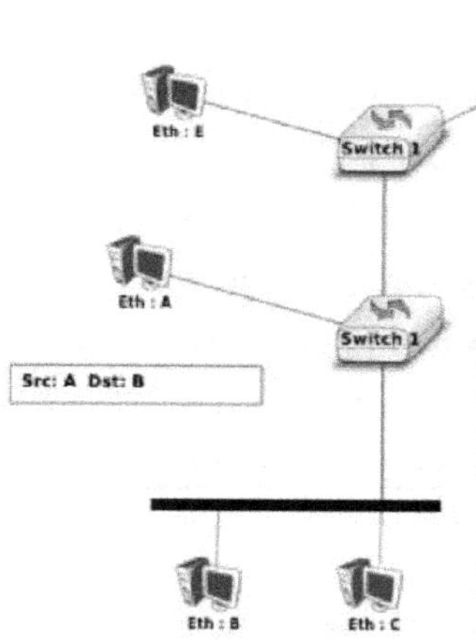

Address	Port
A	West
B	South
C	South
D	North
E	North

Figure 5.25: Operation of Ethernet switches

One of the selling points of Ethernet networks is that, thanks to the utilisation of 48 bits MAC addresses, an Ethernet LAN is plug and play at the datalink layer. When two hosts are attached to the same Ethernet segment or hub, they can immediately exchange Ethernet frames without requiring any configuration. It is important to retain this plug and play capability for Ethernet switches as well. This implies that Ethernet switches must be able to build their MAC address table automatically without requiring any manual configuration. This automatic configuration is performed by the the *MAC address learning* algorithm that runs on each Ethernet switch. This algorithm extracts the source address of the received frames and remembers the port over which a frame from each source Ethernet address has been received. This information is inserted into the MAC address table that the switch uses to forward frames. This allows the switch to automatically learn the ports that it can use to reach each destination address, provided that this host has previously sent at least one frame. This is not a problem since most upper layer protocols use acknowledgements at some layer and thus even an Ethernet printer sends Ethernet frames as well.

The pseudo-code below details how an Ethernet switch forwards Ethernet frames. It first updates its *MAC address table* with the source address of the frame. The MAC *address table* used by some switches also contains a timestamp that is updated each time a frame is received from each known source address. This timestamp is used to remove from the *MAC address table* entries that have not been active during the last *n* minutes. This limits the growth of the *MAC address table*, but also allows hosts to move from one port to another. The switch uses its *MAC address table* to forward the received unicast frame. If there is an entry for the frame's destination address in the *MAC address table*, the frame is forwarded selectively on the port listed in this entry. Otherwise, the switch does not know how to reach the destination address and it must forward the frame on all its ports except the port from which the frame has been received. This ensures that the frame will reach its destination, at the expense of some unnecessary transmissions. These unnecessary transmissions will only last until the destination has sent its first frame. Multicast and Broadcast frames are also forwarded in a similar way.

```
# Arrival of frame F on port P
# Table : MAC address table dictionary : addr->port
# Ports : list of all ports on the switch
src=F.SourceAddress
dst=F.DestinationAddress
Table[src]=P #src heard on port P
if isUnicast(dst) :
if dst in Table:
```

```
ForwardFrame(F,Table[dst])
else:
for o in Ports :
if o!= P : ForwardFrame(F,o)
else:
# multicast or broadcast destination
for o in Ports :
if o!= P : ForwardFrame(F,o)
```

Note: Security issues with Ethernet hubs and switches

From a security perspective, Ethernet hubs have the same drawbacks as the older coaxial cable. A host attached to a hub will be able to capture all the frames exchanged between any pair of hosts attached to the same hub. Ethernet switches are much better from this perspective thanks to the selective forwarding, a host will usually only receive the frames destined to itself as well as the multicast, broadcast and unknown frames. However, this does not imply that switches are completely secure. There are, unfortunately, attacks against Ethernet switches. From a security perspective, the *MAC address table* is one of the fragile elements of an Ethernet switch. This table has a fixed size. Some low-end switches can store a few tens or a few hundreds of addresses while higher-end switches can store tens of thousands of addresses or more. From a security point of view, a limited resource can be the target of Denial of Service attacks. Unfortunately, such attacks are also possible on Ethernet switches. A malicious host could overflow the *MAC address table* of the switch by generating thousands of frames with random source addresses. Once the *MAC address table* is full, the switch needs to broadcast all the frames that it receives. At this point, an attacker will receive unicast frames that are not destined to its address. The ARP attack discussed in the previous chapter could also occur with Ethernet switches [Vyncke2007]. Recent switches implement several types of defences against these attacks, but they need to be carefully configured by the network administrator. See [Vyncke2007] for a detailed discussion on security issues with Ethernet switches.

The *MAC address learning* algorithm combined with the forwarding algorithm work well in a tree-shaped network such as the one shown above. However, to deal with link and switch failures, network administrators often add redundant links to ensure that their network remains connected even after a failure. Let us consider what happens in the Ethernet network shown in the figure below.

When all switches boot, their *MAC address table* is empty. Assume that host *A* sends a frame towards host *C*. Upon reception of this frame, switch1 updates its *MAC address table* to remember that address *A* is reachable via its West port. As there is no entry for address C in switch1's MAC address table, the frame is forwarded to both switch2 and switch3. When switch2 receives the frame, its updates its MAC address table for address A and forwards the frame to host C as well as to switch3. switch3 has thus received two copies of the same frame. As switch3 does not know how to reach the destination address, it forwards the frame received from switch1 to switch2 and the frame received from switch2 to switch1... The single frame sent by host A will be continuously duplicated by the switches until their MAC address table contains an entry for address C. Quickly, all the available link bandwidth will be used to forward all the copies of this frame. As Ethernet does not contain any TTL or HopLimit, this loop will never stop.

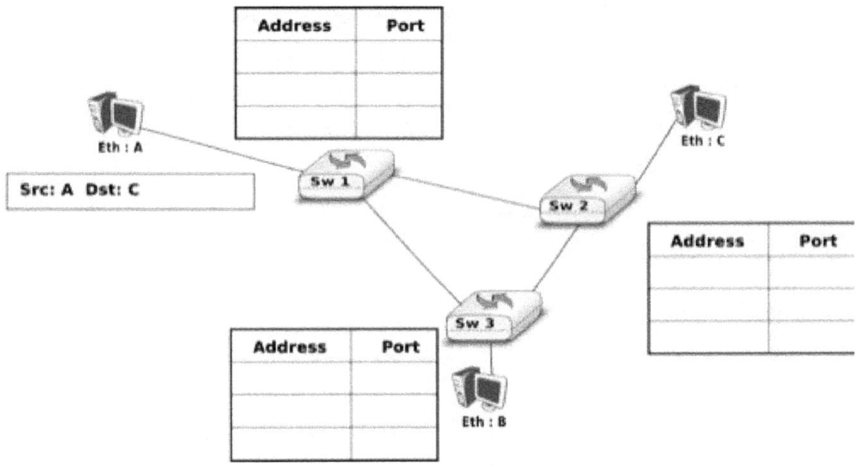

Figure 5.26: Ethernet switches in a loop

The *MAC address learning* algorithm allows switches to be plug-and-play. Unfortunately, the loops that arise when the network topology is not a tree are a severe problem. Forcing the switches to only be used in tree-shaped networks as hubs would be a severe limitation. To solve this problem, the inventors of Ethernet switches have developed the *Spanning Tree Protocol*. This protocol allows switches to automatically disable ports on Ethernet switches to ensure that the network does not contain any cycle that could cause frames to loop forever.

The Spanning Tree Protocol (802.1d)

The *Spanning Tree Protocol* (STP), proposed in [Perlman1985], is a distributed protocol that is used by switches to reduce the network topology to a spanning tree, so that there are no cycles in the topology. For example, consider the network shown in the figure below. In this figure, each bold line corresponds to an Ethernet to which two Ethernet switches are attached. This network contains several cycles that must be broken to allow Ethernet switches that are using the MAC address learning algorithm to exchange frames.

In this network, the STP will compute the following spanning tree. *Switch1* will be the root of the tree. All the interfaces of *Switch1, Switch2* and *Switch7* are part of the spanning tree. Only the interface connected to *LANB* will be active on *Switch9. LANH* will only be served by *Switch7* and the port of *Switch44* on *LANG* will be disabled. A frame originating on *LANB* and destined for *LANA* will be forwarded by *Switch7* on *LANC*, then by *Switch1* on *LANE*, then by *Switch44* on *LANF* and eventually by *Switch2* on *LANA*.

Switches running the *Spanning Tree Protocol* exchange *BPDUs*. These *BPDUs* are always sent as frames with destination MAC address as the *ALL_BRIDGES* reserved multicast MAC address. Each switch has a unique 64 bit *identifier*. To ensure uniqueness, the lower 48 bits of the identifier are set to the unique MAC address allocated to the switch by its manufacturer. The high order 16 bits of the switch identifier can be configured by the network administrator to influence the topology of the spanning tree. The default value for these high order bits is 32768.

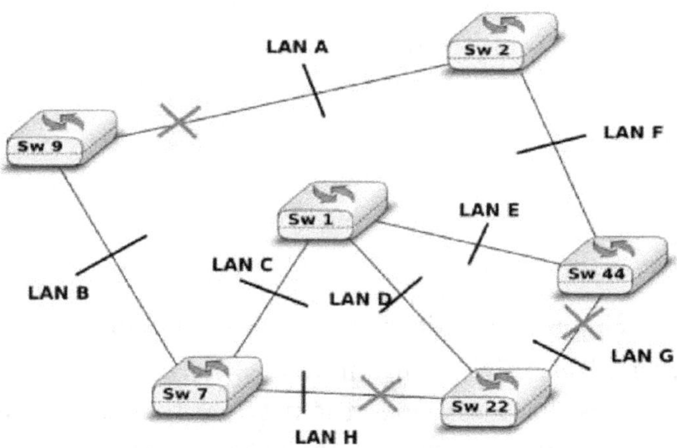

Figure 5.27: Spanning tree computed in a switched Ethernet network

The switches exchange *BPDUs* to build the spanning tree. Intuitively, the spanning tree is built by first selecting the switch with the smallest *identifier* as the root of the tree. The branches of the spanning tree are then composed of the shortest paths that allow all of the switches that compose the network to be reached. The *BPDUs* exchanged by the switches contain the following information :

- the *identifier* of the root switch (R)
- the *cost* of the shortest path between the switch that sent the *BPDU* and the root switch (c)
- the *identifier* of the switch that sent the *BPDU (T)*
- the number of the switch port over which the *BPDU* was sent *(p)*

We will use the notation *<R,c,T,p>* to represent a *BPDU* whose *root identifier* is R, *cost* is *c* and that was sent on the port *p* of switch *T*. The construction of the spanning tree depends on an ordering relationship among the *BPDUs*. This ordering relationship could be implemented by the python function below.

```
# returns True if bpdu b1 is better than bpdu b2
def better( b1, b2) :
return ( (b1.R < b2.R) or
( (b1.R==b2.R) and (b1.c<b2.c) ) or
( (b1.R==b2.R) and (b1.c==b2.c) and (b1.T<b2.T) ) or
( (b1.R==b2.R) and (b1.c==b2.c) and (b1.T==b2.T) and (b1.p<b2.p) ) )
```

In addition to the *identifier* discussed above, the network administrator can also configure a *cost* to be associated to each switch port. Usually, the *cost* of a port depends on its bandwidth and the [802.1d] standard recommends the values below. Of course, the network administrator may choose other values. We will use the notation *cost[p]* to indicate the cost associated to port p in this section.

Bandwidth	Cost
10 Mbps	2000000
100 Mbps	200000
1 Gbps	20000
10 Gbps	2000
100 Gbps	200

The *Spanning Tree Protocol* uses its own terminology that we illustrate in the figure above. A switch port can be in three different states : *Root*, *Designated* and *Blocked*. All the ports of the *root* switch are in the *Designated* state. The state of the ports on the other switches is determined based on the *BPDU* received on each port.

The *Spanning Tree Protocol* uses the ordering relationship to build the spanning tree. Each switch listens to *BPDUs* on its ports. When *BPDU=<R,c,T,p>* is received on port q, the switch computes the port's *priority vector: V[q]=<R,c+cost[q],T,p,q>* , where *cost[q]* is the cost associated to the port over which the *BPDU* was received. The switch stores in a table the last *priority vector* received on each port. The switch then compares its own *identifier* with the smallest root *identifier* stored in this table. If its own *identifier* is smaller, then the switch is the root of the spanning tree and is, by definition, at a distance *0* of the root. The *BPDU* of the switch is then *<R,0,R,p>*, where *R* is the switch *identifier* and *p* will be set to the port number over which the *BPDU* is sent. Otherwise, the switch chooses the best priority vector from its table, *bv=<R,c,T,p>*. The port over which this best priority vector was learned is the switch port that is closest to the *root* switch. This port becomes the *Root* port of the switch. There is only one *Root* port per switch. The switch can then compute its *BPDU* as

BPDU=<R,c,S,p> , where *R* is the *root identifier, c* the cost of the best priority vector, *S* the identifier of the switch and *p* will be replaced by the number of the port over which the *BPDU* will be sent. The switch can then determine the state of all its ports by comparing its own *BPDU* with the priority vector received on each port. If the switch's *BPDU* is better than the priority vector of this port, the port becomes a *Designated* port. Otherwise, the port becomes a *Blocked* port.

The state of each port is important when considering the transmission of *BPDUs*. The root switch regularly sends its own *BPDU* over all of its (*Designated*) ports. This *BPDU* is received on the *Root* port of all the switches that are directly connected to the *root switch*. Each of these switches computes its own *BPDU* and sends this *BPDU* over all its *Designated* ports. These *BPDUs* are then received on the *Root* port of downstream switches, which then compute their own *BPDU*, etc. When the network topology is stable, switches send their own *BPDU* on all their *Designated* ports, once they receive a *BPDU* on their *Root* port. No *BPDU* is sent on a *Blocked* port. Switches listen for *BPDUs* on their *Blocked* and *Designated* ports, but no *BPDU* should be received over these ports when the topology is stable. The utilisation of the ports for both *BPDUs* and data frames is summarised in the table below.

Port state	Receives BPDUs	Sends BPDU	Handles data frames
Blocked	yes	no	no
Root	yes	no	yes
Designated	yes	yes	yes

To illustrate the operation of the *Spanning Tree Protocol*, let us consider the simple network topology in the figure below.

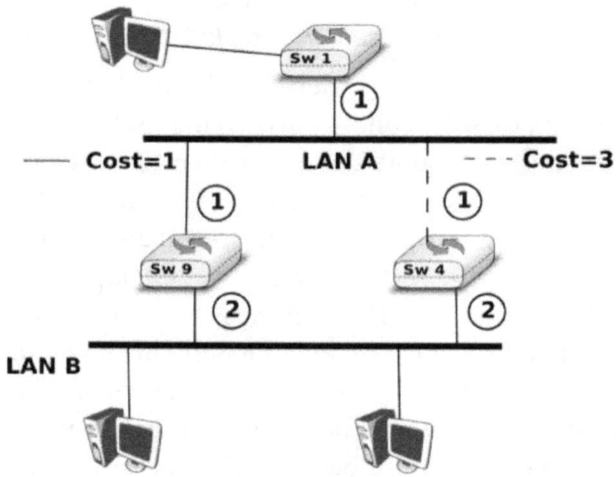

Figure 5.28: A simple Spanning tree computed in a switched Ethernet network

Assume that *Switch4* is the first to boot. It sends its own *BPDU=<4,0,4,?>* on its two ports. When *Switch!* boots, it sends *BPDU=<1,0,1,1>.* This *BPDU* is received by *Switch4,* which updates its table and computes a new *BPDU=<1,3,4,?>.* Port 1 of *Switch4* becomes the *Root* port while its second port is still in the *Designated* state.

Assume now that *Switch9* boots and immediately receives *Switch1* 's BPDU on port 1. *Switch9* computes its own *BPDU=<1,1,9,?>* and port 1 becomes the *Root* port of this switch. This *BPDU* is sent on port 2 of *Switch9* and reaches *Switch4. Switch4* compares the priority vector built from this *BPDU* (i.e. <1,2,9,2>) and notices that it is better than *Switch4* 's *BPDU=<1,3,4,2>.* Thus, port 2 becomes a *Blocked* port on *Switch4.*

During the computation of the spanning tree, switches discard all received data frames, as at that time the network topology is not guaranteed to be loop-free. Once that topology has been stable for some time, the switches again start to use the MAC learning algorithm to forward data frames. Only the *Root* and *Designated* ports are used to forward data frames. Switches discard all the data frames received on their *Blocked* ports and never forward frames on these ports.

Switches, ports and links can fail in a switched Ethernet network. When a failure occurs, the switches must be able to recompute the spanning tree to recover from the failure. The *Spanning Tree Protocol* relies on regular transmissions of the *BPDUs* to detect these failures. A *BPDU* contains two additional fields : the *Age* of the *BPDU* and the *Maximum Age.* The *Age* contains the amount of time that has passed since the root switch initially originated the *BPDU.* The root switch sends its *BPDU* with an *Age* of zero and each switch that computes its own *BPDU* increments its *Age* by one. The *Age* of the *BPDUs* stored on a switch's table is also incremented every second. A *BPDU* expires when its *Age* reaches the *Maximum Age.* When the network is stable, this does not happen as *BPDU* s are regularly sent by the *root* switch and downstream switches. However, if the *root* fails or the network becomes partitioned, *BPDU* will expire and switches will recompute their own *BPDU* and restart the *Spanning Tree Protocol.* Once a topology change has been detected, the forwarding of the data frames stops as the topology is not guaranteed to be loop-free. Additional details about the reaction to failures may be found in [802.1d]

Virtual LANs

Another important advantage of Ethernet switches is the ability to create Virtual Local Area Networks (VLANs). A virtual LAN can be defined as a *set of ports attached to one or more Ethernet switches.* A switch can support several VLANs and it runs one MAC learning algorithm for each Virtual LAN. When a switch receives a frame with an unknown or a multicast destination, it forwards it over all the ports that belong to the same Virtual LAN but not over the ports that belong to other Virtual LANs. Similarly, when a switch learns a source address on a port, it associates it to the

Virtual LAN of this port and uses this information only when forwarding frames on this Virtual LAN.

The figure below illustrates a switched Ethernet network with three Virtual LANs. *VLAN2* and *VLAN3* only require a local configuration of switch S1. Host *C* can exchange frames with host D, but not with hosts that are outside of its VLAN. *VLAN1* is more complex as there are ports of this VLAN on several switches. To support such VLANs, local configuration is not sufficient anymore. When a switch receives a frame from another switch, it must be able to determine the VLAN in which the frame originated to use the correct MAC table to forward the frame. This is done by assigning an identifier to each Virtual LAN and placing this identifier inside the headers of the frames that are exchanged between switches.

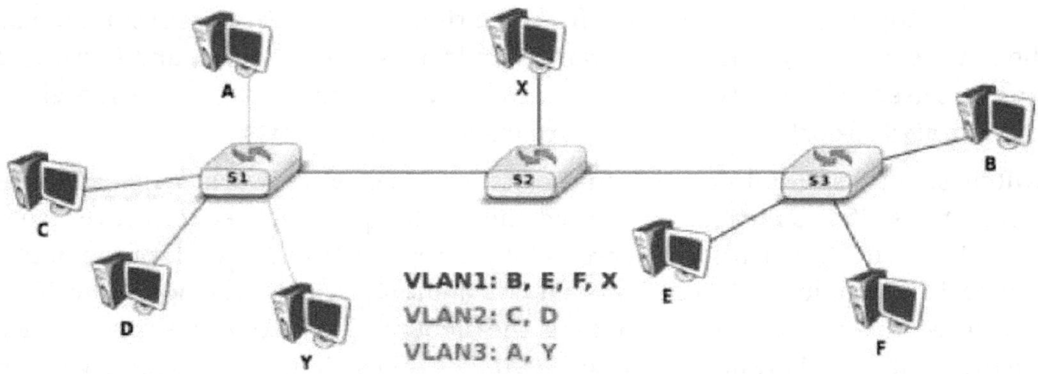

Figure 5.29: Virtual Local Area Networks in a switched Ethernet network

IEEE defined in the [802.1q] standard a special header to encode the VLAN identifiers. This 32 bit header includes a 20 bit VLAN field that contains the VLAN identifier of each frame. The format of the [802.1q] header is described below.

The [802.1q] header is inserted immediately after the source MAC address in the Ethernet frame (i.e. before the EtherType field). The maximum frame size is increased by 4 bytes. It is encoded in 32 bits and contains four fields. The Tag Protocol Identifier is set to 0x8100 to allow the receiver to detect the presence of this additional header. The Priority Code Point (PCP) is a three bit field that is used to support different transmission priorities for the frame. Value 0 is the lowest priority and value 7 the highest. Frames with a higher priority can expect to be forwarded earlier than frames having a lower priority. The C bit is used for compatibility between Ethernet and Token Ring networks. The last 12 bits of the 802.1q header contain the VLAN identifier. Value 0 indicates that the frame does not belong to any VLAN while value 0xFFF is reserved. This implies that 4094 different VLAN identifiers can be used in an Ethernet network.

```
 0                   1                   2                   3
 0 1 2 3 4 5 6 7 8 9 0 1 2 3 4 5 6 7 8 9 0 1 2 3 4 5 6 7 8 9 0 1
+-+-+-+-+-+-+-+-+-+-+-+-+-+-+-+-+-+-+-+-+-+-+-+-+-+-+-+-+-+-+-+-+
| Tag Protocol Identifier       | PCP |C|   VLAN Identifier     |
+-+-+-+-+-+-+-+-+-+-+-+-+-+-+-+-+-+-+-+-+-+-+-+-+-+-+-+-+-+-+-+-+
```

Figure 5.30: Format of the 802.1q header

5.3.3 802.11 wireless networks

The radio spectrum is a limited resource that must be shared by everyone. During most of the twentieth century, governments and international organisations have regulated most of the radio spectrum. This regulation controls the utilisation of the radio spectrum, in order to ensure that there are no interferences between different users. A company that wants to use a frequency range in a given region must apply for a license from the regulator. Most regulators charge a fee for the utilisation of the radio spectrum and some governments have encouraged competition among companies bidding for the same frequency to increase the license fees.

In the 1970s, after the first experiments with ALOHANet, interest in wireless networks grew. Many experiments were done on and outside the ARPANet. One of these experiments was the first mobile phone , which was developed and tested in 1973. This experimental mobile phone was the starting point for the first generation analog mobile phones. Given the growing demand for mobile phones, it was clear that the analog mobile phone technology was not sufficient to support a large number of users. To support more users and new services, researchers in several countries worked on the development of digital mobile telephones. In 1987, several European countries decided to develop the standards for a common cellular telephone system across Europe : the *Global System for Mobile Communications* (GSM). Since then, the standards have evolved and more than three billion users are connected to GSM networks today.

While most of the frequency ranges of the radio spectrum are reserved for specific applications and require a special licence, there are a few exceptions. These exceptions are known as the Industrial, Scientific and Medical (ISM) radio bands. These bands can be used for industrial, scientific and medical applications without requiring a licence from the regulator. For example, some radio-controlled models use the 27 MHz ISM band and some cordless telephones operate in the 915 MHz ISM. In 1985, the 2.400-2.500 GHz band was added to the list of ISM bands. This frequency range corresponds to the frequencies that are emitted by microwave ovens. Sharing this band with licensed applications would have likely caused interferences, given the large number of microwave ovens that are used. Despite the risk of interferences with microwave ovens, the opening of the 2.400-2.500 GHz allowed the networking industry to develop several wireless network techniques to allow computers to exchange data without using cables. In this section, we discuss in more detail the most popular one, i.e. the WiFi [802.11] family of wireless networks. Other wireless networking techniques such as BlueTooth or HiperLAN use the same frequency range.

Today, WiFi is a very popular wireless networking technology. There are more than several hundreds of millions of WiFi devices. The development of this technology started in the late 1980s with the WaveLAN proprietary wireless network. WaveLAN operated at 2 Mbps and used different frequency bands in different regions of the world. In the early 1990s, the IEEE created the 802.11 working group to standardise a family of wireless network technologies. This working group was very prolific and produced several wireless networking standards that use different frequency ranges and different physical layers. The table below provides a summary of the main 802.11 standards.

Standard	Frequency	Typical throughput	Max bandwidth	Range (m) indoor/ outdoor
802.11	2.4 GHz	0.9 Mbps	2 Mbps	20/100
802.11a	5 GHz	23 Mbps	54 Mbps	35/120
802.11b	2.4 GHz	4.3 Mbps	11 Mbps	38/140
802.11g	2.4 GHz	19 Mbps	54 Mbps	38/140
802.11n	2.4/5 GHz	74 Mbps	150 Mbps	70/250

When developing its family of standards, the IEEE 802.11 working group took a similar approach as the IEEE 802.3 working group that developed various types of physical layers for Ethernet networks. 802.11 networks use the CSMA/CA Medium Access Control technique described earlier and they all assume the same architecture and use the same frame format.

The architecture of WiFi networks is slightly different from the Local Area Networks that we have discussed until now. There are, in practice, two main types of WiFi networks: *independent* or *adhoc* networks and *infrastructure* networks[11]. An *independent* or *adhoc* network is composed of a set of devices that communicate with each other. These devices play the same role and the *adhoc* network is usually not connected to the global Internet. *Adhoc* networks are used when for example a few laptops need to exchange information or to connect a computer with a WiFi printer.

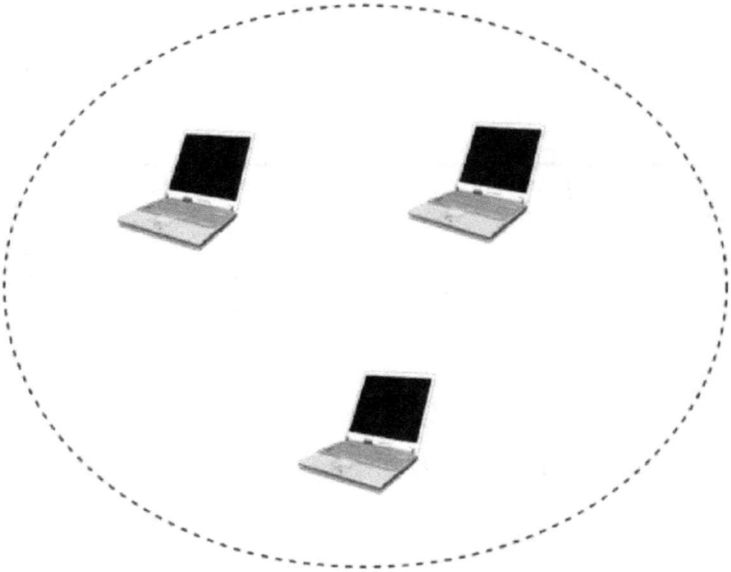

Figure 5.31: An 802.11 independent or adhoc network

Most WiFi networks are *infrastructure* networks. An *infrastructure* network contains one or more *access points* that are attached to a fixed Local Area Network (usually an Ethernet network) that is connected to other networks such as the Internet. The figure below shows such a network with two access points and four WiFi devices. Each WiFi device is associated to one access point and uses this access point as a relay to exchange frames with the devices that are associated to another access point or reachable through the LAN.

An 802.11 access point is a relay that operates in the datalink layer like switches. The figure below represents the layers of the reference model that are involved when a WiFi host communicates with a host attached to an Ethernet network through an access point.

802.11 devices exchange variable length frames, which have a slightly different structure than the simple frame format used in Ethernet LANs. We review the key parts of the 802.11 frames. Additional details may be found in [802.11] and [Gast2002]. An 802.11 frame contains a fixed length header, a variable length payload that may contain up 2324 bytes of user data and a 32 bits CRC. Although the payload can contain up to 2324 bytes, most 802.11 deployments use a maximum payload size of 1500 bytes as they are used in infrastructure networks attached to Ethernet LANs. An 802.11 data frame is shown below.

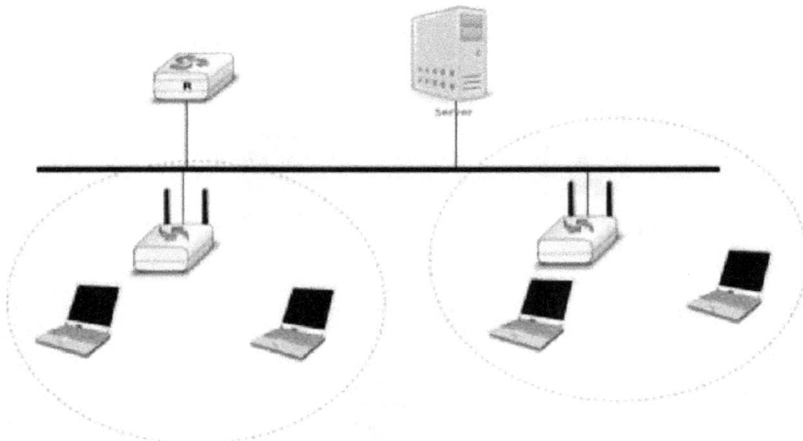

Figure 5.32: An 802.11 infrastructure network

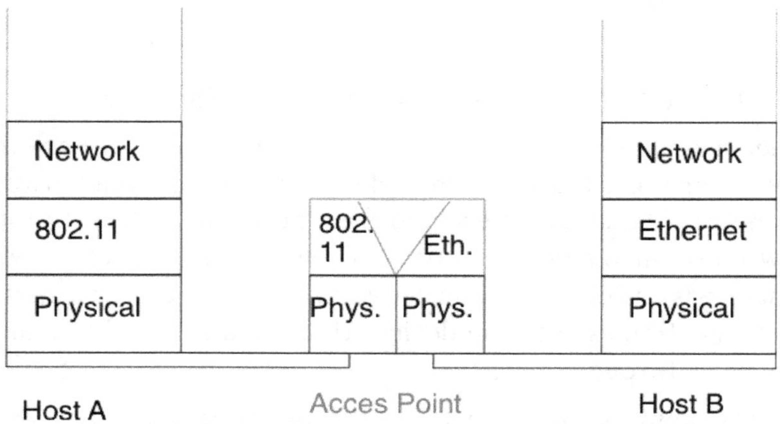

Figure 5.33: An 802.11 access point

Figure 5.34: 802.11 data frame format

The first part of the 802.11 header is the 16 bit *Frame Control* field. This field contains flags that indicate the type of frame (data frame, RTS/CTS, acknowledgement, management frames, etc), whether the frame is sent to or from a fixed LAN, etc [802.11]. The *Duration* is a 16 bit field that is used to reserve the transmission channel. In data frames, the *Duration* field is usually set to the time required to transmit one acknowledgement frame after a SIFS delay. Note that the *Duration* field must be set to zero in multicast and broadcast frames. As these frames are not acknowledged, there is no need to reserve the transmission channel after their transmission. The *Sequence control* field contains a 12 bits sequence number that is incremented for each data frame.

The astute reader may have noticed that the 802.11 data frames contain three 48-bits address fields. This is surprising compared to other protocols in the network and datalink layers whose headers only contain a source and a destination address. The need for a third address in the 802.11 header comes from the *infrastructure* networks. In such a network, frames are usually exchanged between routers and servers attached to the LAN and WiFi devices attached to one of the access points. The role of the three address fields is specified by bit flags in the *Frame Control* field.

When a frame is sent from a WiFi device to a server attached to the same LAN as the access point, the first address of the frame is set to the MAC address of the access point, the second address is set to the MAC address of the source WiFi device and the third address is the address of the final destination on the LAN. When the server replies, it sends an Ethernet frame whose source address is its MAC address and the destination address is the MAC address of the WiFi device. This frame is captured by the access point that converts the Ethernet header into an 802.11 frame header. The 802.11 frame sent by the access point contains three addresses : the first address is the MAC address of the destination WiFi device, the second address is the MAC address of the access point and the third address the MAC address of the server that sent the frame.

802.11 control frames are simpler than data frames. They contain a *Frame Control*, a *Duration* field and one or two addresses. The acknowledgement frames are very small. They only contain the address of the destination of the acknowledgement. There is no source address and no *Sequence Control* field in the acknowledgement frames. This is because the acknowledgement frame can easily be associated to the previous frame that it acknowledges. Indeed, each unicast data frame contains a *Duration* field that is used to reserve the transmission channel to ensure that no collision will affect the acknowledgement frame. The *Sequence Control* field is mainly used by the receiver to remove duplicate frames. Duplicate frames are detected as follows. Each data frame contains a 12 bits *Sequence Control* field and the *Frame Control* field contains the *Retry* bit flag that is set when a frame is transmitted.

Each receiver stores the most recent sequence number received from each source address in frames whose *Retry* bit is reset. Upon reception of a frame with the *Retry* bit set, the receiver verifies its sequence number to determine whether it is a duplicated frame or not.

802.11 RTS/CTS frames are used to reserve the transmission channel, in order to transmit one data frame and its acknowledgement. The RTS frames contain a *Duration* and the transmitter and receiver addresses. The *Duration field of the RTS frame indicates the duration of the entire reservation (i.e. the time required to transmit the CTS, the data frame, the acknowledgements and the required SIFS delays). The CTS frame has the same format as the acknowledgement frame.*

```
 0                   1                   2                   3
 0 1 2 3 4 5 6 7 8 9 0 1 2 3 4 5 6 7 8 9 0 1 2 3 4 5 6 7 8 9 0 1
+-+-+-+-+-+-+-+-+-+-+-+-+-+-+-+-+-+-+-+-+-+-+-+-+-+-+-+-+-+-+-+-+
|     Frame  Control            |          Duration             |
+-+-+-+-+-+-+-+-+-+-+-+-+-+-+-+-+-+-+-+-+-+-+-+-+-+-+-+-+-+-+-+-+
|                                                               |
|     Receiver Address          +-+-+-+-+-+-+-+-+-+-+-+-+-+-+-+-+
|                               |          CRC                  |
+-+-+-+-+-+-+-+-+-+-+-+-+-+-+-+-+-+-+-+-+-+-+-+-+-+-+-+-+-+-+-+-+
|          CRC  (cont.)         |
+-+-+-+-+-+-+-+-+-+-+-+-+-+-+-+-+
```

Figure 5.35: IEEE 802.11 ACK and CTS frames

```
 0                   1                   2                   3
 0 1 2 3 4 5 6 7 8 9 0 1 2 3 4 5 6 7 8 9 0 1 2 3 4 5 6 7 8 9 0 1
+-+-+-+-+-+-+-+-+-+-+-+-+-+-+-+-+-+-+-+-+-+-+-+-+-+-+-+-+-+-+-+-+
|     Frame  Control            |          Duration             |
+-+-+-+-+-+-+-+-+-+-+-+-+-+-+-+-+-+-+-+-+-+-+-+-+-+-+-+-+-+-+-+-+
|                                                               |
|     Receiver Address          +-+-+-+-+-+-+-+-+-+-+-+-+-+-+-+-+
|                               |                               |
+-+-+-+-+-+-+-+-+-+-+-+-+-+-+-+-+   Transmitter Address         |
|                                                               |
+-+-+-+-+-+-+-+-+-+-+-+-+-+-+-+-+-+-+-+-+-+-+-+-+-+-+-+-+-+-+-+-+
|                    32 bits         CRC                        |
+-+-+-+-+-+-+-+-+-+-+-+-+-+-+-+-+-+-+-+-+-+-+-+-+-+-+-+-+-+-+-+-+
```

Figure 5.36: IEEE 802.11 RTS frame format

Note: The 802.11 service

Despite the utilization of acknowledgements, the 802.11 layer only provides an unreliable connectionless service like Ethernet networks that do not use acknowledgements. The 802.11 acknowledgements are used to minimize the probability of frame duplication. They do not guarantee that all frames will be correctly received by their recipients. Like Ethernet, 802.11 networks provide a high probability of successful delivery of the frames, not a guarantee. Furthermore, it should be noted that 802.11 networks do not use acknowledgements for multicast and broadcast frames. This implies that in practice such frames are more likely to suffer from transmission errors than unicast frames.

In addition to the data and control frames that we have briefly described above, 802.11 networks use several types of management frames. These management frames are used for various purposes. We briefly describe some of these frames below. A detailed discussion may be found in [802.11] and [Gast2002].

A first type of management frames are the *beacon* frames. These frames are broadcasted regularly by access points. Each *beacon frame* contains information about the capabilities of the access point (e.g. the supported transmission rates) and a *Service Set Identity* (SSID). The SSID is a null-terminated ASCII string that can contain up to 32 characters. An access point may support several SSIDs and announce them in beacon frames. An access point may also choose to remain silent and not advertise beacon frames. In this case, WiFi stations may send *Probe request* frames to force the available access points to return a *Probe response* frame.

Note: IP over 802.11

Two types of encapsulation schemes were defined to support IP in Ethernet networks : the original encapsulation scheme, built above the Ethernet DIX format is defined in **RFC 894** and a second encapsulation **RFC 1042** scheme, built above the LLC/SNAP protocol [802.2]. In 802.11 networks, the situation is simpler and only the **RFC 1042** encapsulation is used. In practice, this encapsulation adds 6 bytes to the 802.11 header. The first four bytes correspond to the LLC/SNAP header. They are followed by the two bytes Ethernet Type field *(0x800* for IP and *0x806* for ARP). The figure below shows an IP packet encapsulated in an 802.11 frame.

The second important utilisation of the management frames is to allow a WiFi station to be associated with an access point. When a WiFi station starts, it listens to beacon frames to find the available SSIDs. To be allowed to send and receive frames via an access point, a WiFi station must be associated to this access point. If the access point does not use any security mechanism to secure the wireless transmission, the WiFi station simply sends an Association request frame to its preferred access point (usually the access point that it receives with the strongest radio signal). This frame contains some parameters chosen by the WiFi station and the SSID that it requests to join. The access point replies with an Association response frame if it accepts the WiFI station.

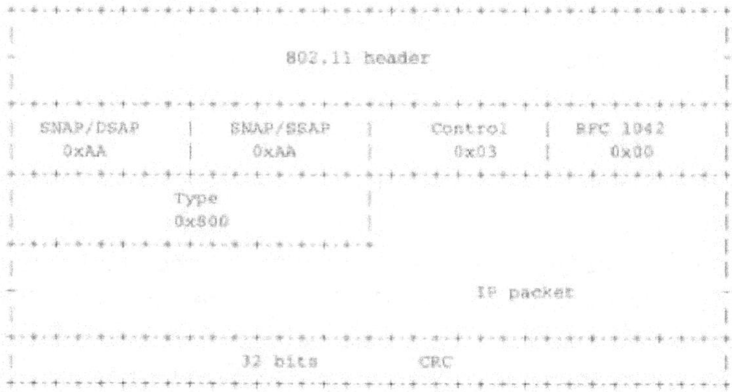

Figure 5.37: IP over IEEE 802.11

5.4 SUMMARY

In this chapter, we first explained the principles of the datalink layer. There are two types of datalink layers: those used over point-to-point links and those used over Local Area Networks. On point-to-point links, the datalink layer must at least provide a framing technique, but some datalink layer protocols also include reliability mechanisms such as those used in the transport layer. We have described the Point-to-Point Protocol that is often used over point-to-point links in the Internet.

Local Area Networks pose a different problem since several devices share the same transmission channel. In this case, a Medium Access Control algorithm is necessary to regulate the access to the transmission channel because whenever two devices transmit at the same time a collision occurs and none of these frames can be decoded by their recipients. There are two families of MAC algorithms. The statistical or optimistic MAC algorithms reduce the probability of collisions but do not completely prevent them. With such algorithms, when a collision occurs, the collided frames must be retransmitted. We have described the operation of the ALOHA, CSMA, CSMA/CD and CSMA/CA MAC algorithms. Deterministic or pessimistic MAC algorithms avoid all collisions. We have described the Token Ring MAC where stations exchange a token to regulate the access to the transmission channel.

Finally, we have described in more detail two successful Local Area Network technologies : Ethernet and WiFi. Ethernet is now the de facto LAN technology. We have analysed the evolution of Ethernet including the operation of hubs and switches. We have also described the Spanning Tree Protocol that must be used when switches are interconnected. For the last few years, WiFi became the de facto wireless technology at home and inside enterprises. We have explained the operation of WiFi networks and described the main 802.11 frames.

5.5 EXERCISES

1. Consider the switched network shown in the figure below. What is the spanning tree that will be computed by 802.1d in this network assuming that all links have a unit cost ? Indicate the state of each port.
2. Consider the switched network shown in the figure above. In this network, assume that the LAN between switches *3* and *12* fails. How should the switches update their port/address tables after the link failure?
3. Many enterprise networks are organized with a set of backbone devices interconnected by using a full mesh of links as shown in the figure below. In this network, what are the benefits and drawbacks of using Ethernet switches and IP routers running OSPF?

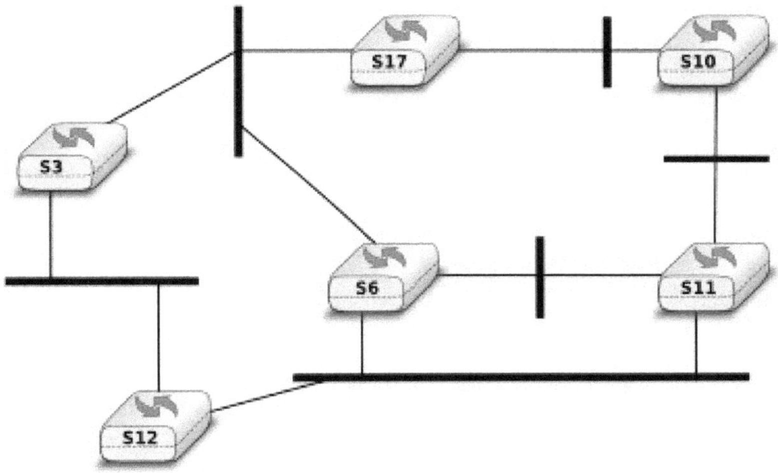

Figure 6.38: A small network composed of Ethernet switches

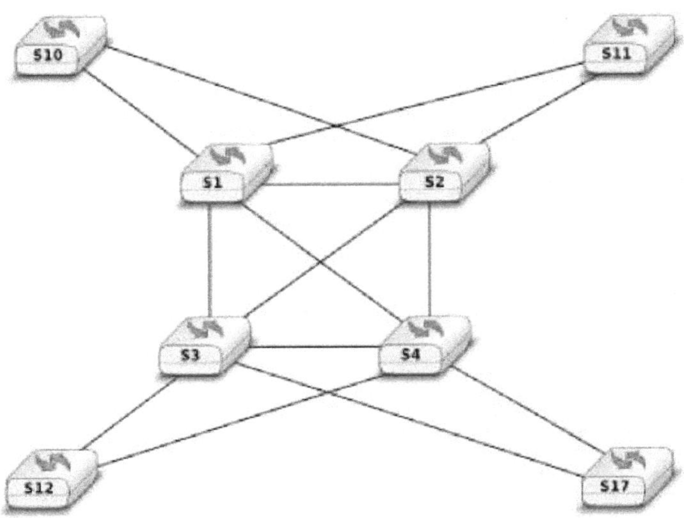

Figure 5.39: A typical enterprise backbone network

4. Most commercial Ethernet switches are able to run the Spanning tree protocol independently on each VLAN. What are the benefits of using per-VLAN spanning trees ?

Glossary

AIMD Additive Increase, Multiplicative Decrease. A rate adaption algorithm used notab*ly by TCP where a host additively increases its transmission rate when the network is not congested and multiplicatively decreases when congested is detected. anycast a transmission mode where an information is sent from one source to one receiver that belongs to a specified group*

API Application Programming Interface

ARP The Address Resolution Protocol is a protocol used by IPv4 devices to obtain the datalink layer address that corresponds to an IPv4 address on the local area network. ARP is defined in RFC 826

ARPANET The Advanced Research Project Agency (ARPA) Network is a network that was built by network scientists in USA with funding from the ARPA of the US Ministry of Defense. ARPANET is considered as the grandfather of today's Internet.

Ascii The American Standard Code for Information Interchange (ASCII) is a character-encoding scheme that defines a binary representation for characters. The ASCII table contains both printable characters and control characters. ASCII characters were encoded in 7 bits and only contained the characters required to write text in English. Other character sets such as Unicode have been developed later to support all written languages.

ASN.1 The Abstract Syntax Notation One (ASN.1) was designed by ISO and ITU-T. It is a standard and flexible notation that can be used to describe data structures for representing, encoding, transmitting, and decoding data between applications. It was designed to be used in the Presentation layer of the OSI reference model but is now used in other protocols such as SNMP.

ATM Asynchronous Transfer Mode

BGP The Border Gateway Protocol is the interdomain routing protocol used in the global Internet.

BNF A Backus-Naur Form (BNF) is a formal way to describe a language by using syntactic and lexical rules. BNFs are frequently used to define programming languages, but also to define the messages exchanged between networked applications. RFC 5234 explains how a BNF must be written to specify an Internet protocol. broadcast a transmission mode where is same information is sent to all nodes in the network

CIDR Classless Inter Domain Routing is the current address allocation architecture for IPv4. It was defined in RFC 1518 and RFC 4632.

Dial-up line A synonym for a regular telephone line, i.e. a line that can be used to dial any telephone number.

DNS The Domain Name System is a distributed database that can be queried by hosts to map names onto IP addresses

eBGP An eBGP session is a BGP session between two directly connected routers that belong to two different Autonomous Systems. Also called an external BGP session.

EGP Exterior Gateway Protocol. Synonym of interdomain routing protocol

EIGRP The Enhanced Interior Gateway Routing Protocol (EIGRP) is a proprietary intradomain routing protocol that is often used in enterprise networks. EIGRP uses the DUAL algorithm described in [Garcia1993]. frame a frame is the unit of information transfer in the datalink layer

Frame-Relay A wide area networking technology using virtual circuits that is deployed by telecom operators. ftp The File Transfer Protocol defined in RFC 959 has been the de facto protocol to exchange files over the Internet before the widespread adoption of HTTP RFC 2616

FTP The File Transfer Protocol is defined in RFC 959

Hosts.txt A file that initially contained the list of all Internet hosts with their IPv4 address. As the network grew, this file was replaced by the DNS, but each host still maintains a small hosts.txt file that can be used when DNS is not available.

HTML The HyperText Markup Language specifies the structure and the syntax of the documents that are exchanged on the world wide web. HTML is maintained by the HTML working group of the W3C

HTTP The HyperText Transport Protocol is defined in RFC 2616

Hub A relay operating in the physical layer.

IANA The Internet Assigned Numbers Authority (IANA) is responsible for the coordination of the DNS Root, IP addressing, and other Internet protocol resources

iBGP An iBGP session is a BGP between two routers belonging to the same Autonomous System. Also called an internal BGP session.

ICANN The Internet Corporation for Assigned Names and Numbers (ICANN) coordinates the allocation of domain names, IP addresses and AS numbers as well protocol parameters. It also coordinates the operation and the evolution of the DNS root name servers.

IETF The Internet Engineering Task Force is a non-profit organisation that develops the standards for the protocols used in the Internet. The IETF mainly covers the transport and network layers. Several application layer protocols are also standardised within the IETF. The work in the IETF is organised in working groups. Most of the work is performed by exchanging emails and there are three IETF meetings every year. Participation is open to anyone. See http://www.ietf.org

IGP Interior Gateway Protocol. Synonym of intradomain routing protocol

IGRP The Interior Gateway Routing Protocol (IGRP) is a proprietary intradomain routing protocol that uses distance vector. IGRP supports multiple metrics for each route but has been replaced by EIGRP

IMAP The Internet Message Access Protocol (IMAP), defined in RFC 3501, is an application-level protocol that allows a client to access and manipulate the emails stored on a server. With IMAP, the email messages remain on the server and are not downloaded on the client.

Internet an internet is an internetwork, i.e. a network composed of different networks. The Internet is a very popular internetwork, but other internets have been used in the path.

Inverse query For DNS servers and resolvers, an inverse query is a query for the domain name that corresponds to a given IP address.

IP Internet Protocol is the generic term for the network layer protocol in the TCP/IP protocol suite. IPv4 is widely used today and IPv6 is expected to replace IPv4

IPv4 is the version 4 of the Internet Protocol, the connectionless network layer protocol used in most of the Internet today. IPv4 addresses are encoded as a 32 bits field.

IPv6 is the version 6 of the Internet Protocol, the connectionless network layer protocol which is intended to replace IPv4. IPv6 addresses are encoded as a 128 bits field.

IS-IS Intermediate System- Intermediate System. A link-state intradomain routing that was initially defined for the ISO CLNP protocol but was extended to support IPv4 and IPv6. IS-IS is often used in ISP networks. It is defined in [ISO10589]

ISN The Initial Sequence Number of a TCP connection is the sequence number chosen by the client (resp. server) that is placed in the SYN (resp. SYN+ACK) segment during the establishment of the TCP connection.

ISO The International Standardization Organisation is an agency of the United Nations that is based in Geneva and develop standards on various topics. Within ISO, country representatives vote to approve or reject standards. Most of the work on the development of ISO standards is done in expert working groups. Additional information about ISO may be obtained from http://www.iso.int

ISO-3166 An ISO standard that defines codes to represent countries and their subdivisions. See http://www.iso.org/iso/country_codes.htm

ISP An Internet Service Provider, i.e. a network that provides Internet access to its clients.

ITU The International Telecommunication Union is a United Nation's agency whose purpose is to develop standards for the telecommunication industry. It was initially created to standardise the basic telephone system but expanded later towards data networks. The work within ITU is mainly done by network specialists from the telecommunication industry (operators and vendors). See http://www.itu.int for more information

IXP Internet eXchange Point. A location where routers belonging to different domains are attached to the same Local Area Network to establish peering sessions and exchange packets. See http://www.euro-ix.net/ or http://en.wikipedia.org/wiki/List_of_Internet_exchange_points_by_size for a partial list of IXPs.

LAN Local Area Network

Leased line A telephone line that is permanently available between two endpoints.

MAN Metropolitan Area Network

MIME The Multipurpose Internet Mail Extensions (MIME) defined in RFC 2045 are a set of extensions to the format of email messages that allow to use non-ASCII characters inside mail messages. A MIME message can be composed of several different parts each having a different format.

MIME document A MIME document is a document, encoded by using the MIME format.

Minicomputer A minicomputer is a multi-user system that was typically used in the 1960s/1970s to serve departments. See the corresponding wikipedia article for additional information : http://en.wikipedia.org/wiki/Minicomputer

Modem A modem (modulator-demodulator) is a device that encodes (resp. decodes) digital information by modulating (resp. demodulating) an analog signal. Modems are frequently used to transmit digital information over telephone lines and radio links. See http://en.wikipedia.org/wiki/Modem for a survey of various types of modems

MSS A TCP option used by a TCP entity in SYN segments to indicate the Maximum Segment Size that it is able to receive.

Multicast a transmission mode where an information is sent efficiently to all the receivers that belong to a given group

Nameserver A server that implements the DNS protocol and can answer queries for names inside its own domain. NAT A Network Address Translator is a middlebox that translates IP packets.

NBMA A Non Broadcast Mode Multiple Access Network is a subnetwork that supports multiple hosts/routers but does not provide an efficient way of sending broadcast frames to all devices attached to the subnetwork. ATM subnetworks are an example of NBMA networks.

Network-byte order Internet protocol allow to transport sequences of bytes. These sequences of bytes are sufficient to carry ASCII characters. The network-byte order refers to the Big-Endian encoding for 16 and 32 bits integer. See http://en.wikipedia.org/wiki/Endianness

NFS The Network File System is defined in RFC 1094

NTP The Network Time Protocol is defined in RFC 1305

OSI Open Systems Interconnection. A set of networking standards developed by ISO including the 7 layers OSI reference model.

OSPF Open Shortest Path First. A link-state intradomain routing protocol that is often used in enterprise and ISP networks. OSPF is defined in and RFC 2328 and RFC 5340 packet a packet is the unit of information transfer in the network layer

PBL Problem-based learning is a teaching approach that relies on problems.

POP The Post Office Protocol (POP), defined RFC 1939, is an application-level protocol that allows a client to download email messages stored on a server.

Resolver A server that implements the DNS protocol and can resolve queries. A resolver usually serves a set of clients (e.g. all hosts in campus or all clients of a given ISP). It sends DNS queries to nameservers everywhere on behalf of its clients and stores the received answers in its cache. A resolver must know the IP addresses of the root nameservers.

RIP Routing Information Protocol. An intradomain routing protocol based on distance vectors that is sometimes used in enterprise networks. RIP is defined in RFC 2453.

RIR Regional Internet Registry. An organisation that manages IP addresses and AS numbers on behalf of IANA. root nameserver A name server that is responsible for the root of the domain names hierarchy. There are currently a dozen root nameservers and each DNS resolver See http://www.root-servers.org/ for more information about the operation of these root servers.

Round-trip-time The round-trip-time (RTT) is the delay between the transmission of a segment and the reception of the corresponding acknowledgement in a transport protocol.

Router A relay operating in the network layer.

RPC Several types of remote procedure calls have been defined. The RPC mechanism defined in RFC 5531 is used by applications such as NFS

SDU (Service Data Unit) a Service Data Unit is the unit information transferred between applications segment a segment is the unit of information transfer in the transport layer

SMTP The Simple Mail Transfer Protocol is defined in RFC 821

SNMP The Simple Network Management Protocol is a management protocol defined for TCP/IP networks. socket A low-level API originally defined on Berkeley Unix to allow programmers to develop clients and servers. spoofed packet A packet is said to be spoofed when the sender of the packet has used as source address a different address than its own.

SSH The Secure Shell (SSH) Transport Layer Protocol is defined in RFC 4253

Standard query For DNS servers and resolvers, a standard query is a query for a A or a AAAA record. Such a query typically returns an IP address.

Switch A relay operating in the datalink layer.

SYN cookie The SYN cookies is a technique used to compute the initial sequence number (ISN)

TCB The Transmission Control Block is the set of variables that are maintained for each established TCP connection by a TCP implementation.

TCP The Transmission Control Protocol is a protocol of the transport layer in the TCP/IP protocol suite that provides a reliable bytestream connection-oriented service on top of IP

Telnet The telnet protocol is defined in RFC 854

TLD A Top-level domain name. There are two types of TLDs. The ccTLD are the TLD that correspond to a two letters ISO-3166 country code. The gTLD are the generic TLDs that are not assigned to a country.

TLS Transport Layer Security, defined in RFC 5246 is a cryptographic protocol that is used to provide communication security for Internet applications. This protocol is used on top of the transport service but a detailed description is outside the scope of this book.

UDP User Datagram Protocol is a protocol of the transport layer in the TCP/IP protocol suite that provides an unreliable connectionless service that includes a mechanism to detect corruption

Unicast a transmission mode where an information is sent from one source to one recipient

vnc A networked application that allows to remotely access a computer's Graphical User Interface. See http://en.wikipedia.org/wiki/Virtual_Network_Computing

W3C The world wide web consortium was created to standardise the protocols and mechanisms used in the global www. It is thus focused on a subset of the application layer. See http://www.w3c.org

WAN Wide Area Network

X.25 A wide area networking technology using virtual circuits that was deployed by telecom operators.

X11 The XWindow system and the associated protocols are defined in [SG1990]

XML The eXtensible Markup Language (XML) is a flexible text format derived from SGML. It was originally designed for the electronic publishing industry but is now used by a wide variety of applications that need to exchange structured data. The XML specifications are maintained by several working groups of the *W3C*

Bibliography

[802.11] LAN/MAN Standards Committee of the IEEE Computer Society. IEEE Standard for Information Technology - Telecommunications and information exchange between systems - local and metropolitan area networks - specific requirements - Part 11 : Wireless LAN Medium Access Control (MAC) and Physical Layer (PHY) Specifications. IEEE, 1999.

[802.1d] LAN/MAN Standards Committee of the IEEE Computer Society, IEEE Standard for Local and metropolitan area networks Media Access Control (MAC) Bridges, IEEE Std 802.1DTM-2004, 2004,

[802.1q] LAN/MAN Standards Committee of the IEEE Computer Society, IEEE Standard for Local and metropolitan area networks— Virtual Bridged Local Area Networks, 2005,

[802.2] IEEE 802.2-1998 (ISO/IEC 8802-2:1998), IEEE Standard for Information technology Telecommunications and information exchange between systems-Local and metropolitan area networks-Specific requirements-Part 2: Logical Link Control. Available from http://standards.ieee.org/getieee802/802.2.html

[802.3] LAN/MAN Standards Committee of the IEEE Computer Society. IEEE Standard for Information Technology - Telecommunications and information exchange between systems - local and metropolitan area networks - specific requirements - Part 3 : Carrier Sense multiple access with collision detection (CSMA/CD) access method and physical layer specification. IEEE, 2000. Available from http://standards.ieee.org/getieee802/802.3.html

[802.5] LAN/MAN Standards Committee of the IEEE Computer Society. IEEE Standard for Information technology-Telecommunications and information exchange between systems-Local and metropolitan area networks-Specific requirements-Part 5: Token Ring Access Method and Physical Layer Specification. IEEE, 1998. available from http://standards.ieee.org/getieee802

[ACO+2006] Augustin, B., Cuvellier, X., Orgogozo, B., Viger, F., Friedman, T., Latapy, M., Magnien, C., Teixeira, R., Avoiding traceroute anomalies with Paris traceroute, Internet Measurement Conference, October 2006, See also http://www.paris-traceroute.net/

[AS2004] Androutsellis-Theotokis, S. and Spinellis, D.. 2004. A survey of peer-to-peer content distribution technologies. ACM Comput. Surv. 36, 4 (December 2004), 335-371.

[ATLAS2009] Labovitz, C., Iekel-Johnson, S., McPherson, D., Oberheide, J. and Jahanian, F., Internet interdomain traffic. In Proceedings of the ACM SIGCOMM 2010 conference on SIGCOMM (SIGCOMM '10). ACM, New York, NY, USA, 75-86.

[AW05] Arlitt, M. and Williamson, C. 2005. An analysis of TCP reset behaviour on the internet. SIGCOMM Comput. Commun. Rev. 35, 1 (Jan. 2005), 37-44.

[Abramson1970] Abramson, N., THE ALOHA SYSTEM: another alternative for computer communications. In Proceedings of the November 17-19, 1970, Fall Joint Computer Conference (Houston, Texas, November 17 - 19, 1970). AFIPS '70 (Fall). ACM, New York, NY, 281-285.

[B1989] Berners-Lee, T., Information Management: A Proposal, March 1989

[Baran] Baran, P., *On distributed communications series,* http://www.rand.org/about/history/baran.list.html,

[BE2007] Biondi, P and A. Ebalard, IPv6 Routing Header Security, CanSecWest Security Conference 2007, April 2007.

[BF1995] Bonomi, F. and Fendick, K.W., The rate-based flow control framework for the available bit rate ATM service, IEEE Network, Mar/Apr 1995, Volume: 9, Issue: 2, pages: 25-39

[BG1992] Bertsekas, D., Gallager, G., Data networks, second edition, Prentice Hall, 1992

[BMO2006] Bhatia, M., Manral, V., Ohara, Y., IS-IS and OSPF Difference Discussions, work in progress, Internet draft, Jan. 2006

[BMvB2009] Bagnulo, M., Matthews, P., van Beijnum, I., NAT64: Network Address and Protocol Translation from IPv6 Clients to IPv4 Servers, Internet draft, work in progress, October 2009,

[BNT1997] Beech, W., Nielsen, D., Taylor, J., AX.25 Link Access Protocol for Amateur Packet Radio, version '2.2, Revision: July 1998

[BOP1994] Brakmo, L. S., O'Malley, S. W., and Peterson, L. L., TCP Vegas: new techniques for congestion detection and avoidance. In Proceedings of the Conference on Communications Architectures, Protocols and Applications (London, United Kingdom, August 31 - September 02,1994). SIGCOMM '94. ACM, New York, NY, 24-35.

[Benvenuti2005] Benvenuti, C., Understanding Linux Network Internals, O'Reilly Media, 2005

[Bush1945] Bush, V. As we may think The Atlantic Monthly 176 (July 1945), pp. 101-108

[Bush1993] Bush, R., FidoNet: technology, tools, and history. Commun. ACM 36, 8 (Aug. 1993), 31-35.

[Bux1989] Bux, W., Token-ring local-area networks and their performance, Proceedings of the IEEE, Vol 77, No 2, p. 238-259, Feb. 1989

[BYL2008] Buford, J., Yu, H., Lua, E.K., P2P Networking and Applications, Morgan Kaufmann, 2008

[CB2003] Cheswick, William R., Bellovin, Steven M., Rubin, Aviel D., Firewalls and internet security - Second edition - Repelling the Wily Hacker, Addison-Wesley 2003

[CD2008] Calvert, K., Donahoo, M., TCP/IP Sockets in Java : Practical Guide for Programmers, Morgan Kaufman, 2008

[CJ1989] Chiu, D., Jain, R., Analysis of the Increase and Decrease Algorithms for Congestion Avoidance in Computer Networks, Computer Networks and ISDN Systems Vol 17, pp 1-14, 1989

[CK74] Cerf, V., Kahn, R., A Protocol for Packet Network Intercommunication, IEEE Transactions on Communications, May 1974

[CNPI09] Gont, F., Security Assessment of the Transmission Control Protocol (TCP),Security Assessment of the Transmission Control Protocol (TCP), Internet draft, work in progress, Jan. 2011

[COZ2008] Chi, Y., Oliveira, R., Zhang, L., Cyclops: The Internet AS-level Observatory, ACM SIGCOMM Computer Communication Review (CCR), October 2008

[CSP2009] Carr, B., Sury, O., Palet Martinez, J., Davidson, A., Evans, R., Yilmaz, F., Wijte, Y., IPv6 Address Allocation and Assignment Policy, RIPE document ripe-481, September 2009

[CT1980] Crane, R., Taft, E., Practical considerations in Ethernet local network design, Proc. of the 13th Hawaii International Conference on Systems Sciences, Honolulu, January, 1980, pp. 166-174

[Cheshire2010] Cheshire, S., Connect-By-Name for IPv6, presentation at IETF 79th, November 2010

[Cheswick1990] Cheswick, B., An Evening with Berferd In Which a Cracker is Lured, Endured, and Studied, Proc. Winter USENIX Conference, 1990, pp. 163-174

[Clark88] Clark D., The Design Philosophy of the DARPA Internet Protocols, Computer Communications Review 18:4, August 1988, pp. 106-114

[Comer1988] Comer, D., *Internetworking with TCP/IP: principles, protocols & architecture,* Prentice Hall, 1988 [Comer1991] Comer D., *Internetworking With TCP/IP : Design Implementation and Internals,* Prentice Hall, 1991

[Cohen1980] Cohen, D., *On Holy Wars and a Plea for Peace,* IEN 137, April 1980, http://www.ietf.org/rfc/ien/ien137.txt

[DC2009] Donahoo, M., Calvert, K., TCP/IP Sockets in C: Practical Guide for Programmers, Morgan Kaufman, 2009,

[DIX] Digital, Intel, Xerox, The Ethernet: a local area network: data link layer and physical layer specifications. SIGCOMM Comput. Commun. Rev. 11, 3 (Jul. 1981), 20-66.

[DKF+2007] Dimitropoulos, X., Krioukov, D., Fomenkov, M., Huffaker, B., Hyun, Y., Claffy, K., Riley, G., AS Relationships: Inference and Validation, ACM SIGCOMM Computer Communication Review (CCR), Jan. 2007

[DP1981] Dalal, Y. K. and Printis, R. S., 48-bit absolute internet and Ethernet host numbers. In Proceedings of the Seventh Symposium on Data Communications (Mexico City, Mexico, October 27 - 29,1981). SIGCOMM '81. ACM, New York, NY, 240-245.

[Dunkels2003] Dunkels, A., Full TCP/IP for 8-Bit Architectures. In Proceedings of the first international conference on mobile applications, systems and services (MOBISYS 2003), San Francisco, May 2003.

[DT2007] Donnet, B. and Friedman, T., Internet Topology Discovery: a Survey. IEEE Communications Surveys and Tutorials, 9(4):2-15, December 2007

[DYGU2004] Davik, F. Yilmaz, M. Gjessing, S. Uzun, N., IEEE 802.17 resilient packet ring tutorial, IEEE Communications Magazine, Mar 2004, Vol 42, N 3, p. 112-118

[Dijkstra1959] Dijkstra, E., A Note on Two Problems in Connection with Graphs. Numerische Mathematik, 1:269- 271, 1959

[FDDI] ANSI. *Information systems - Fiber Distributed Data Interface (FDDI) - token ring media access control (MAC).* ANSIX3.139-1987 (R1997), 1997

[Fletcher1982] Fletcher, J., An Arithmetic Checksum for Serial Transmissions, Communications, IEEE Transactions on, Jan. 1982, Vol. 30, N. 1, pp. 247-252

[FFEB2005] Francois, P., Filsfils, C., Evans, J., and Bonaventure, O., Achieving sub-second IGP convergence in large IP networks. SIGCOMM Comput. Commun. Rev. 35, 3 (Jul. 2005), 35-44.

[FJ1994] Floyd, S., and Jacobson, V., The Synchronization of Periodic Routing Messages, IEEE/ACM Transactions on Networking, V.2 N.2, p. 122-136, April 1994

[FLM2008] Fuller, V., Lear, E., Meyer, D., Reclassifying 240/4 as usable unicast address space, Internet draft, March 2008, workin progress

[FRT2002] Fortz, B. Rexford, J. ,Thorup, M., Traffic engineering with traditional IP routing protocols, IEEE Communication Magazine, October 2002

[FTY99] Theodore Faber, Joe Touch, and Wei Yue, The TIME-WAIT state in TCP and Its Effect on Busy Servers, Proc. Infocom '99, pp. 1573

[Feldmeier95] Feldmeier, D. C., Fast software implementation of error detection codes. IEEE/ACM Trans. Netw. 3, 6 (Dec. 1995), 640-651.

[GAVE1999] Govindan, R., Alaettinoglu, C., Varadhan, K., Estrin, D., An Architecture for Stable, Analyzable Internet Routing, IEEE Network Magazine, Vol. 13, No. 1, pp. 29-35, January 1999

[GC2000] Grier, D., Campbell, M., A social history of Bitnet and Listserv, 1985-1991, Annals of the History of Computing, IEEE, Volume 22, Issue 2, Apr-Jun 2000, pp. 32 - 41

[Genilloud1990] Genilloud, G., X.400 MHS: first steps towards an EDI communication standard. SIGCOMM Comput. Commun. Rev. 20, 2 (Apr. 1990), 72-86.

[GGR2001] Gao, L., Griffin, T., Rexford, J., Inherently safe backup routing with BGP, Proc. IEEE INFOCOM, April 2001

[GR2001] Gao, L., Rexford, J., Stable Internet routing without global coordination, IEEE/ACM Transactions on Networking, December 2001, pp. 681-692

[GSW2002] Griffin, T. G., Shepherd, F. B., and Wilfong, G., The stable paths problem and interdomain routing. IEEE/ACM Trans. Netw. 10, 2 (Apr. 2002), 232-243

[GW1999] Griffin, T. G. and Wilfong, G., An analysis of BGP convergence properties. SIGCOMM Comput. Commun. Rev. 29, 4 (Oct. 1999), 277-288.

[GW2002] Griffin, T. and Wilfong, G. T., Analysis of the MED Oscillation Problem in BGP. In Proceedings of the 10th IEEE international Conference on Network Protocols (November 12 - 15, 2002). ICNP. IEEE Computer Society, Washington, DC, 90-99

[Garcia1993] Garcia-Lunes-Aceves, J., Loop-Free Routing Using Diffusing Computations, IEEE/ACM Transactions on Networking, Vol. 1, No, 1, Feb. 1993

[Gast2002] Gast, M., 802.11 Wireless Networks: The Definitive Guide, O'Reilly, 2002

[Gill2004] Gill, V., Lack of Priority Queuing Considered Harmful, ACM Queue, December 2004

[Goralski2009] Goralski, W., The Illustrated network : How TCP/IP works in a modern network, Morgan Kaufmann, 2009

[HFPMC2002] Huffaker, B., Fomenkov, M., Plummer, D., Moore, D., Claffy, K., Distance Metrics in the Internet, Presented at the IEEE International Telecommunications Symposium (ITS) in 2002.

[HRX2008] Ha, S., Rhee, I., and Xu, L., CUBIC: a new TCP-friendly high-speed TCP variant. SIGOPS Oper. Syst. Rev. 42, 5 (Jul. 2008), 64-74.

[ISO10589] Information technology — Telecommunications and information exchange between systems — Intermediate System to Intermediate System intra-domain routeing information exchange protocol for use in conjunction with the protocol for providing the connectionless-mode network service (ISO 8473), 2002

[Jacobson1988] Jacobson, V., Congestion avoidance and control. In Symposium Proceedings on Communications Architectures and Protocols (Stanford, California, United States, August 16 - 18, 1988). V. Cerf, Ed. SIGCOMM '88. ACM, New York, NY, 314-329.

[JSBM2002] Jung, J., Sit, E., Balakrishnan, H., and Morris, R. 2002. DNS performance and the effectiveness of caching. IEEE/ACM Trans. Netw. 10, 5 (Oct. 2002), 589-603.

[Kerrisk2010] Kerrisk, M., The Linux Programming Interface, No Starch Press, 2010

[KM1995] Kent, C. A. and Mogul, J. C., Fragmentation considered harmful. SIGCOMM Comput. Commun. Rev. 25, 1 (Jan. 1995), 75-87.

[KP91] Karn, P. and Partridge, C., Improving round-trip time estimates in reliable transport protocols. ACM Trans. Comput. Syst. 9,4 (Nov. 1991), 364-373.

[KPD1985] Karn, P., Price, H., Diersing, R., Packet radio in amateur service, IEEE Journal on Selected Areas in Communications, 3, May, 1985

[KPS2003] Kaufman, C., Perlman, R., and Sommerfeld, B. DoS protection for UDP-based protocols. In Proceedings of the 10th ACM Conference on Computer and Communications Security (Washington D.C., USA, October 27 - 30, 2003). CCS '03. ACM, New York, NY, 2-7.

[KR1995] Kung, N.T. Morris, R., Credit-based flow control for ATM networks, IEEE Network, Mar/Apr 1995, Volume: 9, Issue: 2, pages: 40-48

[KT1975] Kleinrock, L., Tobagi, F., Packet Switching in Radio Channels: Part I-Carrier Sense Multiple-Access Modes and their Throughput-Delay Characteristics, IEEE Transactions on Communications, Vol. COM-23, No. 12, pp. 1400-1416, December 1975.

[KW2009] Katz, D., Ward, D., *Bidirectional Forwarding Detection,* **RFC 5880**, June 2010

[KZ1989] Khanna, A. and Zinky, J. 1989. The revised ARPANET routing metric. SIGCOMM Comput. Commun. Rev. 19,4 (Aug. 1989), 45-56.

[KuroseRoss09] Kurose J. and Ross K., Computer networking : a top-down approach featuring the Internet, Addison-Wesley, 2009

[Licklider1963] Licklider, J., Memorandum For Members and Affiliates of the Intergalactic Computer Network, 1963

[LCCD09] Leiner, B. M., Cerf, V. G., Clark, D. D., Kahn, R. E., Kleinrock, L., Lynch, D. C., Postel, J., Roberts, L. G., and Wolff, S., A brief history of the internet. SIGCOMM Comput. Commun. Rev. 39, 5 (Oct. 2009), 22-31.

[LCP2005] Eng Keong Lua, Crowcroft, J., Pias, M., Sharma, R., Lim, S., A survey and comparison of peer-to- peer overlay network schemes, Communications Surveys & Tutorials, IEEE, Volume: 7 , Issue: 2, 2005, pp. 72-93

[LFJLMT] Leffler, S., Fabry, R., Joy, W., Lapsley, P., Miller, S., Torek, C., An Advanced 4.4BSD Interprocess Communication Tutorial, 4.4 BSD Programmer's Supplementary Documentation

[LSP1982] Lamport, L., Shostak, R., and Pease, M., The Byzantine Generals Problem. ACM Trans. Program. Lang. Syst. 4, 3 (Jul. 1982), 382-401.

[Leboudec2008] Leboudec, J.-Y., Rate Adaptation Congestion Control and Fairness : a tutorial, Dec. 2008 [Malamud1991] Malamud, C., Analyzing DECnet/OSI phase V, Van Nostrand Reinhold, 1991

[McFadyen1976] McFadyen, J., Systems Network Architecture: An overview, IBM Systems Journal, Vol. 15, N. 1, pp. 4-23, 1976

[McKusick1999] McKusick, M., Twenty Years of Berkeley Unix : From AT&T-Owned to Freely Redistributable, in Open Sources: Voices from the Open Source Revolution, Oreilly, 1999, http://oreilly.com/catalog/opensources/book/toc.html

[ML2011] Minei I. and Lucek J. ,'MPLS-Enabled Applications: Emerging Developments and New Technologies <http://www.amazon.com/MPLS-Enabled-Applications-Developments-Technologies-

Communications/dp/0470665459>'_ (Wiley Series on Communications Networking & Distributed Systems), Wiley, 2011

[MRR1979] McQuillan, J. M., Richer, I., and Rosen, E. C., An overview of the new routing algorithm for the ARPANET. In Proceedings of the Sixth Symposium on Data Communications (Pacific Grove, California, United States, November 27 - 29, 1979). SIGCOMM '79. ACM, New York, NY, 63-68.

[MSMO1997] Mathis, M., Semke, J., Mahdavi, J., and Ott, T. 1997. The macroscopic behavior of the TCP congestion avoidance algorithm. SIGCOMM Comput. Commun. Rev. 27, 3 (Jul. 1997), 67-82.

[MSV1987] Molle, M., Sohraby, K., Venetsanopoulos, A., Space-Time Models of Asynchronous CSMA Protocols for Local Area Networks, IEEE Journal on Selected Areas in Communications, Volume: 5 Issue: 6, Jul 1987 Page(s): 956 -96

[MUF+2007] Muhlbauer, W., Uhlig, S., Fu, B., Meulle, M., and Maennel, O., In search for an appropriate granularity to model routing policies. In Proceedings of the 2007 Conference on Applications, Technologies, Architectures, and Protocols For Computer Communications (Kyoto, Japan, August 27-31, 2007). SIGCOMM '07. ACM, New York, NY, 145-156.

[Malkin1999] Malkin, G., RIP: An Intra-Domain Routing Protocol, Addison Wesley, 1999

[Metcalfe1976] Metcalfe R., Boggs, D., Ethernet: Distributed packet-switching for local computer networks. Communications of the ACM, 19(7):395-404, 1976.

[Mills2006] Mills, D.L., Computer Network Time Synchronization: the Network Time Protocol. CRC Press, March 2006, 304 pp.

[Miyakawa2008] Miyakawa, S., From IPv4 only To v4/v6 Dual Stack, IETF72 IAB Technical Plenary, July 2008

[Mogul1995] Mogul, J., The case for persistent-connection HTTP. In Proceedings of the Conference on Applications, Technologies, Architectures, and Protocols For Computer Communication (Cambridge, Massachusetts, United States, August 28 - September 01, 1995). D. Oran, Ed. SIGCOMM '95. ACM, New York, NY, 299313.

[Moore] Moore, R., *Packet switching history,* http://rogerdmoore.ca/PS/

[Moy1998] Moy, J., OSPF: Anatomy of an Internet Routing Protocol, Addison Wesley, 1998

[Myers1998] Myers, B. A., A brief history of human-computer interaction technology. interactions 5, 2 (Mar. 1998), 44-54.

[Nelson1965] Nelson, T. H., Complex information processing: a file structure for the complex, the changing and the indeterminate. In Proceedings of the 1965 20th National Conference (Cleveland, Ohio, United States, August 24 - 26, 1965). L. Winner, Ed. ACM '65. ACM, New York, NY, 84-100.

[Paxson99] Paxson, V. , End-to-end Internet packet dynamics. SIGCOMM Comput. Commun. Rev. 27, 4 (Oct. 1997), 139-152.

[Perlman1985] Perlman, R., An algorithm for distributed computation of a spanning tree in an extended LAN. SIGCOMM Comput. Commun. Rev. 15, 4 (Sep. 1985), 44-53.

[Perlman2000] Perlman, R., Interconnections : Bridges, routers, switches and internetworking protocols, 2nd edition, Addison Wesley, 2000

[Perlman2004] Perlman, R., RBridges: Transparent Routing, Proc. IEEE Infocom , March 2004.

[Pouzin1975] Pouzin, L., The CYCLADES Network - Present state and development trends, Symposium on Computer Networks, 1975 pp 8-13.

[Rago1993] Rago, S., UNIX System V network programming, Addison Wesley, 1993

[RE1989] Rochlis, J. A. and Eichin, M. W., With microscope and tweezers: the worm from MIT's perspective. Commun. ACM 32, 6 (Jun. 1989), 689-698.

[RFC20] Cerf, V., *ASCII format for network interchange,* **RFC 20**, Oct. 1969

[RFC768] Postel, J., *User Datagram Protocol,* **RFC 768**, Aug. 1980

[RFC789] Rosen, E., *Vulnerabilities of network control protocols: An example,* **RFC 789**, July 1981

[RFC791] Postel, J., *Internet Protocol,* **RFC 791**, Sep. 1981

[RFC792] Postel, J., *Internet Control Message Protocol,* **RFC 792**, Sep. 1981

[RFC793] Postel, J., *Transmission Control Protocol,* **RFC 793**, Sept. 1981

[RFC813] Clark, D., *Window and Acknowledgement Strategy in TCP,* **RFC 813**, July 1982

[RFC819] Su, Z. and Postel, J., *Domain naming convention for Internet user applications,* **RFC 819**, Aug. 1982 [RFC821] Postel, J., *Simple Mail Transfer Protocol,* **RFC 821**, Aug. 1982

[RFC822] Crocker, D., *Standard for the format ofARPA Internet text messages, :rfc:'822,* Aug. 1982

[RFC826] Plummer, D., "Ethernet Address Resolution Protocol: Or Converting Network Protocol Addresses to 48.bit Ethernet Address for Transmission on Ethernet Hardware', **RFC 826**, Nov. 1982

[RFC879] Postel, J., *TCP maximum segment size and related topics,* **RFC 879**, Nov. 1983

[RFC893] Leffler, S. and Karels, M., *Trailer encapsulations,* **RFC 893**, April 1984

[RFC894] Hornig, C., *A Standard for the Transmission of IP Datagrams over Ethernet Networks,* **RFC 894**, April 1984

[RFC896] Nagle, J., *Congestion Control in IP/TCP Internetworks,* **RFC 896**, Jan. 1984

[RFC952] Harrenstien, K. and Stahl, M. and Feinler, E., *DoD Internet host table specification,* **RFC 952**, Oct. 1985

[RFC959] Postel, J. and Reynolds, J., *File Transfer Protocol,* **RFC 959**, Oct. 1985

[RFC974] Partridge, C., *Mail routing and the domain system,* **RFC 974**, Jan. 1986

[RFC1032] Stahl, M., *Domain administrators guide,* **RFC 1032**, Nov. 1987

[RFC1035] Mockapteris, P., *Domain names - implementation and specification,* **RFC 1035**, Nov. 1987

[RFC1042] Postel, J. and Reynolds, J., *Standard for the transmission of IP datagrams over IEEE 802 networks,* **RFC 1042**, Feb. 1988

[RFC1055] Romkey, J., *Nonstandard for transmission of IP datagrams over serial lines: SLIP,* **RFC 1055**, June 1988

[RFC1071] Braden, R., Borman D. and Partridge, C., *Computing the Internet checksum,* **RFC 1071**, Sep. 1988 [RFC1122] Braden, R., *Requirements for Internet Hosts - Communication Layers,* **RFC 1122**, Oct. 1989

[RFC1144] Jacobson, V., *Compressing TCP/IP Headers for Low-Speed Serial Links,* **RFC 1144**, Feb. 1990

[RFC1149] Waitzman, D., *Standard for the transmission of IP datagrams on avian carriers,* **RFC 1149**, Apr. 1990

[RFC1169] Cerf, V. and Mills, K., *Explaining the role ofGOSIP,* **RFC 1169**, Aug. 1990

[RFC1191] Mogul, J. and Deering, S., *Path MTU discovery,* **RFC 1191**, Nov. 1990

[RFC1195] Callon, R., *Use of OSIIS-IS for routing in TCP/IP and dual environments,* **RFC 1195**, Dec. 1990

[RFC1258] Kantor, B., *BSD Rlogin,* **RFC 1258**, Sept. 1991

[RFC1321] Rivest, R., *The MD5 Message-Digest Algorithm,* **RFC 1321**, April 1992

[RFC1323] Jacobson, V., Braden R. and Borman, D., *TCP Extensions for High Performance,* **RFC 1323**, May 1992

[RFC1347] Callon, R., TCP and UDP with Bigger Addresses (TUBA), *A Simple Proposal for Internet Addressing and Routing,* **RFC 1347**, June 1992

[RFC1518] Rekhter, Y. and Li, T., *An Architecture for IP Address Allocation with CIDR,* **RFC 1518**, Sept. 1993

[RFC1519] Fuller V., Li T., Yu J. and Varadhan, K., *Classless Inter-Domain Routing (CIDR): an Address Assignment and Aggregation Strategy,* **RFC 1519**, Sept. 1993

[RFC1542] Wimer, W., *Clarifications and Extensions for the Bootstrap Protocol,* **RFC 1542**, Oct. 1993

[RFC1548] Simpson, W., *The Point-to-Point Protocol (PPP),* **RFC 1548**, Dec. 1993

[RFC1550] Bradner, S. and Mankin, A., *IP: Next Generation (IPng) White Paper Solicitation,* **RFC 1550**, Dec. 1993

[RFC1561] Piscitello, D., *Use of ISO CLNP in TUBA Environments,* **RFC 1561**, Dec. 1993

[RFC1621] Francis, P., *PIP Near-term architecture,* **RFC 1621**, May 1994

[RFC1624] Risjsighani, A., *Computation of the Internet Checksum via Incremental Update,* **RFC 1624**, May 1994

[RFC1631] Egevang K. and Francis, P., *The IP Network Address Translator (NAT),* **RFC 1631**, May 1994 [RFC1661] Simpson, W., *The Point-to-Point Protocol (PPP),* **RFC 1661**, Jul. 1994

[RFC1662] Simpson, W., *PPP in HDLC-like Framing,* **RFC 1662**, July 1994

[RFC1710] Hinden, R., *Simple Internet Protocol Plus White Paper,* **RFC 1710**, Oct. 1994

[RFC1738] Berners-Lee, T., Masinter, L., and McCahill M., *Uniform Resource Locators (URL),* **RFC 1738**, Dec. 1994

[RFC1752] Bradner, S. and Mankin, A., *The Recommendation for the IP Next Generation Protocol,* **RFC 1752**, Jan. 1995

[RFC1812] Baker, F., *Requirements for IP Version 4 Routers,* **RFC 1812**, June 1995

[RFC1819] Delgrossi, L., Berger, L., *Internet Stream Protocol Version 2 (ST2) Protocol Specification - Version ST2+,* **RFC 1819**, Aug. 1995

[RFC1889] Schulzrinne H., Casner S., Frederick, R. and Jacobson, V., *RTP: A Transport Protocol for Real-Time Applications,* **RFC 1889**, Jan. 1996

[RFC1896] Resnick P., Walker A., *The text/enriched MIME Content-type,* **RFC 1896**, Feb. 1996

[RFC1918] Rekhter Y., Moskowitz B., Karrenberg D., de Groot G. and Lear, E., *Address Allocation for Private Internets,* **RFC 1918**, Feb. 1996

[RFC1939] Myers, J. and Rose, M., *Post Office Protocol - Version 3,* **RFC 1939**, May 1996

[RFC1945] Berners-Lee, T., Fielding, R. and Frystyk, H., *Hypertext Transfer Protocol - HTTP/1.0,* **RFC 1945**, May 1996

[RFC1948] Bellovin, S., *Defending Against Sequence Number Attacks,* **RFC 1948**, May 1996

[RFC1951] Deutsch, P., *DEFLATE Compressed Data Format Specification version 1.3,* **RFC 1951**, May 1996 [RFC1981] McCann, J., Deering, S. and Mogul, J., *Path MTU Discovery for IP version 6,* **RFC 1981**, Aug. 1996 [RFC2003] Perkins, C., *IP Encapsulation within IP,* **RFC 2003**, Oct. 1996

[RFC2018] Mathis, M., Mahdavi, J., Floyd, S. and Romanow, A., *TCP Selective Acknowledgment Options,* **RFC 2018**, Oct. 1996

[RFC2045] Freed, N. and Borenstein, N., *Multipurpose Internet Mail Extensions (MIME) Part One: Format of Internet Message Bodies,* **RFC 2045**, Nov. 1996

[RFC2046] Freed, N. and Borenstein, N., *Multipurpose Internet Mail Extensions (MIME) Part Two: Media Types,* **RFC 2046**, Nov. 1996

[RFC2050] Hubbard, K. and Kosters, M. and Conrad, D. and Karrenberg, D. and Postel, J., *Internet Registry IP Allocation Guidelines,* **RFC 2050**, Nov. 1996

[RFC2080] Malkin, G. and Minnear, R., *RIPng for IPv6,* **RFC 2080**, Jan. 1997

[RFC2082] Baker, F. and Atkinson, R., *RIP-2 MD5 Authentication,* **RFC 2082**, Jan. 1997

[RFC2131] Droms, R., *Dynamic Host Configuration Protocol,* **RFC 2131**, March 1997

[RFC2140] Touch, J., *TCP Control Block Interdependence,* **RFC 2140**, April 1997

[RFC2225] Laubach, M., Halpern, J., *Classical IP and ARP over ATM,* **RFC 2225**, April 1998

[RFC2328] Moy, J., *OSPF Version 2,* **RFC 2328**, April 1998

[RFC2332] Luciani, J. and Katz, D. and Piscitello, D. and Cole, B. and Doraswamy, N., *NBMA Next Hop Resolution Protocol (NHRP),* **RFC 2332**, April 1998

[RFC2364] Gross, G. and Kaycee, M. and Li, A. and Malis, A. and Stephens, J., *PPP Over AAL5,* **RFC 2364**, July 1998

[RFC2368] Hoffman, P. and Masinter, L. and Zawinski, J., *The mailto URL scheme,* **RFC 2368**, July 1998 [RFC2453] Malkin, G., *RIP Version 2,* **RFC 2453**, Nov. 1998

[RFC2460] Deering S., Hinden, R., *Internet Protocol, Version 6 (IPv6) Specification,* **RFC 2460**, Dec. 1998 [RFC2464] Crawford, M., *Transmission of IPv6 Packets over Ethernet Networks,* **RFC 2464**, Dec. 1998

[RFC2507] Degermark, M. and Nordgren, B. and Pink, S., *IP Header Compression,* **RFC 2507**, Feb. 1999

[RFC2516] Mamakos, L. and Lidl, K. and Evarts, J. and Carrel, J. and Simone, D. and Wheeler, R., *A Method for Transmitting PPP Over Ethernet (PPPoE),* **RFC 2516**, Feb. 1999

[RFC2581] Allman, M. and Paxson, V. and Stevens, W., *TCP Congestion Control,* **RFC 2581**, April 1999

[RFC2616] Fielding, R. and Gettys, J. and Mogul, J. and Frystyk, H. and Masinter, L. and Leach, P. and Berners- Lee, T., *Hypertext Transfer Protocol - HTTP/1.1,* **RFC 2616**, June 1999

[RFC2617] Franks, J. and Hallam-Baker, P. and Hostetler, J. and Lawrence, S. and Leach, P. and Luotonen, A. and Stewart, L., *HTTP Authentication: Basic and Digest Access Authentication,* **RFC 2617**, June 1999

[RFC2622] Alaettinoglu, C. and Villamizar, C. and Gerich, E. and Kessens, D. and Meyer, D. and Bates, T. and Karrenberg, D. and Terpstra, M., *Routing Policy Specification Language (RPSL),* **RFC 2622**, June 1999

[RFC2675] Tsirtsis, G. and Srisuresh, P., *Network Address Translation - Protocol Translation (NAT-PT),* **RFC 2766**, Feb. 2000

[RFC2854] Connolly, D. and Masinter, L., *The 'text/html' Media Type,* **RFC 2854**, June 2000

[RFC2965] Kristol, D. and Montulli, L., *HTTP State Management Mechanism,* **RFC 2965**, Oct. 2000

[RFC2988] Paxson, V. and Allman, M., *Computing TCP's Retransmission Timer,* **RFC 2988**, Nov. 2000

[RFC2991] Thaler, D. and Hopps, C., *Multipath Issues in Unicast and Multicast Next-Hop Selection,* **RFC 2991**, Nov. 2000

[RFC3021] Retana, A. and White, R. and Fuller, V. and McPherson, D., *Using 31-Bit Prefixes on IPv4 Point-to- Point Links,* **RFC 3021**, Dec. 2000

[RFC3022] Srisuresh, P., Egevang, K., *Traditional IP Network Address Translator (Traditional NAT),* **RFC 3022**, Jan. 2001

[RFC3031] Rosen, E. and Viswanathan, A. and Callon, R., *Multiprotocol Label Switching Architecture,* **RFC 3031**, Jan. 2001

[RFC3168] Ramakrishnan, K. and Floyd, S. and Black, D., *The Addition of Explicit Congestion Notification (ECN) to IP,* **RFC 3168**, Sept. 2001

[RFC3243] Carpenter, B. and Brim, S., *Middleboxes: Taxonomy and Issues,* **RFC 3234**, Feb. 2002

[RFC3235] Senie, D., *Network Address Translator (NAT)-Friendly Application Design Guidelines,* **RFC 3235**, Jan. 2002

[RFC3309] Stone, J. and Stewart, R. and Otis, D., *Stream Control Transmission Protocol (SCTP) Checksum Change*, **RFC 3309**, Sept. 2002

[RFC3315] Droms, R. and Bound, J. and Volz, B. and Lemon, T. and Perkins, C. and Carney, M., *Dynamic Host Configuration Protocol for IPv6 (DHCPv6)*, **RFC 3315**, July 2003

[RFC3330] IANA, *Special-Use IPv4 Addresses*, **RFC 3330**, Sept. 2002

[RFC3360] Floyd, S., *Inappropriate TCP Resets Considered Harmful*, **RFC 3360**, Aug. 2002

[RFC3390] Allman, M. and Floyd, S. and Partridge, C., *Increasing TCP's Initial Window*, **RFC 3390**, Oct. 2002 [RFC3490] Faltstrom, P. and Hoffman, P. and Costello, A., *Internationalizing Domain Names in Applications (IDNA)*, **RFC 3490**, March 2003

[RFC3501] Crispin, M., *Internet Message Access Protocol - Version 4 revl*, **RFC 3501**, March 2003

[RFC3513] Hinden, R. and Deering, S., *Internet Protocol Version 6 (IPv6) Addressing Architecture*, **RFC 3513**, April 2003

[RFC3596] Thomson, S. and Huitema, C. and Ksinant, V. and Souissi, M., *DNS Extensions to Support IP Version 6*, **RFC 3596**, October 2003

[RFC3748] Aboba, B. and Blunk, L. and Vollbrecht, J. and Carlson, J. and Levkowetz, H., *Extensible Authentication Protocol (EAP)*, **RFC 3748**, June 2004

[RFC3819] Karn, P. and Bormann, C. and Fairhurst, G. and Grossman, D. and Ludwig, R. and Mahdavi, J. and Montenegro, G. and Touch, J. and Wood, L., *Advice for Internet Subnetwork Designers*, **RFC 3819**, July 2004

[RFC3828] Larzon, L-A. and Degermark, M. and Pink, S. and Jonsson, L-E. and Fairhurst, G., *The Lightweight User Datagram Protocol (UDP-Lite)*, **RFC 3828**, July 2004

[RFC3927] Cheshire, S. and Aboba, B. and Guttman, E., *Dynamic Configuration of IPv4 Link-Local Addresses*, **RFC 3927**, May 2005

[RFC3931] Lau, J. and Townsley, M. and Goyret, I., *Layer Two Tunneling Protocol - Version 3 (L2TPv3)*, **RFC 3931**, March 2005

[RFC3971] Arkko, J. and Kempf, J. and Zill, B. and Nikander, P., *SEcure Neighbor Discovery (SEND)*, **RFC 3971**, March 2005

[RFC3972] Aura, T., *Cryptographically Generated Addresses (CGA)*, **RFC 3972**, March 2005

[RFC3986] Berners-Lee, T. and Fielding, R. and Masinter, L., *Uniform Resource Identifier (URI): Generic Syntax*, **RFC 3986**, January 2005

[RFC4033] Arends, R. and Austein, R. and Larson, M. and Massey, D. and Rose, S., *DNS Security Introduction and Requirements*, **RFC 4033**, March 2005

[RFC4193] Hinden, R. and Haberman, B., *Unique Local IPv6 Unicast Addresses*, **RFC 4193**, Oct. 2005

[RFC4251] Ylonen, T. andLonvick, C., *The Secure Shell (SSH) Protocol Architecture*, **RFC 4251**, Jan. 2006

[RFC4264] Griffin, T. and Huston, G., *BGP Wedgies*, **RFC 4264**, Nov. 2005

[RFC4271] Rekhter, Y. and Li, T. and Hares, S., *A Border Gateway Protocol 4 (BGP-4)*, **RFC 4271**, Jan. 2006

[RFC4291] Hinden, R. and Deering, S., *IP Version 6 Addressing Architecture*, **RFC 4291**, Feb. 2006

[RFC4301] Kent, S. and Seo, K., *Security Architecture for the Internet Protocol*, **RFC 4301**, Dec. 2005

[RFC4302] Kent, S., *IP Authentication Header*, **RFC 4302**, Dec. 2005

[RFC4303] Kent, S., *IP Encapsulating Security Payload (ESP)*, **RFC 4303**, Dec. 2005

[RFC4340] Kohler, E. and Handley, M. and Floyd, S., *Datagram Congestion Control Protocol (DCCP)*, **RFC 4340**, March 2006

[RFC4443] Conta, A. and Deering, S. and Gupta, M., *Internet Control Message Protocol (ICMPv6)for the Internet Protocol Version 6 (IPv6) Specification,* **RFC 4443**, March 2006

[RFC4451] McPherson, D. and Gill, V., *BGP MULTI_EXIT_DISC (MED) Considerations,* **RFC 4451**, March 2006

[RFC4456] Bates, T. and Chen, E. and Chandra, R., *BGP Route Reflection: An Alternative to Full Mesh Internal BGP (IBGP),* **RFC 4456**, April 2006

[RFC4614] Duke, M. and Braden, R. and Eddy, W. and Blanton, E., *A Roadmap for Transmission Control Protocol (TCP) Specification Documents,* **RFC 4614**, Oct. 2006

[RFC4648] Josefsson, S., *The Base16, Base32, and Base64 Data Encodings,* **RFC 4648**, Oct. 2006

[RFC4822] Atkinson, R. and Fanto, M., *RIPv2 Cryptographic Authentication,* **RFC 4822**, Feb. 2007

[RFC4838] Cerf, V. and Burleigh, S. and Hooke, A. and Torgerson, L. and Durst, R. and Scott, K. and Fall, K. and Weiss, H., *Delay-Tolerant Networking Architecture,* **RFC 4838**, April 2007

[RFC4861] Narten, T. and Nordmark, E. and Simpson, W. and Soliman, H.,'Neighbor Discovery for IP version 6 (IPv6)', **RFC 4861**, Sept. 2007

[RFC4862] Thomson, S. and Narten, T. and Jinmei, T., *IPv6 Stateless Address Autoconfiguration,* **RFC 4862**, Sept. 2007

[RFC4870] Delany, M., *Domain-Based Email Authentication Using Public Keys Advertised in the DNS (DomainKeys),* **RFC 4870**, May 2007

[RFC4871] Allman, E. and Callas, J. and Delany, M. and Libbey, M. and Fenton, J. and Thomas, M., *DomainKeys Identified Mail (DKIM) Signatures,* **RFC 4871**, May 2007

[RFC4941] Narten, T. and Draves, R. and Krishnan, S., *Privacy Extensions for Stateless Address Autoconfiguration in IPv6,* **RFC 4941**, Sept. 2007

[RFC4944] Montenegro, G. and Kushalnagar, N. and Hui, J. and Culler, D., *Transmission of IPv6 Packets over IEEE 802.15.4 Networks,* **RFC 4944**, Sept. 2007

[RFC4952] Klensin, J. and Ko, Y., *Overview and Framework for Internationalized Email,* **RFC 4952**, July 2007

[RFC4953] Touch, J., *Defending TCP Against Spoofing Attacks,* **RFC 4953**, July 2007

[RFC4954] Simeborski, R. and Melnikov, A., *SMTP Service Extension for Authentication,* **RFC 4954**, July 2007

[RFC4963] Heffner, J. and Mathis, M. and Chandler, B., *IPv4 Reassembly Errors at High Data Rates,* **RFC 4963**, July 2007

[RFC4966] Aoun, C. and Davies, E., *Reasons to Move the Network Address Translator - Protocol Translator (NAT-PT) to Historic Status,* **RFC 4966**, July 2007

[RFC4987] Eddy, W., *TCP SYN Flooding Attacks and Common Mitigations,* **RFC 4987**, Aug. 2007

[RFC5004] Chen, E. and Sangli, S., *Avoid BGP Best Path Transitions from One External to Another,* **RFC 5004**, Sept. 2007

[RFC5065] Traina, P and McPherson, D. and Scudder, J., *Autonomous System Confederations for BGP,* **RFC 5065**, Aug. 2007

[RFC5068] Hutzler, C. and Crocker, D. and Resnick, P. and Allman, E. and Finch, T., *Email Submission Operations: Access and Accountability Requirements,* **RFC 5068**, Nov. 2007

[RFC5072] Varada, S. and Haskins, D. and Allen, E., *IP Version 6 over PPP,* **RFC 5072**, Sept. 2007

[RFC5095] Abley, J. and Savola, P. and Neville-Neil, G., *Deprecation of Type 0 Routing Headers in IPv6,* **RFC 5095**, Dec. 2007

[RFC5227] Cheshire, S., *IPv4 Address Conflict Detection,* **RFC 5227**, July 2008

[RFC5234] Crocker, D. and Overell, P., *Augmented BNFfor Syntax Specifications: ABNF,* **RFC 5234**, Jan. 2008

[RFC5321] Klensin, J., *Simple Mail Transfer Protocol,* **RFC 5321**, Oct. 2008

[RFC5322] Resnick, P., *Internet Message Format,* **RFC 5322**, Oct. 2008

[RFC5340] Coltun, R. and Ferguson, D. and Moy, J. and Lindem, A., *OSPF for IPv6,* **RFC 5340**, July 2008

[RFC5598] Crocker, D., *Internet Mail Architecture,* **RFC 5598**, July 2009

[RFC5646] Phillips, A. and Davis, M., *Tags for Identifying Languages,* **RFC 5646**, Sept. 2009

[RFC5681] Allman, M. and Paxson, V. and Blanton, E., *TCP congestion control,* **RFC 5681**, Sept. 2009

[RFC5735] Cotton, M. and Vegoda, L., *Special Use IPv4 Addresses,* **RFC 5735**, January 2010

[RFC5795] Sandlund, K. and Pelletier, G. and Jonsson, L-E., *The RObust Header Compression (ROHC) Framework,* **RFC 5795**, March 2010

[RFC6068] Duerst, M., Masinter, L. andZawinski, J., *The 'mailto' URIScheme* , **RFC 6068**, October 2010

[RFC6144] Baker, F. and Li, X. and Bao, X. and Yin, K., *Framework for IPv4/IPv6 Translation,* **RFC 6144**, April 2011

[RFC6265] Barth, A., *HTTP State Management Mechanism,* **RFC 6265**, April 2011

[RFC6274] Gont, F., *Security Assessment of the Internet Protocol Version 4,* **RFC 6274**, July 2011

[RG2010] Rhodes, B. and Goerzen, J., Foundations of Python Network Programming: The Comprehensive Guide to Building Network Applications with Python, Second Edition, Academic Press, 2004

[RJ1995] Ramakrishnan, K. K. and Jain, R., A binary feedback scheme for congestion avoidance in computer networks with a connectionless network layer. SIGCOMM Comput. Commun. Rev. 25, 1 (Jan. 1995), 138156.

[RY1994] Ramakrishnan, K.K. and Henry Yang, The Ethernet Capture Effect: Analysis and Solution, Proceedings of IEEE 19th Conference on Local Computer Networks, MN, Oct. 1994.

[Roberts1975] Roberts, L., ALOHA packet system with and without slots and capture. SIGCOMM Comput. Commun. Rev. 5, 2 (Apr. 1975), 28-42.

[Ross1989] Ross, F., An overview of FDDI: The fiber distributed data interface, IEEE J. Selected Areas in Comm., vol. 7, no. 7, pp. 1043-1051, Sept. 1989

[Russel06] Russell A., Rough Consensus and Running Code and the Internet-OSI Standards War, IEEE Annals of the History of Computing, July-September 2006

[SAO1990] Sidhu, G., Andrews, R., Oppenheimer, A., Inside AppleTalk, Addison-Wesley, 1990

[SARK2002] Subramanian, L., Agarwal, S., Rexford, J., Katz, R.. Characterizing the Internet hierarchy from multiple vantage points. In IEEE INFOCOM, 2002

[Sechrest] Sechrest, S., An Introductory 4.4BSD Interprocess Communication Tutorial, 4.4BSD Programmer's Supplementary Documentation

[SG1990] Scheifler, R., Gettys, J., X Window System: The Complete Reference to Xlib, X Protocol, ICCCM, XLFD, X Version 11, Release 4, Digital Press

[SGP98] Stone, J., Greenwald, M., Partridge, C., and Hughes, J., Performance of checksums and CRC's over real data. IEEE/ACM Trans. Netw. 6, 5 (Oct. 1998), 529-543.

[SH1980] Shoch, J. F. and Hupp, J. A., Measured performance of an Ethernet local network. Commun. ACM 23, 12 (Dec. 1980), 711-721.

[SH2004] Senapathi, S., Hernandez, R., Introduction to TCP Offload Engines, March 2004

[SMKKB2001] Stoica, I., Morris, R., Karger, D., Kaashoek, F., and Balakrishnan, H., Chord: A scalable peer- to-peer lookup service for internet applications. In Proceedings of the 2001 conference on Applications, technologies, architectures, and protocols for computer communications (SIGCOMM '01). ACM, New York, NY, USA, 149-160

[SMM1998] Semke, J., Mahdavi, J., and Mathis, M., Automatic TCP buffer tuning. SIGCOMM Comput. Commun. Rev. 28, 4 (Oct. 1998), 315-323.

[SPMR09] Stigge, M., Plotz, H., Muller, W., Redlich, J., Reversing CRC - Theory and Practice. Berlin: Humboldt University Berlin. pp. 24.

[STBT2009] Sridharan, M., Tan, K., Bansal, D., Thaler, D., Compound TCP: A New TCP Congestion Control for High-Speed and Long Distance Networks, Internet draft, work in progress, April 2009

[Seifert2008] Seifert, R., Edwards, J., The All-New Switch Book : The complete guide to LAN switching technology, Wiley, 2008

[Selinger] Selinger, P., *MD5 collision demo,* http://www.mscs.dal.ca/~selinger/md5collision/

[SFR2004] Stevens R. and Fenner, and Rudoff, A., UNIX Network Programming: The sockets networking API, Addison Wesley, 2004

[Sklower89] Sklower, K. 1989. Improving the efficiency of the OSI checksum calculation. SIGCOMM Comput. Commun. Rev. 19, 5 (Oct. 1989), 32-43.

[Smm98] Semke, J., Mahdavi, J., and Mathis, M., Automatic TCP buffer tuning. SIGCOMM Comput. Commun. Rev. 28,4 (Oct. 1998), 315-323.

[Stevens1994] Stevens, R., TCP/IP Illustrated : the Protocols, Addison-Wesley, 1994

[Stevens1998] Stevens, R., UNIX Network Programming, Volume 1, Second Edition: Networking APIs: Sockets and XTI, Prentice Hall, 1998

[Stewart1998] Stewart, J., BGP4: Inter-Domain Routing In The Internet, Addison-Wesley, 1998

[Stoll1988] Stoll, C., Stalking the wily hacker, Commun. ACM 31, 5 (May. 1988), 484-497.

[TE1993] Tsuchiya, P. F. and Eng, T., Extending the IP internet through address reuse. SIGCOMM Comput. Commun. Rev. 23, 1 (Jan. 1993), 16-33.

[Thomborson1992] Thomborson, C., The V.42bis Standard for Data-Compressing Modems, IEEE Micro, September/October 1992 (vol. 12 no. 5), pp. 41-53

[Unicode] The Unicode Consortium. The Unicode Standard, Version 5.0.0, defined by: The Unicode Standard, Version 5.0 (Boston, MA, Addison-Wesley, 2007

[VPD2004] Vasseur, J., Pickavet, M., and Demeester, P., Network Recovery: Protection and Restoration of Optical, SONET-SDH, IP, and MPLS. Morgan Kaufmann Publishers Inc., 2004

[Varghese2005] Varghese, G., Network Algorithmics: An Interdisciplinary Approach to Designing Fast Networked Devices, Morgan Kaufmann, 2005

[Vyncke2007] Vyncke, E., Paggen, C., LAN Switch Security: What Hackers Know About Your Switches, Cisco Press, 2007

[WB2008] Waserman, M., Baker, F., *IPv6-to-IPv6 Network Address Translation (NAT66),* Internet draft, November 2008, http://tools.ietf.org/html/draft-mrw-behave-nat66-02

[WMH2008] Wilson, P., Michaelson, G., Huston, G., *Redesignation of 240/4 from "Future Use" to "Private Use"*, Internet draft, September 2008, work in progress, http://tools.ietf.org/html/draft-wilson-class-e-02

[WMS2004] White, R., Mc Pherson, D., Srihari, S., Practical BGP, Addison-Wesley, 2004

[Watson1981] Watson, R., Timer-Based Mechanisms in Reliable Transport Protocol Connection Management. Computer Networks 5: 47-56 (1981)

[Williams1993] Williams, R. *A painless guide to CRC error detection algorithms*, August 1993, unpublished manuscript, http://www.ross.net/crc/download/crc_v3.txt

[Winston2003] Winston, G., NetBIOS Specification, 2003

[WY2011] Wing, D. and Yourtchenko, A., *Happy Eyeballs: Success with Dual-Stack Hosts*, Internet draft, work in progress, July 2011, http://tools.ietf.org/html/draft-ietf-v6ops-happy-eyeballs-03

[X200] ITU-T, recommendation X.200, Open Systems Interconnection - Model and Notation, 1994

[X224] ITU-T, recommendation X.224, Information technology - Open Systems Interconnection - Protocol for providing the connection-mode transport service, 1995

[XNS] Xerox, Xerox Network Systems Architecture, XNSG058504, 1985

[Zimmermann80] Zimmermann, H., OSI Reference Model - The ISO Model of Architecture for Open Systems Interconnection, IEEE Transactions on Communications, vol. 28, no. 4, April 1980, pp. 425 - 432.

Index

www.ingramcontent.com/pod-product-compliance
Lightning Source LLC
LaVergne TN
LVHW081939200926
848484LV00009B/2474